T0189465

Adversarial Machine Learning

Aneesh Sreevallabh Chivukula • Xinghao Yang •
Bo Liu • Wei Liu • Wanlei Zhou

Adversarial Machine Learning

Attack Surfaces, Defence Mechanisms, Learning Theories in Artificial Intelligence

Aneesh Sreevallabh Chivukula
BITS Pilani Hyderabad Campus
Department of Computer Science &
Information Systems
Secunderabad, Hyderabad, Telangana,
India

Xinghao Yang
Computer Science
University of Technology Sydney
Sydney, NSW, Australia

Bo Liu
Computer Science
University of Technology Sydney
Sydney, NSW, Australia

Wei Liu
Computer Science
University of Technology Sydney
Sydney, NSW, Australia

Wanlei Zhou
Computer Science
University of Technology Sydney
Sydney, NSW, Australia

ISBN 978-3-030-99774-8   ISBN 978-3-030-99772-4   (eBook)
https://doi.org/10.1007/978-3-030-99772-4

This Springer imprint is published by the registered company Springer Nature Switzerland AG
The registered company address is: Gewerbestrasse 11, 6330 Cham, Switzerland

Preface

A significant robustness gap exists between machine intelligence and human perception despite recent advances in deep learning. Deep learning is not provably secure. A critical challenge in deep learning is the vulnerability of deep learning networks to security attacks from malicious adversaries. Even innocuous perturbations to the training data can be used to manipulate the behavior of the deep network in unintended ways. For example, autonomous AI agents in unmanned autonomous systems such as self-driving vehicles can play multistage cyber deception games with the learning algorithms. Adversarial deep learning algorithms are specifically designed to exploit such vulnerabilities in deep networks. These vulnerabilities are simulated by training the learning algorithm under various attack scenarios. The attack scenarios are assumed to be formulated by an intelligent adversary. The optimal attack policy is formulated as solving for optimization problems. The attack scenarios have led to the development of adversarial attack technologies in computer vision, natural language processing, cybersecurity on multidimensional, textual and image data, sequence data, and spatial data.

In discriminative learning models, adversarial learning problems are formulated with deep neural networks computing statistical divergence metrics between training data features and adversarial data features. Latent space on high-dimensional training data can also be searched by deep networks to construct adversarial examples. Depending on the goal, knowledge, and capability of an adversary, adversarial examples can be crafted by prior knowledge, observation, and experimentation on the loss functions in deep learning. Adversarial examples are known to transfer between data-specific manifolds of deep learning models. Thus predictive performance of deep learning models under attack is an interesting area for research. Randomized adversarial algorithms for discrimination can be extended with efficiency, complexity, reliability, learnability, etc. tradeoffs in the game theoretical optimization. The resultant convergence properties of game theoretical optima can be investigated with adaptive dynamic programming to produce numerical computational methods for adversarial deep learning.

The existing adversarial learning algorithms differ in design assumptions regarding adversary's knowledge, attack strategies, attack influence, and security violation.

In this book, we conduct a literature review to provide new insights on the relation between adversarial learning and cyberattacks. We contrast the adversarial threats found in the learning assumptions of machine learning models as well as attack vectors in deep learning models. We also seek to survey and summarize non-stationary data representations and concept classes learnt by adversarial deep learning networks with respect to the sensitivity landscape and loss functions in each application domain. The robustness of the adversarial deep learning networks has been surveyed to produce a taxonomy of adversarial examples characterizing the defense of learning systems with game theoretical adversarial learning algorithms. The game theoretic learning profiles analyze adversarial robustness of the learning system with respect to adversary's objectives, assumptions, models, etc. in a dynamic optimization of the learning robustness and its solution stability over a changing fitness landscape.

We then review the use of game theory, convex optimization, and stochastic optimization in securing the adversarial deep learning formulations by providing algorithmic comparisons summarizing the theories and applications of game theoretical adversarial deep learning. Another interesting study is that of defence mechanisms available for deep learning models deployed in real world environments. We propose future research directions in adversarial learning applications specialized to data analytics models applicable to cybersecurity, deep learning, and artificial intelligence. They can realize the practical verifications, numerical approximations, and formal specifications of adversarial deep learning integrated into complex systems. Computational intelligence techniques such as multitask learning and multiobjective optimization relevant to the adversarial loss design are also summarized. We thus propose to bound the attacker's gain under an optimal policy with respect to formal as well as empirical verification in the game theoretic models extensible into learning system design techniques.

From a data privacy perspective, we review the cybersecurity risks, threats, and vulnerabilities in privacy preservation and physical world attacks. Detection and response options are provided for specific deep learning algorithms, attacks and threats in complex learning systems, adversarial deep learning, robust optimization, and intelligent control. Such research themes are applicable to resilient systems design with privacy preserving data mining to analyze the threat data, metadata, and attack patterns. It can also be used in the study of data quality and provenance of shared information in adversarial data mining to produce IoT systems with defences in the learning algorithms that combine security algorithmics with privacy systemics to produce cybersecurity capacities. Then security orchestrations can provision cybersecurity solutions as a service on the Internet for reliable access to real-world machine learning systems.

Further, we contrast the existing literature with recent research into game theoretical adversarial deep learning. We had studied adversarial attacks on game-theoretic learning models involving evolutionary adversaries, stochastic adversaries, and variational adversaries targeting the misclassification performance of deep neural networks and convolutional neural networks. Our game theoretical adversarial deep learning is applicable to cyberspace security classification problems in the training stage and testing stage. Such learning problems study feature manipulations, misclassifications costs, and distributional robustness in adversarial learning applications. The adversarial loss functions and training procedures in recently done research are applicable to the study of trustworthiness of deep learning in deployment. They can simulate the cyberspace security safeguards, risks, and challenges in cyber-physical systems as computational algorithms design and statistical inference analysis problems.

This book is relevant for adversarial machine learning practitioners and adversarial artificial intelligence researchers working in the design and application of adversarial deep learning theories in machine learning, deep learning, data mining, and knowledge discovery algorithms design. Particular emphasis is placed on the real-world application domains of Adversarial Deep Learning in the development of data science, big data analytics, and cybersecurity solutions. The adversarial deep learning theories are summarized with reference to capabilities of computational algorithms in pattern recognition, game theory, computational mathematics, and numerical analysis. The resultant analytics algorithmics, deep neural networks, and adversarial loss functions review the state of the art in the implementation of adversarial algorithms, their attack surfaces, concepts, and methods from the perspective of game theoretical machine learning. The book explores the systems theoretic dependence between randomization in adversarial manipulations and generalizability in blackbox optimizations of the game theoretical adversarial deep learning. It aids future research, design, development, and innovations in the game theoretical adversarial deep learning algorithms applicable to cyberspace security data mining problems.

The book also serves as a reference on the existing literature that can be implemented by researchers as baseline models to empirically compare the relevant attack scenarios and defense mechanisms for adversarial deep learning. The known invasive techniques and their countermeasures to develop future cybersecurity capabilities are reviewed. The security issues and vulnerabilities in the machine/deep learning solutions are mainly located within the deep layers of mathematical formulation and mechanism of the learning methods. The game theoretical formulations of the adversarial learning in the book leverage deep learning and big data to solve for adversarial samples that effect data manipulation on the learnt discriminative learning baselines. Several such learning baselines must be built to generate an adversary's attack hypothesis and consequent defense mechanisms available for adjusting the decision boundaries in discriminative learning. Thus the research questions covered in the book can set the stage for strategies and expectations in the adversarial deep learning capabilities offered around cyber adversaries' Tools, Tactics, Techniques, and Procedures (TTPs) in the cyber kill chain. They can assess, prioritize, and select the high-risk use case scenarios of cyber threats targeting deep learning models in security detection/prevention layers.

One significant barrier to the widespread adoption of deep learning methods is their complexity in both learning and reasoning phases that make it difficult to understand and test the potential vulnerabilities and also suitable mitigations. Learning from data for decision making within cyberspace domain is still a current and important challenge due to its complexity in design and development. This challenge is also interweaving with complexities from adversarial attacks targeting manipulated results for machine/deep learning models. The resilience of the machine learning models is a critical component for trustworthy systems in cybersecurity and artificial intelligence, but one that is poorly understood and investigated by mainstream security research and industry community. The book provides a survey of the security evaluation of machine learning algorithms with the design-for-security paradigm of adversarial learning to complement the classical design-for-performance paradigm of machine learning. The security evaluation is useful for the purpose of alleviating prediction bias in machine learning systems according to the security attributes defined for a given adversarial learning models algorithmics operational in dynamic learning environments. Formalized adversarial learning assumptions around the attack surface then constructs adversarial deep learning designs with reference to signal processing characteristics in the robustness properties of machine learning systems TTPs.

This book begins with a review of adversarial machine learning in Chap. 1 along with a comparison of new versus existing approaches to game theoretical adversarial machine learning. Chapter 2 positions our research contributions in contrast to related literature on (i) adversarial security mechanisms and generative adversarial networks, (ii) adversarial examples for misleading deep classifiers and game theoretical adversarial deep learning models, and (iii) adversarial examples in transfer learning and domain adaptation for cybersecurity.

The adversarial attack surfaces for the security and privacy tradeoffs in adversarial deep learning are given in Chap. 3. They summarize the cyber, physical, active, and passive attack surfaces in interdependent, interconnected, and interactive security-critical environments for learning systems. Such attack surfaces are increasing vertically in numbers, volumes and horizontally in types, functionality over Internet, social networks, smartphones, and IoT devices. Autonomic security in self-protecting and self-healing threat mitigation strategies must consider such attack surfaces in control mechanisms of the networking domains to identify threats and choose appropriate machine learning and data mining methods for adversarial learning.

Chapter 4 describes game theoretical adversarial deep learning. The computational algorithms in our research are contrasted with stochastic optimization techniques in the game theory literature. Several game formulations are illustrated with examples to construct cost-sensitive adversaries for adversarial data mining. Proper quantification of the hypothesis set in decision problems of this research leads us into various functional problems, oracular problems, sampling tasks, and optimization problems in the game theoretical adversarial learning. We can then develop a theory of sample complexity, formal verification, and fuzzy automata in the adversarial models with reliable guarantees. The resultant sampling dynamics are applicable into the Adversarial Signal Processing of soft matching patterns and their feature embeddings in cybersecurity attack scenarios and defense mechanisms. In terms of information-theoretic efficiency of machine learning, this is a study of the sample complexity of the function classes in adversarial learning games to devise each attack scenario as a blackbox attack where the adversaries have no prior knowledge of the deep learning training processes and its best response strategies.

Chapter 5 presents theories and algorithms for adversarial deep learning. These algorithmics can also be used to check the learning system specifications for consistency and applicability to merge the attack data and harden the specifications into a new adversarial learning model with vulnerability assessment metrics, protocols, and countermeasure fusions. Example applications of the adversarial attacks due to game theoretical adversarial deep learning proposed in our research are presented in Chap. 6. We work in the context of statistical spam and autonomous systems applications with images and videos. But we have found literature in several cybersecurity analytics applications for the adversarial deep learning in real-world domains. For instance, it is applicable in cryptanalysis, steganalysis, IoT malware, synthetic data generators, network security, biometrics recognition, object detection, virtual assistants, cyber-physical control systems, phishing detection, computational red teaming, natural language generation, etc. But the data analytics results from adversarial data mining are not always formulated in terms of game theoretical modelling and optimization although game theory provides an excellent abstraction for generative-discriminative modelling in adversarial deep learning that is intractable in shallow architectures for machine learning.

Chapter 7 develops a discussion on the utilization of adversarial learning in privacy enhancing technologies. By defining the trust, resilience, and agility ontologies for each threat agent the privacy preserving data mining techniques can extend our research in game theoretical adversarial deep learning to operate in accordance with privacy-by-design paradigm for contractual, statutory, and regulatory requirements regarding the use of computing and internet technologies in machine learning. We can produce security and dependability metrics ontologies to reflect the quality of an adversarial system with respect to its privacy functionality, performance, dependability, coupled with security costs and complexities, transparency and fairness, interpretability, and explainability in modelling the adversarial AI agents within multivector, multistage, and hybrid kill-chain strategies for cyberattacks. Computational difficulties for measuring utility and associated information loss can be addressed in game theory to provision security service offerings satisfying lightweightness, heterogeneity, early detection of attacks, high availability, high accuracy, high reliability, fault tolerance, resilience, robustness, scalability, and energy efficiency. Such adversarial AI agents can discover new attacks and learn over time to respond better to threats in cybersecurity as seen in intelligent scanners, firewalls, anti-malware, intelligent espionage tools, and autonomous weapons.

Secunderabad, Hyderabad, Telangana, India   Aneesh Sreevallabh Chivukula
Qingdao, Shandong, China   Xinghao Yang
Sydney, NSW, Australia   Bo Liu
Sydney, NSW, Australia   Wei Liu
Sydney, NSW, Australia   Wanlei Zhou

Contents

The original version of the book has been revised. A correction to this book can be found at
https://doi.org/10.1007/978-3-030-99772-4_8

Author Biography

Dr. Aneesh Sreevallabh Chivukula is an assistant professor in the Department of Computer Science & Information Systems at the Birla Institute of Technology and Science (BITS), Pilani, Hyderabad Campus. He has a PhD in data analytics and machine learning from the University of Technology Sydney (UTS), Australia. He holds a Master of Science by Research in computer science and artificial intelligence from the International Institute of Information Technology Hyderabad, India. His research interests are in Computational Algorithms, Adversarial Learning, Machine Learning, Deep Learning, Data Mining, Game Theory, and Robust Optimization. He has taught subjects on advanced analytics and problem solving at UTS. He has been teaching academic courses on computer science at BITS, Pilani. He has industry experience in engineering, R&D, consulting at research labs, and startup companies. He has developed enterprise solutions across the value chains in the open source, Cloud, and Big Data markets.

List of Figures

List of Tables

Chapter 1
Adversarial Machine Learning

This chapter investigates the robustness gap between machine intelligence and human perception in machine learning for cyberspace security with game theoretical adversarial learning algorithms. In this chapter, we shall conduct a literature review to provide new insights on the relation between adversarial learning and cybersecurity. We seek to survey and summarize non-stationary data representations learnt by machine learning models. The modelling robustness shall be surveyed to produce a summarization of adversarial examples and adversarial algorithms. We shall also survey the use of convex optimization, stochastic optimization, and evolutionary computing in adversarial deep learning formulations. Another interesting study shall be that of defense mechanisms available for deep learning models deployed in real-world environments.

Data mining is the study of automatically learning mathematical patterns from the information in a database. It is a process of knowledge discovery that requires developing computational algorithms [182] for preprocessing, modelling, and post-processing data given a database system. The design of those algorithms, however, must be based on a machine learning paradigm. Machine learning paradigms are modes of computational learning based on some underlying statistical assumptions, such as the level of human oversight in the training data or the data's underlying distribution. Example paradigms include supervised learning, unsupervised learning, semi-supervised learning, reinforcement learning, meta-learning, and deep learning.

A standard statistical assumption, called the stationarity assumption, is that the training data used by a model to learn a mathematical pattern and the testing data used to evaluate how well it recognizes those patterns are sampled from the same underlying probability distribution of independent and identically distributed (i.i.d) random variables. Yet the stationarity assumption does not hold in most real-world applications; training and testing data seldom share exactly the same distributions and are not often i.i.d. Therefore, a robust learning paradigm for non-stationary data analytics has become something of a goal in adversarial learning. Adversarial learning has applications in areas like spam filtering, virus detection,

A. Sreevallabh Chivukula et al., *Adversarial Machine Learning*,
https://doi.org/10.1007/978-3-030-99772-4_1

intrusion detection, fraud detection, biometric authentication, network protocol verification, computational advertising, recommender systems, social media web mining, complex system performance modelling, and so on [31, 56].

Adversarial learning algorithms are specifically designed to exploit vulnerabilities in a given machine learning algorithm. These vulnerabilities are simulated by training the learning algorithm under various attack scenarios and policies. The attack scenarios are assumed to be formulated by an intelligent adversary [285], and the optimal attack policy is one that can solve one or many optimization problems over one or many attack scenarios, noting that various adversarial learning algorithms may differ in their statistical assumptions over the adversary's knowledge, security violations, attack strategies, and attack influences [63].

As such, a learning algorithm that has been designed to offset an attack becomes robust to that attack; its vulnerabilities are no longer vulnerable. Thus, the goal of adversarial learning can be thought of as one of finding solutions for the objective functions in search and optimization algorithms that defend against attack scenarios. Once found, these solutions can be incorporated into the design of many machine learning algorithms as defense mechanisms to guard against attack.

Deep learning refers to a particular class of neural network algorithms. These algorithms consist of many stages of non-linear information processing in hierarchical architectures exploited for pattern classification and feature learning [156]. Deep learning research aims to discover machine learning algorithms at multiple levels of data abstraction.

Deep learning with high-dimensional data has been found to be susceptible to adversarial attacks. Such attacks are crafted by prior knowledge, observation, and experimentation on the loss functions in the deep learning models [226]. A systematic investigation into the design of deep learning loss functions to defend against adversaries is a novel and practical area of research. Furthermore, statistical error analyses of the data-driven loss functions must consider conflicting optimization goals in the models under attack, such as accuracy, scalability, runtime, and diversity, defined over underlying data distributions.

Loss functions have been defined in the context of multiple machine learning paradigms applicable to deep learning. In supervised learning, loss functions are defined as fitting criteria for class probability estimation [92]. In statistical learning, loss functions are defined as minimizers of empirical risk in training data [524]. In computational learning, loss functions are said to minimize Bayes decision rule for predictors by computing the expected probability of classification error [415]. Energy-based learning models [349, 350] are a theoretical framework for statistical inference and computational learning characterized by loss functions.

Adversarial learning problems in discriminative learning loss functions are typically formulated with statistical divergence metrics between training data features and adversarial data features. The latent space on high-dimensional training data can also be searched by deep networks to construct adversarial examples. Depending on the goal, knowledge, and capability of an adversary, adversarial examples can also be crafted by prior knowledge, observation, and experimentation on the loss functions in deep learning.

Thus the existing adversarial learning algorithms differ in design assumptions regarding adversary's knowledge, attack strategies, attack influence, and security violation. Furthermore, adversarial examples are known to transfer between data-specific manifolds of machine learning models. Therefore the predictive performance of deep learning models under attack is an interesting area for research.

Adversarial attack technologies exist in computer vision, natural language processing, cyberspace security on multidimensional, textual and image data, sequence data, and spatial data. Such problems study feature manipulations, misclassifications costs, and distributional robustness in deep learning models misspecification. Resultant machine learning algorithms have applications to model cybersecurity risks in web security, malware analysis, anti-spoofing techniques, rare pattern mining, imbalanced classification, out-of-distribution examples detection, concept drift, and motif mining. The related adversarial loss functions and training procedures are applicable to the evaluation of deep learning deployments trustworthiness. They can simulate the cyberspace security safeguards, risks, and challenges as computational optimization and statistical inference problems. Generating and explaining the adversarial data manipulations allows a study of the effects of algorithmic bias in deep learning. Further it can be the conduit for robust optimization theories developed around adversarial machine learning.

In image processing and computer vision, data provenance has applications in image forensics for the detection of manipulated images in strategic intelligence. Questions on the origin of suspect images have gained prominence with the increase in deepfakes on the Internet. Deepfakes are deep learning networks that are able to generate fake news and fake evidence on the Internet. They are of public concern in the online social media and search engine landscape. Misinformation threats due to fake data can try to target the weakest links in the information chain for falsification purposes. They can be used to manipulate public opinion during elections, discredit, and blackmail people. New approaches to recognizing synthetic media must be provided into browser extensions and analytics toolsets. Further adversarial attacks to scramble objects in images can disrupt computer vision result to increase misclassification rates and spread false information. Deepfakes have applications in creative arts, advertising, film production, and video games [617]. They can affect the politics of evidence involving audiovisual manipulation in witness testimony. It can be recontextualized, reinterpreted, and broadcasted on the Internet. Nguyen et al. [460] give a survey of the deep learning models to create deepfake content. Carlini et al. [103] have an approach to construct robustness bounds in neural networks that have to contend with such adversarial examples designed to mislead image classifications to take unwanted actions.

Integrating data provenance into machine learning shall create robust, scalable, and generalizable methods for knowledge discovery that can support authenticity of digital media to obtain accurate and reliable results in augmented intelligence with adversarial training. Explainable artificial intelligence is a research area advancing machine learning in digital media forensics and predictive technologies. Robust models for data-driven decision-making in machine learning assume imperfect information is available for learning system parameters and optimizing probability distributions on uncertain data and erroneous estimations. In robust optimization, random variables underlying the machine learning features are modelled as uncertain parameters belonging to a convex uncertainty set and the decision-maker protects the machine learning system against the worst case within that set. Data-driven optimization objectives then use observations of the random variables as training inputs to mathematical programming problems. Robust decision-making involves stochastic programming and optimization under probabilistic constraints. Robust optimization problems can also be studied as risk aversion problems with an empirical risk measure for feature engineering [692] with adversarial robustness. Deep generative modelling of the adversarial data manipulations investigates the dependencies between generative modelling and causal attributions in the latent variables. It has applications in computer vision tasks acting as control pipelines in physical systems where the main challenge with generating robust physical perturbations is environmental variability.

1.1 Adversarial Learning Frameworks

Traditional machine learning models assume training data samples, testing data samples, and validation data samples follow the same, independent, and identically distributed data distribution. This assumption creates security vulnerabilities in machine learning models subject to attack from intelligent adversaries with a malicious intent. Given training data samples, such adversaries design adversarial examples to increase model error. Securing learning systems from such adversarial examples is an active area of research in artificial intelligence, security diagnostics, generative learning, deep learning, information security, autonomous systems, intelligent systems, and data analytics.

Adversarial examples can mislead learning models as long as adversary's attack is planned after learning model has completed training and therefore cannot react to new samples. From this observation, adversarial algorithms incorporate adversary into training process of learning models. Thus, adversarial algorithms model adversarial machine learning as an interaction between two agents—the learning model and one or more intelligent adversaries.

Game theory provides a framework to study interactions between learning model (or learner for short) and intelligent adversary (or adversary for short) in terms of interaction between evolving strategies of the learner and the adversary. Game theory interactions were first formulated in life sciences as non-linear differential equations that study interactions between populations of biological systems.

In machine learning, loss functions quantify the impact of information uncertainty over a distribution of analytics predictions. Adversarial algorithms formulate machine learning loss functions for a training process that prevents model overfitting to training data in presence of rational, adaptive adversaries that simulate evolving changes to learning environment as adversarial examples.

In game theoretical adversarial learning, adversarial examples are generated by designing machine learning algorithms under various attack scenarios in adversary's strategy space. Optimal attack strategy for adversarial manipulation is formulated as solution to (often non-linear and non-convex) optimization problems.

Adversarial examples are hard to detect because machine learning models trained on limited data are required to produce expected output for every possible input. Reinforcement learning agents can also be manipulated by adversarial examples to result in degraded agent performance in the presence of perturbations too subtle to be perceived by a human.

In the following literature review, we provide an overview of the existing adversarial machine learning algorithms, each differing in attack scenarios and defense mechanisms for deploying reliable data analysis systems and robust pattern recognition systems. We also summarize the state-of-the-art techniques in game theoretical adversarial learning and adversarial reinforcement learning for software-based inference and decision-making.

1.1.1 Adversarial Algorithms Comparisons

This section presents a literature review and attack taxonomy of adversarial learning algorithms. The adversarial algorithms are summarized in Tables 1.1 and 1.2 in terms of algorithm design and algorithm application. The algorithms are primarily compared on the adversarial cost function (or cost function for short). It is a measure of the expected performance of the learning algorithm in the presence of an adversary. It is formulated differently for different adversarial learning algorithms. The tables' columns list the various features for comparing adversarial learning algorithms. Our algorithm is termed "game theory : deep learning." The tables' rows list the various algorithms under comparison. Across the rows, we list computational models vulnerable to adversarial data for feature extraction, deep learning, support vector machines, and classifier ensembles where the input data for simulating adversarial attacks is taken to be text spam, image spam, and biometric spam. The algorithms are compared on cost function, search algorithm, convergence conditions, attack strategy, attack influence, security violation, adversary's knowledge, algorithm moves, and learning games. The "cost function" is the objective function to solve for adversarial data. The "search algorithm" is the algorithm used to find an optimal solution. The "convergence conditions" is the search criteria for creating adversarial data. The "attack strategy" is the attack scenario under which the adversary operates. The "attack influence" of a strategy determines the access that the adversary has to train data and test data input to the learning algorithm. The "security violation" is the purpose of the adversary's attack. The "adversary's knowledge" is the semantic information of the adversary. The "algorithm moves" are the actions taken by learning algorithm to adapt to adversarial data manipulation. From the tables, we see that most of the existing research works do not add game theory formulations to the cost function. Thus most of the existing learning

Table 1.1 Adversarial algorithms comparison 1

Adversarial algorithm	Cost function	Search algorithm	Convergence conditions	Attack strategy	Attack influence	Security violation	Adversary's knowledge	Algorithm moves	Learning games
Classifier ensembles [59]	$E = 2 - \frac{2}{n}\sum_{k=1}^{n} F(k),\ F(k) = \frac{\sum_{i=1}^{k}\lvert w_i\rvert}{\sum_{j=1}^{n}\lvert w_j\rvert}.$ (1.1)	Randomized sampling	Ensemble size, feature subset size	Reorder features by importance for discriminant function	Causative	Targeted, availability	Training features	Average discrimination functions	None
Feature weighting [321]	$min_w \frac{\lambda}{2} w^T w + \frac{1}{m}\sum_{i=1}^{m} l(w^T(S^{-1}x), y),$ $l(f, y) = max(0, 1 - yf).$ (1.2)	Feature bagging	Number of base models	Addition/deletion of binary features	Causative	Indiscriminate, availability	Training features	Average estimated weights	None
SVM: inputs [65]	$max_{x_c} L(x_c) = \sum_{k=1}^{m}(1 - y_k f_c(x_k))$ $\frac{\partial L}{\partial u} = \sum_{k=1}^{m} M_k \frac{\partial Q_{kc}}{\partial u} + \frac{\partial Q_{kc}}{\partial u}\alpha_c.$ (1.3)	Gradient ascent	Change in test error	Train noise injection	Causative	Targeted, integrity	Gradient of loss	Incremental learning svms	None
SVM: labels [664]	$L(D_{tr}) = argmin_{f\in F}[\Omega(f) + C.\hat{R}(f, D_{tr})],$ $\hat{R}(f, D_{tr}) = \frac{1}{n}\sum_{i=1}^{n} l(f(x_i), y_i),\ C > 0,$ (1.4) $V_L(D_{tr}, D_{vd}) = f_{Dtr}^2 + C.\hat{R}(f_{Dtr}, D_{vd}),$ $f_{Dtr} = L(D_{tr}),\ V_L(z, y) = V_L((x_i, z_i), (x_i, y_i)).$	Gradient ascent	svm margin support vectors by lp and qp	Label noise injection	Causative	Targeted, integrity	Training labels	Update svm weights and hyperplanes	None

		Backpropagation with L-BFGS	Early stopping on adversarial validation set error	Linear perturbation on x	Causative	Targeted, integrity	Training and testing data	Update decision function parameters	None
Deep learning [227]	$\hat{J}(\theta, x, y) = \alpha J(\theta, x, y) + (1 - \alpha) J((\theta, x + \epsilon$ (1.7) $sign(\nabla_x J(\theta, x, y))))$.	Backpropagation with L-BFGS	Early stopping on adversarial validation set error	Linear perturbation on x	Causative	Targeted, integrity	Training and testing data	Update decision function parameters	None
Adversarial networks: DNN [480]	$S_{p+1} = x + \lambda_{p+1} sgn(J_F[\hat{O}(x)])U S_p,$ $\hat{O}(x) = argmax_{j=0...N-1} O_j(x),$ (1.6) $\delta_x = \epsilon sgn(\Delta_x c(F, x, y)),$ $c(F, x, y) = p(y = 1|x) = exp((x - \mu)^T \beta(x - \mu)),$ $F(x) = f_n(\theta_n, f_{n-1}(\theta_{n-1}, \ldots f_2(\theta_2, f_1(\theta_1, x)))).$	Jacobian-based dataset augmentation	Early stopping on adversarial validation set error	Observe DNN outputs given inputs chosen by the adversary	Exploratory	Targeted, integrity	Testing data	Jacobian-based regularization and distillation	None

Table 1.2 Adversarial algorithms comparison 2

Adversarial algorithm	Cost function	Search algorithm	Convergence conditions	Attack strategy	Attack influence	Security violation	Adversary's knowledge	Algorithm moves	Learning games
Adversarial networks: DAE [238]	$J_{DCN}(\theta) = \Sigma_{i=1}^{m}(L(t^i, y^i) + \Sigma_{j=1}^{H+1}\lambda_j\|\frac{\partial h_j^i}{\partial h_{j-1}^i}\|_2)$ (1.7) $min_r c|r|_2 + L(x+r, l).$	Stacking DAEs into a feedforward neural network	Training error	Gaussian additive noise	Exploratory	Indiscriminate, availability	Testing data	Penalty function smoothing the adversarial data	None
Game theory: regularized loss [385]	$max_\alpha min_w - \lambda\alpha^T\alpha + \lambda w^T w + C\Sigma_{i=1}^{n}$ (1.8) $Loss(y_i, w^T(x_i + \alpha)).$	Trust region	Adversary's payoff does not increase or the maximum number of iterations is reached	Move positive data toward negative samples	Causative	Targeted, availability	Training and testing data	Rebuild classifiers though his regularized loss function	Zero sum game
Game theory: sparse attacks [628]	$min_{w\in R^d}|y - Xw|_2 + \Sigma_{i=1}^{d}\lambda_i|w_i|_1.$ (1.9)	Minimum budget	Accumulated cost more than minimum budget	Select features affect estimated weights	Causative	Indiscriminate, privacy	Estimated weights	Robust regularization	Non-zero sum game
Game theory: support vector machines [220]	$min\frac{1}{2}|w|^2 + C\Sigma_i[1 - y_i w^T x_i + t_i]$ $t_i \geq Kz_i + \Sigma_j v_{ij}$ (1.10) $t_i \geq Kz_i + \Sigma_j v_{ij}$ $v_i \geq 0$ $z_i + v_i \geq (y_i x_i w).$	Quadratic programming	Training error subject to regularization terms	Delete different features from different data points	Causative	Targeted, integrity	Training features	Parameters regularization	Non-zero sum game
Game theory: deep learning (Our method)	$Maxmin: (\alpha^*, w^*) = argmax_{\alpha\in A}$ (1.11) $J_L(\alpha, argmin_{w\in W} J_L(\alpha, w)).$	Evolutionary algorithm	Nash equilibrium	Move positive samples toward negative samples	Causative	Targeted, integrity	Training data	Update estimated weights for adversarial manipulation	Constant sum game

algorithms cannot adapt to continuous adversarial data manipulations. As shown in the column "Learning games," it is the only adversarial learning algorithm that has a game theory-based formulation of training and testing data distributions input to deep learning models.

1.2 Adversarial Security Mechanisms

In addition to Tables 1.1 and 1.2, the existing adversarial learning algorithms and their application domains can also be classified by the learner's defense mechanisms and corresponding adversary's attack scenarios [33, 59, 63, 531]. Learner's defense mechanisms have been proposed by designing secure learning algorithms [63], multiple classifier systems [59], privacy-preserving machine learning [531], and use of randomization or disinformation to mislead the adversary [33].

Biggio et al. [63] discuss learner's defense mechanism in terms of an empirical framework extending the model selection and performance evaluation steps of pattern classification by Duda et al. [166]. The framework recommends training the learner for "security by design" rather than "security by obscurity." The framework recommends following additional steps to validate the defense mechanisms proposed in case of both generative learning models and discriminative learning models under attack.

- Proactively anticipate the most relevant adversarial attacks through a what-if analysis simulating potential attack scenarios.
- Define attack scenarios in terms of goal, knowledge, and capability of adversary.
- Propose a generative data distribution model on conditional probabilities that can formally account for a large number of potential attacks and cross-validation samples on training data and testing data.

Following assumptions are made regarding the learning algorithm's security. The model performance is then evaluated under an optimal attack strategy simulated according to the framework proposed by Biggio et al. [63].

- An adversary's goal is formulated as the optimization of an objective function. The objective function is designed on the desired security violation (that is integrity, availability, or privacy) and attack specificity (from targeted to indiscriminate).
- An adversary's knowledge is defined as knowledge of the components of the classifier, viz., training data, feature set, learning algorithm, decision function and its parameters, available and feedback.
- An adversary's capability is defined as the control adversary has on training data and testing data taking into account application-specific constraints such as attack influence (either causative or exploratory), effect on class priors, fraction of samples, and features manipulated by adversary.

Depending on the goal, knowledge, and capability of the adversary, these assumptions are also classified in terms of attack influence, security violation, and attack specificity.

The attack influence can be causative or exploratory. Causative attack affects both training and testing data. Exploratory attack affects only testing data.

The security violation can target either integrity or availability or privacy of the learner. A machine learning algorithm whose integrity is compromised cannot detect malicious behavior of the adversary. The integrity of an algorithm with many false negatives gets compromised. A machine learning algorithm whose availability is compromised exhibits severely degraded performance for legitimate users. The availability of an algorithm with many false positives gets compromised. The privacy of an algorithm whose detailed feedback is made public also gets compromised.

The attack specificity can be either targeted or indiscriminate for attacks that influence prediction or action of the algorithm. In targeted attacks the attack is directed at only a few instances of the training or testing data. In indiscriminate attacks the attack is directed at an entire class of instances or objects.

Our adversarial algorithms have causative attack influence, integrity security violation, and targeted attack specificity.

The typical adversary's attack scenarios range across (i) adding noise to features/labels, (ii) adding/deleting features/labels, (iii) slight change or manipulation or perturbation to data distributions, and (iv) slight change to decision boundaries. The corresponding optimization problems are solved using search algorithms with sampling and gradients methods. The sampling methods range across incremental sampling, bagging sampling, stacking sampling, and randomized sampling. The gradient methods range across linear methods, quadratic methods, convex methods, and stochastic methods. These optimization problems are solved on finding a local optimum solution determined by convergence conditions ranging across (i) number of features, (ii) number of regularization terms, and (iii) changes to estimated errors over training/testing data.

Our adversarial algorithms cause slight change to data distributions simulated by stochastic optimization and randomized sampling methods. Our optimization problems converge onto solutions computed at Nash equilibria in Stackelberg games. From the adversary's standpoint, the equilibrium solution is a local optimum in case of worst-case attack scenarios and a global optimum in case of best-case attack scenarios. The strength and relevancy of our attack scenarios is determined by the performance of the deep learning models under attack.

1.2.1 Adversarial Examples Taxonomies

Papernot et al. [482] provide a threat model summarizing various attack scenarios in adversarial learning algorithms. The adversarial classifier's defense mechanisms are then supposed to improve model robustness to its validation data samples.

Here, validation data samples are deployed into the trained model's runtime data distribution to be non-iid with respect to testing data samples in trained model's training data distribution.

Papernot et al. [482] express their machine learning threat model in steps of adversarial manipulations found during machine learning training process and machine learning inference process. During machine learning training process, adversary is supposed to manipulate either online data collection processes or offline data collection processes. Such an adversarial manipulation either injects adversarial examples or modifies training data with intent of modifying learning model's decision boundaries. During machine learning inference process, adversary is supposed to plan either blackbox attacks or whitebox attacks on learning model's parameters. Such attack settings cause distribution drifts between training and runtime data distributions.

Papernot et al. [482] also view machine learning security through the prism of confidentiality, integrity, and availability models where adversary targets classifier's parameters, labels, and features, respectively. In contrast to machine learning security, machine learning privacy is explored in terms of model performance when (i) training and runtime data distributions differ, (ii) amount of data exposed by learning model is bound by a differential privacy budget, and (iii) learning model's defenses provide fairness, interpretability, and transparency to learning outputs. Adversarial environments affecting model complexity, model accuracy, and model resilience are formulated in terms of no free lunch theorem for adversarial learning. Papernot et al. [482] also motivate game theoretical adversarial learning during machine learning inference within a probably approximately correct (PAC) learning framework.

Biggio et al. [68] survey adversarial machine learning for pattern classifiers. The adversarial examples for pattern classifiers are supposed to be created at either training time or testing time. Recent research in adversarial examples for deep network applications in computer vision and cybersecurity is also discussed. Attack scenarios at training time are called poisoning attacks, while attack scenarios at testing time are called evasion attacks. To integrate with deep learning terminology, poisoning attacks are also called adversarial training attacks while evasion attacks are also called adversarial testing attacks. Then security evaluation and defense mechanisms of pattern classifiers under attack are discussed. Here, a proactive security-by-design learning model incorporating adversary designs in learning process is also presented. It is shown in Fig. 1.1.

Biggio et al. [68] categorize adversary designs as optimization problem-solving for best attack strategy defined by adversary's goal in attack scenario, adversary's knowledge of targeted learning system and adversary's capability of manipulating input data. Under various assumptions on such adversary designs, optimal attack strategies are then shown to be possible for not only supervised learning algorithms but also unsupervised learning algorithms such as clustering algorithms and feature selection algorithms. Adversary's goal is further categorized into (i) security violation that compromises one of integrity, availability, and privacy of learning system and (ii) attack specificity and error specificity that cause misclassification

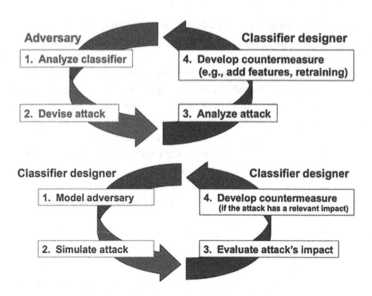

Fig. 1.1 Reactive and proactive arms race between adversary and learner

of specific set of samples and specific set of classes, respectively. Here, adversary's knowledge of targeted learning system is further categorized into following

- **Perfect-knowledge whitebox attacks** with complete knowledge of learning parameters. In this case, security evaluation provides upper bound on performance degradation in attack scenario.
- **Limited-knowledge gray-box attacks** with prior knowledge about feature representation and learning algorithm but not training data and learning parameters. Here security evaluation is conducted on a surrogate classifier learning a surrogate dataset available from similar data source as training data. Adversarial examples for surrogate classifier are then tested against targeted classifier to evaluate transferability of attack scenarios between learning algorithms.
- **Zero-knowledge blackbox attacks** without any knowledge of learning algorithm but partial knowledge of feature representation and training data distribution. Here security evaluation checks whether optimal attack strategy transfers between an optimally trained surrogate model and targeted classifier model. Reinforced feedback on classifier decisions can be used to refine surrogate model.

Biggio et al. [68] also categorize adversary's knowledge by application-specific data manipulation constraints on input data distributions, features, and classes. A high-level formulation of adversary's optimal attack strategy and classifier's security evaluation curves is also provided. Such a security evaluation considers both differentiable and non-differentiable learning algorithms like neural networks and decision trees, respectively. Here sensitivity analysis of deep networks is defined as a study of the phenomenon of minimally perturbing training samples, whereas a more general security evaluation of pattern classifiers is defined to be a study of adversary's attack strength and attack confidence in manipulating classifier's decision boundaries for the targeted classes. Proactive defense techniques summarized across such attack settings include (i) randomizing training data and classifier output, (ii) domain experts correcting classifier decisions, (iii) data sanitization with robust statistics, (iv) automatic drift detection, (v) properly combining classifier ensembles, (vi) iterative adversarial training heuristics, (vii) game theoretical adversarial learning, and (viii) robust optimization in regularized learning that effectively tackle the curse of dimensionality on large datasets and non-linear classifiers. Future research of data-driven adversarial machine learning security evaluation is proposed to lie at intersection of software testing, formal verification, robust artificial intelligence, and interpretable machine learning.

1.3   Stochastic Game Illustration in Adversarial Deep Learning

Figure 1.2 illustrates the learning process in the game formulation of our research as a flow chart. The $CNN_{original}$ is trained on training data X_{train} and evaluated on testing data X_{test} to give "learner performance" in the experiments. Figure 1.2

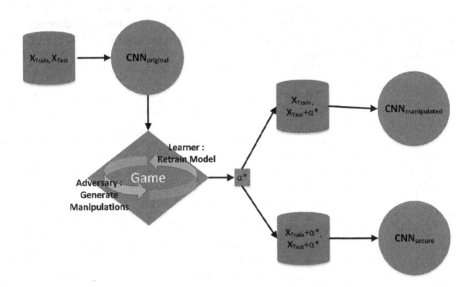

Fig. 1.2 A flow chart illustrating the benefits of a game theoretic learner. The two-player game is played by a single adversary and one learner. The game produces a final deep learning network CNN_{secure} that is better equipped to deal with the adversarial manipulations than the initial deep learning network $CNN_{original}$

illustrates a two-player game. The game has moves executed by each of the adversaries and the learner during each interaction. In these moves, an adversary targets the learner by the adversarial sample produced from the evolutionary operators. The learner then adapts the deep learning operators for the adversarial data by retraining the CNN on the new cross-validation sample.

A set L of M adversaries $L = \{L_1, L_2, L_3, \ldots, L_M\}$ targets this performance by engaging the CNN in multiple two-player sequential games. In each two-player game, the CNNs trained on the original and generated data samples and tested on the adversarial data are $CNN_{manipulated-cnn}$ and $CNN_{manipulated-gan}$, respectively. All these CNNs are given under the umbrella term "manipulated learner performance." We find that $CNN_{manipulated-cnn}$ as well as $CNN_{manipulated-gan}$ are significantly worse performing than the original CNN $CNN_{original}$ trained on the original training and testing data (X_{train}, X_{test}). Thus we conclude adversarial manipulation succeeds in attacking the learner. A new convolutional neural network CNN_{secure} is then retrained on $(X_{train} + \mathbb{A}_S^*, X_{test} + \mathbb{A}_S^*)$ to adapt to adversarial manipulations. It is given as "secure learner performance." CNN_{secure} is our proposed model. It is found to be better than the manipulated CNN's $CNN_{manipulated-cnn}$ and $CNN_{manipulated-gan}$.

Therefore, we conclude that the new CNN_{secure} has successfully adapted to adversarial data generated by multiple adversaries, while the given $CNN_{original}$ is vulnerable to each adversarial manipulation α_i^* generated by each adversary L_i playing a game i on the given training/testing data distributions. Our algorithm is able to find a data sample that affects the performance of a CNN. The CNN that is able to recover from our adversarial attack is better equipped to deal with unforeseen changes in the underlying data distribution. The game between adversary and learner allows us to produce adversarial data manipulations for a CNN trained on the underlying data distribution.

Chapter 2
Adversarial Deep Learning

Deep learning is not provably secure. Deep neural networks are vulnerable to security attacks from malicious adversaries, which is an ongoing and critical challenge for deep learning researchers. This chapter studies adversarial deep learning algorithms in exploiting vulnerabilities of deep neural networks. The core focus is on a series of game theoretical adversarial deep learning algorithms for improved network robustness especially under zero-knowledge black-box attack scenarios. Although there are many recent works that study network vulnerabilities, few are proposed for zero-knowledge black-box attacks, and even fewer are on game theoretical-based approach. Even innocuous perturbations in training data can change the way a deep network behaves in unintended ways. This means that imperceptibly and immeasurably small departures from the training data can result in a completely different label classification when using the model for supervised deep learning. The algorithmic details proposed in this chapter have been used in game theoretical adversarial deep learning with evolutionary adversaries, stochastic adversaries, randomized adversaries, and variational adversaries proposed in our research. In designing the attack scenarios, the adversarial objective was to make small, undetectable changes to the test data. The adversary manipulates representation parameters in the input data to mislead the learning process of the deep neural network, so it successfully misclassifies the original class labels as the targeted class labels.

Deng [156] surveys existing literature on deep learning for representation learning and feature learning where a hierarchy of higher-level features or concepts are defined from lower-level ones. Deep learning models, architectures, and algorithms are categorized into three classes—generative, discriminative, and hybrid models:

- Generative models characterize the joint probability distributions of the observed data and their associated classes with high-order correlation properties between the observed variables and the hidden variables.

A. Sreevallabh Chivukula et al., *Adversarial Machine Learning*,
https://doi.org/10.1007/978-3-030-99772-4_2

- Discriminative models distinguish between patterns by characterizing the posterior distributions of classes conditioned on the observed data.
- Hybrid models are discriminative models assisted by generative models in a significant way via better optimization or/and regularization of discriminative criteria used to learn parameters from data.

Deep learning is also understood by Deng [156] as an extension of previous research work on shallow architectures solving well-constrained problems such as generalized linear models, multi-layer perceptrons, support vector machines, maximum entropy models, conditional random fields, Gaussian mixture models, and hidden Markov models. For the typical problems addressed by deep architectures, such shallow architectures and their statistical methods tend to produce intractable computational algorithms for class inference.

The commonly used deep learning models such as deep belief networks, variational autoencoders, and convolutional neural network extract structures and regularities in the input features by avoiding difficulties with global optimization. Parameter optimization is done by designing a greedy layer-by-layer training algorithm that helps alleviate the overfitting problem observed in many shallow architectures training millions of parameters. Thus, deep learning models are useful for end-to-end learning of intelligent systems embedding domain knowledge and interpreting uncertainty.

2.1 Learning Curve Analysis for Supervised Machine Learning

No free lunch (NFL) theorems for supervised learning and optimization [649–651] state that, averaged over all learning theoretic situations represented in data samples, machine learning models preferring simple to complex training fail as often as they succeed. This means that the random process generating training data distribution may not always be the same as the random process governing the testing data distribution. There are many alternative models to consider for the analysis of data mixed with noise. There is no guarantee that the statistical model chosen is the right one or adequately captures patterns in all the data samples. Smoothing and regularization techniques are a simple approach to uncover patterns in training data with a minimum of preconceptions and assumptions as to what those patterns should be in testing data. In general, we have to contend with a model selection criteria for the chosen analytics algorithm.

In predictive analytics models built with supervised machine learning algorithms, the model selection criteria carries out an optimization of the goodness of fit to a training and a testing data sample. This is called cross-validation which assumes that a statistical model is as good as its prediction. This model evaluation scheme is unable to estimate counterfactual predictions when the world changes. So Fig. 2.1 shows additional validation data samples to compare predicted classes

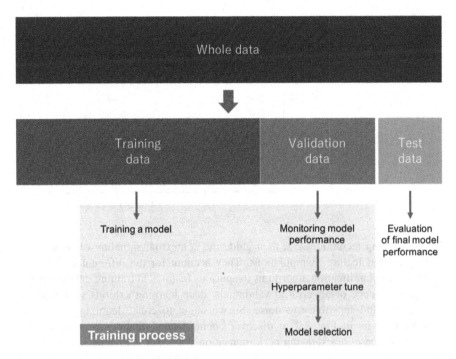

Fig. 2.1   Adversarial loss functions training process

with actual classes. In adversarial learning, such comparisons are done with the adversarial cost functions accounting for both class and cost distribution information in generating the predictions of supervised learning algorithms. Thus, adversarial data can be considered to be part of the validation data samples in model selection. An adversarial training process trains the machine learning models on both training data samples given by the user and validation data samples created by the adversary. Further, the validation data samples are used to fine-tune the hyperparameters for training the machine learning models.

In experimental evaluation of adversarial machine learning, we may run statistical tests to find counterfactual scenarios in the training data. Causal inference can also be used to estimate the impact of counterfactual scenarios. For systematic model selection in machine learning, the counterfactual modeling focus is on estimating what would happen in the event of a change that may or may not actually happen in the training data. Such adversarial machine learning models may sacrifice predictive performance in the current environment for machine learning to discover new counterfactual features in a changing validation environment for machine learning. The resultant counterfactual policies comparing training data with validation data can be used to define new sensitivity analysis, anomaly detection, and concept drift applications for adversarial learning. Cost-sensitive evaluation metrics account for severity differences in false alarms versus missed fraud cases.

Fig. 2.2 Custom loss functions learning curves

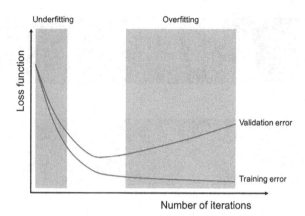

Feature ranking techniques can then guide the contextual signaling of fraudulent predictions and feature manipulations. They account for the different degrees of sensitivity of classification algorithms to spurious features in training data samples.

In the presence of adversarial validations, deep learning exhibits slow rate of convergence and sensitivity to noise. So we ought to create learning curves on deep learning as in Fig. 2.2 to discover counterfactual features in color-coded classification baselines showing performance on y-axis for parameter ranges on x-axis. According to the bias-variance tradeoffs in machine learning, complex models that tend to overfit noisy data exhibit high variance, while simplistic models that lack flexibility to approximate complex processes exhibit high bias.

We wish to arrive at a goodness of fit criteria for model selection that is neither underfitting with high bias nor overfitting with high variance to the training data samples. Practically, we want to select the regions of Fig. 2.2 that exhibit low errors on all of training, validation, and testing data samples. Overfitting occurs when training error is low but testing error is high. Underfitting occurs when testing error is low but training error is high. In analyzing the prediction error, bias-variance decomposition separates the analysis of bias and variance in the machine learning model evaluation. By bootstrapping samples from the data given in cross-validation experiments, we create training, validation, and testing data samples to estimate models from the machine learning algorithms. Bagging, boosting, and stacking are commonly used data sampling methods to create the cross-validation datasets. Bias-variance decomposition is applicable to the generalization errors resulting from loss functions in both classification and regression [160].

Learning curves represent the generalization performance of the models produced by a learning algorithm. Based on estimated probabilities for class membership, learning curves compare different classification algorithms to explore the relationship between training dataset size and the learning/induction algorithm. They allow us to see patterns that are common across different datasets. Without an examination of the learning curves, we cannot draw conclusions on one algorithm being better than another algorithm for a particular application domain. A summary of learning curve analysis is given by Perlich et al. [491].

Comparison between analytics modeling for robust theoretical evidence is to be done with performance metrics on the cost imbalance due to misclassification errors in the predictions. Predictive performance of the model's ability to distinguish between adversarial data and training data can be analyzed with accuracy and area under the receiver operating curve (AUC). Additionally, performance metrics that reflect the imbalance in class labels can be used to calculate the classification errors. They include sensitivity, F1-score, and F2-score. Learning curves papers. It is important to incorporate such data protection safeguards in the analytics value chain built with cross-validation or hold out testing to choose the "most accurate" algorithm for analyzing a given dataset.

A cyber risk analytics for the information leaks in deep learning has become necessary to analyze machine learning models trained on sensitive datasets. Learning curves can consider the bias-variance decomposition in adversarial loss functions to derive such regularizations in the learning objectives of supervised machine learning. During model validation experiments, the information divergence between the validation data samples and the training data samples may be computed as the discretized data distributions obtained from sampling schemes within adversarial deep learning.

The extent to which noise on modeling parameters and their training data can benefit the overall quality of the data distributions in sampling schemes depends on the specific adversarial noise processes and the nature of the generated target distribution in game theoretical adversarial learning. Our proposals study the interplay of adversarial cost function and classification error functions to design game theoretical classifiers that deteriorate at a slower rate than regular classifiers on adversarial data. With deep generative modeling of the adversary's best response strategies, we construct the data resampling dynamics from measurement studies on cost-sensitive adversaries for discriminative learning. We simulate encodings of the resultant decision boundaries as storing-retrieving problems in data mining.

2.2 Adversarial Loss Functions for Discriminative Learning

Adversarial examples can be crafted by experimentation on the loss functions in deep learning. Such experiments result in empirical data analytics around adversarial loss functions and corresponding training procedures in discriminative learning. This research is then applicable to the study of trustworthiness of deep learning in cyber-physical systems in real-world deployments.

We can formulate and customize the adversarial loss functions with adversarial learning objective functions solved by optimization algorithms. The adversarial learning algorithms can then devise training data manipulations with adversaries targeting to mislead deep neural networks. After demonstrating the vulnerability of deep learning in this way, we can propose defense mechanisms to make robust neural networks.

Specific to supervised learning applications, loss functions evaluate the statistical error of predictive analytics. Typically, the loss function reduces bias in a predictive classification model and variance in a predictive regression model [69]. Here, adversarial loss functions reduce the predictive model's sensitivity to model noise.

Our proposal is to analyze this type of noise in a game theoretical adversarial deep learning paradigm. It involves the design of adversarial payoff functions that generate adversarial data manipulations by optimizing the adversarial cost functions for different types of adversaries. Such adversaries include evolutionary, stochastic, randomization, variational, and generative adversaries.

The intuition of our adversarial loss functions is derived from the concept of actions and moves in game theory. During learning, the attack scenarios are modeled as moves made by a learning algorithm and countermoves made by an intelligent adversary. Our game theory studies interactions between independent self-interested agents or players working toward a goal. Each player has a set of associated strategies/moves/actions that optimize a payoff function or utility function for achieving the goal. The game eventually converges to an equilibrium state from which none of the players have any incentive to deviate.

Through optimizations of the proposed adversarial learning, we can empirically analyze the discriminative loss functions in deep learning to generate misclassified data points and hence adversarial manipulations to the training data. Further, in contrast to traditional deep learning methods, we propose adversarial payoff functions that are non-differentiable and discontinuous over the search space of the adversarial manipulations. Within an empirical risk minimization framework for supervised learning and game theory, we study adversarial loss functions for discriminative learning involving classification and regression.

Rich data science problems and machine learning features can be engineered from our algorithms by modeling a wide variety of data analytics application scenarios involving discriminative learning. For example, we propose adversarial loss functions to learn moments and cumulants of time-dependent data distributions in regression modeling. The proposed loss functions can be extended for non-linear algorithm-oriented approaches to robust regression. The sensitivity of our loss function could be customized with patterns constructed to improve application-dependent model selection. Here, deep generative models are helpful for feature engineering and learning generalizations in specific application domains.

Our adversarial payoff functions can model the discrimination hypotheses around class labels and their decision boundaries in classification modeling. The proposed payoff functions optimize the search for data manipulations on an original pixel data space as well as a latent data space representing pixel distributions by a Gaussian mixture model. The payoff functions were then optimized by the parameter settings in simulated annealing, variational learning, and generative learning algorithms. The deep neural network's misclassification performance at the time of Nash equilibrium was measured in terms of t-statistics hypothesized over recall, true positive rate, and the f_1-score of targeted class labels.

We experimented with adversarial payoff functions over randomized strategy spaces by changing the Stackelberg game formulation. Here, the attack scenarios over the strategy spaces determined the convergence criteria of Stackelberg games over multi-label datasets. In Nash equilibrium, the game converged on adversarial manipulations that affect testing performance across targeted labels in both two-label and multi-label classification models. The results led us to a proposal for a secure learner that is immune to that type of adversarial attack, and an empirical analysis confirms that this classification model is significantly more robust than a traditional deep neural network under attack by an adversary.

2.3 Adversarial Examples in Deep Networks

Papernot et al. [480] present a practical demonstration of adversarial samples known to transfer between deep learning models. Such adversarial examples are constructed to control the integrity of a target deep neural network (DNN) without access to the target DNN's architecture, parameters, and training data. A substitute DNN is then trained to approximate the target DNN's learned model. The substitute DNN also has no knowledge of the probability vectors encoding the target DNN's belief of the relation between training input and classes. The attack is defined by assuming that the adversary can observe target DNN's outputs given the inputs chosen by the adversary. The adversary model has access to the same training data distribution as the target model.

The substitute DNN is trained through a Jacobian-based dataset augmentation technique. This step in the algorithm is called substitute model training. This dataset augmentation technique allows adversary to select data points that are representative of the target DNN's behavior in the input domain. The adversarial attack is made tractable by limiting the number of queries put to the target DNN. The queries are formulated by an efficient search heuristic over the input data domain.

After finding adversarial examples, the algorithm fine-tunes the perturbations in the adversarial examples to maximize the transferability of adversarial samples. The fine-tuning is based on the observation that the substitute DNN's and target DNN's cost gradient sign matrices are correlated. This step in the algorithm is called adversarial sample crafting. In all, the adversarial algorithm goes through phases of initial collection, architecture selection, labeling, training, and augmentation. The adversarial algorithm produces a substitute training set that represents the target model's decision boundaries.

Two algorithms are implemented to search for the adversarial samples. Both search algorithms evaluate the target model's sensitivity to substitute model's input so that a small perturbation in the target model's input achieves the adversarial misclassification goal. Both search algorithms differ in computational efficiency of producing adversarial examples. Defenses proposed against such attacks include the use of adversarial sample training, Jacobian-based regularization and distillation, and a careful analysis of the distribution of queries.

Gu et al. [238] study the robustness of DNNs by studying pre-processing and training strategies accounting for the structure of adversarial examples as well as the targeted model's network topology. The pre-processing is done with denoising autoencoders (DAEs). Autoencoder is chosen as the deep learning model because it preserves the original non-adversarial data distribution by mapping original training data back to itself. The experiments in Gu et al. [238] demonstrate that DAEs are able to remove adversarial noise in DNN training strategies. Furthermore, an end-to-end training procedure with a penalty function smoothing the adversarial data is proposed by stacking DAEs into a feedforward neural network called a contractive autoencoder (CAE). The additional penalty in CAE minimizes the squared norm of the Jacobian of the hidden representation of input data.

DNNs achieve high performance because deep cascades of non-linear units allow to generalize non-locally in data-specific manifolds. The ability of DNNs to automatically learn non-local generalization priors from data is both a strength and weakness for adversarial learning in real-world environments. Adversarial examples in DNNs are attributed to the following reasons by Gu et al. [238].

- In high-dimensional data, the smoothness assumption that underlies kernel methods does not hold for deterministic feedforward neural network architectures
- Applying kernel methods in manifold space does not guarantee local generalization in the input space
- Due to cross-model cross-dataset generalization properties of adversarial examples, the attacker can generate adversarial examples from independent models
- Fewer degrees of freedom in data are captured as the layers of deep neural network increase

Therefore, according to Gu et al. [238], the challenge in DNN's design is to train a deep network that not only generalizes in abstract manifold space to achieve good recognition accuracy but also retains local generalization in the input space. In both shallow models and deep models, adversarial examples are also universal and unavoidable by this definition. Thus, deep learning architectures that are robust to adversarial data must be trained to incorporate input invariance with respect to the final network output accounting for adversarial data.

2.4 Adversarial Examples for Misleading Classifiers

Although neural networks achieve high performance by expressing an arbitrary computation in terms of massively parallel non-linear steps, Szegedy et al. [590] make observation that neural network layers do not disentangle basis distributions from semantic information. Szegedy et al. [590] find that deep networks learn discontinuous input-output mappings so that imperceptible perturbations increase deep network's prediction error even when it is trained on different subsets of a dataset. Such imperceptible perturbations are called adversarial examples. Learning adversarial examples is intrinsically connected to deep network structure and input data distributions. In experiments by Szegedy et al. [590], a significant amount of adversarial examples were found to be misclassified by deep networks. These adversarial examples were created by changing deep network's hyperparameter settings such as the number of layers, weight's initialization, and weight's regularization. Thus, Szegedy et al. [590] conclude that adversarial examples are not the result of a particular deep learning model's overfitting.

In high-dimensional input signals to a simple linear model, Goodfellow et al. [227] observe that many infinitesimal changes to the input from adversarial examples add up to one large change to the output in deep learning. Goodfellow et al. [227] hypothesize that deep network classifiers exhibit such linear behavior in high-dimensional spaces. Adversarial examples are then analyzed as a property of high-dimensional dot products. Stability of underlying model weights is said to result in stability of adversarial examples. To get adversarial perturbation, cost function for training a deep network is linearized around current parameter values. This method for generating adversarial examples is called fast gradient sign method (FGSM). In FGSM, the direction of adversarial perturbation is hypothesized to be more important than its position in the data space. Then, adversarial training of deep learning models is proposed as a non-linear regularization that secures deep networks by minimizing their worst-case error on FGSM's adversarial examples. Adversarial training is also viewed as an active learning where learning model obtains new labels for the adversarial examples from a heuristic labeler copying labels of the nearby points. Papernot et al. [481] introduce a black-box attack strategy to generate adversarial examples without knowledge of the target deep neural network internals.

Nguyen et al. [458] generate adversarial examples with evolutionary algorithms and call them "fooling images." Fooling images are unrecognizable to human eyes but classified as recognizable objects with high confidence by deep neural networks (DNNs). A population of fooling images is evolved by designing an evolutionary algorithm called multidimensional archive of phenotypic elites (MAP-Elites). MAP-Elites keeps best individual found so far for each objective. Then it mutates a randomly chosen organism from the population and replaces the current champion for any objective if new individual has higher fitness on that objective. DNN's prediction score is taken as fitness function in MAP-Elites. For any class that has been seen before, a fooling image generated with higher prediction score becomes champion for that class. Image pixels of MNIST dataset and image pixels generated by compositional pattern-producing network (CPPN) represent the genomes in MAP-Elites. Various activation functions of a CPPN provide different geometric regularities to a fooling image. Evolution operators of MAP-Elites determine topology, weights, and activation units of each CPPN network in population. For various hypotheses on relations between training dataset and DNN architecture, prediction scores and Mann-Whitney U tests validate the fooling image distribution output by MAP-Elites.

Carlini et al. [102] devise white-box as well as black-box attack scenarios for feedforward neural networks acting as classifiers. Across multiple detection mechanisms, new adversarial loss functions are proposed for fooling the neural network classifiers. Experiments are then proposed to explore the data space and transferability properties of targeted adversarial examples. To formulate the attacks, three threat models of zero-knowledge adversary, perfect-knowledge adversary, and limited-knowledge adversary are defined. A zero-knowledge adversary has no knowledge of detector's presence while targeting class label predictions of the classifier. The zero-knowledge adversary thus acts as a baseline for targeting any proposed detector. In comparison, a perfect-knowledge adversary has full knowledge of both classifier parameters and detector's detection scheme. Perfect-knowledge adversary thus performs a white-box attack. To perform a black-box attack, Carlini et al. [102] assume that a limited-knowledge adversary knows detector's detection scheme but has no access to trained classifier, trained detector, or their training data.

The detector schemes studied by Carlini et al. [102] include (i) a second neural network to classify images as natural or adversarial, (ii) principal component analysis (PCA) to detect statistical properties of images or network parameters, (iii) statistical hypothesis tests (such as maximum mean discrepancy tests and Gaussian mixture models comparing adversarial data distribution with original data distribution), and (iv) input normalization with randomization and blurring. A ℓ_2 distance between adversarial examples and training examples is assumed to be the adversarial loss function measuring robustness of defense in the detection mechanisms. In an iterative gradient descent attack, the adversarial loss function has an additional regularization term that compares the deep network's log-likelihood of predicting target class with the next-most-likely class. A user-defined threshold on ranked log-likelihood's then assigns either a high-confidence or low-confidence to the generated adversarial examples. The evaluation of the properties of the adversarial examples is recommended to be done according to the following evaluation criteria:

- Evaluating adversarial examples across multiple datasets (such as MNIST and CIFAR) with defenses that did not operate directly on pixels
- Evaluating new schemes for strength of an attack which demonstrate an adversary who can generate attacks to evade detection when aware of proposed defense
- Reporting false positive rates in addition to true positive rates in the performance evaluation.

Here, a neural network is said to be robust if finding adversarial examples that bypass its detector is a difficult proposition.

Baluja et al. [25] proposed a targeted attack where feedforward neural networks called adversarial transformation networks (ATNs) are trained to generate adversarial examples. ATNs generate adversarial examples that minimally modify classifier's outputs given original input. By contrast, Moosav et al. [439] constructed an untargeted attack technique, i.e., DeepFool, which is optimized by distance metrics between adversarial examples and normal examples.

In our research in [124, 125], we generate adversarial examples to effect a poisoning attack on the classification training data. The adversarial examples are generated by the adversarial manipulations learned during our game theoretical attacks on the training process of the learner. In our black-box attack scenarios generating testing data distributions, no prior knowledge about the learning model is assumed. Our adversary knows neither the learning model's training process nor the learning model's best response strategies across the Stackelberg game's plays. Our adversary does a targeted attack to manipulate multiple positive labels into a single negative label. The attack strength of our adversarial manipulations is defined in terms of search randomization parameters in ALS and SA. The scalar optima in SA are used to generate the vector optima in ALS. The local optima in ALS converge onto the non-convex stochastic optima solving the Stackelberg game to produce output of optimal adversarial manipulations. The optimal adversarial manipulations are able to encode the adversarial data in terms of the multivariate statistical parameters of a Gaussian mixture model produced in multi-label datasets.

2.5   Generative Adversarial Networks

Goodfellow et al. [226] state that the primary cause of deep learning networks' vulnerability to adversarial examples is their linear nature in high-dimensional search spaces. Also the deep learning networks perform poorly on testing data examples that do not have high probability in the training data distribution. Thus, adversarial examples can be generated by applying a worst-case perturbation to the training data. The perturbed input results in an incorrect output prediction with high confidence. Thus, Goodfellow et al. [226] argue for the need of having an adversarial training procedure whose objective is to minimize the worst-case error when the training data is perturbed by the adversary. Goodfellow et al. [226] then formulate the adversarial training as a min-max game between two deep neural networks. The resulting deep generative model is called generative adversarial networks (GANs).

A variety of deep generative methods are available to create the perturbation between training and testing data distributions [485]. Radford et al. [500] propose a stable GAN called DCGAN. Gulrajani et al. [400] design IWGAN which undertakes a theoretical analysis of the generative learning process. Berthelot et al. [46] propose BEGAN with a new loss function in the training algorithm. Chen et al. [119] propose InfoGAN which uses generative learning models for unsupervised representation learning.

Insofar as the learner's defense mechanisms are concerned, our game formulation is similar to the GAN game formulation. However, the objective of our research is to simulate a real adversarial attack scenario on two-label and multi-label classification model in terms of the cost to the adversary. We seek to increase the classification performance when the data distribution is changed with a malicious intent. By contrast, the objective of GAN is to generate synthetic data that is indistinguishable from the original data. Our objective function has cost and error terms defining the attack scenarios in adversarial data generation settings. By contrast, the objective function in GAN is defined in terms of the loss functions of the deep neural networks learning the given training and testing data distributions.

In a min-max game formulation, we seek to create the datasets for attack scenarios in a discriminative learning model and supervised learning problem, while GAN addresses a generative learning model and unsupervised learning problem. Furthermore, the generator is the leader of the game in min-max formulation for GAN, whereas in our min-max formulation, the intelligent adversary leads the game. While searching for the Nash equilibrium in a min-max game, GANs solve a convex optimization problem with gradient-based optimization algorithms, whereas we solve a non-convex stochastic optimization problem with evolutionary learning algorithms. Thus, we are able to estimate the best cost for the adversary in effecting the adversarial attack.

Generative adversarial networks (GANs) [226] estimate data likelihood with an adversarial framework involving a two-player game between a generator network G and a discriminator network D. IWGAN [241] improves GAN's estimations with regularization that does not introduce correlations between generated examples.

The objective of our game formulation with variational autoencoders is not to improve classification accuracy by augmenting the original data training the autoencoders. Importantly, we note that the fundamental difference between our research with variational autoencoders and generative networks objective is deceiving the classifier rather than mimicking the original data [241, 500]. We solve a supervised learning problem with variational adversaries, while deep generative models generally solve either unsupervised learning or semi-supervised learning problems with generative adversaries.

2.6 Generative Adversarial Networks for Adversarial Learning

Adversarial examples have been defined for deep generative models [325]. The distribution of adversarial manipulations in white-box attacks as well as black-box attacks has been modeled with AdvGAN [659]. A thread of research on adversarial autoencoders [606] imposes a prior distribution on the output of an encoder network learning training data, where autoencoder discriminatively predicts whether a sample comes from its latent space or from prior distribution determined by the user. By contrast, our game theoretical optimization problem is independent from a particular training data distribution and classification model.

Larsen et al. [346] propose generative adversarial learning in the reconstruction loss of a variational autoencoder. Tran et al. [605] propose constraints on the distance function to train generative adversarial networks in the latent spaces of an autoencoder. Gregor et al. [233] propose an attention mechanism-based autoencoder to learn the latent spaces in a sequential variational autoencoder framework. Ha et al. [246] propose a recurrent neural network for sketch generation in images. Makhzani et al. [405] propose an adversarial training mechanism for probabilistic autoencoders.

A taxonomy of adversarial attack scenarios in deep learning is provided by Gilmer et al. [219] and Biggio et al. [68]. Our attack scenario with Stackelberg games proposes new adversarial payoff functions. We represent feature space for adversarial manipulations in terms of adversarial cost functions, stochastic operators, and game strategies in a simulated annealing algorithm.

Wang et al. [629] survey theories and implementations of generative adversarial networks. A taxonomy of the existing generative adversarial network formulations relevant for the game theoretical adversarial learning algorithms is summarized in Tables 2.1, 2.2, 2.3, and 2.4. Across the rows in tables, the algorithm comparisons are made on generator network's attack scenario, loss function, strategy space, and objective function. Most of the deep generative models do not analyze data distributions in terms of game theoretical optimization of the objective functions. In comparison, our methods propose adversarial payoff functions for optimization and adversarial cost functions for regularization in the objective functions.

2.6.1   Causal Feature Learning and Adversarial Machine Learning

Causality methods have been applied to deep learning problems such as semi-supervised learning and transfer learning. In these problems, informed priors retrieved from other networks are used to center the weights in hybrid deep learning networks. Such networks are then used to construct statistical hypotheses on patterns, structure, context, and content in actual data [431].

Backpropagation learning algorithms for deep networks have been improved by training probabilistic graphical models. Such training is inherently Bayesian where prior distributions inform and constrain analytics models predicting posterior distributions [567]. The improved deep learning algorithms result in a predicted output informed by causal inference. Within a Bayesian framework, causality methods also enhance the interpretability of deep networks operating in an uncertain environment [314].

We are interested in the attack scenarios with latent variable models in game theoretical adversarial learning. Kumari et al. [336] study white-box attacks at the level of the latent layers of the adversarially trained image classification models. Higher robustness at the feature layers is achieved by the adversarial training of latent layers with an iterative variant of FGSM. By contrast, our research creates deep generative models for the adversarial manipulations that provide game theoretical regularizers on the targeted classifier's loss function.

Chattopadhyay et al. [112] propose a structural causal model for causal influence of an input feature on a neural network's output. Such causal influences on the prediction function's output are called neural network attributions. They are said to be more interpretable artifacts of the deep network causations rather than regression features that primarily map correlations between the input and the output of the

Table 2.1 Generative adversarial network comparison 1

Adversarial network	Attack scenario	Discriminator loss function	Generator loss function	Information divergence function	Game type	Payoff function	Cost function	Optimization constraints
Defense-GAN [535]	Model the distribution of unperturbed images in white-box attacks as well as black-box attacks	Same as WGAN	Same as WGAN	MSE, L_2 norm	Min-max game	Reformer network, latent codes	Adversarial training augments the training data	Representative GAN to reconstruct adversarial examples
GANGs [474]	Resource-bounded best responses on synthetic data	Classifier score that is function of both real data and fake data	Generator payoff as a function of the fake data only	Deterministic and non-deterministic resource-bounded Nash equilibrium	Zero-sum strategic-form game	Player payoff under a profile of mixed strategies, Definition 2	Measuring function in Definition 6 and Theorem 10	Finite GANGs on discrete data
AdvGAN [659]	Semi-white-box adversarial perturbations with target class and ground truth	Static and dynamic distillation model training with alternative minimization approaches	Targeted attack loss for LSGAN given in Equation 4	Ensemble adversarial learning	Min-max game	Same as Goodfellow GAN	Hinge loss	Cross-entropy loss
DeLiGAN [245]	Limited training data to capture the diversity across the image modality	Same as DCGAN	Same as DCGAN	m-IS a KL divergence measuring intra-class sample diversity along with the sample quality	Min-max game	Reparameterization of the latent space in prior distribution	L_2 regularizer to prevent local maxima in generator	Uniform mixture weights in gradient descent

EBGAN [702]	Handcrafted and regularized contrastive sample generation in supervised, weakly supervised, and unsupervised settings	Reconstruction loss and energy function in autoencoder	Same as Goodfellow GAN	Inception score	Min-max game	Adversarial training	Reconstruction error	Grid search over architectural choices and hyperparameters
Fisher GAN [445]	Standardized discrepancies in two-sample hypothesis testing and semi-supervised learning	Mahalanobis distance between the feature means embeddings of real and fake distributions	Mean embedding distance	Integral probability metrics (IPM) and inception score parametrized by generative neural networks	Min-max game	Same as DCGAN	Same as DCGAN	Second-order moments of the critic that discriminates between the two distributions, cross-entropy regularization term in semi-supervised learning
Improved f-GAN [496]	Generator divergence ordered from the most mode seeking to most mode covering	Same as Goodfellow GAN	Estimate of the model density-to-data density ratio from the current discriminator	f-Divergence	Min-max game	Expectation maximization	Real-fake data learning intractable likelihoods	Image quality/diversity metrics/factors without dropping modes

Table 2.2 Generative adversarial network comparison 2

Adversarial network	Attack scenario	Discriminator loss function	Generator loss function	Information divergence function	Game type	Payoff function	Cost function	Optimization constraints
CausalGAN [319]	True/feasible causal graph structured on data labels for both the observational and interventional distributions over images and labels jointly	Conditional GAN losses mixed with label losses	Same as DCGAN with label gradients	Total variation distance (TVD)	Same as WGAN, DCGAN	Same as WGAN, DCGAN	Two-stage procedure on multiple label and binary label conditioned image distributions	Margin-coefficient tuples in stochastic gradient descent
AM-GAN [714]	Predefined labeling and dynamic labeling for image generation, image quality, and image diversity	Cross-entropy for multi-class classification	Same as DCGAN	Inception score, AM score	Min-max game	None	None	Class-aware gradient
MBGAN [140]	None	Non-linear metric in Equation 9 and Equation 10	Same as DCGAN	Inception score	Min-max game	None	None	Weight clipping, center penalty
Triangle-GAN [208]	Semi-supervised image classification, image-to-image translation, and attribute-based image generation	Conditional GAN and bidirectional GAN losses	Two conditional GAN generators corresponding to two discriminators	Jensen-Shannon divergence (JSD) plus a Kullback-Leibler (KL) divergence	Min-max game	None	None	None

f-CLSWGAN [657]	No labeled examples of certain classes in multimodal embedding	Softmax classifier for zero-shot learning (ZSL) and generalized zero-shot learning (GZSL)	Same as WGAN	Multimodal embedding model with labeled examples of seen classes and deep CNN features conditioned on class-level semantic information	Min-max game	None	Generated data is much lower dimensional than high-quality images necessary for discrimination	Class embeddings that model the semantic relationship between classes
LSGAN [410]	Penalize samples based on their distances to the decision boundary	Equation 2	Equation 2 to generate samples toward the decision boundary and manifold of real data	f-Divergence, Pearson chi-square divergence	Min-max game	None	None	Deterministic equations between labels for fake data, real data, and generated data for one-hot encoding and dimensionality reduction
D2GAN [459]	Image generation	Kullback-Leibler (KL) and reverse KL divergences	Any multi-mode density function	Inception score and MODE score	Min-max game	None	None	Minimal enclosing ball, surrogate objectives, multiple players, etc. in generator's density function

Table 2.3 Generative adversarial network comparison 3

Adversarial network	Attack scenario	Discriminator loss function	Generator loss function	Information divergence function	Game type	Payoff function	Cost function	Optimization constraints
GAN [226]	Adversarial framework for likelihood estimation which backpropagates discriminator derivatives through generative processes	Maxout activation networks	Rectifier linear activations and sigmoid activation networks	Kullback-Leibler divergence, Jensen-Shannon divergence	Min-max game	None	None	G and D are given enough capacity and training time; no overfitting in D; G must not be trained too much without updating D
IWGAN [241]	Better GAN training algorithm	Critic loss in WGAN	Adversary loss in WGAN	Earth mover distance	Min-max game	None	None	Penalty on the gradient norm, normalization schemes which don't introduce correlations between examples

InfoGAN [119]	Disentangle interpretable representations from unlabeled data	Same as DCGAN	Information-regularized generator on incompressible noise and structured semantic features	Mutual information and differential entropy	Min-max game	None	None	Sleep-wake algorithm with variational regularization
ss-InfoGAN [569]	Extracted and controllable data representations where latent variables correspond to label categories and learn both continuous and categorical codes	Same as DCGAN	Mutual information between a code vector and real labeled samples and synthetic unlabeled samples, cross-entropy for categorical latent codes, mean squared error for continuous latent codes	Mutual information and differential entropy	Min-max game	None	None	Factors not corresponding to labels will not be discovered in supervised and semi-supervised settings, real and synthetic data distributions are independent, and labels follow a fixed distribution and hence have a fixed entropy

Table 2.4 Generative adversarial network comparison 4

Adversarial network	Attack scenario	Discriminator loss function	Generator loss function	Information divergence function	Game type	Payoff function	Cost function	Optimization constraints
McGan [446]	Mean and covariance feature statistics	Same as WGAN along with a cross-entropy loss on labeled data	Mean L_q norm, covariance Ky-Fan norm (nuclear norm of truncated covariance difference), feature matching integral probability metrics (IPM); IPMs are bounded linear functions defined in the non-linear feature space induced by the parametric feature map	Geodesic distances between the covariances and probability measures in a multimodal setting	Min-max game	None	None	Bounded modes of the feature embeddings of real and fake distribution, sufficient samples from "real" and "fake" data for training both "generator" and the "critic" feature space
DCGAN [500]	Reusable feature representations from large unlabeled datasets, hierarchical clustering of the intermediate representations	Leaky rectified activation	Deconvolutions and filtering the maximal activations of each convolution filter in the network	Percentage accuracy on training, testing, validation data	Min-max game	None	None	Batch normalization

BEGAN [46]	Matching the distribution of the errors instead of the distribution of the samples, dynamically weighing regularization terms or other heterogeneous objectives	Discriminator has two competing goals in closed-loop feedback control: autoencode real images and discriminate real from generated images	Negative of discriminator loss	Global measure of convergence by using the boundary equilibrium concept from proportional control theory	Min-max game	None	None	Correct hyper-parameter selection to maintain a balance between the generator and discriminator losses
BGAN [274]	Same as DCGAN	Same as DCGAN	Boundary-seeking REINFORCE objective with policy gradient training where reward is the normalized importance weights	f-Divergence and Jensen-Shannon divergence with importance weights for generated samples	Min-max game	None	None	Approximated the expectations in normalized importance weights by using the Monte-Carlo sampling
AnoGAN [540]	Imaging markers relevant for disease progression and treatment monitoring	Discrimination loss enforces the generated image to lie on the learned manifold	Residual loss that enforces visual similarity between generated image and query image	Anomaly/novelty detection score from feature matching classification functions in latent spaces	Same as DCGAN	None	None	Suitable feature representation in discriminator

neural network. In sequence prediction tasks with such a structural causal model, the causal dependencies between different input neurons are assumed to be jointly caused by a latent confounder such as a data-generating mechanism applied to time-series models.

Yang et al. [677] study the pixel-level features for causal reasoning in pixel-wise masking and adversarial perturbation. Ancona et al. [15] and Lundberg et al. [400] discuss attribution methods in Shapley values from cooperative game theory.

Our research investigation is in creating such interpretable artifacts of the game theoretical adversarial manipulations. Toward this end, we have created Granger-causal features of the regression predictions. In future work, we shall create predictive baselines in latent variable models of the data-generating mechanisms in neural network attributions. We expect such baselines shall discover counterfactual features in application-specific rule-based classifiers.

2.6.2 Explainable Artificial Intelligence and Adversarial Machine Learning

We are interested in explainable artificial intelligence (XAI) of the deep generative models applicable to game theoretical adversarial learning in black-box attacks. Lou et al. [393] introduced generalized additive models (GAMs) as an interpretable extension of generalized linear models (GLMs). Guidotti et al. [240] survey the explainability of black-box models. Rudin [533] compares XAI models with inherently interpretable models. Wang et al. [631] propose hybrid rule sets that integrate interpretable models with black-box models. Frosst et al. [205] create a decision tree that generalizes a neural network's learning. Ribeiro et al. [516] provide textual anchor explanations for image classification and visual question answering. Ignatiev et al. [290] propose a constraint reasoning system to explain predictions.

Strumbelj et al. [573] explain predictions with coalitional game theory. Bulo et al. [528] define a randomized prediction game that is a non-cooperative game theoretical formulation in which the classifier and the attacker make randomized strategy selections according to some probability distribution defined over the respective strategy set in handwritten digit recognition, spam detection, and malware detection. Peake et al. [488] create interpretable structure of association rules from latent factor recommendation system training a matrix factorization black-box model. Lakkaraju et al. [343] create rule-based models with decision set learning designed for interpretability of submodular function optimization. Baehrens et al. [23] propose explanation methods for the decisions of any classification method. Ribeiro et al. [514] explain predictions of any classifier as a submodular optimization problem. Shrikumar et al. [556] compute importance scores for neuron activation in a neural network that show significant advantages over gradient-based methods. Koh et al. [320] use influence functions from robust statistics to explain predictions.

Bastani et al. [35] propose metrics to evaluate the robustness of deep neural nets. Narodytska et al. [453] create Boolean representation of a deep neural network to verify its properties. Tomsett et al. [599] survey connections between interpretability and adversarial attacks. Liu et al. [381] develop adversary-resistant detection framework by utilizing the interpretation of machine learning models. Tao et al. [593] propose an adversarial sample detection technique for face recognition models, based on interpretability. Fidel et al. [194] propose a method for detecting adversarial examples with SHapley Additive exPlanations (SHAP) values computed for the internal layers of a DNN. Ilyas et al. [294] attribute adversarial examples to the presence of non-robust features. Ignatiev et al. [291] demonstrate that the explanations (XPs) of machine learning (ML) model predictions and of adversarial examples (AEs) are related by a first-order logic (FOL) framework called hitting set duality.

2.6.3 Stackelberg Game Illustration in Adversarial Deep Learning

Figure 2.3 is a flowchart for our adversarial autoencoder-based Stackelberg game model. A multi-label classifier $CNN_{original}$ (henceforth shortened as CNN_o) with weights $w^* \in W$ is trained on labeled training data X_{train} and evaluated on labeled testing data X_{test} sourced from an image database. CNN_o participates in a two-player game with our game theoretical adversary. Adversary attacks CNN_o on a targeted positive label $target = pos$ by generating optimal attack $\alpha^* \in A$ at Nash equilibrium for every negative label $neg \in Neg$ that targeted positive label pos is manipulated into. In this research, pos and Neg are class labels where $overall = pos \cup Neg$ and $A = Enc(X_{train})$ is determined by an autoencoder function Enc trained on X_{train}.

In each iteration of game, adversarial manipulation α_{best} is generated by a simulated annealing algorithm. For training data X_{train}, each α_{best} generates

Fig. 2.3 A flowchart illustrating the adversarial autoencoder-based Stackelberg game theoretical modeling

adversarial data $Enc(X_{train}) + \alpha_{best}$ in encoded space. It is then decoded as $Dec(Enc(X_{train}) + \alpha_{best})$ to be evaluated against CNN_o.

Upon convergence game outputs optimal α^* inferred for each pair of *pos* and *neg*. All α^*'s are then combined to effect a multi-label adversarial attack on CNN_o to output manipulated classifier $CNN_{manipulated}$ (henceforth shortened as CNN_m). CNN_m is finally retrained into secure classifier CNN_{secure} (henceforth shortened as CNN_s) that is robust to multi-label adversarial attacks.

2.7   Transfer Learning for Domain Adaptation

In machine learning, transfer learning applies learnable knowledge obtained from one data analytics problem onto another problem. Storing, reusing, and transferring information and knowledge from previous datasets and tasks have the potential to improve sample efficiency in new machine learning problems such as those involving reinforcement learning agents. After supervised learning, transfer learning is a big driver of success in commercial machine learning and scalable deep learning. As a form of multi-task learning, transfer learning can be used in supervised learning to improve the multi-label classification in applications of adversarial machine learning such as spam filtering and multicriteria classifiers.

Domain adaptation is a field of transfer learning that is applicable to spam filtering. In it, a source distribution is used to learn a well-performing model for a target distribution that is related to but different from the source distribution. The source distribution could be spam emails received by a source user where domain adaptation seeks to model the spam emails for a different target user. Thus, the source and target data distributions have the same feature space but different data distribution in domain adaptation. Unlike domain adaptation, the feature space of source data for transfer learning can be same as well as different to the target data.

Domain adaptation can be used to model distributional shift in data available for training and the machine learning algorithms and validating the corresponding distributional robustness of adversarial learning algorithms. So the modern machine learning community has several strategies for gaining domain adaptation between training datasets and validation datasets in practical applications of artificial intelligence. Such strategies lead us to conditional, semi-supervised, weakly supervised, multimodal, and multi-structured variants of supervised learning algorithms. They are weaker forms of supervised learning where hand-labeled training data is not available without mistakes and noise in the class labels [680]. They result in adversarial machine learning paradigms such as incremental learning, utility learning, reinforcement learning, and online learning with class and cost distribution information for transferable feature representations in adversarial examples due to outlier detection, novelty detection, and change point detection within the distributional shift's information filtering. Here, we can inject domain expertise with functions to label the new generated training data [693].

2.7.1 Adversarial Examples in Transfer learning

Tramer et al. [604] propose methods to find the dimensionality of adversarial examples that can transfer between deep learning models. Adversarial subspaces with a large number of dimensions are more likely to enable transferability between deep learning models. A decision boundary analysis of supervised learning is used to study the limits of transferability between data distributions. Deep learning models in computer vision are used to craft adversarial examples that humans can recognize but computers misclassify. Reinforcement learning agents operating in game theoretical data environments are proposed to make computers misclassify the adversarial examples. Adversarial examples are found to occur in contiguous regions of feature subspaces relevant to transfer learning among misclassified points. These subspaces are found for linear and quadratic models for deep learning in the digit classification problem using MNIST dataset and the malware detection problem using DREBIN dataset. Model-agnostic adversarial perturbations are obtained by shifting training data points in the directions obtained by difference in the labeled class means in the input feature space. Multiple independent directions for crafting the adversarial data manipulations are also obtained to measure the dimensionality of the adversarial subspaces. They are generated with variants of the fast gradient sign method that constrain adversarial perturbations with l_p norms of the classification loss functions. The transferability of adversarial examples between deep learning models is studied with distances proposed between decision boundaries of the undefended models and adversarially trained models.

Ma et al. [667] assess the dimensionality of adversarial examples with distance distribution of an adversarial example and its neighbors. The decision boundaries of adversarial subspaces are found to be transferable depending on the proximity of legitimate data points to them in the adversarial directions. Such transferability increases with the number of independent orthogonal adversarial directions of these subspaces. Wang et al. [627] create adversarial examples for transfer learning models used in the context of image recognition applications such as face recognition, iris recognition, flower recognition, and traffic sign recognition. Adversarial data manipulations mimic the internal representation of the target image after transfer learning.

Papernot et al. [479] train substitute learning models to craft transferable adversarial examples between several deep learning and machine learning models. The targeted classifier is designated an oracle that uses reservoir sampling to label the training datasets and in turn increase efficiency for training the substitutes on augmented datasets. The augmentation iteration alternates between augmentations of the datasets used to train the substitute model and the labelings provided by the oracle to fine-tune the augmentations. Reservoir sampling affects the quality of the substitute by constraining the number of randomly generated labeling queries made from the substitute to the oracle. Such a sampling method is suitable for real-world environments where adversary is constrained by quotas on being detected by a defender. The transferability of adversarial samples is studied between deep neural networks, logistic regression, support vector machines, decision trees, nearest neighbors, and classifier ensembles. Even commercial machine learning classifiers hosted by Amazon and Google are considered in the experimental evaluation. Substitutes are designed for black-box attacks where adversaries target remote classifiers without knowledge about model architecture, parameters, and training datasets. Experiments indicate that knowledge transfer occurs between many machine learning models to a deep neural network mimicking the decision boundaries of the original classifier.

To study transfer learning with target labels, Liu et al. [388] distinguish between non-targeted and targeted adversarial examples. Adversarial examples are generated to transfer to particular target labels as misclassified by deep learning models. Chin et al. [122] propose a new transfer learning method for fine-tuning the robustness of transferred neural network obtained from regularizing the pre-trained models in deep learning. The adversary has access to the pre-trained model's weights and architecture but does not have access to task-specific transferred model and query.

Baluja et al. [26] train a neural network called adversarial transformation network (ATN) to craft a targeted adversarial attack. Instead of solving per-sample optimization problems to create the adversarial data, ATN creates minimally modified adversarial examples for every input training image. ATNs accommodate various threat models such as training black-box and white-box targets over targeted and untargeted attack scenarios on the rank orders in the target neural network's outputs. Further ATN can be trained to generate either an adversarial perturbation from a variant of residual networks or an adversarial autoencoding of the input reconstructed with adversarial noise signal.

Wu et al. [654] identify transferable adversarial examples due to the skip connections in supervised deep learning. Gradients from the skip connections are proposed to craft the adversarial examples. They transfer to the state of the art in deep neural networks including ResNets, DenseNets, Inceptions, Inception-ResNet, and Squeeze-and-Excitation Networks. Furthermore, such adversarial examples can be combined with existing black-box techniques for adversarial attacks to obtain improvements in the state-of-the-art transferability methods. Such adversarial examples raise security concerns in the deployment of deep neural networks in applications such as face recognition, autonomous driving, video analysis, and medical diagnosis.

2.7.2 Adversarial Examples in Domain Adaptation

Su et al. [575] propose adversarial domain adaptation with active learning. Importance sampling combined with adversarial training is used to account for distribution shifts between domains. It acts as a sample selection scheme for active learning especially when the target domain does not have as many labeled examples as the source domain. In the importance sampling, a diversity of samples is generated with the help of adversarial loss. Such a semi-supervised domain adaptation improves classification performance and reduces labeling cost with domain adversarial learning on object classification and detection tasks.

Zhang et al. [700] extend unsupervised domain adaptation in semantic segmentation with adversarial learning. Pixel-level annotated samples in the source domain are used to segment unlabeled samples in the target domain. In adversarial learning, a discriminator is built to distinguish between source and target domains. A segmentation model then targets to deceive the domain discriminator with deep learning. The task of semantic segmentation is to assign class labels to all pixels in an image. Semantic segmentation serves as the backbone for computer vision systems like autonomous vehicles operating in urban environments. Vu et al. [624] address the task of unsupervised domain adaptation in semantic segmentation with losses based on the entropy minimization of the pixel-wise predictions. Adversarial training analyzes residual nets for semantic segmentation to construct feature maps on the source domain that are similar to those in the target domain. The neural network for semantic segmentation is learned on generated images with the content of the source domain and style of the target domain for which source segmentation map serves as the ground truth. Several semi-supervised learning paradigms for domain adaptation can benefit from the design of such adversarial losses.

Yang et al. [678] study domain adaptation in semantic segmentation. Adversarial learning is used to match the marginal distribution of feature representations across domains. Attack objectives are proposed on intermediate feature maps that learn domain-invariant task-discriminative representations. They are supervised by semantic segmentations in the source domain. By improving robustness of the supervised learning, transferable adversarial examples fill the gap between domains from adaptions in the classification decision boundaries. Such an adversarial learning can also be understood as a form of active learning or hard example mining where the model minimizes the worst-case error when features are perturbed by adversaries. Adversarial features are generated by accumulating gradient maps of the attack objectives in semantic segmentation classifiers. Prediction maps of adversarial features intended to confuse the segmentation classifier are further optimized according to an entropy minimization technique that provides extra supervision in the training objectives.

Kim et al. [315] reformulate the mapping function in domain adaptation for translating images from one visual domain to another as a conditional image generation problem for generative adversarial networks (GANs). Proposed DiscoGAN does not require explicit labels on the images being generated. An image reconstruction loss is proposed to encourage mapping between multi-modal image domains. A new GAN architecture is given to define cross-domain relations changing specified attributes such as hair color, gender, and orientation. So GANs can generate images of objects in domain adaptation based on specified image characteristics, styles, and viewpoints. Encoded text description of images can be used as conditional information to generate images. Pre-trained face recognition modules can also be used as conditional inputs to GANs.

Sankaranarayanan et al. [539] give a learned embedding for unsupervised domain adaptation. It is robust to distribution shift between source and target domains.

Unsupervised data from target distribution is sampled to guide the supervised learning procedures in data sampled from source distribution. An adversarial image generation approach learns the feature embeddings with a classification loss and an image generation procedure. Proposed approach yields better results than feature embeddings based on denoising autoencoders and domain classifiers. Thus, adversarial losses can perform domain adaptation.

Mancini et al. [407] discover latent domains for domain adaptation. They are embedded into a CNN architecture to learn robust target classifiers. Domain membership information aligns the distribution of CNN feature representations to a reference distribution. Such classifiers span multiple domain distributions without the need for labeled training data. Such latent domains represent the manifolds in source domain images and learn information about their semantic categories. Tzeng et al. [613] combine discriminative modeling with GAN losses to handle larger distribution shifts that are not handled by GANs alone. Such adversarial adaptation methods seek to minimize an approximate domain discrepancy distance through an adversarial objective for a domain discriminator. This work on adversarial losses for domain adaptation subsumes previous design choices made in deep learning for domain adaptation. Domain-specific feature extraction is allowed to be learned by not sharing the neural network weights between source and target domains. The target domain classifiers are adversarially trained until they match the source domain classifier's predictions. Applications are demonstrated on cross-modality adaptation tasks.

Shen et al. [554] learn domain-invariant representations with Wasserstein distance-guided representation learning (WDGRL). By providing an adversarial objective to a domain classifier, a min-max game is designed for domain adaptation to make source and target feature representations indistinguishable. The domain classifier distinguishes between source and target representations where Wasserstein distance acts as the domain discrepancy measure for adversarial loss. WDGRL is optimized with iterative adversarial training strategy to minimize the estimated Wasserstein distance between source and target feature representations. Thus, deep learning acts as a powerful framework to learn feature representations for domain adaptation. Specifically, Wasserstein distance is able to relate the source and target errors.

Wang et al. [635] propose an adversarial objective loss function to bridge source and target domains by learning a domain-invariant deep representation on the transferable regions in images. Such a transfer learning is able to produce a discriminative model that reduces dataset shift between training and testing distributions. The resulting domain-invariant representations can be embedded into deep neural network architectures to minimize the discrepancy between source and target feature distributions with adversarial learning. The attention mechanism in deep learning is highlighted to extract fine-grained features considering different regions of images obtained from different domains. A transferable local attention mechanism is proposed to generate multiple region-level domain discriminators, and a complementary transferable global attention mechanism is proposed to generate a single image-level domain discriminator to highlight transferable images.

Further, the adversarial model training can be extended to multiple discriminators to enhance the distribution matching where discriminator designs can range from formidable adversary to forgiving teacher. Here, a min-max game is proposed between a discriminator and a generator such that the domain discriminator distinguishes between source and target data, while the generator is a feature extractor trained adversarially to deceive the domain discriminator. These designs in deep domain adaptation are an extension to the classical ideas in statistics of defining a statistical distance in probabilistic metric space. Such a distance is then minimized by learning a representation of source and target data that is able to bridge the distribution discrepancy between different domains. Such transferable attention models based on adversarial loss transferring attention between objects in source and target domains have applications in image captioning, image segmentation, and image classification. Resulting deep network classifiers can be trained on labeled source data domain and generalize well to unlabeled target data domain. They can be refined further toward classifier adaptation by minimizing the entropy of class-conditional distribution to be regularized on target domain. The local attention generation mechanism creates an attentive entropy value for each image's entropy loss to enhance the matching of similar images across source and target domains. The attentive entropy loss is combined with the domain adaptation objective and the adversarial classification objective to obtain a unified optimized problem for adversarial training. The optimal solution to create feature representations is then obtained with a backpropagation procedure on errors that can be computed on differentiable losses. Such feature representations can be extended into multimodal optimization problems involving adversarial feature selection in robust machine learning.

2.7.3 Adversarial Examples in Cybersecurity Domains

Adversarial examples were first created in image classification. Due to depth of architectures in deep learning classifiers such as CNNs, the interpretability of the millions of learned parameters in such models comes at a premium. They have been extended to more complex mechanisms for attacking face recognition, video action recognition, and physical-world adversarial attacks on road signs. Wei et al. [640] generate transferable adversarial examples for image and video object detection. Transferability of the adversarial examples is enhanced by manipulating the low-level feature maps from multiple layers of the object detectors. An attention weighting mechanism is integrated into the feature loss to manipulate feature subregions. A high-level class loss is used to train the generators. The adversarial example generation is formulated as an image-to-image translation problem. Such adversarial examples can be created for two common types of models for object detection categorized as proposal-based models and regression-based models.

Adversarial examples can be crafted by changing pixel-level values in image classification. They have also been created by applying patches of changes to images used in object detection over stop signs, for example. Thys et al. [598] craft adversarial patches in person detectors. Here, the target classes contain lots of intra-class variety unlike stop sign's dataset. Such adversarial attacks can be used as cloaking devices to circumvent surveillance systems where intruders can sneak around undetected by holding a small cardboard plate in front of their body aimed toward the surveillance camera. They can augment the human-annotated images to determine the model performance for person detection. Such test sets account for adversarial examples designed to steer the model in the wrong way and further target to fool the model. Such vulnerabilities in person detection models of a security surveillance camera can be highlighted as risks of such an attack on the detection system. The bounding box for adversarial patches is predicted according to an object score and a class score components in the adversarial losses. Adversarial patches are then applied to the images after various transformations to fool the detectors even more. This allows the generation of targeted attacks where data is available for particular scenes in the footage environment. Some of the factors influencing an adversarial patch generation are lighting changes, viewing angle differences, rotations in patch, size of patch. They can change with respect to person size, camera can add noise or blur the patch. They optimize an image to minimize different probabilities related to the appearance of a person in the output of a detector. In experiments, the effects of generated patches are compared with that of random patches to determine the most effective patches minimizing object loss. Optimizing the adversarial losses for different detector architectures ensures the transferability of the adversarial patches.

Elsayed et al. [172] create adversarial examples that transfer from computer vision models to time-limited human observers. The effect of adversarial examples in machine learning is investigated in contrast to cognitive biases and optical illusions in human visual perception studied by neuroscience. So it is possible to craft adversarial examples with human-meaningful features. They can be designed to cause a mistake not only in visual object recognition but also in human perception. Elsayed et al. [172] design psychophysics experiments to compare the pattern of errors made by humans to the misclassification validations in neural network classifiers.

Brown et al. [87] create targeted adversarial image patches that can attack any scene in the physical world to cause an image classifier to output any target class under a wide variety of mathematical transformations. Prior knowledge of lighting conditions, camera angle, and classifier types being targeted is not required to create such a physical-world attack. In image classification tasks, the classifier must detect the most salient feature in an image to determine its class label. The adversarial path exploits this feature to produce adversarial features that are much more salient than objects in the physical world. So large local perturbations that are not imperceptible can also mislead machine learning classifiers that operate without human validation. So adversarial examples can be crafted for the physical world by modeling adversarial examples from physical transformations where robots are perceiving the world through cameras, sensors, and phones to deal with image, sound, and video data representations.

Athalye et al. [19] synthesize 3D adversarial objects that are adversarial over a chosen distribution of transformations such as viewpoint shifts, camera noise, and affine transformation. An expectation over transformation algorithm is designed in a white-box attack scenario where adversary has access to classifier, its gradient, possible classes, and a space of valid inputs. In the optimization procedure for creating adversarial examples, the adversarial perturbations are modeled with respect to an expectation defined on a chosen distribution of transformation functions. Instead of selecting the log-likelihood of a single example as the optimization objective, the effective distance between adversarial and original inputs is minimized. This is the expected or perceived distance as seen by the classifier. The optimal solution resulting in adversarial data is obtained by a stochastic gradient descent algorithm of the expected value where the gradient is computed through differentiation through each of the sampling transformations. Such an adversarial attack scenario treats the cyber world as a domain whose transformations transfer to the physical world acting as a codomain. The distribution of transformations acts as a perturbation budget to produce successful adversarial examples.

Machine learning systems are vulnerable to adversarial attacks especially in non-stationary adversarial environments within the cybersecurity domains. Beyond image recognition domains such as deepfakes in detection systems, adversarial learning applications in the cybersecurity domains include malware identification, spam detection, risk scoring, SQL injection, ransomware development, biometrics recognition systems, traffic sign detection, autonomous driving, anomaly detection, entity classification, dictionary learning, cyber-physical systems, and industrial control systems. In cybersecurity domains, modifying an API call or an executable's content byte might cause the modified executable to perform a different functionality. So adversaries in the cybersecurity domains must implement methods to modify executable's features that will not break its functionality due to the perturbed data samples in feature vectors within URL characters, spam emails, network packets, phishing detectors, sensor signals, physical processes, etc. Some of the targeted attacks in neural networks built for cybersecurity domains are dedicated APT attack, Trojan attack, backdoor attack, and distributed denial-of-service (DDoS) attack. In cyber-physical systems, adversarial learning applications play a role in the optimization of critical infrastructure such as electric power grids, transportation networks, water supply networks, and nuclear plants. In biometrics recognition systems, adversarial learning has applications in handwritten signature verification, fingerprint classification, face recognition, sentiment analysis, speaker recognition, network forensics, and iris code generation. A survey of adversarial attacks in cybersecurity in contrast to computer vision is given by [656] and [616]. It can be used to build threat-knowledge databases in sensitive real-time applications for artificial intelligence and soft computing.

Chapter 3
Adversarial Attack Surfaces

In this chapter, we explore adversarial attack surfaces. We examine how they can exploit vulnerabilities in machine learning and how to make learning algorithms robust to attacks on security and privacy of the learning system. To explore the vulnerabilities, we can simulate various model training processes under a range of various attack scenarios in supervised and unsupervised settings. Each attack strategy is assumed to be formulated by an intelligent adversary that is capable of either feature manipulation, label manipulation, or both. The optimal attack policy of the adversaries is determined by the solution for optimization problems that output the adversarial data. We can then apply the knowledge that we learned to improve and reinforce the learning procedure so as to better defend against attacks. The sensitivity analysis summarized in this chapter can be used to develop computational algorithms for optimization objectives and statistical inferences in adversarial learning algorithm's capacity for randomization, discrimination, reliability, and learnability. It creates research pathways into robustness, fairness, explainability, and transparency of machine learning models.

3.1 Security and Privacy in Adversarial Learning

Evasion Attacks Biggio et al. [54] discuss adversarial security at test time of a deployed classifier system. Security evaluation is then performed at different risk levels of non-linear classifier performance in malware detection. A secure classifier is proposed by using a gradient descent approach on a differentiable discriminant function. Adversary's goal is defined in terms of minimizing classifier's loss function with positive adversarial samples that cross decision boundary. This model can also incorporate application-specific adversarial knowledge in the definition of adversarial attack scenarios. Such adversarial knowledge includes prior knowledge

A. Sreevallabh Chivukula et al., *Adversarial Machine Learning*,
https://doi.org/10.1007/978-3-030-99772-4_3

about training data, feature representation, type of learning algorithm and its decision function, classification weights, and feedback from classifier.

Poisoning Attacks In security-sensitive settings, machine learning algorithms cannot assume training data is from a natural and well-behaved distribution. By injecting adversarial examples into training data such that testing error increases, Biggio et al. [66] investigate poisoning attacks against support vector machines (SVMs) with linear kernel, polynomial kernel, and RBF kernel. A gradient ascent procedure is used to compute adversarial examples as local maxima of SVM's non-convex error surface. In gradient ascent iteration, after each update to attack example, optimal decision boundary is computed from solution to an incremental SVM. Search procedure takes many tiny gradient steps. It is stopped when attack example deviates too much from training data. The changes to SVM's decision boundaries due to malicious input are shown to be important in application domains such as spam, worm, intrusion, and fraud detection.

Xiao et al. [664] propose adversarial label noise to maximize SVM's worst-case classification error by flipping labels in the training data. Attack strategies for creating the adversarial label noise are motivated by a structural risk minimization framework. In this framework, SVM learning minimizes a sum of a regularizer risk and empirical risk in data. Here, a regularizer penalizes excessive hypothesis complexity to avoid overfitting in a convex optimization quadratic programming problem. The adversary then optimizes empirical risk on malicious data so that the SVM is misled into shifting decision boundary away from the original data distribution. Empirical risk optimization is further decomposed into two iterative sub-problems solved by quadratic programming and linear programming. Further labels of samples in different classes are flipped in a correlated way to force the hyperplane forming decision boundary to rotate as much as possible. Adversary is assumed to have full knowledge of the feature set in the training data with equal cost assigned to each label flip.

Inference Attacks Shokri et al. [555] investigate privacy breach problem of commercial classification models leaking information about their training data on Internet applications. Adversary queries target model as a black-box to retrieve model's output on a given input. Such inputs are generated by training shadow models that imitate the behavior of the target model. In contrast to the black-box target model, shadow models know ground truth label for the inferred record. The black-box models are neural network models in Amazon ML and Google Prediction API trained on datasets of images. The details of black-box models are hidden from their data owners. The datasets are obtained from retail purchases, location traces, and hospital inpatient stays. Here, a privacy breach is said to occur if the adversary can use model's output to infer the values of sensitive attributes in the model input. The attribute inference is defined by Shokri et al. [555] in terms of class membership inference of given data record's presence in model's training dataset. The success of the proposed class membership inference is measured in terms of attack precision and attack recall of target model. The shadow model is trained on a synthetic dataset with a hill-climbing algorithm generating candidate records which are classified with high confidence by the target model. In each iteration of hill-climbing, a candidate record is proposed by changing randomly selected features of latest accepted record. A candidate record is accepted in hill-climbing algorithm only if it increases the probability of being correctly classified by target model. Several defense strategies are proposed against class membership queries. These strategies include restricting prediction vector to top classes, rounding classification probabilities, increasing entropy of prediction vector such that output becomes almost uniform and independent of input, and regularizing classification loss function to penalize large parameters during training.

3.1.1   Linear Classifier Attacks

Dalvi et al. [142] analyze classifier performance by viewing classification as a game between the classifier adapting to an adversary seeking to make the classifier produce false negatives. Here, the cost-sensitive adversary is contrasted with the cost-sensitive classifier where data-generating process in adversarial classification not only is allowed to change over time but also allows this change to be a function of classifier parameters. Adversarial classification is thus defined in terms of a game between two players—the adversary and the classifier—where the classifier maximizes its payoff function characterized by classifier's expected payoff over adversary's cost parameters.

Dalvi et al. [142] propose that the adversary's goal is to find a classification feature change strategy that maximizes adversary's expected payoff. Adversarial examples are generated by standard feature selection algorithms with naive Bayes classifier's payoff function as evaluation function. The theory of computationally tractable Nash equilibria strategies in adversarial classification is left as an open question analyzing the two-player non-zero sum games.

Lowd et al. [394] introduced adversarial learning algorithms for linear classifiers under attack. The goal of adversarial learning is to learn and attack part of classifier's decision boundary by learning feature weights without (i) constructing domain-specific feature representations and (ii) assuming a stochastic process for training data distribution.

Lowd et al. [394] assume that adversary can send membership queries to classifier to distinguish between malicious examples and non-malicious examples. The computational complexity of possible membership queries is bound by a polynomial number of line searches along each feature dimension. Adversarial learning algorithm then minimizes a linear adversarial cost function over non-malicious instance space to be learned by the adversary. Optimal adversarial cost function produces non-malicious examples that are most similar to a base adversarial example accessible to the adversary.

Lowd et al. [394] also demonstrate adversarial training experiments on linear classifiers like naive Bayes models, support vector machines with linear kernels, and maximum entropy models learning Boolean features for spam filtering. The proposed learning framework (called ACRE) is useful to study both the attacker or adversary and the defender or classifier. It can be used to determine whether an adversary can efficiently learn enough about defeating a classifier by minimizing an adversarial cost function.

3.2   Feature Weighting Attacks

Traditionally, machine learning algorithms assume that algorithm training can be performed on controlled and high-quality data. In the real world, machine learning is performed on noisy and uncertain data. Here, a robust classifier can anticipate noisy features during testing only when it is trained assuming noisy features are present during training. Moreover, robust classifiers must be dense classifiers that train on as many informative or important features as possible. Such considerations are the focus of feature weighting techniques in adversarial environments. Here, adversarial data created by an intelligent adversary is different from the random noise found in the natural world.

Since traditional classifiers cannot continuously adjust to changes in adversarial environments, Kolcz et al. [321] attempt to design classifiers that degrade gracefully as the distribution of testing data diverges from the distribution of the original training data. This is done by a feature selection process reweighting less important features for classification. The feature weighting improves model performance by making it robust to concept drift in data at the expense of extra computational cost in the model. The intuition behind this approach is that weight distribution over features for the learning algorithm reflects the importance of the features for unsupervised and supervised learning.

Kolcz et al. [321] envision a two-stage approach to robust classifier training where classifier is used to assign weights to features in the first stage which are then transformed through feature weighting to induce the final model in the second stage. The final model satisfies an objective function to be optimized. Since a single best reweighting scheme for both supervised and unsupervised learning is not available in the literature, Kolcz et al. [321] experiment with several choices for feature weighting. The objective function for feature weighting is formally analyzed by Kolcz et al. [321] as a particular case of regularized risk minimization with a quadratic form regularizer and convex loss function.

The feature weighting methods in experiments by Kolcz et al. [321] include feature bagging, partitioned logistic regression, confidence-weighted learning, feature noise injection, and sample selection bias correction. These details are described below:

- Feature bagging trains a probabilistic model as arithmetic or geometric mean of several base models. Each base model is trained on possibly overlapping subset of the original features. The performance of the bagged model is supposed to more robust than the performance of any base model because weights of less important features will be overwhelmed by the weights of more important features during the training process.

- Partitioned logistic regression is a special case of feature bagging where feature subsets and class labels are non-overlapping.
- To prevent undertraining, confidence-weighted learning aggressively updates weights of rare features in the data by maintaining a normal distribution over the weight vector of a linear classifiers. The feature weights are updated such that the Kullback-Leibler divergence between the training data distribution and testing data distribution is minimized without reducing model performance.
- Feature noise injection alleviates the problem of model overfitting to training data by introducing artificial feature noise during model training.
- Sample selection bias correction assigns feature weights such that reweighted training data resembles the available testing data. The correct weights are inferred without explicit density estimation. However, sample selection bias correction assumes the testing data is also available during training in the input domain.

Liu et al. [378] design supervised learning algorithms secure to adversarial poisoning attacks that do not make independence assumptions on feature distributions. Poisoning attacks are assumed on both dimensionality reduction and predictive regression steps. High-dimensional features are projected into a low-dimensional subspace with high data density. Then linear regression models best characteristics of data. A matrix factorization algorithm is proposed to recover low-dimensional subspace in the presence of training data corrupted by both noise and adversarial examples. A principal component regression uses trimmed optimization to estimate regression parameters in low-dimensional subspace.

In the adversarial attack scenario proposed by Liu et al. [378], the regression model can choose its training process and defense strategy without access to training data before adversarial manipulation. The adversary has full knowledge of training algorithm and parameters. The adversarial attack scenario is simulated as a zero-sum Stackelberg game where adversary's payoff function minimizes a certain budget of poisoning training data, while regressor's payoff function is regression accuracy. The learning process is formally characterized in terms of a model function relating the adversarial input and the predicted output. A quadratic loss function and a threshold function bounding loss function are also analyzed in the regression. An alternative maximization solves the proposed optimization problem on HTTP logs. The adversarial data is generated by moving training data samples along a direction to manipulate the regressor until it cannot predict correctly. Results are benchmarked against robust regression models like OLS linear regression and ridge regression predictions in the presence of noise.

3.3   Poisoning Support Vector Machines

According to the previously discussed adversarial security mechanisms, poisoning attacks are causative attacks where specially crafted attack points are injected into the training data. In a poisoning attack, an adversary cannot access the training database but can provide new training data. Poisoning attacks compromise the security of a large-scale learning system that infers hidden patterns in large complicated datasets to support decision-making with behavioral statistics. Previous poisoning attacks have been studied with anomaly detection methods.

In the probably approximately correct (PAC) model, the structural risk minimization of SVM learning is studied in the context of a convex quadratic programming problem. The impact of stochastic and adversarial label noise on support vector machine (SVM) classification errors has been theoretically analyzed under the PAC learning model. Poisoning attacks in SVMs have been addressed by considering data sanitization as a form of outlier detection, multiple classifier systems, incremental learning, and robust statistics. Evasion attacks in SVMs have been addressed by explicitly embedding knowledge of adversarial data manipulation into the learning algorithm using (i) game theoretical models for classification, (ii) probabilistic models of data distribution drift under attack, and (iii) multiple classifier systems.

Biggio et al. [65] demonstrate that an intelligent adversary can predict change in SVM's decision function due to adversarial input. Poisoning attacks against an SVM inject adversarial examples into training data to increase the SVM's testing error. The attack proposed by Biggio et al. [65] has an incremental learning technique with a gradient ascent strategy. The gradient is computed based on properties of the SVM's optimal solution. Since the attack depends on gradient (of dot products between points in input space), the attack is also kernelized by using both linear and non-linear kernels in the input space. For increasing the testing error, the gradient ascent procedure converges to local maxima of the non-convex validation error surface. The proposed gradient ascent strategy assumes that the adversary knows the training data used by the learning algorithm. In real-world attack scenario, a substitute training dataset could be used instead of the original training dataset. The convergence of proposed gradient ascent strategy depends on the smoothness of SVM parameters and the manifold geometry of data points found in the solution of a quadratic programming problem. The proposed attack strategy can also be extended to a coalition of attacks where choosing the best subset of data points for attack is a subset selection problem.

Huang et al. [664] propose an adversarial learning algorithm for attacks on SVMs that maximize classification error by flipping labels in the training data. The proposed contamination attack is a poisoning attack because it targets SVM's testing error (also called empirical risk in PAC model) by contaminating the training data labels. The proposed adversarial data manipulation is called label noise injection. Two attack algorithms are proposed to account for adversarial data manipulations. Both algorithms assume that the adversary has access to the feature set of training data. Each label flip by adversary is assumed to have equal cost that is independent of the feature values in the sample. The first algorithm greedily maximizes SVM's test error through continuous relaxation of the label values in a gradient ascent procedure. The second algorithm does a breadth-first search to greedily construct sets of candidate label flips that are correlated to the SVM's testing error. Both algorithms can be understood as a search for labels that achieve maximum difference between empirical risk for classifiers trained on original data and contaminated data. The algorithms can also be used to simulate a constant sum game between the attacker and the classifier whose aim is to, respectively, maximize and minimize testing error on the untainted test dataset. Different game formulations can be simulated if the players use non-antagonistic objective functions. Improvements to the algorithms are possible by the study of an incremental SVM under label perturbations. The problem of label noise injection creating the attacker manipulation in an SVM is also related to the classification problems for SVMs in semi-supervised learning, active learning, and structured prediction.

3.4 Robust Classifier Ensembles

Biggio et al. [59] propose that an ensemble of linear classifiers can improve not only accuracy but also robustness of supervised learning. That is because more than one classifier has to be evaded or poisoned to compromise the whole ensemble of classifiers. The training strategy evenly distributes the feature weights between discriminative and non-discriminative features in data. Undermining the discriminative weights in the classifier can then undermine the accuracy of the classifier. The objective of robust classifier ensembles is then to find such a correct tradeoff between robustness and accuracy. Here, an adversary is forced to modify a large nature of feature values to manipulate the classifier.

Biggio et al. [59] design boosting and random subspace method (RSM) to distribute weights in the adversarial algorithm. The adversarial behavior is modeled in terms of two scenarios—a worst-case scenario where the adversary has complete knowledge of the classifier and an average-case scenario where the adversary has only an approximate knowledge of the classifier. The ensemble discrimination function is then obtained by averaging different linear classifiers trained on different randomly selected subsets of the original feature set.

The averaging method by Biggio et al. [59] to find ensemble performance is an extension of the idea to use average performance of linear classifier to prevent overfitting or underfitting in imbalanced data. By reducing the variance component of classification or estimation error, the randomized sampling used in the algorithm reduces instability in decision or estimation function. Such a stable decision function is not supposed to undergo large changes in output for small perturbations in input data due to adversarial data or stochastic noise.

In Biggio et al. [59], the experimental evaluation has two objectives. The first objective is to understand the conditions under which randomized sampling produces an evenly distributed weight distribution in an ensemble of classifiers. The second objective is to evaluate whether the evenly distributed weights improve the robustness of classifier's ensemble as compared to a single base classifier. Thus, randomization-based sampling techniques are shown to be useful in the design of pattern recognition systems in adversarial environments.

Biggio et al. [60] extend adversarial environments in linear classifiers to randomization-based multiple classifier systems (MCS). The MCS combines linear base classifiers via bagging and random subspace sampling. For improvements to classification accuracy and robustness, MCS's weight distributions are investigated for more even distribution of weight values than single classifier weights. In worst-case attacks, adversary is assumed to have complete knowledge of the feature set, classifier parameters, and the decision function. In non-worst-case attacks, adversary is assumed to have an incomplete knowledge of classifier's decision function. Classifier robustness is then evaluated as a function of attack strength, representing maximum number of features which can be modified by the adversary. In non-worst-case attacks, adversary approximates feature weights by overestimating or underestimating the importance of most discriminant features in classification performance. In worst-case attacks, adversary is supposed to modify the features to minimize decision function and maximize decrease in the classifier performance.

Biggio et al. [58] formally measure hardness of evasion for an adversary targeting pattern classification systems in general and an ensemble classifier architecture in particular. Hardness of evasion is taken into account in the choice of features and choice of classifier architecture. It is defined as the expected value of minimum number of features to be modified by an adversary who seeks to evade classifier. It is calculated on disjoint subsets of discriminant (class-conditioned iid) features' weights assumed to be equally distributed among multiple classifiers with the same decision functions. Classifier parameters are chosen to minimize a classification cost given in terms of the false positive and the false negative errors.

3.5   Robust Clustering Models

Adversarial clustering problems cannot be solved by clustering stability criteria that address stochastic noise in dataset, rather than targeted adversarial manipulations. Biggio et al. [67] devise poisoning and obfuscation attacks for single-linkage hierarchical clustering. In such poisoning attacks, the adversary's goal is injecting adversarial examples in the clustering quality measure. In obfuscation attacks, the adversary's goal is to hide data samples in existing cluster by manipulating the feature values. In these attacks, a cluster is defined as not only the hard partition (and the soft partition) of partitional clustering algorithms but also as the dominant sets (and parameterized hierarchy of subsets) in linkage-type clustering algorithms.

Biggio et al. [67] put additional constraints on attack scenarios with a distance metric between non-manipulated training data and manipulated adversarial data.

Degree of knowledge of the adversary is encoded by entropy of a probability distribution in an attack sample. The probability distribution is defined over the knowledge space of the adversary giving information about the dataset and its parameterization in the clustering algorithm. Supposing such an adversarial knowledge, adversary's goal is an objective function expressed in terms of a (i) real-valued distance measure between clusterings evaluating attack samples for poisoning attacks and (ii) non-negative real scalar divergence measure between attack samples and target samples. Here, a greedy heuristic dendrogram cut criteria represents the single-linkage hierarchical clustering output as a binary matrix of probabilities assigning samples to clusters.

3.6 Robust Feature Selection Models

Xiao et al. [663] provide an adversarial framework to investigate poisoning attacks on feature selection methods such as LASSO, ridge regression, and elastic net. Such feature selection is used to derive security-sensitive actionable information in large-scale high-dimensional data-driven technologies like spam detection, malware detection, web page ranking, and network protocol verification. Xiao et al. [663] assume feature selection to be a problem of filtering a relevant feature subset inferring an iid random process for the training data. Feature selection criteria is then represented as an optimization of an objective function such as classification error and prediction information gain.

Xiao et al. [663] define the adversary's goal in terms of a security violation which can be categorized as any one of integrity violation, availability violation, and privacy violation in feature selection. Integrity violation slightly modifies selected feature subset to facilitate subsequent evasion attack. Availability violation compromises feature selection algorithm to produce an output feature subset with largest generalization error. Privacy violation reverse-engineers feature selection process to infer information about feature subset, training data, and system users. A targeted attack affects specific feature subset, while indiscriminate attack affects selection of any feature.

Xiao et al. [663] suppose that adversary's knowledge can be about assumptions on training data, feature representation, feature selection algorithm, and feature selection criteria. Then adversary's influence can be either causative or exploratory to affect either training data or testing data, respectively. Here, poisoning attacks for feature selection manipulate feature values and labels in training data to construct poisoning samples that will be misclassified subsequently. Evasion attacks for feature selection manipulate testing data to evade detection by proposing distance measures and adversarial strategies to compare original data, non-manipulated attack sample, and attack sample. Such adversarial strategies are expressed in terms of the adversary's knowledge, the adversary's capability, the adversary's goal, and the adversary's influence in affecting the computation of an adversarial loss function empirically simulating feature selection algorithms on poisoned data.

For each feature selection algorithm in the experiments, Xiao et al. [663] optimize an adversarial loss function with a (sub)gradient ascent algorithm solving a convex optimization problem. The feature spaces are assumed to define continuous and discrete features and differentiable and non-differentiable features. To evaluate the feature selection under attack settings, a stability index is proposed to indicate anti-correlation rankings between feature subsets of the feature selection algorithm. Experiments show that an adversary can easily compromise feature selection algorithms that promote sparsity in the feature representation. The poisoning attacks and evasion attacks are said to mislead model's decision-making by introducing model bias and model variance, respectively, into the feature selection algorithm's mean squared error decomposition.

Mei et al. [419] poison latent Dirichlet allocation (LDA) corpus so that LDA produces adversarially manipulated topics in LDA user decisions. Adversarial attack is formulated as a bilevel optimization problem for variational inference under budget constraints. It is solved by a computationally efficient gradient descent method based on implicit functions. The optimization employs a KL divergence between LDA learner's word-topic distribution and fully factorized variational distribution constrained by Karush-Kuhn-Tucker (KKT) conditions. The adversary poisons training corpus such that topics learned by LDA are guided toward target multinomial distributions defined by the adversary. Adversary's goal is to minimize an attacker risk function which defines the distance between adversarial multinomial distribution and training multinomial distribution. Adversary's risk combined with learner's KL divergence gives a bilevel optimization framework for constructing the adversarial examples. Adversarial examples on words and sentences misleading LDA topics are created on a corpus sourced from the United States House of Representatives floor debate transcripts, online new year's wishes, and TREC AP newswire articles.

3.7 Robust Anomaly Detection Models

Kloft et al. [318] explore adversarial examples for an (online centroid) anomaly detection algorithm. The adversarial attack scenario is expressed in terms of the efficiency and the constraints of formulating an optimal attack on outlier detection. The outlier detection finds unusual events across finite sliding windows in computer security applications such as automatic signature generation and intrusion detection systems. A poisoning attack is assumed to create adversarial examples on training data where a certain percentage of training data is controlled by the adversary. An anomalous data point is then measured according to the Euclidean distance from the empirical mean of the training data. The empirical mean is calculated on training data by a finite sliding window online algorithm for non-stationarity data. By pushing the empirical mean point toward adversarial examples, the adversary forces the anomaly detection algorithm to accept anomalous data point as normal training data.

Kloft et al. [318] express the relative displacement of original empirical mean in terms of the attack direction vector between the attack point and the mean point. A greedy optimal attack is then proposed to locate attack points in a Voronoi cell on data points that maximize relative displacement of the empirical mean. For a Euclidean norm, the greedy attack is optimized with either a linear program or a quadratic program. The mixing of normal points and attack points is modeled by Bernoulli random variables which are iid in a kernel Hilbert space. The attack progress is measured by projecting the current empirical mean onto an attack direction vector. Theoretical analysis is provided for bounding the expectation and the variance of relative displacement by the number of training points and attack points in the current sliding window. The adversary is assumed to have full knowledge of the training data and the anomaly detection algorithm. The anomaly detector's defense to adversarial attack is proposed in terms of controlling the false positive rate.

Rubinstein et al. [532] evaluate poisoning attacks and training defenses for principal component analysis (PCA)-subspace anomaly detection where principal components maximize robust measures of training data dispersion. Adversary's goal is expressed as increasing false positives and false negatives of model under attack. A time series of traffic volumes between pairs of points is the dataset representing a routing matrix. Robust PCA of the routing matrix then identifies volume anomalies in an abnormal subspace. Adversary's poisoning strategies consider attacks with increasing amounts of variance information in the attack scenarios. The weakest attack strategy knows nothing about the traffic flows and adds random noise as adversarial examples. In locally informed attack strategy, the adversary intercepts the information about current traffic volume on network links under attack. In globally informed attack strategy, the adversary has knowledge of traffic volumes on all network links and network levels. In short-term attack, the anomaly detector is retrained for each week of training data during which adversary attacks network. In long-term attack, anomaly detector's principal components are slowly poisoned by the adversary over several weeks. In each attack scenario, the adversary decides the quantity of data to add to the target traffic flow according to a Bernoulli random variable. A robust PCA analysis on adversarially altered routing matrix then produces adversarial examples which are classified as innocuous by the anomaly detector. A tractable analytic solution to robust PCA is derived by Rubinstein et al. [532] from an objective function with relaxation approximations maximizing the attack vectors projected onto normal subspace covariance matrices. A projection pursuit method then produces feasible solutions for the objective function in direction of its gradient.

Feng et al. [186] present adversarial outliers for logistic regression. Linear programming procedure estimates logistic parameters in the presence of adversarial outliers in the covariance matrix in binary classification problems. Non-robustness of logistic regression to adversarial outliers is calculated from the maximum likelihood estimate of log-likelihood's influence function as well as the loss function in high-dimensional training data that has been corrupted by the adversarial outliers. In the attack scenario, adversarial outliers seek to dominate correlations in the objective function of the logistic regression model. Robustness bounds are then derived on the population risk and the empirical risk with Lipschitz continuous loss functions.

3.8 Robust Task Relationship Models

Zhao et al. [703] propose data poisoning attacks on relatedness of tasks in multi-task relationship learning (MTRL). Optimal attacks in MTRL solve a bilevel optimization problem adaptive to arbitrary target tasks and attacking tasks. Such attacks are found by a stochastic gradient ascent procedure. The vulnerability of MTRL to adversarial examples is categorized into feature learning approaches, low-rank approaches, task clustering approaches, and task relationship approaches where the learning goal is to jointly learn a prediction function. Then MTRL of linear prediction functions with arbitrary convex loss functions and positive semi-definite covariance matrices is studied. Adversary's goal is defined as degradation of the performance of a set of target tasks by injecting poisoned data to a set of attacking tasks. Adversary's payoff function is defined as empirical loss of training data on target tasks where the adversary has complete knowledge of the target MTRL model. In the gradient ascent procedure, poisoning data is iteratively updated in the direction maximizing the adversarial payoff function. The prediction function is a least squares loss function for regression tasks and squared hinge loss function for classification tasks. The prediction performance is evaluated by maximizing area under curve for classification tasks and minimizing normalized mean squared error for regression tasks.

3.9 Robust Regression Models

Liu et al. [703] study adversarial supervised learning in high-dimensional regression problems. The target of adversarial manipulation is the training data. The attack scenario is called poisoning attack. In contrast to robust supervised learning models that make strong statistical assumptions about the underlying input distribution and subsequent nature of feature matrix, feature independence, and signal-noise ratios, the proposed adversarial supervised learning relaxes such assumptions to approximate the feature matrix with a low-rank matrix suitable for robust regression. The resultant performance guarantees are compared with robust principal component regression acting as a baseline model. Such machine learning models have application in spam filtering, traffic analysis, and fraud detection to enforce security against powerful adversaries. The learning challenges to be addressed in algorithm design are that the dimensionality reduction can reliably recover the low-rank subspace patterns and the regression performed on the subspace can recover accurate predictions. Further, these design goals have to be achieved despite adversarially poisoned samples in the training dataset. Toward these ends, the authors develop a robust matrix factorization algorithm which correctly recovers the subspace wherever possible and use its features in a trimmed principal component regression, which uses the recovered basis and trimmed optimization to estimate linear model parameters. A noise residual is the solution of robust regression. It is used to study the interference of adversarial data with the regression model design and the ability of the adversary to significantly skew the estimator. This leads to the design of bounded loss function for adversarial learning. The adversary can then be assumed to create poisoning strategies to trigger the worst-case performance in the dimensionality reduction algorithm and regression models. The most effective of such attacks move the data samples along the direction to maximally modify the learned estimator. Experimental results are compared with linear regression models designed to be robust to the adversarial data poisoning. Such adversarial learning models tend to focus more on the defense against adversary to produce adversarial learning algorithms with distributional robustness rather than setting up the attack scenarios for validating their misclassification error costs. The non-linear regression modeling predictions can further benefit from security feature engineering based on adversarial learning theories involving deep representation learning models such as factorization machines [511]. Factorization machines are a low-rank approximation of a sparse data tensor when most of its predicted elements are unknown. In security feature engineering, they can model the interactions between features using factorized parameters. They are applicable not only to dimensionality reduction tasks but also to general prediction tasks in high-dimensional settings. As proposed by Blondel et al. [73], higher-order factorization machines can be estimated with dynamic programming algorithms tailored for prediction tasks in adversarial learning. Applications can be demonstrated for link prediction applications in complex networks. In game theoretical adversarial learning, the dynamic programming algorithms can be proposed to study the convergence properties of game theoretical optima. The game theoretical loss functions and training procedures in such a research are applicable to the study of learning and resampling dynamics within neural computing mechanisms tailored to adversarial learning. The complex dynamics expressed in adversarial data distributions can then be modeled as randomization algorithmics in data mining systems and machine learning models.

Amin et al. [215] study adversarial regression in cyber-physical systems (CPS). CPS are the critical infrastructure such as electric power grid, transportation networks, water networks, and nuclear plants. A supervised regression model is proposed to detect anomalous sensor readings in such infrastructures. Then a game theoretical model is built on the interaction between the CPS defender and adversary. In it, the defender chooses detection thresholds, while the attacker deploys a stealthy attack in response. Such an attack is due to carefully modify readings of compromised sensors that go undetected. Stuxnet attack is given as a well-known example of targeting physical infrastructure through cyber means. It is defined as the corruption of sensor readings to ensure that an attack on the controller code either is undetected or indirectly impacts controller behavior. The learning problem solves adversarial anomaly detection in the context of integrity attacks on a subset of sensors in CPS. The supervised regression task in the anomaly detection model predicts a measurement for each sensor as a function of readings from other sensors. The robust anomaly detection is modeled as a Stackelberg game between defender and adversary. An ensemble predictor containing a combination of neural network regression and linear regression is explored in the regression-based detector. The adversarial objective is expressed as a mixed-integer linear programming problem. Thus, an adversarial loss function can be derived for sampling, prediction, and optimization problems in deep learning regression. Such regression baselines can be built for multivariate prediction problems in adversarial learning. Stackelberg games can be used to model the strategic interactions assuming rational agents in markets on which there is some hierarchical competition. Strategic interactions between payoff functions for both players reflect the relative ranking of each player's application scenario in terms of the final outcome expected in machine learning. The search space of strategies for each player in a game is normally assumed to be bounded and convex, and the corresponding payoff function is assumed to be differentiable. The equilibrium solution for all payoff functions in the game is determined by the solution to an optimization objective function. Game theory provides the mathematical tools to model behaviors of the defender and the adversary behaviors in machine learning in terms of defense and attack strategies. Game theoretical adversarial learning takes into account tradeoff made by the attacker between the cost of adapting to the classifier and the benefit from attack. On the other hand, the tradeoff made by the defender balances between the benefit of a correct attack detection and the cost of a false alarm.

Zhang et al. [698] consider robust regression models in online and distributed environments. Here, the data mining applications of adversarial learning theories have to accommodate new challenges on the data analytics methodologies imposed by big data, where it is usually impossible to store an entire high-dimensional data stream or to scan it multiple times due to its tremendous volume and changing dynamics to the underlying data distribution over time. We would have to consider the amortized computational cost of pattern mining on high-dimensional and multi-dimensional data distributions. The pattern validation metrics in adversarial learning must also consider physical domain knowledge as ground truth for supervised learning. The modeling will require to learn dense substructures, rare classes, and condensed patterns over transactional, sequential, and graph datasets where random process generating training data may not be the same as that governing testing data. The implemented approach will have to be merged with approaches for adaptive discriminative learning with continuous optimization. Here, the adversarial examples can be put into sparse, measured, dense attack scenarios for adversarial learning. They must account for the operational latency-sensitive stream data analytics and knowledge representation learning over limited resources specified in terms of time, power, and communication costs. Adversarial manipulations must be defined over incremental learning and distributed processing of adversarial attacks at big data speeds and scales. Zhang et al. [698] identify heterogeneously distributed data corruption due to adversaries. They have proposals for corruption estimation when the data cannot be entirely loaded into computer memory. The robust regression is done with a scalable least-squares regression model that learns a reliable set of regression coefficients. Online and distributed algorithms are proposed for such robust regression. The true regression coefficients are recovered with a constant upper bound on the error of the state-of-the-art batch methods under the arbitrary corruption assumptions that are not uniformly distributed in the training data mini-batches provided to the online algorithm.

3.10 Adversarial Machine Learning in Cybersecurity

Adversarial attacks have several applications in computer vision, natural language processing, cyberspace security, and the physical world [499]. In computer vision, adversarial attacks are created for image classification [439] and object detection [665]. In natural language processing, adversarial attacks are created for text classification [536] and machine translation [168]. In cyberspace security, adversarial attacks are created for cloud services [389], malware detection [235, 526], and intrusion detection [289].

In the physical world, adversarial attacks are created to scale adversarial training to large models and datasets [340]. Kurakin et al. [339] discuss physical-world scenarios with cameras and other sensors as input. Eykholt et al. [177] generate robust visual adversarial perturbations under different physical conditions for the real-world case of road sign classification. Here, computer vision tasks act as control pipelines in physical systems where the main challenge with generating robust physical perturbations is environmental variability. Melis et al. [420] create physical-world attacks on robot-vision systems. Sharif et al. [552] create physical-world attacks on facial biometric systems using face recognition models for surveillance and access control. Xiao et al. [661] discuss spatial transformation of adversarial perturbations with Lp distance acting as a metric of the perceptual quality in the penalizing adversarial perturbations. Akhtar et al. [6] survey adversarial attacks on deep learning in computer vision. In comparison to game theoretical attacks, the physical-world attacks physically change the appearance of an object to deceive trained detection. They are restricted to once-only attack plays applied to targeted threats [580] in the game theoretical settings. They seem applicable to generating the stochastic search policy in our game with search heuristics such as Monte Carlo tree search [88] in combinatorial game theory.

Deep learning methods can be used to advance cybersecurity objectives such as detection, modeling, monitoring, analysis, and defense against various threats to sensitive data and security systems [406]. Rossler et al. [527] discuss synthetic image generation and manipulation benchmarks based on DeepFakes, Face2Face, FaceSwap, and NeuralTextures as prominent representatives for facial manipulations in data-driven forgery detectors. Matern et al. [416] exhibit artifacts from face tracking and editing to expose manipulations in face editing algorithms like DeepFakes and Face2Face.

Further applications of adversarial machine learning in cybersecurity include malware detection, malware classification, spam detection, phishing detection, botnet detection, intrusion detection and intrusion prevention, and anomaly detection. Tong et al. [600] discuss evasion attacks in PDF malware detection. Melis et al. [421] apply explainable machine learning models in Android malware detection. Marino et al. [411] explain incorrect classifications in data-driven intrusion detection systems. Corona et al. [136] provide a taxonomy of adversarial attacks in intrusion detection systems (IDSs) and computing infrastructures. Demetrio et al. [153] propose feature attribution to provide meaningful explanations to the classification of malware binaries. Fleshman et al. [198] quantify system robustness of machine learning-based anti-virus products using malware detection models.

3.10.1 Sensitivity Analysis of Adversarial Deep Learning

Understanding the machine learning model is useful to validate its correctness, detect algorithmic bias and information leakages, and learn new patterns from data. In complex machine learning models especially, state-of-the-art performance for the model comes at the price of interpretability. We shall have to tradeoff between learnability and robustness of the supervised machine learning. By "learnability," we mean the ability of the classifier to predict correct labels (without regard to noise), and by "robustness," we mean that the prediction is the same with or without noise (without regard to correctness). The tradeoff we observe is that more learnability comes at the price of less robustness, and vice versa. Sensitivity analysis is the study of effects on a dependent variable with respect to changes in the independent variables. It is useful in the study of black-box attack scenarios in adversarial learning where the outputs of the learning model and process are an opaque function of several inputs. That is, the exact relationship between inputs and outputs for machine learning is not well understood analytically. Sensitivity analysis in machine learning has a key role to play in the analysis of complex systems for artificial intelligence. It can be used to determine a model of the system under study. It can identify model parameters that contribute to data analytics output variability factors. It can identify the optimal search region of interest in a calibration study on analytics factors and their interactions. Finally, it can evaluate the analytics models to create an output distribution of influential responses assessed within analytics methods for correlation/classification/regression, Bayesian inference, and machine learning. A review of sensitivity measures such as in the analysis of variance is given by Frey et al. [130]. As risk assessment methods in adversarial learning representations, sensitivity measures can be used to prioritize additional data collection, identify critical control points in the dataset, and verify model validation. Sensitivity analysis can be done for knowledge discovery, feature ranking, dimensionality reduction, and model tuning.

In contrast to sensitivity analysis, scenario analysis examines a specific application scenario for machine learning in great detail to discover all the relevant variables aligned to the scenario. These variables would in turn support the creation of a knowledge base understanding the full range of outcomes given a specific set of input variables defining the real-world scenario. By testing the machine learning models across a wide range of scenarios, sensitivity analysis adds credibility to it by informing data-driven decision-making toward tangible conclusions and optimal decisions. Particular attention can be paid to algorithmic bias favoring rare features with strong sensitivity toward probability estimation errors and adversarial noise processes. Adversarial training refers to the incorporation of adversarial examples into the training process of machine learning models. Adversarial training is sensitive to not only the parameters but also the hyperparameters affecting the training process. Duesterwald et al. [167] present a sensitivity analysis of the hyperparameter landscape in the adversarial training of deep learning networks. Hyperparameter optimization techniques are applied to tune the adversarial training to maximize robustness while keeping the loss in accuracy within a defined budget.

Wexler et al. [646] develop a What-If Tool that allows analyses of machine learning systems to probe and visualize their inputs and outputs. It can be used to analyze feature importance, test performance in hypothesis testing, and visualize model behavior across multiple input datasets. Such a tool is of interest to practitioners of machine learning to answer questions on the effect of adversarial manipulations to data points on modeling predictions. It can also be used to analyze the distributional robustness of machine learning model across data samples acting as training, testing, and validation datasets. Users of the What-If Tool have a visual interface to perform counterfactual reasoning, investigate decision boundaries, and explore changes to predictions with respect to changes in data points. Thus, it supports the rapid prototyping and exploration over multiple statistical hypotheses in adversarial learning. Without access to the modeling details, generalizable explanations can be generated for adversarial manipulations using such hypotheses in a model-agnostic manner. This flexibility with explanations and their representations improves the interpretability of adversarial learning. It can be combined with exploratory data analysis processes to deal with complexity in input data types, modeling tasks, and optimization strategies. The workflow for testing hypothetical scenarios in the What-If Tool supports general sense-making around the data in addition to the evaluation of performance metrics optimized toward fairness constraints on machine learning. The data points in output predictions can be visualized with confusion matrices and ROC curves.

In supervised machine learning, sensitivity analysis studies the probability of misclassification due to weight perturbations in the learning model caused by machine imprecision and noisy input. To validate the distributional robustness of supervised learning on various inputs, sensitivity analysis has been extended into optimization techniques for neural networks such as sample reduction, feature selection, active learning, and adversarial learning. After discussing the geometrical and statistical approaches to machine learning sensitivity analysis, Yeung et al. [685] showcase its application in dimensionality reduction, network optimization, and selective learning. Provided a neural network contains the optimal number of hidden units and is able to construct optimal discriminating boundaries between classes, it can be used for feature extraction and rule induction with sensitivity analysis on informative patterns expressed in terms of the decision boundaries. Engelbrecht et al. [174] propose a sensitivity analysis on neural network decision boundaries and present their visualization algorithms. The dynamic patterns discovered from the sensitivity analysis are used in a selective learning algorithm. Thus, we can extract accurate rules from trained neural networks. Patwary et al. [486] conduct a sensitivity analysis-based investigation of semi-supervised learning. A divide-and-conquer strategy based on fuzziness in the training dataset is shown to improve the performance of classifiers. Here, a classifier classifies an instance to a class with a degree of belief on the extent to which the instance belongs to the specific class. In an initial training step, a classifier is trained on a small volume of training data with class labels. In a final training step, a large volume of unlabeled data is used for assigning each data point to one of several class labels. The classifier's generalization ability on unseen validation datasets is interlinked with the fuzziness of a classifier in arriving at its prediction accuracy. Low fuzziness samples from testing dataset are added to the original training dataset to retrain the learning model with improved accuracy. Resampling methods are used to study the generalization error bounds. Such a theory of learning from noisy data can be used to build semi-supervised learning classifiers involving learning methods such as self-training, co-training, multi-view learning, expectation maximization with generative mixture models, graph pattern mining, and transductive SVM.

Suresh et al. [585] propose risk-sensitive loss functions to solve the multi-category classification problems that minimize both the approximation and estimation error. Here, approximation error depends on the closeness of the prediction to the actual classifier, and estimation error depends on the closeness of the estimated input distribution on the underlying input distribution. The error analysis incorporates the risk-sensitive loss functions into a neural network classifier architecture. Performances are compared on imbalanced training samples using other well-known loss functions to approximate the posterior probability. The proposed loss functions improve the overall and per class classification accuracy. Such risk-sensitive loss functions on the decision performance are required to extend the results of binary classification to multi-category classification problems. In neural networks, the classifier employs loss functions that minimize the expected misclassification for all classes. Here, the risk-sensitive loss functions measure the confidence level in the class label prediction and corresponding risk associated with the action behind every classifier decision. The cost of misclassification is fixed a priori. In game theoretical modeling, such misclassification costs can be incorporated into the design of adversarial payoff functions. In multi-category classification problems, the adversarial payoff functions must be able to deal with strong overlap between classes in sparse data and high imbalance in samples per class. Neural network architectures then find joint probability distributions over the observation data to arrive at an accurate estimation of the desired coded class label. The risk factors on estimated posterior probability in the loss function designs penalize the misclassification patterns and their costs. The training process of the classifier is guided by both a confusion matrix and a risk matrix. Difficulty in obtaining the ground truth about original classes in the input data distribution increases the computational complexity in model development.

Cortez et al. [137] propose visualization for extracting human understandable knowledge from supervised learning black-box data mining models using sensitivity analysis. The data mining models considered are neural networks, support vector machines, random forest, and decision trees. Sensitivity responses are used to create measures of input importance for both regression and classification tasks in data mining. Such sensitivity-augmented regression trends and classification patterns discovered by data mining can be used to improve data-driven decision-making in the real world. Here, the data-driven analytics model learns an unknown underlying function that maps several input variables to one output target within a supervised learning paradigm. Interpretability of the data mining models can be improved with feature engineering strategies such as extraction of rules and multidimensional visualization techniques. The proposed sensitivity analysis treats the machine learning models as black boxes to query them with sensitivity samples and record the obtained responses. It does not utilize additional information such as the model fitting criteria and feature importance attributions. The rationale for sensitivity analysis is that a relevant input should produce substantial output changes when varying its input levels. Such input relevance is quantified by using a sensitivity measure. A baseline vector is proposed to capture input interactions with less computational effort. Sensitivity measures model the target outcome with either output class labels or the probability of classes. The total area under the receiver operating characteristic curve (AUC) calculation and the ensemble sampling methods are used as the sensitivity measure in multi-label classification tasks. Regression errors such as the mean absolute error (MAE) are used as the sensitivity measure in multivariate regression tasks. The sensitivity measures are first computed for each individual class, and then a weighted average is performed to compute a global sensitivity measure. The effects of these sensitivity measures on tree ranking and hyperplane separation are then studied in data visualizations for various inputs in the cross-validation experiments estimating the data mining performance metrics. Several new sensitivity analysis methods, measures, aggregation functions, and visualization techniques are proposed. Feature selection methods can be further designed to improve the relative ranking in the sensitivity measures to guide the search through the variables relevant for data mining tasks at hand.

Engelbrecht [173] does a sensitivity analysis of the decision boundaries learned by a neural network output function with respect to input perturbations. A sensitivity analysis of each hidden unit activation function reveals which boundary is implemented by which hidden unit. Here, a decision boundary is treated as the region of uncertainty in the classification of input feature space. A unique discriminating decision boundary can be obtained by pruning an oversized network that is overfitting the data, by growing an undersized network that is underfitting the data, or by adding regularization terms to the objective function for machine learning. Optimal decision boundaries lead to a statistically good generalization performance of classifiers produced with reference to the equations for decision boundaries. Data sampling methods on modeling outputs are used to locate decision boundaries in terms of the modeling inputs for a classifier. Modeling parameters that do not define any decision boundary can be pruned since they do not contribute to the classification function. Selecting patterns in the regions across decision boundaries, we can perform numerosity and dimensionality reduction in the training dataset.

Fawcett [180] surveys the characteristics of receiver operating characteristics (ROC) graphs in a tutorial. ROC curves can be used to organize classifier outputs and visualize their performance. They are rooted in signal detection theory but have been adopted by the machine learning community to analyze skewed class distributions, classification error costs, and cost-sensitive learning in the presence of unbalanced classes. An ROC graph depicts relative tradeoffs between benefits (true positive rate) and costs (false positive rate). Since neural networks can be considered as probabilistic classifiers yielding a relative instance probability or class membership score, they can be ranked with thresholds to produce a discrete classifier which can trace a curve through the ROC space to discriminate between positive and negative instances. A combination of scoring and voting can be produced to augment discrete classifiers to generate not only a class label but also a probability estimate required for creating a data point in the ROC curve. While machine learning performance metrics derived on the confusion matrix are sensitive to changes in the class to record proportions in the training data, ROC curves are insensitive to changes in class distribution. Area under an ROC curve (AUC) is equivalent to the probability that the classifier will rank a randomly chosen positive instance higher than a randomly chosen negative instance. It is closely related to Wilcoxon test of ranks and Gini index. AUC can be used to compare several classification baselines. It is possible for a high-AUC classifier to perform worse in a specific region of ROC space than a low-AUC classifier. Averaging ROC curves allows us to select the best classifier for a given training data sample. Using probability estimation trees, multi-class AUCs can be generated to study the discrimination between multiple pairs of classes combining pairwise discriminability values. Illustrating the bounding regions of new classifiers in an ROC graph can be used to direct rule induction and feature construction in an application domain for data mining. Such feature engineering can produce pattern discovery in terms of classification models, association rules, sequential patterns, etc. Such a classifier selection remains invariant to class skew and error costs which serve as the operating conditions in cost-sensitive learning. Finally, all conclusions drawn from the ROC curves are relevant only in the training data samples. Separate performance evaluation of the machine learning models is required on testing data samples and validation data samples. Here, adversarial data samples can be considered to be the validation data samples.

Flach [197] discusses machine learning metrics that are able to optimize tradeoffs due to skewed class and misclassification cost distributions obtained from machine learning models in training and deployment. A type of contour plots called ROC isometric plots are used to analyze and characterize the behavior of a variety of machine learning metrics. The machine learning metrics are sourced from contingency tables tabulating the model quality statistics in decision tree splitting criteria, rule induction patterns, classification, information retrieval, and subgroup discovery. True and false positive rates are assumed to sufficient statistics for characterizing the performance of a classifier in any target context. The derived machine learning metrics are interpreted to add statistical meaning to the conventional metrics. For example, accuracy calculation is interpreted in terms of expected yield as follows: (i) Disregarding misclassification costs, accuracy estimates the probability that a randomly chosen example is correctly classified. (ii) With misclassification costs, accuracy estimates the probability that a randomly chosen example incurs zero cost. (iii) With misclassification costs and correct classification profits, accuracy estimates the probability that a randomly chosen example incurs a profit. Thus, ROC curves can be used to detect a discriminative signal in the presence of adversarial noise in adversarial deep learning. They can be used to refine the proposals on game theoretical modeling that considered misclassification costs. They can be used to characterize the statistical differences between training and validation data samples where adversarial datasets act as validation samples skewing the class distributions in training data samples.

Ribeiro et al. [515] explain modeling predictions by learning an interpretable model from them. It solves a submodular optimization problem to provide the trust modeling of a classifier. Building users' trust in machine learning models is important because users will not use a black-box model or an individual prescriptive decision they do not trust. Trust is a vital concern for directly using machine learning classifiers as tools as well as deploying machine learning models within other products. Therefore, to evaluate machine learning models in real-world datasets, we can plan to inspect individual predictions and their explanations acting as metrics of interest over feature engineering augmenting the performance measures such as accuracy, precision, recall, and F-score. Ribeiro et al. [515] identify the desired characteristics of explanation methods. They include interpretable explanations that provide a qualitative understanding between the input variables and the response, local fidelity explanations corresponding to the model behavior in the neighborhood of the instance being predicted, model-agnostic explanations that are able to treat the learning model as a black box, and global perspective explanations to ascertain trust in the learning model. Goldstein et al. [224] discuss the visualization of black-box algorithms with plots such as individual conditional expectation (ICE) plots and partial dependence plots (PDPs). The techniques for visualization include decision boundary visualization in high dimensions, visualization of the hidden layers of neural networks to understand dependencies between the inputs and model outputs with insights into classification uncertainty, graphical representation of the contribution of variables to the model fit in support vector machines, game theoretical approaches to assess the contributions of different features to predictions, and quasi-regression estimation of black-box functions.

Thiagarajan et al. [597] conduct a sensitivity analysis of deep neural networks. Prediction uncertainties are analyzed in the sensitivity analysis with probabilistic networks. The learning objective is to lead to more robust and generalizable models without compromising on model interpretation. A new regularization of the predictions is introduced to demonstrate neural networks that generalize to unseen data. Finally, the prediction uncertainties are decomposed and explained in the input domain to improve the validation and interpretation of deep learning models. The notion of interpretability in this chapter is restricted to understanding model predictions in terms of simple actionable constructs on the input features. The experimental results are compared with conventional statistical modeling that adopts a Bayesian inferencing pipeline on pre-trained models for deep learning with point estimates. Such approaches may not be able to deal with out-of-distribution test samples. Prediction uncertainties are classified into epistemic uncertainty also known as model uncertainty that can be explained given enough training data and aleatoric uncertainty that depends on noise or randomness in the input sample. To address aleatoric uncertainty assuming a prior distribution on the inputs, the authors include mean and variance estimates for the prediction in the sensitivity analysis. When such sensitivity measures are used as regularizers for the learning objectives, they are said to lead to better generalization performance. At the same time, features that contribute maximally to the model uncertainty are tracked. Then a model that assigns uncertainties to reliable outputs suggests learning problems in either the training process or the input data. The output of deep learning is taken to be the prediction of a continuous regression response variable. A conditional likelihood-based loss function is selected to train the neural network toward such a response. Feature sensitivities are computed with a first-order Taylor expansion of the model's decision function decomposed into relevance scores for each input feature. The feature sensitivities then regularize the conditional entropy centered on the critical parameters in the deep neural network's loss function and training process. In experimental evaluation of the deep neural networks, the proposed approach produces improved validation performance compared to baseline models that did not take uncertainties into account. The effect of masking insensitive features is calculated from the R-squared statistic measuring the prediction variance in the dependent variable for regression from each of the independent variables.

Zhang et al. [699] conduct a sensitivity analysis of one-layer convolutional neural networks (CNNs) for sentence classification. It is unknown how CNNs are dependent on unexpected changes to input word vector representations, filter region size, activation functions, pooling strategy, regularization parameters, number of feature maps, hyperparameters, and other free parameters in the model architecture. The search space of all possible model architectures is huge. SVM for sentence classification are used as baseline models to improve the CNN results. The experimental results can be used to guide hyperparameter optimization techniques such as grid search, random search, and Bayesian optimization. As part of spam detection in the real world, Pruthi et al. [498] conduct a sensitivity analysis of word recognition with recurrent neural networks (RNNs) in the presence of adversarial misspellings. Adversarially crafted spelling mistakes are created in attack scenarios such as dropping, adding, and swapping internal characters within word input to text classification having to deal with adversarial edits. Experiments demonstrate that an adversary can degrade the classifier's performance to that achieved by random guessing. To limit the number of different inputs to the classifier, the sensitivity analysis reduces the number of distinct word recognition outputs that an adversary can induce. Thus, the learning objective is to design a low sensitivity system with a low error rate. Helton et al. [269] review sampling methods for sensitivity analysis such as random sampling, importance sampling, and Latin hypercube sampling. They help in the construction of distributions to characterize stochastic and subjective uncertainty in the adversarial datasets that propagates through machine learning models to eventually affect the model predictions. The sensitivity analysis procedures reviewed include examination of scatterplots, regression analysis, correlation and partial correlation, rank transformations, and identification of non-monotonic and non-random patterns.

Xu et al. [670] derive generalization bounds for machine learning algorithms based on their robustness properties. Here, generalization error can be understood as an estimation of the risk of learning algorithms. It is empirically measured in terms of performance errors on the training dataset. Complexity measures on supervised learning bound the gap between the expected risk and the empirical risk by the complexity of the hypothesis set for machine learning. They include Vapnik-Chervonenkis (VC) dimension, Kolmogorov complexity, and Rademacher complexity. Xu et al. [670] define algorithmic robustness with reference to a min-max optimization objective found in the theory of robust optimization. Informally, a learning algorithm is robust if it achieves "similar" performance on a testing sample and a training sample that are "close." Many machine learning models such as LASSO regression, support vector machines, and deep neural networks can be reformulated to have learning objectives in such a robust optimization framework to target minimizing the empirical performance error under the worst possible input perturbation in some properly defined uncertainty set for optimization. Here, the generalization ability of learning algorithms can be investigated in terms of the expected value of loss function of the learned hypotheses on samples that statistically deviate from training samples. In adversarial training settings, such an expected loss is customized for minimizing the feature manipulations in adversarial learning and misclassification costs in game theoretical modeling. In other analyses of machine learning models, the expected loss can be tailored for metric learning, transfer learning, reinforcement learning, and learning with outliers. The generalization bounds on expected loss derived from the proposed algorithmic robustness framework can handle transfer learning setups due to mismatched datasets in domain adaptation. They can be extended into investigations on robustness of unsupervised and semi-supervised learning algorithms.

To correct mistakes in classification settings, Asif et al. [18] create cost-sensitive classifiers that can be penalized on application-dependent predicted and actual class labels. A robust min-max game theoretical approach produces classifiers that minimize the cost of mistakes in classification as a convex optimization problem. Such an optimization is tractable in comparison to the NP-hard empirical risk minimization approaches that address the cost of mistakes in cost-sensitive classification with non-convex loss functions. This is the approach to minimize expected cost in robust machine learning. It directly minimizes the cost-sensitive loss on an approximation of the training data. The proposed zero-sum game is solved using linear programming. The machine learning performance evaluation is done on a confusion cost matrix. Cost sensitivity can be used for reweighting available training data, incorporating confusion costs into the formulation of the classifier, and boosting an ensemble of weak classifiers to produce a cost-sensitive learner. Further, the loss functions for training processes can directly incorporate cost sensitivity into multiclass generalizations of binary classifiers. An adversarial learning perspective on cost sensitivity brings an added dimension of classification modeling, statistical estimation, and decision-making under uncertainty. Here, the relevant adversarial learning methods include maximin model of decision-making as a sequential adversarial game, mini-max optimization of the regret of decisions, statistical estimates under uncertainty that minimize worst-case risk, and maximum entropy models using the logarithmic loss on exponential family distributions. Probability distributions are estimated as the solutions of such min-max games. Cost-sensitive learning that incorporates such adversarial learnings becomes more robust not only to distributional shifts in the dataset but also to uncertainty due to conditional distributions over labels in the loss function. Without assuming any closed-form equation in parametric forms for the given data, this approach allows us to incorporate training data properties and conditional data distributions as classi-fication constraints due to the adversary's conditional label distribution. Viewing the cost-sensitive classification task as a two-player game between an estimator and an adversary constrains the adversary to choose data manipulation distributions that match a vector of moment statistics of the underlying input distribution. The computational complexity of the estimator implicitly grows with the dimensionality of such constraints. Thoughtful feature selection and regularization can avoid such issues.

Lundberg et al. [401] present a framework called SHAP (SHapley Additive exPlanations) for interpreting the predictions in deep learning. An explanation of a model's prediction is taken to be a model itself. It is called explanation model and defines a class of additive feature attribution methods. Game theoretical modeling then guarantees a unique solution for the entire class of additive feature attribution methods. Such explanation models use simplified inputs that map to original inputs through a mapping function. They are solved as penalized linear regression models. Shapley regression values from cooperative game theory are used to find the feature importances for linear models in the presence of multicollinearity. Samek et al. [538] introduce the need for explainable artificial intelligence in AI domains such as image classification, sentiment analysis, speech understanding, and strategic game playing. The latest developments for visualizing, explaining, and interpreting deep learning models are then surveyed. Two sensitivity analysis methods are presented for explaining predictions in black-box deep learning classifiers. One method computes sensitivity of prediction with respect to changes in the input. Another method decomposes the decision in terms of input variables. Das et al. [144] review the explainable artificial intelligence (XAI) landscape. A taxonomy of XAI techniques is provided. Their usage to build trustworthy, interpretable, and self-explanatory deep learning models is surveyed. In addition to the creation of adversarial examples in misleading classifier decisions, XAI must have a feature engineering realization centered around ethical, judicial, security reasons. "Interpretability" is defined as a desirable quality or feature of an algorithm which provides enough expressive data to understand how the algorithm works. "Interpretation" is defined as a simplified representation of a complex domain, such as outputs generated by a machine learning model, to meaningful concepts which are human-understandable and reasonable. An "explanation" is defined as the additional meta information, generated by an external algorithm or by the machine learning model itself, to describe the feature importance or relevance of an input instance toward a particular output classification. Each explanation should be consistent across similar data points and generate stable or similar explanation on the same data point over time. So Das et al. [144] study XAI in production systems of machine learning for trustability, transparency, bias, and fairness. A deep learning model is considered "transparent" if it is expressive enough to be human-understandable. Here, transparency can be a part of the algorithm itself or using external means such as model decomposition or simulations. "Trustability" of deep learning models is a measure of confidence, as humans, as end-users, in the intended working of a given model in dynamic real-world environments. "Fairness" in deep learning is the quality of a learned model in providing impartial and just decisions without favoring any populations in the input data distribution. Fairness mitigates biases introduced to the AI decision from either input datasets or poor neural network architecture.

The game theoretical adversarial learning proposed in this book can be used to develop computational algorithms for optimization objectives and statistical inferences in adversarial learning algorithm's capacity for randomization, discrimination, reliability, and learnability. Studying the computational complexity of the game theoretical modeling in adversarial learning accommodates research extensions into robustness, fairness, explainability, and transparency of machine learning models. We can simulate the variational encodings of the learnable decision boundaries resulting from game theoretical adversarial deep learning as storing-retrieving problems in data mining on adversarial manipulations. The trustworthiness of machine learning in deployment can be simulated by computational optimization and statistical inference problems in advanced analytics of game theoretical adversaries in deep learning. In addition to operation constraints in the security policies, distance and budget constraints in the adversarial cost functions are our research interest. Here, constraint-driven game theories and evolutionary computations are needed to solve multi-objective, constrained, large-scale, and uncertain optimization problems in black-box attack scenarios.

Further computational difficulties for measuring utility and associated information loss can be addressed in game theory formulations. Then decision theory-based adversarial learning gives adaptive data analytics. After training the learning algorithms on statistically significant datasets produced by game theoretical adversaries, deep learning can scale and validate the machine learning modeling onto big data settings with computational models from human-in-the-loop decision-making. Robust models for data-driven decision-making in game theoretical adversarial machine learning assume imperfect information is available for learning the modeling parameters. They optimize probability distributions on uncertain data to avoid erroneous estimations. In terms of robust optimization, random variables underlying the machine learning features are modeled as uncertainty parameters belonging to a convex uncertainty set. The data-driven decision-maker is then protected with the machine learning system built against the worst-case scenario within that set. Such approaches to construct robustness bounds in adversarial deep learning have to contend with adversarial examples designed to mislead image classifications to take unwanted actions. Thus, the robustness in data-driven decision-making can be researched within adversarial machine learning. We can then design loss functions in deep learning with game theoretical objectives.

Chapter 4
Game Theoretical Adversarial Deep Learning

This chapter summarizes the game theoretical strategies for generating adversarial manipulations. The adversarial learning objective for our adversaries is assumed to be to inject small changes into the data distributions, defined over positive and negative class labels, to the extent that deep learning subsequently misclassifies the data distribution. Thus, the theoretical goal of our adversarial deep learning process becomes one of determining whether a manipulation of the input data has reached a learner decision boundary, i.e., where too many positive labels have become negative labels. The adversarial data is generated by solving for optimal attack policies in Stackelberg games where adversaries target the misclassification performance of deep learning. Sequential game theoretical formulations can model the interaction between an intelligent adversary and a deep learning model to generate adversarial manipulations by solving a two-player sequential non-cooperative Stackelberg game where each player's payoff function increases with interactions to a local optimum. With a stochastic game theoretical formulation, we can then extend the two-player Stackelberg game into a multiplayer Stackelberg game with stochastic payoff functions for the adversaries. Both versions of the game are resolved through the Nash equilibrium, which refers to a pair of strategies in which there is no incentive for either the learner or the adversary to deviate from their optimal strategy. We can then explore adversaries who optimize variational payoff functions via data randomization strategies on deep learning designed for multi-label classification tasks. Similarly, the outcome of these investigations is an algorithm design that solves a variable-sum two-player sequential Stackelberg game with new Nash equilibria. The adversary manipulates variational parameters in the input data to mislead the learning process of the deep learning, so it misclassifies the original class labels as the targeted class labels. The ideal variational adversarial manipulation is the minimum change needed to the adversarial cost function of encoded data that will result in the deep learning incorrectly labeling the decoded data. The optimal manipulations are due to stochastic optima in non-convex best response strategies. The adversarial data generated by this variant

A. Sreevallabh Chivukula et al., *Adversarial Machine Learning*,
https://doi.org/10.1007/978-3-030-99772-4_4

of the Stackelberg games simulates continuous interactions with the classifier's learning processes as opposed to one-time interactions. The learning process of the CNNs can be manipulated by an adversary at the input data level as well as the generated data level. We can then retrain the original deep learning model on the manipulated data to give rise to a secure adversarial deep learning model that is robust to subsequent performance vulnerabilities from game theoretical adversaries. Alternative hypotheses for such adversarial data mining in the game theoretical adversarial deep learning strategies are provided in cybersecurity applications with machine learning that is designed for security requirements. The game theoretical solution concepts lead to a deep neural network that is robust to subsequent data manipulation by a game theoretical adversary. This promising result suggests that learning algorithms based on game theoretical modeling and mathematical optimization are a significantly better approach to building more secure deep learning models.

Stochastic games defining strategy spaces for adversarial manipulations have been used to generate adversarial examples [309]. Such a strategy space is defined in terms of two or more adversaries' actions and corresponding payoff functions. Each of such an adversary can engage one or more learners in a game and vice versa. From the learner's standpoint, adjusting parameters of a game theoretical model is computationally less expensive than building a new model that is robust to the adversarial manipulation. From the adversary's standpoint, the attack scenarios can be characterized by the stochastic optimization parameters estimated in the game theoretical interactions with the learner.

4.1 Game Theoretical Learning Models

The ideas of two-player sequential games (or Stackelberg game) and multiplayer cooperative games have been employed as game theoretical frameworks training adversarial learning algorithms. To search for equilibrium in such games is equivalent to solving a high-dimensional optimization problem. The eventual model performance is then estimated by stochastic optimization methods based on computationally efficient heuristic search algorithms. So long as the objective function is bounded, global optimization methods such as genetic algorithms, simulated annealing, and stochastic hill-climbing can be applied to search for the convergence criteria that lead to subgame perfect equilibria.

Globerson et al. [220] discuss a classification algorithm with a game theoretical formulation. The proposed algorithm is robust to feature deletion according to a min-max objective function optimized by quadratic programming. In Liu et al. [385], the interactions between an adversary and data miner are modeled as a two-player sequential Stackelberg zero-sum game where the payoff for each player is designed as a regularized loss function. The adversary iteratively attacks the data miner using the best possible strategy for transforming the original training data. The data miner independently reacts by rebuilding the classifier based on the data miner's observations of the adversary's modifications to the training data. Such a game is repeated until the adversary's payoff does not increase or the maximum number of iterations is reached. Liu et al. [387] propose an extension to Liu et al. [385] where a one-step game is used to reduce the computing time of the minimax algorithm. The one-step method converges to Nash equilibrium by utilizing singular value decomposition (SVD). Liu et al. [686] formulate a bilevel optimization problem from a non-zero sum game on adversarial data transformations. The game experiments with sparse regularizers for designing robust classification objectives.

A game ends in an equilibrium with payoffs to each player based on their objectives and actions. The learner has no incentive to play a game that leads to too many false positives with too little increase in true positives. The adversary has no incentive to play a game that increases the utility of false negatives not detected by the learning algorithm. At equilibrium, the adversary is able to find testing data that is significantly different from the training data, whereas the learner is able to update its model for new threats from adversarial data.

All players are assumed to act in their rational interest to maximize the payoffs. This assumption, at every stage of game, eliminates Nash equilibria with non-credible threats to the learner and creates an equilibrium called the subgame perfect equilibrium. Here, perfect equilibrium assumes that each player knows about the other's utility function. The players' utility functions vary by application domain.

4.1.1 Fundamentals of Game Theory

Game theory provides the mathematical tools to model behaviors of the defender and the adversary behaviors in machine learning in terms of defense and attack strategies. Game theoretical adversarial learning takes into account the tradeoff made by the attacker between the cost of adapting to the classifier and the benefit from the attack. On the other hand, the tradeoff made by the defender balances between the benefit of a correct attack detection and the cost of a false alarm. The optima in adversarial learning are able to determine what suitable strategy is needed to reduce the defender's loss from adversarial attacks. Strategic interactions between payoff functions for both players reflect the relative ranking of each player's application scenario in terms of the final outcome expected in machine learning. Stackelberg games are usually used to model the strategic interactions assuming rational agents in markets on which there is some hierarchical competition. The search space of strategies for each player in a game is normally assumed to be bounded and convex, and the corresponding payoff function is assumed to be differentiable. The equilibrium solution for all payoff functions in the game is determined by the solution to an optimization objective function. Game theory has application in economics, political theory, evolutionary science, and military strategy.

Webb et al. [639] present an introduction to game theory. It covers the decision models and decision processes for determining a rational agent participating in static games, dynamic games, and evolutionary games. Various notions of game theoretical equilibrium lead to either descriptive or prescriptive notions of data analytics. In formulating a game, we have to define the players, actions and information available to the players, timing information about interaction between players that are either simultaneous or sequential, order of play and any repetitions in the interactions, payoffs to various players as a result of interaction, and estimations on the costs-benefits of each set of potential choices for all players. Osborne et al. [476] design a textbook for a graduate course in game theory. It covers strategic games, extensive games, and coalitional games.

Leyton-Brown et al. [352] define game theory as the mathematical study of interaction among independent, self-interested agents. The main classes of games, their representations, and the main concepts used to analyze them are summarized. A utility theory is developed to modeling an agent's interests and preference across a set of available alternatives in games such as normal form games, extensive-form games, imperfect-information games, repeated games, stochastic games, Bayesian games, and coalitional games. Agents faced with uncertainty in the learning environment then define the expected value of the utility function with respect to the appropriate probability distribution over states. In a simple manner, utility can be interpreted as the amount of happiness an agent (player) gets from a particular outcome or payoff. Game theoretical outcomes of interest in the machine learning system can be categorized within subsets of possible outcomes as solution concepts such as found due to Pareto optimality and Nash equilibrium. So strategic games in machine learning ought to model the adversarial learning components such as a set of players, a set of strategies for each player, and a payoff function indicating desirable outcomes in the game for a player. The game theoretical context (due to skill or strategy) of decisions for each player is useful for analyzing the data-driven decision-making made by machine learning systems under risk. It has been applied to social sciences to create a rational choice theory as an adaptation of the philosophy of methodological individualism for maximizing the utility/currency/value of individual actions among collective behaviors. A choice is considered to be "rational" in economics if it leads to preference ranking over a set of items characterizing the alternatives for a decision-maker where all comparisons are consistent. More advanced consistency notions ought to account for uncertainty in the learning environments and decision-making over time when a player does not have precise information and cognitive ability about the outcomes of the choices and comparisons between them, respectively. So the decision-making processes in rational choice theory have to be validated on an empirically basis for ideas such as "reason," "preferences," "rationality," and "learnability" with useful formal mathematical properties in the machine learning systems.

Depending on the player's interactions in the game theoretical objectives, the equilibrium solution is called either a Stackelberg equilibrium or a Nash equilibrium. In our research, we apply such a game theoretical modeling to supervised machine learning problems inferring the decision boundaries and corresponding data distributions in training data samples and validation data samples. We represent the costs of participating in the game in terms of the misclassification performances and retraining costs in deep learning. Evolutionary search and optimization algorithms are used to solve the game to find adversarial manipulations to training data. Depending on the importance of the costs incurred to generate an attack and to retrain the classifier, we find different equilibria solutions for the game. Further, we assume a black-box attack scenario where the adversary is unable to observe the classifier's strategies before choosing its strategy. We then experiment with variants in the attack scenarios where the defender's utility losses in the game are inferior to the utility of the adversary in a non-zero sum game.

Our research extends into Bayesian game models in which players have incomplete information about other players. This is more likely as the defender might not know the exact cost of generating adversarial data and the attacker might not know the exact classification cost for the defender. They only have beliefs about these costs. This modeling approach transforms games of incomplete information into games of imperfect information. Thus, adversarial learning techniques that rely on a game theory-based framework can be relevant as it models behaviors of the learner and the adversary based on the benefits and costs incurred for retraining the model and generating an attacker. Training a classifier with adversarial examples in synthetic adversarial data is similar to regularization of the classifier. In this context, game theory provides useful tools to model the behavior of the adversary and the learner as it includes, on the one hand, the benefit for the adversary to attack and the cost to generate the adversarial data and, on the other hand, the costs of the learner to update the model. Thus, game theory-based approaches cast light on the tradeoff adversaries and learners both made and can be used to assess the risks of implementing a specific cybersecurity technology for data-driven decision-making.

From a computational point of view, decision-making procedures can be encoded into algorithms and heuristics simulating rationality effectively. One important way to study rationality is to propose agents on the assumptions adopted by different algorithms and heuristics. We can then study the equilibrium of a market of interactions between such agents as quantification of the impact of algorithms and heuristics in the data analytics models. Game theory can be used to derive the market equilibrium mathematically. Such agent-based studies also involve computational intelligence. Because the combinatorial explosion of the optimal algorithms and heuristics is usually computationally intractable, our ability to effectively use the available computational power to find a good solution is determined by the computational intelligence algorithms that we implement. The level of optimality that we can reasonably achieve in an agent-driven paradigm then defines our effective rationality in a machine learning problem. Decision procedures in computational intelligence can be evolved with evolutionary learning algorithms. They are able to separate domain-specific knowledge from the reasoning mechanism. Thus, rationality in the real world can be studied within the context of decision problems in computational intelligence. By visualization of data transformations in computational intelligence including analysis of perturbation data, fuzzy membership functions can be designed to mitigate the effect of outliers and perturbations on the classification decision boundaries by penalizing training errors differently.

General problem-solvers in computational intelligence are a field of artificial intelligence in planning. They involve knowledge representation on beliefs, actions, and their effects, causal reasoning about actions and their consequences, and resource allocation about timing performance across actions. Finite choice decision problems are the topic for constraint satisfaction that is at the intersection of artificial intelligence, logic programming, and operations research. It appears in applications such as industrial scheduling and production planning. Search and optimization algorithms can be designed to use constraint satisfaction for finding efficient solutions. Computational intelligence algorithms called local search procedures can mimic strategic thinking in human beings. They can automate iterative improvements to the current situation, look for possible changes experimentally, and change strategies in response to actual or anticipated changes. Dynamic procedures for local search can model human rationality and reinforcement learning with evolutionary algorithms that evolve solutions instead of designing them. Such procedures can be either evolutionary computation procedures or procedures generated by evolutionary computation. By specifying stationary and evolutionary procedures in different agents, we are able to identify trading strategies and market behaviors. Representation, explanation, reasoning, and learning with computational intelligence agents ought to ensure the statistical goodness of fit for computational intelligence algorithms.

Camerer et al. [99] describe game theory as a mathematical system for analyzing and predicting strategic situations. The game theoretical equilibrium is based on mutually consistent strategic thinking and best response strategies in the equilibrium. Best responses are determined by the beliefs on the optimization of the attack surfaces of adversaries. The machine learning system is assumed to act rationally in any given situation. It's presence as a rational player then changes the game theoretical optimum reached by both the players and the heterogeneous population of the adversaries. A reinforcement learning model is proposed to empirically analyze the predictive power of repeated games. Adversarial examples are interpreted as counter-examples and deviations from the success criteria. They are able to dynamically change the parameterization of the game theoretical rationality. The refinement and selection of game theoretical strategies of a player subject to beliefs about the strategies of remaining players in the game are then found by stochastic better response solutions in the path to the statistical equilibrium of a game. The rationality that can be observed in the game theoretical decision-making for the learner and the adversaries then leads to a concept of "bounded rationality" that has information about decisions, payoffs, computational capabilities, and intelligences in the game theoretical formulation of the learning objectives designed to produce functional behavior for each player. The resultant game theoretical concept classes consist of machine learning systems with abilities to learn and evolve over time.

A "reasonable-case" analysis of the adversaries and their optimization constraints leads to a quantitative security evaluation of the machine learning methods expressed in terms of computation of an optimal attack and derivation of an upper bound on the adversarial risk for statistical learning algorithms. Here, reasoning frameworks built around knowledge representations of adversarial examples include case-based reasoning, rule-based reasoning, and data-driven reasoning. They can provide not only maximin optimization strategies for learning algorithms but also provision game theoretical criteria for system design with mathematical programming on discontinuous and noisy fitness functions having multiple types of design, system, and operational constraints. In addition to operation constraints in the security policies, distance and budget constraints in the adversarial cost functions are our research interest. The trustworthiness of machine learning in deployment can be simulated by computational optimization and statistical inference problems in advanced analytics with game theoretical adversarial deep learning. It can also incorporate dynamical system control in black-box optimizations of the deep learning. Here, constraint-driven game theories and evolutionary computations are needed to solve multi-objective, constrained, large-scale, and uncertain optimization problems. Application-specific constraints are determined by decision-making in data mining. By modeling the information leakage as loss functions in deep learning, our optimization solutions in game theoretical equilibrium are able to formulate the information leaks of private information available in the AI platforms as adversarial settings. We also conduct a study of the existing adversarial cost functions with respect to robustness bounds and privacy budgets in the deep representation learning models for adversarial learning. We wish to achieve convergence to an approximation of the target distributions with deep generative learning. The extent to which adversarial noise can benefit the training process as well as the overall quality of the distributions generated by game theoretical adversarial learning depends on the specific nature of the generated target distribution. Here, we can frame data mining extensions of the adversarial deep learning into web data mining, time series analysis, cyber-physical systems, autonomous systems manipulation, multimedia pattern recognition, and network security analytics.

As limited thinking models in economics, such reasoning frameworks have application in explaining price bubbles, speculation and betting, competition neglect in business strategy, simplicity of incentive contracts, and persistence of nominal shocks in macroeconomics. Resultant learning algorithms have application in explaining the evolution of pricing, repeated contracting, industrial organization, trust-building, and policy-makers setting inflation rates in macroeconomic institutions. In economic analysis of market behavior, game theoretical equilibrium is assumed to exist in models such as supply and demand analysis. The seller's goal is profit maximization in the production of goods and services. Opportunity costs are associated with drawing resource inputs to produce goods. They lead to increase in prices due to increase in costs of production. Separately, the buyer's goal is to maximize utility. Buyer's purchasing power increases with decrease in market price. Competition between sellers and buyers on price adjustments leads to an equilibrium price. Surpluses among sellers force price decreases. Shortages among buyers force price increases. Here, macroeconomic theory is an area of economics that studies the employment of resources, price stability, economic growth, and interactions among nations in the world economy. By contrast, microeconomics describes the economic behavior and decisions made by individual economic agents. Their behaviors affect relative prices that act as signals in a market economy to guide production and consumption. Such game theoretical analysis is applicable to markets that are the outcome of strategic interactions rather than stochastic natural processes such as digital markets, cloud computing, energy marketplaces, and crowdsourcing systems. Here, computing machines create strategic interactions through communication and commerce. Resultant statistical inference problems in game theoretical optimization can benefit from econometrics literature on parametric inference from observed strategic interactions.

Halpern et al. [248] survey the main themes at the intersection of game theory and computer science. The computational complexity of modeling bounded rationality is analyzed with reference to algorithmic mechanism design in game theory. Such mechanism design has application in combinatorial auctions for voting mechanisms, spectrum auctions, airport time slots, and industrial procurement. Here, a "mechanism" is a protocol for interactions between players to determine the solution for an underlying optimization problem. A complex dependence exists between elicited data and specified behavior in a mechanism. In general, algorithmic game theory differs from microeconomics in terms of focusing on the optimization problems with optimal solutions, impossibility results, feasible approximation guarantees, etc. in Internet-like networks. Narahari et al. [448] write about the application of game theory and mechanism design to problem-solving in engineering, computer science, microeconomics, and network science. Illustrative examples are provided for the key ideas of mechanism design such as social choice theory, direct mechanisms, and indirect mechanisms. Narahari et al. [449] is another research monograph on mechanism design theory. Optimal mechanisms are described as a research direction to optimize a performance metric such as the adversarial payoff functions in game theoretical adversarial deep learning. Cost-sharing mechanisms are proposed as a protocol to design computationally efficient adversarial cost functions with incentives and budgets. Iterative mechanisms can be used to reduce the cost of computing valuations and allocations in game theoretical adversarial deep learning.

Further research on game theoretical learning can be found in proceedings of conferences such as Decision and Game Theory for Security (GameSec) and Logic and the Foundations of Game and Decision Theory (LOFT).

4.1.2 Game Theoretical Data Mining

Fayyad et al. [183] define a framework called knowledge discovery in database (KDD) to unify data mining algorithms with data analytics activities. KDD is a design process that utilizes data mining algorithms for the analysis, design, and discovery of useful patterns in databases. KDD is defined as the overall process for discovering useful knowledge from data. Data mining is referred to as the application of specific machine learning theories to particular steps of advanced problem-solving algorithms in the KDD process. Without the context provided by KDD process, data mining algorithms can discover meaningless patterns. The KDD process draws ideas from several research areas of computer science such as machine learning, pattern recognition, databases, statistics, artificial intelligence, expert systems, data visualization, and high-performance computing. The unifying goal is to extract high-level knowledge patterns from low-level data models in the context of complex datasets obtained from real-world data sources. Scaling the mathematical properties of data mining algorithms to large datasets is one of the primary goals. KDD systems offer statistical procedures for sampling and modeling data, evaluating hypotheses, and handling adversarial noise processes. KDD methods employ more search in model extraction to operate in the context of large datasets with rich data structures. The KDD goals distinguish between verification of learning hypothesis and autonomous discovery of patterns. The discovery goal is further grouped into the well-known prediction modeling and descriptive analytics. The relative importance of prediction and description tasks varies between data mining applications. The primary data mining methods to implement applications are selection, extraction, classification, regression, clustering, association, summarization, optimization, randomization, approximation, dependency modeling, and change detection. The components of a data mining algorithm are identified as model representation features, model evaluation criteria, model learning algorithms, and model search methods. Begoli et al. [40] propose knowledge discovery process to analyze massive data. Design principles are given for data collection processes, system organization, and data dissemination practices. They are able to accommodate a variety of analytics methods such as statistical analysis, data mining and machine learning, and data visualization and exploratory data analysis in the data analysis pipeline. They can incorporate lightweight architectures that reduce cost, maximize performance, and track provenance to store, process, and analyze structured data, semi-structured data, unstructured data, and polystructured data.

Triantaphyllou et al. [607] discuss efficient and effective methods for data mining and knowledge discovery (DM&KD) in mathematical logic and artificial intelligence. Such DM&KD methods have application in the formal verification of adversarial deep learning. Search techniques and incremental learning algorithms are discussed to infer monotone Boolean functions, association rules, and guided learning from adversarial examples and validation examples in adversarial machine learning. A rejectability graph can be created on the adversarial examples based on interesting properties derived for positive and negative classes in adversarial learning. Clique subgraphs are obtained as connected components from decomposing the rejectability graph. They provide computational insight into minimizing the size of the inferred rules on training examples. Thus, the rejectability graph also provides an intuition for partitioning the original data in large-scale adversarial learning problems. Maimon et al. [403] survey a taxonomy of data mining methods. Several data mining algorithms are surveyed for analytics tasks such as data cleansing, missing value imputation, feature extraction, dimensionality reduction, feature selection, discretization methods, outlier detection, rule induction, decision trees, Bayesian networks, regression frameworks, support vector machines, data visualization, association rules, clustering, classification, frequent set mining, link analysis, multi-objective optimization, neural networks, reinforcement learning, granular computing, fuzzy logic, fractal mining, wavelet methods, information fusion, model comparison, interestingness measures, query languages, text mining, data stream mining, spatial data mining, relational data mining, web data mining, collaborative data mining, and parallel data mining.

L'Huillier et al. [353] introduce adversarial data mining for classification tasks. It is applied to phishing fraud detection with malicious email messages where spam filtering techniques are ineffective. An online version of a weighted margin support vector machine is designed with game theory. In experimental evaluation, it performs better than the state of the art in online classification algorithms operating in an adversarial environment. Server-side phishing filtering techniques can incorporate such adversarial machine learning theories to extract relevant features from phishing emails. They can then use data mining algorithms to determine hidden patterns in the relationships between the extracted features. A game theoretical data mining framework models the signaling game between the adversary and the classifier to solve adversarial classification problems. The signaling game imposes security requirements for sequential rationality on the adversarial payoff functions. The equilibria and their refinements in dynamic games of incomplete information can create an online learning theory around the incremental events presented to an online classifier operating in an adversarial environment. Online algorithms and generative algorithms have to be considered as the adversarial machine learning to minimize the computational cost in the cost function design for the learner even at the expense of lower predictive power for its discriminative learning. The resultant adversarial classifier has applications in deceptive phishing and malware phishing for automatic phishing filtering. It has better performance than countermeasures such as blacklisting and whitelisting, content-based filtering, network authentication, and encryption.

Bruckner et al. [91] model the interaction between a learner and a generator in email spam filtering as a Stackelberg competition of adversarial learning. By accounting for adversarial data distributions generated at application time as well as training data distributions available for learning, a Stackelberg prediction game generalizes the existing predictive modeling solutions in the context of email spam filtering. A non-zero sum game is proposed where the adversary and learner act sequentially without information about the opponent's course of action. By committing to a predictive model, the learner acts as the leader of the game. When the parameters of learner's model, adversary's transformation, and both players' loss functions satisfy a well-defined mathematical criterion, the prediction game has a unique Nash equilibrium that can be solved as an optimization problem. The game theoretical learning solves a bilevel mathematical program with equilibrium constraints with solutions obtained by sequential quadratic programming methods. Wang et al. [636] discuss the integration of game theory with data mining, artificial intelligence, and cybernetics. Incorporating data mining into game theory allows for the game theoretical analysis of complex data in databases with knowledge discovery processes of data mining. The learned knowledge is represented by data mining features such as prediction rules, classification rules, association rules, and clustering rules. Such representations can lead to operational improvements to the game theoretical modeling by supporting data-driven decision-making in adversarial deep learning. Data mining methods can be applied in evolutionary game dynamics for not only data pre-processing but also strategy selection in real-world scenarios selected by data mining features leading to the research area called game mining. Further, according to the nature of the game theoretical players, the types of game mining are defined as game content mining, game structure mining, and game usage mining.

Cesa-Bianchi et al. [108] write a book on prediction of individual sequences taking ideas from statistical decision theory, information theory, game theory, machine learning, and mathematical finance. Prediction problems are defined in terms of short-term evolution of natural phenomena. Formalization of prediction is given in terms of sequential prediction to be the realization of stationary stochastic process in statistical decision theory. Here, the statistical properties of the probabilistic process are estimated from the sequence of past observations to derive prediction rules on the estimates. The risk of a prediction rule is then defined as the expected values of a loss function measuring the discrepancy between predicted value and true outcome. The performance of the predictor is then measured on cumulative loss accumulated over many loops of prediction. Without an underlying stochastic process for the predictor, there is no baseline for comparing the predictor's performance. Such baselines are then modeled from a class of models called reference forecasters that incorporate domain expertise to advise on the next outcome. The domain expert can also include black-box models of unknown computational power and access to private sources of side information. The class of experts can be a statistical model built around states of natural phenomena. The difference between the cumulative loss of an expert and a predictor is defined as regret. Machine learning strategies are devised to minimize the regret with respect to all experts in the concept class for adversarial learning. Adversarial robustness can also be defined in terms of such regret minimization. Randomization prediction algorithms can then be designed to play repeated games to predict sequential compound decisions compressing the prediction sequences into compound decisions. Here, information theory can be utilized to do the data compression with reference to particular loss functions. A probability distribution is determined over the set of possible outcomes using Bayesian statistics for maximum likelihood estimation in online pattern recognition. The stochastic environment generating the prediction sequences can be studied with game theory. Minimax theorems in game theory can derive bounds on the performance of sequential prediction algorithms. Generalized minimax theorems can be used to define performance guarantees for adversarial deep learning algorithms without assuming any closed-form probability distribution underlying the adversarial data distributions. Then regret minimization strategies in game theoretical adversarial learning induce attack-defense dynamics that lead to several notions of game theoretical equilibria.

Rezek et al. [512] establish a common vocabulary for statistical inference in game theory and machine learning. Analogies are formed between best responses in fictitious play and Bayesian inference methods. An update rule for fictitious variational play is proposed for variational learning algorithms. They exhibit better convergence properties in strongly connected graphical models and have application for clustering a mixture distribution. The optimization objective is solved with respect to the joint distributions of the learning features chosen by all the players in the game. Kleinberg et al. [317] present a robust optimization framework for the evaluation of data mining operations in decision-making such as associations and clustering with utility functions in game theory. The interestingness and value of the data mining patterns are determined by the extent to which they can be used for the data-driven decision-making processes in an enterprise to increase game theoretical utility/value of decisions made by the enterprise during its interactions with other agents in the market such as customers, suppliers, employees, competitors, governments, etc. Such a utilitarian view of data mining needs to address several research questions in combinatorial optimization, linear programming, and game theory. Matrix games are proposed to solve clustering problems with approximation algorithms. Their computational complexity can be improved in an iterative manner by methods for data sampling and greedy learning. A sensitivity analysis of the optimization problem is conducted to propose a new interestingness measure for data mining patterns. It is then developed into a theory of predicting the value of data mining operations with knowledge discovery methods and artificial intelligence tools that are able to explicitly account for the goals and objectives of data mining tasks.

Freitas et al. [202] survey evolutionary algorithms (EAs) that act as stochastic search algorithms in data mining. Genetic algorithms (GAs) and genetic programming (GPs) are a popular class of EAs that are presented as robust, adaptive search techniques in solving data mining tasks such as discovery of classification rules, attribute construction and selection, and clustering. Multi-objective EAs can find Pareto-optimal solutions in several data mining tasks that are applicable to crafting the adversarial examples in our research on game theoretical adversarial learning algorithms. EAs also cope better with diverse attribute interactions in the adversarial data mining tasks. The custom loss functions proposed for each adversary type can be modeled as fitness functions evaluating candidate solutions for adversarial examples according to multiple quality criteria in EAs. Instance-based machine learning is amenable to the adversarial data representations for data mining with EAs in a synergistic manner for the design of individual representation, fitness function, and genetic operators specific to the adversarial data mining task being solved. By automatically discovering computer programs with GPs, EAs can be used for algorithm induction going beyond rule induction in adversarial deep learning.

Ficici et al. [192] distinguish between evolutionary algorithms and co-evolutionary algorithms in terms of the interactions between co-evolving entities. Game theory is used to describe such interactions by assuming co-evolution as an optimization method leading to an extension of the Markov chain models for evolutionary algorithms. Computational learning theory (COLT) can be used to analyze competitive games to construct co-evolutionary algorithms dynamics and constraints. Ficici et al. [190] use evolutionary game theory for feature selection in co-evolutionary algorithms of data mining. Variable-sum games are proposed for linear ranking, Boltzmann selection, and tournament selection of the features. Boltzmann selection converges onto a polymorphic Nash equilibrium according to a point attractor from chaos theory in theoretical physics and dynamical systems. Polymorphic Nash equilibria are Nash equilibria for mixed strategy games expressing polymorphic data populations. Co-evolutionary algorithms are understood as a search method or a problem-solver and a model of a dynamical system. Ficici et al. [191] examine feature selection methods such as fitness-proportional, linear rank, truncation, and ES selection in the context of two-population co-evolution with game theoretical learning. The selection methods add regions of phase space that lead to cyclic dynamics in non-Nash attractors.

Herbert et al. [271] apply game theory techniques to assess the optimization quality of competitive learning clusters with a self-organizing map (SOM). SOMs offer a flexible robustness model for clustering with several configurable aspects in many different applications. It can take advantage of dynamic and adaptive data structures to decide the neuron updates in competitive learning with reference to several performance measures and selection criteria in machine learning. Here, game theoretical learning is used to improve the quality of updates to not only one neuron but also the entire neuron clusters with a training algorithm called GTSOM. Garg et al. [210] apply game theoretical techniques to feature clustering. Features are viewed as rational players in a coalitional game where the coalitions are the clusters. Clusters are then formed to maximize individual payoffs at the solution concept called Nash stable partition (NSP). NSP is solved by an integer linear program (ILP). ILP is modified into a hierarchical clustering approach to find clusters over a large number of features. Thus, game theory is used in feature selection to distinguish between relevant and irrelevant features and substitutable and complementary features.

Shah et al. [550] survey game models in privacy preservation, network security, intrusion detection, and resource optimization. Game theory is one of the approaches to privacy-preserving data mining (PPDM). PPDM has utilized association rules to achieve privacy-preserving distributed association rule mining (PPRADM) algorithms. Game theory can also be used to design the tradeoffs between data utility and privacy preservation with a sequential game model. Privacy games can be designed from Cooperative Game Theory to create Cooperative Privacy in coalitions. Game theory can be used in the analysis of network attacks such as browser attacks, denial-of-service (DDoS) attacks, worm attacks, and malware attacks. Bayesian honeypot game models have been proposed for solving the problems caused by distributed denial-of-service attacks. Stackelberg models have been proposed for network hardening problems where the defender optimally adds honeypots in the network to detect the attacker. Dynamic game models have been proposed for intrusion detection systems (IDS) in ad hoc wireless network. IDS optimizations can be categorized into resource allocation optimization, IDS configuration optimization, and countermeasure optimization. Resource allocation optimization problems are concerned with optimization of network link sampling, resource sharing between nodes, cluster defense strategy in sensor networks, etc. IDS configuration optimization is concerned with optimization of IDS sensitivity, survivability, and attack mitigation in wireless sensor network. Countermeasure optimization is concerned with optimization unavailability time of network nodes, computation of the optimal response in multi-stage attacks, computation of optimal countermeasures in a wireless sensor network, etc.

He et al. [262] uses game theory for the keyword auction mechanisms in sponsored search to select ads in search engine monetization. The auction mechanism is formulated within a bilevel optimization framework solved by game theoretical machine learning. Ad selection is determined by the ranking and pricing ads for keyword auctions. A Markov model on historical data describes the changes in advertiser's bids in response to the auction mechanism. The key performance indices (KPIs) satisfying the Markov property include signals to the search engine such as the number of impressions, the number of clicks, and the average cost per click. Each advertiser is assumed to not have any details of the remaining advertiser's bidding behaviors for the keywords in the auction mechanism. Further, each advertiser has no knowledge of the internals of the auction mechanism. So mechanism-dependent advertiser behavior models can be built from historical auction logs. The Markov model is then able to predict future bid sequences. The auction mechanism is then empirically designed for revenue maximization on the predicted bid sequences. The empirical revenue model converges when the prediction time period approaches infinity. A genetic programming algorithm optimizes the empirical revenue model. Thus, game theoretical machine learning has application in electronic commerce and artificial intelligence. The genetic programming algorithm can handle complex, non-linear functional relationships in the prediction sequences to take best response bid strategies.

Narayanam et al. [451] devise a game theoretical learning algorithm to detect non-overlapping communities in social networks formed by the actions of rational individuals in Internet networks. The results are comparable to state of the art in graph clustering such as due to multilevel partitioning approaches to clustering. The utility of a node in the community is defined as the number of neighbors of that node in its community and a weighted fraction of the neighbors in its community that are connected themselves. Modularity and coverage of nodes are the performance measures in the clustering experiments for finding communities in a social network. Bulo et al. [93] extract hypergraph clustering groups by using game theory to formalize the notion of a cluster. The clustering problem of using high-order similarities between objects is called the hypergraph clustering problem. A non-cooperative multiplayer clustering game is devised to discover clustering quality in accordance with the solution concepts of the game theoretical equilibrium. Finding the equilibrium of the clustering game is shown to be equivalent to locally optimizing a polynomial function with linear constraints. Discrete-time dynamics are used to optimize the polynomial function. Results are compared with clique expansion methods in edge-weighted hypergraphs. The resultant clusters exhibit robustness against outliers.

Freund et al. [203] discuss the connections between game theory and online learning. Randomized prediction problem in online machine learning is defined as the learning model in which the agent predicts the classification of a sequence of items while minimizing the total number of prediction errors. A boosting algorithm is proposed to combine the learning models obtained from multiple runs across multiple data distributions. It combines the several selected hypotheses into a final hypothesis with arbitrarily small error rate. The generalization error of the final hypothesis can be bounded with reference to the VC theory of computational learning theory.

4.1.3 Cost-Sensitive Adversaries

Nelson et al. [456] study how an adversary can efficiently query a classifier. Undetected adversarial examples are crafted at minimum cost to the adversary using polynomial number of queries in the training feature space. Thus, a cost-sensitive adversary can discover blind spots of a detector by observing the membership query responses of the detector for negative labels to construct low-cost adversarial examples that have maximum impact on the detector's intended performance. This problem of finding low-cost negative instances with few queries is termed the problem of near-optimal evasion. The targeted classifiers are called convex-inducing classifiers. They include linear classifiers and anomaly detectors that learn hypersphere decision boundaries. There is no need to reverse engineer the decision boundary of the classifier. The adversarial objective of query-based optimization is comparable but not similar to the research area of active learning. The adversary's notion of utility to craft adversarial examples is represented by an adversarial cost function. Lanckriet et al. [344] analyze misclassification probabilities of the correct classification of future data points in a worst-case setting for classifiers. The resultant minimax problem is interpreted geometrically as minimizing the maximum of the Mahalanobis distances between two classes in binary classification problems optimized by quadratic programs. Classifier robustness is defined on the estimation errors of means and covariances of the classes. It is found to be competitive with non-linear classifiers such as support vector machines. This is a discriminative approach to measuring the adversarial robustness of classifiers. It can be contrasted with generative approach that makes distributional assumptions about the class-conditional densities in the adversarial data to estimate and control the relevant probabilities.

Asif et al. [18] discuss application-dependent penalties for mistakes between predicted and actual class labels in robust classifiers. The cost of mistakes is formulated as a convex optimization problem on the non-convex cost-sensitive loss. This approach to adversarial robustness is contrasted with empirical risk minimization on a convex surrogate loss that is tractable. But, the statistical difference between the actual loss and its convex surrogate can lead to a statistically significant mismatch between the optimal parameter estimation under surrogate loss function and original performance objective. The penalties for mistakes are represented as a confusion cost matrix for classification tasks. In contrast to reweighting methods and mistake-specific losses, the goal for supervised machine learning is to minimize the expected misclassification cost. The classifier construction is framed as a game against an adversarial evaluator. Parameter estimates in the classifier are expressed as the solution to a zero-sum game payoff parameter efficiently found by linear programming. Performance bounds are provided on the generalization error to demonstrate empirical benefits of the proposed approach to classifier construction. The proposed cost-sensitive learning has an adversarial loss function that depends on the actual and the predicted classes. It is more general than the zero-one loss used in binary classification to learn the best class prediction. But estimating the conditional-class distributions for cost-sensitive learning requires more training data that is either found in the data source or generated synthetically. A cost-sensitive learner can be utilized during either training or prediction time to iteratively reweight the available training datasets so that the classifier is sensitive to costly mistakes in multi-class prediction tasks. The confusion costs can also be incorporated into the classification criteria. Cost-sensitive boosting techniques can combine multiple cost-sensitive weak learners to produce a strong learner. Here, the adversarial perspective to cost-sensitive classifiers introduces statistical estimation and decision-making under uncertainty into the classifier construction. The statistical procedures for data-driven decision-making include Wald's maximin model, sequential adversarial games, Savage's minimax optimization of the regret of decisions, statistical estimates under uncertainty that minimize worst-case risk, and maximum entropy modeling for exponential family distributions in the adversarial loss. Such formulations of adversarial machine learning are robust to adversarial shifts acting as constraints in the moment statistics of the training feature sets and uncertainty in the cost-sensitive loss function estimates on the conditional label distributions. A parameterized cost matrix defines each player's game outcomes. The training feature sets can incorporate kernel methods to consider richer feature spaces that adversarially approximate the training data.

 To account for differences in data creation and transmission procedures, De Silva et al. [148] take into consideration vulnerability characteristics of test data in the design of adversarial classifier's countermeasures. So the attack cost structure can learn in an environment of sensor-to-decision protocols such as in an Internet of Things system. It can also be used to conduct a vulnerability analysis of the machine learning system deployed in the real world. The main contribution of the proposed cost-aware adversarial learning (CAL) framework is projection operator to mitigate the impact of falsification. It projects falsified test instances to the space of legitimate feature vectors with reference to an attack cost function acting as the distance metric. CAL approach is evaluated on Gaussian mixture model (GMM) with principal component analysis (PCA) and deep neural network (DNN) classifier. The GMM parameters are estimated using an expectation-maximization (EM) algorithm on class-conditional distributions. The cost function is defined to be a quadratic norm function in addition to a L_1 norm cost function. Adversarial attack is assumed to be a white-box attack and a gray-box attack where the architecture of the deep neural network is known to the adversary but the learned parameters may or may not be known. Rios Insua et al. [518] review the state of the art in adversarial classification from the considerations of game theoretical frameworks that is contrasted with adversarial risk analysis. The proposed adversarial risk analysis is a Bayesian decision analysis problem. It does not assume that game theoretical agents share information about their beliefs and preferences according to a common knowledge hypothesis in game theoretical frameworks. Adversarial robustness strategies depend on whether generative or discriminative classifiers as base models. Monte Carlo (MC) simulation solves for the optimal attack. Approximate Bayesian computation (ABC) techniques generate adversarial data distributions. Binary classification problems are evaluated in evasion attack and integrity-violation attack settings. Here, game theoretical frameworks can make real-time inference about the adversary's decision-making process at operation time. The adversarial risk analysis is suitable for applications having computational bottlenecks with possible changes in adversary's behavior being incorporated into classifier retraining. The proposed adversarial classification has cybersecurity applications in automation process found in spam detection, autonomous driving, fraud detection, phishing detection, content filtering, cargo screening, predictive policing, and terrorism.

Fawzi et al. [181] analyze the robustness of classifiers to adversarial perturbations to derive upper bounds for adversarial robustness measures on the difficulty of the classification task. The robustness measures depend on distinguishability measure between classes. Adversarial instability is attributed to low flexibility of classifiers in comparison to the difficulty of the classification task. A distinction is made between robustness of a classifier to random noise and its robustness to adversarial perturbations. In real-world classification tasks, weak concepts of adversarial robustness correspond to partial information about the classification task, while strong concepts capture the essence of fixed classification families such as piecewise linear functions for the classification task. A more flexible family of non-linear classifiers and a better training algorithm are found to achieve better robustness. Experimental evaluation suggests that increasing depth of the neural network helps with increasing its adversarial robustness but adding layers to an already deep network only moderately changes the robustness. Biggio et al. [57] improve classifier robustness with information hiding strategies that introduce randomness in the decision function. It is used in a multiple classifier system architecture. A game theoretical formulation between classifier and adversary is proposed for creating better-performing adversary-aware classifiers. Lack of information about the exact decision boundary leads to the adversary making too conservative or too risky choices in deciding adversarial manipulations for a malicious pattern. Thus, the classifier can benefit by increasing the uncertainty of the adversary. However, excessive randomization can also lead to a drop in the performance of the selected classifier. This tradeoff between the randomization strategies is analyzed with a repeated game of strategies to allow the classifier to retrain according to the strategies selected by the adversary. Schmidt et al. [542] analyze the sample complexity of robust learning in state-of-the-art classifiers subject to adversarial perturbations. It is important in analyzing the robustness properties of learning systems deployed in safety- and security-critical environments. The sample complexity of standard benign generalization of classifiers is compared with the sample complexity of adversarially robust generalization in specific distributional models such as the Gaussian model and Bernoulli model. Upper and lower bounds are provided as finite sample guarantees for the sample complexity in case of worst-case distributional shifts. The existence of an adversary is argued to significantly increase the loss for any hypothesis in a hypothesis class for classifier design. Less adversarial forms of robustness such as learning a robust classifier in benign settings are applicable to problems in transfer learning and domain adaptation. The sample complexity analysis is extensible with more constrained and lower-dimensional perturbations in different perturbation sets. Further robustness properties are understood in terms of the properties of adversarial distributions that make robust generalization hard or easy in a model class of interest.

Miller et al. [427] examine adversarial active learning to discover strategies for allocation of finite resources in machine learning for labeling training data and feature extraction. Active learning techniques are presented in adversarial contexts where accurate labeling of new content in a timely fashion is required to maintain detection performance in applications such as anti-phishing platforms and malicious advertisement detection. In active learning, the learning algorithm actively engages an oracle to request information for labeling a training dataset. The learner uses a query strategy for selecting the instance to be labeled. It can select instances that don't even occur in the dataset. So the learner is limited to a pool of observed but unlabeled instances where human labeling is expensive. The active learning selection strategies can be used to prioritize human labeling by fine-tuned prioritization algorithms that predict optimal levels of human resources. Noisy oracles provide weak adversarial environments for active learning. Adversaries attempt to disguise malicious instances effectively without incurred costs. Defenders try to efficiently identify malicious instances by measuring features with low cost. Such an active learning can be modeled within the frameworks for game theoretical adversarial learning. The cost of measuring features during training or testing is then a subject for active learning. Here, the query oracle is supposed to label instances and rate features to improve the performance of the learning system. In a white-box attack, the adversary is assumed to be able to estimate the decision function by repeated probing at every round of active learning with arbitrary precision. The adversary has knowledge of the stochastic process generating the data around benign and malicious labels but not the actual realizations of the training data. At every round of the active learning, the adversary injects utmost one instance in the training set to reflect non-stationarity in the learning process by including outlying instances of a given label. Oracle types are categorized as expert oracle that supplies highly accurate labeling supported by expensive technical experts, noisy oracle representing crowdsourced information with accuracy varying as a function of instance, and malicious oracle that employs adversarial strategies to mislabel specific targeted samples. Adversarial sample creation plays a role in designing malicious oracles producing decoy examples to reduce the quality of active learning. Miller et al. [428] review adversarial active learning with mixed sample selection strategies. Such a security-sensitive machine learning has applications in network intrusion detection systems (NIDS); biometric authentication; email spam; image, character, and speech recognition; and document classification. A taxonomy of training time attacks is called tampering. A taxonomy of testing/use time attacks is called foiling. In tampering attacks, the adversarial objective is given as mislabeling oracle predictions on correctly labeled examples and feature manipulations chosen to bias the learning process with black-box optimizations. The noisy oracles vary in accuracy when the ground truth is unknown. Uncertainty sampling and Max-Expected Utility are chosen as the strategies for sample selection criteria in active learning. In uncertainty sampling, the most uncertain sample receives the most uncertain score. Random sampling selection criteria act as the baseline. Other query strategies include density-based, query-by-committee, and variance reduction sampling methods. Mixed strategies can be devised to discover unknown classes in the training data. In security applications, such unknown classes are expected because the data exhibits adversarial drift with non-stationarity properties of the data distribution that change over time. Adversarial learning techniques address data drift with sampling techniques such as uncertainty sampling with randomization, handling noisy labels generated by non-adaptive, covariate shift setting theories for adaptive adversaries. Here, active learning in adversarial contexts must include experimentation around learning system performance with respect to real-time concept drift, performance degradation over time, return on human effort to label the data, coping with attacks and defenses against malicious adversaries labeling the data, feature extraction costs in static and dynamic analysis of malware, query strategy performance to learn a concept and react to its drift, and query strategy robustness to adversarial manipulations of the human oracle.

Our research into constrained optimization theories in the objective functions for adversarial learning is driven by the adversary's capability and control on training data and validation data taking into account application-specific constraints, effect on class priors, fraction of samples, and features manipulated by the adversary. Depending on the goal, knowledge, and capability of the adversary, these constraints are also classified in terms of attack influence, security violation, and attack specificity. Such constrained optimization problems on shallow architectures tend to produce intractable computational algorithms for class estimation and inference in supervised learning. The proposed adversarial cost functions and adversarial training procedures necessitate the need for deep learning architectures in the statistical methods solving the optimization problems in adversarial payoff functions. Cybersecurity approaches to sampling problems in adversarial learning may then focus on resilience enhancements to Markov chain methods and Bayesian Stackelberg games. In this context, we can derive robust classification models in the adversarial learning frameworks.

The evolutionary search algorithms of our research can be extended into Markov decision processes and cellular automata by an extension of the local optimization procedures maximizing the adversarial payoff functions. Here, mixture density networks can express conditional data distributions on latent variables and class labels in the training data and adversarial data. We can also measure information divergence between minimal representations of training data and adversarial data feature embeddings with deep metric learning-based adversarial cost functions.

We may also enforce a prior distribution on the latent factors for coherent data generation in supervised learning. The trustworthiness of such machine learning in deployment can be simulated by computational optimization and statistical inference problems in advanced analytics with game theoretical adversaries and dynamical system control in black-box optimizations of the deep learning. We can then analyze the bias-variance decomposition in adversarial payoff functions to derive utility bounds for deep learning in a mistake bound framework for cybersecurity. We study the existing adversarial cost functions with respect to robustness bounds and privacy budgets in the sparse representation learning models for adversarial learning. To derive reliable guarantees on the security of neural networks, we conduct a data-driven adversarial machine learning security evaluation at the intersection of software testing, formal verification, robust artificial intelligence, and interpretable machine learning. Here, model complexity (otherwise called generalization error) can be defined as the discrepancy between the out-of-sample error and the in-sample error in formal verification applicable to the cyber information processing methods in adversarial learning classification and optimization problems.

Our game theoretical adversarial learning framework can automate the detection, classification, generation, and optimization of trustworthy machine learning in the web and mobile apps. The generative representations in our adversarial manipulations are able to quantify the security threats that exploit the active and passive measurements in big data application domains. We model the malicious activities of adversaries in game theoretical optimization objective functions. Then the deep learning solutions in equilibrium are able to identify the information leaks of private information available in the AI platforms. By modeling the information leakage as loss functions in deep learning, we can formulate adversarial settings in a game theoretical learning framework. We can include sensitive attack scenarios and defense approaches from application domains such as biometric recognition into such a learning theory framework. In this context, we can also explore the privacy-enhancing technologies that impose controls on data sharing and collaborative analytics in Internet measurements. Here, we can design data analysis, knowledge discovery, and machine learning algorithms for data sharing frameworks. In them, domain constraints can be modeled as adversarial cost functions, and design constraints can be modeled as adversarial payoff functions. Security information can be represented with complex networks. Then deep learning baselines can perform in terms of data mining processes and machine learning features. Secure scalable federated learning can also be implemented into distributed systems and database systems. Our research in adversarial learning provides the frameworks to analyze the security and privacy in machine learning. In a high-performance computing infrastructure, we can implement it in tools and frameworks for serial algorithms, parallel algorithms, and distributed computations of big data.

4.1.4 Adversarial Training Strategies

Zhou et al. [712] survey game theoretical approaches to adversarial machine learning with particular focus on cybersecurity applications due to attacks from active adversaries. Such applications include intrusion detection, banking fraud detection, spam filtering, and malware detection. The corresponding security games are formed between the learning system and an intelligent adversary where both players attempt to play best response strategies that maximize their payoffs. Each player determines an optimal strategy based on prediction of the opponent's strategy choice. The adversarial learning process then results in a robust classifier less susceptible to being misled by adversarial manipulations. Simultaneous games and sequential games are the most popular security games to study the strategic interactions between the intelligent adversary and the learning system. In Stackelberg games, either the adversary or the learner is the leader of the game. They can be extended to single-leader-multi-follower games such as the Bayesian Stackelberg games.

Alpcan et al. [11] discuss decision-making in high-dimensional high-volume feature spaces with strategic games in complex systems such as communication networks, smart electricity grids, cyber-physical systems, and network security. Here, game theoretical adversarial learning can be used in non-linear optimization in large systems of variables where players have limited information and resources to effectively identify their preference parameters at low cost in dynamic online settings. The challenges of such limited information are escalated in high-dimensional datasets for big data analytics. At the same time, the non-linear optimization problems present computational challenges. So the proposed game theoretical formulations focus on low-dimensional data representations reduced with linear transformations such as random projection and sampling methods in arriving at the Nash equilibrium solution concepts. The novel randomized projections are constructed to approximately preserve inter-point distances and inner products used in learning algorithms. Big strategic games and quadratic games are designed to approximate the solution concepts in optimization. Thus, large-scale strategic games can study the statistical inference in machine learning under adversarial contexts. In computer security, such approaches to secure learning can be contrasted with theoretical frameworks for secure multi-party computation and differential privacy. They can also conceptualize multiple iteration attack strategies that seek to mislead classifiers used in spam detection, polymorphic worm detectors, and network anomaly detectors. Regret minimizing learners and non-parametric statistical methods that can deal with large numbers of parameters are also comparable to adversarial learning algorithms. So game theoretical adversarial learning algorithm design and adversarial machine learning game analysis can benefit from optimization theories found in robust statistics, online learning theory, and theory of regret minimization.

Li et al. [355] extend adversarial machine learning to account for operational constraints in randomized decisions. A conceptual separation is made between learning attacker preferences and operational decisions with respect to machine learning predictions. The task of adversarial classification with reinforcement is separated into the task of learning to predict attack preferences and the task of optimizing operational policy that explicitly abides by the operational constraints on the predictor. Then adversary's best response strategies are computed as randomized operational decisions. Training data is interpreted as the revealed preferences of the attackers in adversarial evasion. A basis representation is proposed for compactly estimating the operational decision function in a linear program. A randomized operational policy explicitly abides by operational constraints. An iterative constraint generation approach creates the adversary's best response. Thus, a principled way to embed randomization into adversarial classification with off-the-shelf machine learning techniques is introduced. The baseline linear program estimating the operational decisions has an exponential number of variables and constraints. Its scalable approximation is arrived at by the Fourier representation of Boolean functions combined with constraint generation to compute randomized operational decisions under budget constraints. Hart et al. [253] discuss adaptive strategies in repeated games that include smooth fictitious play and regret matching. The empirical distribution of play is a correlated equilibrium with vector payoffs. Such games can be used for adaptive discriminative learning with continuous optimization in the game theoretical adversarial learning.

Jia et al. [299] combine Internet of Things (IoT) and advanced data analytics to learn game theoretical agents utility functions from data. Such data-driven methods derive utility models from observed decisions in equilibrium with computational algorithms for statistical inference such as inverse optimization and inverse optimal control. They can incorporate agile frameworks for analytics development to predict agents' behaviors and design incentives to achieve game theoretical objectives in the forecasts for the agents in shared resource games. Such a game theoretical agent's behaviors modeled in an energy game are applicable to demand response programs in markets such as formed by commodity, energy, and ride-sharing systems. For example, in a smart building energy game, the occupants consume shared resources such as lighting, heating, ventilation, and air conditioning. An energy game then incentivizes to use energy efficiently through monetary rewards on the energy consumption. The utility functions for individual agents are estimated in a non-cooperative game on their historical actions. Projected gradient ascent (PGA) is used to develop an optimal poisoning attack strategy in the utility learning adversarial algorithm. The utility learning adversarial algorithm synthesizes malicious attack points to imitate normal behaviors. Stationary conditions on normal behaviors are expressed as regression residuals. The agents' decisions and behaviors are then computed at the Nash equilibrium of the estimated utility functions. A strong threat model is devised from Kerckhoffs's principle then targeted by adversaries who poison training datasets to mislead predictions and achieve malicious goals. The gradient in PGA is interpreted as training sensitivity capturing the change in the learned utility models with respect to the adversarial data. Similarly, a testing sensitivity estimates the variation in the Nash equilibria with respect to the parameters of an agent's utility function. PGA is then shown to reduce the predictive power of the learned utility functions. Experiments are conducted on synthetic and real-world game datasets. A powerful attacker can then generate malicious poisoning attacks that result in large errors in the agent's behaviors and predictions that remain indistinguishable from normal actions. A tradeoff is found between attack efficacy and detectability. This tradeoff is used to propose a defense mechanism of detecting malicious actions and applying robust learning methods for utility estimation.

Dritsoula et al. [165] explore an intruder classification game as a security game where a strategic defender classifies an intruder as spy or spammer based on the solution to a non-zero sum game. The classifier is designed to detect file server and mail server attacks. The defender's objective function randomizes between a set of thresholds to balance missed detections and false alarms. The attacker tradeoffs between increasing attack strength and chances of getting caught. Nash equilibria in mixed strategies are computed for the non-zero sum game in polynomial time. The focus of the game theoretical framework is attacker classification rather than intrusion detection. The spammer is a non-strategic player represented with a fixed and known probability distribution. The spy is a strategic player that selects the number of attacks on the main target according to an adversarial cost function. The security game is compared with a signaling and dynamic game with multiple stages where the players update their beliefs and distributions based on Bayesian statistics. The spy's cost matrix influences the best response strategies of the defender in its payoff formulation. The spammer's attack distribution influences the spy's Nash equilibrium strategy. The defender's Nash equilibrium strategy is randomization across a contiguous set of thresholds where the parameters of the game satisfy conditions for randomizing between the set of thresholds.

4.2   Game Theoretical Adversarial Learning

Dalvi et al. [142] analyzed classifier performance by viewing classification as a game with the classifier adapting to an adversary, aiming to make the classifier produce false negatives. Here, a cost-sensitive adversary is combined with a cost-sensitive classifier to define adversarial classification in a game theoretical framework. In adversarial classification, the data-generating process is allowed to change over time such that the data change can be expressed as a function of classifier parameters. Classifier is then assumed to maximize an expected payoff over adversary's cost parameters. In turn, the adversary's strategy is to find classification feature changes that maximize adversary's expected payoff. Nash equilibria are demonstrated for both sequential games and repeated games where parameters of both players are known to each other.

Lowd et al. [394] introduced adversarial algorithms to learn a linear classifier's decision boundary. An ACRE learning framework is used to determine whether an adversary can efficiently learn enough about defeating a classifier by minimizing a linear adversarial cost function. Biggio et al. [66] defined poisoning attacks against support vector machines (SVMs) by injecting adversarial examples into training data. A gradient ascent procedure computes adversarial examples as local maxima of SVM's non-convex error surface.

Bruckner et al. [90] proposed prediction games to model interaction between a learner building predictive models and a data generator controlling data generation process. Kantarcioglu et al. [310] designed a subgame perfect Nash equilibrium, which optimizes attribute selection with cost functions in an adversarial classification Stackelberg game. Liu et al. [386] modeled competing behavior between a rational adversary and a black-box data miner as a sequential Stackelberg game. Chivukula et al. [123] enhanced [386] proposals for deep learning models, while Yin et al. [687] extended them for sparse attack scenarios. Zhou et al. [709] explored a nested game framework, where adversarial strategy is chosen according to a probability of making prediction about classifier's decision boundary in a single-leader-multi-follower game.

Kantarcioglu et al. [308] develop a game theoretical framework to analyze adversarial learning applications such as intrusion detection and fraud detection. In it, a classifier's equilibrium performance indicates its eventual success or failure. A security game is solved to predict the end state of an equilibrium. The conditions under which an equilibrium exists estimate the classifier performance and adversary's behavior. So the game theoretical equilibria provide guidance on constructing classifiers that are useful in data mining and knowledge discovery. The solution concepts to the security games are solved by stochastic simulated annealing and Monte Carlo integration to find the equilibrium strategies. In experimental evaluation, the classification cost for misclassifying positive labels is found to be much higher than that for misclassifying negative labels. Under equal misclassification costs and equal population size for positive and negative labels, the classifier would minimize the total number of misclassification errors. Liu et al. [384] model the interactions and outcome between an intelligent adversary and learning system as a two-person sequential non-cooperative linear Stackelberg game. The Nash equilibrium solution concepts are obtained by solving discrete and continuous optimization problems in the Stackelberg game formulated as a bilevel programming problem. The strategy space for the adversary can be both finite and infinite. In the infinite case, the players in the game need not know about all the payoff functions. Genetic algorithms solve the Stackelberg game for the infinite case.

The unexpected predictions in the training data distribution can be studied in terms of adversarial learning where perturbations in training data can change the way a deep network predicts in unintended ways. Rakhlin et al. [504] provide an online learning no-regret algorithm with game theory. It is called optimistic mirror descent. It is used for online optimization problems in predictable sequences. It converges to a minimax equilibrium in a finite zero-sum matrix game in logarithmic time. So black-box regret guarantees can be found for predictive analytics on arbitrary sequences representing worst-case performance of the game theoretical interactions in adversarial deep learning. They can be used to design custom loss functions for sampling, prediction, and optimization problems in adversarial deep learning. The benign sequences are due to the smoothness of the inner optimization and the corresponding saddle-point optimization structure in game formulations. Here, predictable/normal sequences refer to benign class labels, and unexpected/abnormal sequences refer to adversarial class labels. The predictability of sequences comes from the predictability of gradients in optimization and convergence criteria to discover the minimax value. The optimization objective is to minimize cumulative regret between predictable and adversarial sequences interleaved among the game theoretical payoff sequences for all players participating in the security game. In optimistic mirror descent algorithm, Bregman divergence defined on a custom loss function determines the step sizes in the predictive sequences and adapts the step sizes to sequences observed so far. We may also use a custom loss function in the moments and cumulants of data distributions to explore "abnormal" prediction values and their corresponding causal feature "explanations" suitable for explainable artificial intelligence. Here, we can experiment with the feature selection procedures and loss function designs involving generalized variance, non-parametric Bayesian networks and probabilistic causal structures in multivariate deep network regression/interpolation between sequences. Here, attention-based and generative mechanisms in deep learning can be the regression baselines for the analysis of variance and model evaluation in multivariate structured prediction. We may also use any descriptive statistics, summary statistics, sufficient statistics, and order statistics suitable for analysis of variance in the predictable sequences. Motwani et al. [443] is a standard text on randomized algorithms for online learning problems in game theoretical adversarial learning.

Blum et al. [74] present a sequential resource-sharing game to achieve social welfare with privacy-preserving, publicly announced information. The motivating use case is taken from multi-agent settings in financial decision-making where players play the game with imperfect information. The idea of social welfare in the game depends on actions of the past players. Its applicability is then shown on machine-scheduling and cost-sharing games. Deferentially private information dissemination is the recommended adversarial defense mechanism that is at the intersection of mechanism design and privacy-preserving machine learning. A privacy-preserving mechanism collects information from players to compute an approximate correlated equilibrium that has advice to the players on optimal plays according to player types and behaviors. The tradeoff between increase in private approximate information about the state of play and decrease in social welfare is analyzed with best response dynamics in greedy matching games that have noisy cost functions. Unlike adversarial deep learning, the noisy cost functions are estimated on states of play in the game rather than the payoff of the game abstracting the values of players' actions. Thus, we can augment the players' payoff functions with state equations of a dynamical system to result in stochastic control in the game theoretical interactions of the adversarial deep learning.

In our research, we evaluate multi-label adversarial learning algorithms in stochastic optimization settings. We empirically generate adversarial manipulations at Nash equilibrium in a constant-sum and a variable-sum sequential Stackelberg game. Our adversary's strategy space is determined by evolutionary parameters and variational parameters learned on the input data distribution. Therefore, the optimal adversarial manipulations found by our adversaries define a generative model for the adversarial data found in classifier's input data space.

Furthermore, we define adversarial cost functions on a strategy space encoding original data distribution. Our adversarial payoff functions are optimized by a simulated annealing algorithm randomizing step changes in adversary's strategy spaces. Randomization in our adversarial attack strategies is also defined by the latent space reconstructing original data distribution with a variational autoencoder (VAE). The proposed (variational non-linear non-convex) adversarial cost function leads to better regularization of the adversarial payoff function converging to a Nash equilibrium in our Stackelberg game.

4.2.1 Multilevel and Multi-stage Optimization in Game Theoretical Adversarial Learning

Based on visual interpretation of probabilistic classifiers, Di Nunzio et al. [469] survey the gamification of supervised machine learning techniques to label objects at an affordable cost that is not time-consuming. A pricing model is devised for constructing a reasonably accurate classifier with small size samples of labeled objects where the performance is comparable to state-of-the-art classification algorithms. The game is organized into ten levels according to separability criteria between the positive and the negative classes. The goal in each level is to find the best classifier maximizing F1-score with the least amount of computational resources. Liaghati et al. [367] discuss maximin optimization approaches to resilient system design operating in a co-evolutionary environment. Here, adversarial manipulations are considered to be unexpected emergent behaviors exhibited by complex systems. Emergent behaviors arise due to diversity, connectivity, interactivity, and adaptivity of a system in its environment. Mathematical programming is used in such system design to optimize the system with respect to complexities and tradeoffs in the operating environments. Complexity multiple different interactions, problem formulation, stakeholders, and the operational environment. Such complexities include multiple players, different interactions between players, learning problem formulation, stakeholders of the data mining, and the operational environment for machine learning. In this context, adversarial examples lead to black swan events in complex systems. System resilience and adversarial robustness are then achieved by thoughtful, informed design that makes systems effective and efficient in a wide range of contexts. The definition of resilience is extended to maintain capability in the face of disruption by absorbing external stresses. Resilience is defined in terms of probability of recovery according to correct prognostics and correct diagnosis. Mathematical programming for system design includes mixed integer non-linear programming, evolutionary algorithms with multiple constraints and non-linear fitness functions, Bayesian optimization of uncertain security requirements, and minimax/maximin robust optimization suitable for non-linear problems. The application of game theory to systems engineering leads to the design of systems where the adversarial operational environment is uncontrollable and uncertain. The operating environments in the resilient system designs are tested against uniform distributions derived according to the maximum entropy principle. Air defense system is chosen as the representative of a complex system operating in adversarial environments with associated computational costs. Yair et al. [675] interpret the statistical procedure called contrastive divergence (CD) learning as adversarial learning where a discriminator classifies whether a Markov chain generated from the statistical model has been time reversed. CD is also contrasted with the learning in generative adversarial networks (GANs) to conclude that CD's update rules cannot be expressed in terms of the gradients of any fixed objective function. CD has empirical advantages on maximum likelihood estimation (MLE) due to short Markov chains initialized at the data samples found across a wide range of application domains. CD adjusts contrastive distribution to generate samples that are close to the manifold yet traverse large distances along it.

Multilevel optimization is suitable for competitive games where there is no chance player. Multi-stage optimization is suitable for cooperative games in which all players receive the same payoff, but there are chance players. The players' moves in a cooperative game alternate between cooperating players and chance players. Decision problems in game theoretical adversarial learning can be formulated as optimization problems in multilevel and multi-stage optimization theories that include multiple independent decision-makers, sequential or multi-stage decision processes, and multiple possibly conflicting objectives. Here, multilevel optimization has multiple stages, multiple objectives, and multiple decision-makers. By contrast, multilevel optimization generalizes mathematical programming with models on decision problems and complexity classes for determining each player's move as a solution to optimization problems in game theoretical adversarial learning. Practical applications for such multi-stage optimization include hierarchical decision systems such as government agencies and large corporations with multiple subsidiaries, controlled optimization systems such as electrical networks, and biological systems. Multilevel optimization theories also allow us to quantify the computational resource tradeoffs between privacy and security, adversary cost and learner cost, and attack scenario and defense mechanism in game theoretical adversarial learning in terms of duality formulations in optimization such as separation versus optimization, inverse optimization versus forward optimization, pricing versus sensitivity, and primal versus dual functions in optimization. Chalkiadakis et al. [109] write a book on cooperative game theory on the strategic behaviors of self-interested agents with binding agreements among them. The computational aspects of cooperative game theory are summarized such as transferable utility in games, solution concepts such as Shapley value, compact representations for games, and efficiently computing solution concepts for games. The game theoretical algorithms suitable for adversarial learning include welfare-maximizing coalition structures, methods to form coalitions under uncertainty, and bargaining algorithms.

A game can be interpreted as a multi-agent model of relationships between agent's actions and incentives. When agents are self-interested, the game models an optimization process to describe an uncertain process with an underlying probabilistic model. Here, multi-objective optimization simultaneously optimizes multiple objectives to discover Pareto-optimal curves which are a set of points where each objective function cannot grow larger with decreasing another. In game theory, each objective function belongs to a separate agent, and the decision variables are partitioned into the domain of each player's objective function. Here, pursuit and evasion games and strategic resource deployment game can be formulated for algorithmic warfare. Economics games are related to auctions; buying/selling can be used in computational advertising, resource procurement, stock market analysis, and dynamic price discovery. Graphical games are designed on network formation between players in social, corporate, and P2P networks. Recreational games such as chess, checkers, go involve full information about the opponents. Deb et al. [150] discuss the real-world applications of evolutionary multi-objective optimization (EMO). Pareto-optimal solutions are found by an optimization methodology for EMO that can handle a large number of objectives, a large computational cost, and difficulty in visualization of the objective space. The EMO procedure progresses to Pareto-optimal regions by adaptively finding the correct lower-dimensional interactions. It is implemented with elitist non-dominated sorting GA or NSGA-II algorithm that can scale to many number of objectives. Such Pareto optima can model the game's randomized strategy space in game theoretical adversarial learning. We can formulate the adversarial manipulations as stochastic optimization and randomized sampling parameters of a variational autoencoder generating the adversarial data within a Stackelberg game. Such a game is designed to mislead the adversary with robust statistics in terms of EMO algorithms such as simulated annealing (SA) and alternating least squares (ALS). The scalar optima in SA are used to generate the vector optima in ALS. The strength and relevancy of our attack scenarios are determined by the performance of the deep learning models under attack.

Zhang et al. [696] survey the intersection between evolutionary computation (EC) algorithms and machine learning techniques. They include genetic algorithms (GA), evolutionary programming (EP), evolutionary strategies (ES), genetic programming (GP), learning classifier systems (LCS), differential evolution (DE), estimation of distribution algorithms (EDAs), ant colony optimization (ACO), particle swarm optimization (PSO), and memetic algorithms (MA). The machine learning techniques that use EC algorithms include statistical methods, interpolation and regression, clustering analysis (CA), principal component analysis (PCA), orthogonal experimental design (OED), opposition-based learning (OBL), artificial neural networks (ANN), support vector machines (SVM), case-based reasoning, reinforcement learning, competitive learning, and Bayesian networks. A taxonomy is produced for comparing the evolutionary steps enhancing each machine learning technique. Game theoretical adversarial learning can use the evolutionary steps for parameter adaptation, operator adaptation, local search, and computational costs to produce numerical computational methods in evolutionary game theory with evolutionary adversaries crafting dynamical algorithms for producing adversarial manipulations. The game theoretical strategy spaces for algorithmic randomization and data manipulation in our research are determined by the stochastic operators in evolutionary algorithms and variational networks defining the attack scenarios. The evolutionary search algorithms of my research can be extended into Markov decision processes and cellular automata by an extension of the local optimization procedures maximizing the adversarial payoff functions. Here, mixture density networks can express conditional data distributions on latent variables and class labels in the training data and adversarial data. We can also measure information divergence between minimal representations of training data and adversarial data feature embeddings with deep metric learning-based adversarial cost functions. We may also enforce a prior distribution on the latent factors for coherent data generation in supervised learning.

4.3 Game Theoretical Adversarial Deep Learning

In Liu et al. [385], the interactions between an adversary and data miner are modeled as a two-player sequential Stackelberg zero-sum game where the payoff for each player is designed as a regularized loss function. Each player's move is based on the observation of the opponent's last play. The adversary iteratively attacks the data miner by best strategy for transforming the original training data. The data miner reacts by rebuilding classifier based on data miner's observations of the adversary's modifications to the training data. The adversary's strategy of play is determined independently by the adversary. The game is repeated until adversary's payoff does not increase or the maximum number of iterations is reached.

The maximin problem for optimization proposed in Liu et al. [385] is solved without making assumptions on the distribution underlying training and testing data. The empirical evaluation of the optimization algorithm is conducted on image spam and text spam data. Different settings of loss functions yield different types of classifiers such as logistic regression with log linear loss function and support vector machines with hinge loss function. For the chosen loss functions, the optimization objective is formulated as an unconstrained convex optimization problem. The optimization problem is solved by the trust region method minimizing objective function on a constrained neighborhood of polar coordinates. At Nash equilibrium, the solution of the maximin problem achieves the highest false negative rate and lowest data transformation cost simultaneously. This leads to robust classification boundaries at the test time. The weight vector computed at Nash equilibrium also gives features that are more robust to adversarial data manipulations.

Liu et al. [387] propose an extension to Liu et al. [385] where one-step game is used to reduce computing time of the minimax algorithm. The one-step method converges to Nash equilibrium by utilizing singular value decomposition (SVD). SVD gives orthogonal basis vectors or singular vectors acting as the "principal components" of training data. Thus, the singular vectors characterize each type of class present in the training data. The label of a test data is then taken by Liu et al. [385] to be the training class generating smaller residue vector. This

SVD-driven classification algorithm is taken to be the initial state of the game theoretical model. The adversary goal is to transform target class (or positive class) instances into the negative class. This goal is achieved in the testing data by shifting positive instances in training data by a small amount such that the class distribution is skewed toward positive class label. Moreover, the payoff function for the adversary is formulated as the difference in singular vectors before and after the adversarial data manipulation. Thus, a rational adversary not only attempts to minimize the distance between distributions of negative instances and transformed positive instances but also minimizes the transformation itself. The payoff for the adversary is then approximately solved using a trust region sub-problem which is solved using a subspace approximation while avoiding the expensive computation of the gradient matrix and hessian matrix of the adversary's loss function and classifier's loss function, respectively. In validating the algorithm, the adversarial examples are constructed to produce high false positive rate for the classifier at the initial step of the game. At the end of the game, the false positive rate of the learning algorithm is reduced by taking into account adversarial data manipulations.

Wang et al. [628] assume that the adversary changes any feature of the classifier at will and pays a cost proportional to the size of the feature subset that has been changed. Such an attack on classifier is called sparse feature attack in the paper. The min-max optimization problem is then formulated as a non-zero sum game. In a non-zero sum game, the gain of classifier is not necessarily the loss of adversary. Regularized loss functions are proposed for both the data miner and adversary to make the game's objective a convex bilevel optimization problem. Both l_1 and l_2 regularizers are examined with respect to the proposed sparse models. The adversary is assumed to apply change in data by minimizing the changes to loss function. The adversary selects an attack strategy with full knowledge of the data miner's feature weighting strategy. In regularizing the adversary's loss function, both the number of positive samples and the number of negative samples are used to account for imbalance in the data. Then the data miner chooses the feature weights based on samples in the manipulated data space. The goal of data miner is to determine a decision boundary based on continuously manipulated data in each step. The goal of adversary is to determine a manipulating vector based on a given budget in each step. These steps are repeated sequentially until convergence. Upon convergence, the classifier finds feature weights that are robust against the proposed sparse feature attacks. For solving a l_2 regularized least squares objective, the adversary's data manipulations are assumed to be bounded by a perturbation matrix of l_1 norms that set a reasonable budget (or accumulated cost) as the convergence criteria for the adversary. The elements of perturbation matrix are tuned to the input data by cross-validation over training and testing data ordered in time. The various games are then simulated by various l_1 and l_2 regularizers on the perturbation matrix. The choice of regularizers for the data miner leads to tradeoffs between sparsity and accuracy and bias and variance of the classifiers. Experimental evaluation validates that game theoretical classifiers deteriorate at a slower rate than regular classifiers on both near-future and far-future data.

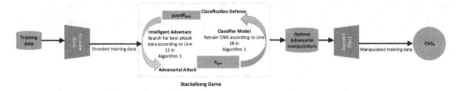

Fig. 4.1 A flowchart illustrating the variational Stackelberg game theoretical adversarial learning

To derive the payoff functions in the game, we assume that the adversary has no knowledge of either the deep neural network layers or loss functions in the deep learning model. Our proposed game theoretical optimization problems are solved without making assumptions on the learner's training and testing data distributions. The strategy space for algorithmic randomization and data manipulation in our game is determined by the stochastic operators in evolutionary algorithms and variational networks defining the attack scenarios.

4.3.1   Overall Structure of Learning Model in Variational Game

Figure 4.1 is a flowchart of our adversarial learning process that accounts for the presence of a variational adversary in supervised learning [126]. The final outcome of our adversarial learning is a CNN classification model CNN_{secure} (henceforth shortened as CNN_s) that is robust to the adversarial attacks.

We generate the adversarial data in a two-player Stackelberg game between the adversary and the classifier. The adversary creates a variational model by searching for adversarial manipulations on encoded training data. Every statistical parameter of the encoded training data is searched according to a simulated annealing (SA) procedure. The aggregation of adversarial manipulations to all statistical parameters in the encoded training data is optimized according to an alternating least squares (ALS) procedure. The ALS optimization is invoked at each time when the adversary generates adversarial data X_{gen} in the Stackelberg game. X_{gen} acts as a validation data for the classifier under attack. For every X_{gen}, the classifier re-optimizes its training weights to update itself.

The result of such a game theoretical interaction between the learner's and classifier's best moves is quantified by the adversary's payoff $payoff_{best}$. The adversary engages the classifier in the Stackelberg game as long as the $payoff_{best}$ increases. A decrease of $payoff_{best}$ indicates that Nash equilibrium exit condition has been reached in the Stackelberg game. At the end of the game, the adversary has optimal adversarial manipulations from the most recent X_{gen}. Such manipulations are applied on the training data to obtain attacked training data. Then the classifier's learning process adds the attacked data into the original training data so that the CNN_s can be optimally retrained by our adversarial attacks. While the CNN classifier is trained in the original data space, the adversary generates data manipulations in the encoded data space. A variational representation of the encoded data space allows the adversary to propose a generative model for the adversarial manipulations.

4.3.2 The Differences Between Our Method and GANs

Although both GAN and our method [126] are based on the framework of game theory and both of them are seeking for the Nash equilibrium, they have some great differences. In this section, we summarize these differences into three aspects, including the model construction, the model optimization, and the optimization results.

Model Construction Firstly, our variational Stackelberg game is a variable-sum problem, while the GANs construct a constant-sum game. Secondly, our method defines the adversary as the game leader, whereas the GAN is led by a generator. Lastly, the GANs define attack scenarios to discover generative models underlying given data distribution, while we optimize adversarial payoff functions with evolutionary attack parameters defining our attack scenarios in randomized strategy spaces.

Model Optimization Firstly, GANs solve a convex optimization problem with gradient-based optimization algorithms. By contrast, we solve a stochastic optimization problem with a simulated annealing algorithm. Specifically, our game's Nash equilibrium is computed by solving non-convex optimization problem. Secondly, during game theoretical adversarial training, we query CNN about the attack performance $error_{pos}(w)$, while GANs query CNN to distinguish between "real" data and "fake" data.

Optimization Results This is the most significant difference between GANs and our model. Firstly, GAN's objective at the Nash equilibrium is to learn a generative model that mimics the original distribution of data, while our method learns the optimal adversarial manipulations $(\alpha_*^{\mu}, \alpha_*^{\sigma})$ that are not the original true distribution of the data but are *manipulations* to the original distribution. Secondly, GAN's discriminator at Nash equilibrium is unable to classify between labels, while our classifier is robust to adversarial manipulation, and its defense performance is measured by $error_{Pos}(w)$. Thirdly, in our black-box attack scenario, different proposals on adversarial payoff functions and adversarial cost functions lead to different Nash equilibria for learning objective function and corresponding adversarial manipulations. In contrast, a GAN always tries to converge to training data distribution.

4.3.3   Comparisons of Game Theoretical Adversarial Deep Learning Models

In our research, game theoretical adversarial deep learning is applied to cyberspace security classification problems in the training stage and testing stage. Such problems study feature manipulations, misclassifications costs, and distributional robustness in adversarial learning applications. Adversarial examples are then crafted by experimentation on the loss functions in deep learning. The adversarial loss functions and training procedures in our research are applicable to the study of trustworthiness of deep learning in cyber-physical system deployment. They can simulate the cyberspace security safeguards, risks, and challenges as computational optimization and statistical inference problems. For the sensitivity analysis on such big data, we can analyze the analytics validation metrics that tune the deep neural network parameters according to misclassification trends in structured predictions. Common validation metrics for this purpose include confusion matrix, precision-recall curve, ROC curve, lift curve, and kappa statistic. We can also define synopsis data structures on tensors and graphs to derive the adversarial machine learning features. Our interest is in those data structures that aid similarity search and metric learning across probability distributions to evaluate the security of machine learning algorithms according to a design-for-security machine learning paradigm rather than the traditional design-for-performance paradigm. In this context, causality and stationarity of Markov chains can be used to define expectation maximization and minimum description length principles for statistical inference in adversarial data distributions. We have applied the learned features in clustering, classification, and association analysis. They can be extended into feature learning for structured prediction, change detection, event mining, and pattern mining. Here, the learned features can be one of sampled features, constructed features, extracted features, inferred features, and predictive features. The adversarial cost optimization over various types of learned features can be parameterized tractably with custom loss functions in supervised deep learning models and adversarial cost functions in robust optimization.

Sun et al. [584] discuss feature selection in machine learning and pattern recognition that is based on information theoretic features to remove redundant and irrelevant features from high-dimensional data. A cooperative game theoretical framework is proposed for feature evaluation and weighting to optimize the learning performance of dimensionality reduction. Shapley values evaluate the weight of each feature in interdependent feature subsets to produce a feature selection algorithm. Thus, game theory can be used for the analysis of learned feature's relevance, interdependence, and redundancy analysis in adversarial deep learning. In general, game theoretical feature selection has artificial intelligence applications where optimal combination of feature selection algorithm and classifiers is necessary for efficient model selection in machine learning theories dealing with uncertain information. Sun et al. [582] develop a cooperative game theory framework to evaluate the relative feature importance. Information theoretic measurements are proposed to distinguish between the redundancy, interdependence, and independence between learned features. A Banzhaf power index is derived for each feature. It is averaged over a coalition of feature subsets to which it belongs to propose context of feature selection within a voting game. The impact of a feature is calculated in terms of winning coalitions reflecting the feature's relevance to a target class.

Gore et al. [229] apply cooperative game theory to the feature selection in the Relief algorithm. By assuming a probability distribution on the training data, information theoretic measures are derived to rank the learned features, select feature subsets, and quantify the individual contribution of every feature belonging to a feature subset. Such feature selection based on game theory is useful for learning target concept to optimize the adversarial criterion functions and improve adversarial robustness performance to approximate the underlying class-conditional distributions in adversarial deep learning. By handling the curse of dimensionality, it can enhance the prediction performance, reduce measurement and storage requirements, reduce training complexity and prediction time, and provide better understanding of the stochastic process generating the adversarial data. The Relief algorithm acts as a discriminator between different classes grouping the feature subsets. Shapley values decide the feature's importance across iterations of the feature selection algorithm computing game theoretical coalitions. Cohen et al. [132] design a contribution-selection algorithm (CSA) for feature selection based on multiperturbation Shapley analysis (MSA) framework. Game theoretical learning assesses the usefulness of features selected according to either forward selection or backward elimination search algorithms. The CSA algorithm can be optimized according to performance measures such as accuracy, balanced error rate, and area under receiver operating characteristic curve. Coalitional games in CSA lead to a game theoretical iteration estimating Shapley values for features according to the MSA framework. In experiments, feature subsets are produced to empirically generate a high-performing classifier.

We design Stackelberg games between two players where one of two players, a follower data miner (learner), acts in response to the moves of the other player, an intelligent adversary (adversary) leader, with the goal of converging on an equilibrium state called Nash equilibrium. We have formulated the objective functions in (two-player sequential) Stackelberg (zero-sum) games as bilevel optimization problems, where the game theoretical goal is defined to simultaneously optimize two payoff functions that influence one another according to a leader-follower interaction that allows the learner to retrain after each attack. Stochastic search algorithms are then designed to solve the optimization problems. The optimal attack policy is thus formulated in terms of stochastic optimization operators and evolutionary computing algorithms. The adversary's payoff function simulates their attack processes, and the learner's simulates its learning processes. The solution to attack processes specifies the adversary's optimal attack policy under constraints. The solution to learning processes specifies the learner's gain given the adversary's gain under the optimal attack policy. In white-box attack scenarios, attack policies can be formulated as multiple EM-like steps that attempt to estimate an adversary's cost functions (sparse as well as dense) as a black-box attack and a learner's loss functions as a white-box attack. Introducing metric learning models that measure image representation and information divergence between legitimate and illegitimate data will allow us to explore white-box substitution attacks on the expected behavior of loss functions in multi-label classification networks.

4.3.4 Comparisons Between Single Play Attacks and Multiple Play Attacks on Custom Loss Functions

Adversarial attack technologies exist in computer vision, natural language processing, and cyberspace security on multidimensional, textual, and image data, sequence data, and spatial data. Such problems study feature manipulations, misclassification costs, and distributional robustness in malware analysis, concept drift, object detection, novelty detection, outlier detection, event detection, imbalanced classification, distribution shifts, rare pattern mining, out-of-distribution example detection, structured prediction, motif mining, model misspecification, and nonstationary feature learning. Here, our research into game theory is able to generate convergence criteria of stochastic search policies and game theoretical optima in the large-scale robust optimization algorithm design necessary in computational intelligence of cyber-physical systems. The resulting adversarial loss functions and training procedures in our research are applicable to the study of trustworthiness of deep learning deployment and evaluation.

Bear et al. [37] discuss the role of loss functions in rewarding accuracy and penalizing inaccuracy. Convex loss functions are found to favor simpler models that have more bias and less variance. By contrast, concave loss functions are found to favor complex models that have less bias and more variance. Such optimality tradeoffs between bias and variance in predicting the target class labels and associated concept classes shape the objective function landscape of the adversarial loss functions that inform statistical inference in game theoretical adversarial deep learning. Generating and explaining the adversarial manipulations requires us to study the effects of algorithmic bias in deep learning problems and subsequent robust optimization in adversarial learning problems. The bias-variance decomposition in adversarial payoff functions can be analyzed to derive utility bounds for deep learning in a mistake bounds framework for cybersecurity applications of adversarial learning. We can then express the bias-variance tradeoffs learning robustness, fairness, and transparency in deep learning frameworks for explainable artificial intelligence. Here, we can explore the signal filtering, detection, and estimation in tensors with information divergence mechanisms built around the game theoretical adversarial manipulations. Domingos [160] presents a unified bias-variance decomposition applicable to squared loss, zero-one loss, variable misclassification costs, and adversarial loss functions. It is utilized in the design of decision tree learning, instance-based learning, and boosting. Loss function is defined as the mathematical function to measure a model's cost of predicting a classification label or regression value. The goal of machine is stated as producing a model with the smallest possible loss. The optimal model is obtained by minimizing the expected loss over all the training examples, validation examples, and adversarial examples. In the case of zero-one loss, the optimal model is the Bayes classifier with a loss function called the Bayes rate. Since loss is a function of training dataset, the same adversarial learning algorithm produces different machine learning models for different training datasets. This dependency is reduced by averaging the expected loss over several training datasets that include the adversarial learning datasets. Here, bias-variance decompositions decompose the expected loss into bias, variance, noise terms that are computed with a computational algorithm. Adversarial data distributions are accounted for in the noise term. The bias term is independent of the training set and is zero for a learner that always makes the optimal prediction. The variance term is independent of the true value of the predicted variable. It is zero for a learner that always makes the same prediction regardless of the training set. The distribution of margins for correctly classifying the predictions with high confidence can then be used to derive bounds on the generalization error of adversarial loss functions proposed in game theoretical adversarial deep learning. The smaller the probability of a lower margin, the lower the bound on generalization error on training examples augmented with the adversarial examples. Maximizing classification margins and minimizing misclassification errors are a combination of reducing the number of biased examples, decreasing model variance on unbiased examples, and increasing model variance on biased examples. The related work is on adversarial deep learning theories in data mining patterns and machine learning theories in computational learning algorithms. It has application in malware analysis, agent mining, intelligent control, and cyber risk analysis in trust modeling of the security and privacy of machine learning.

Belkin et al. [43] study the model capacity of neural network's interpolation with double descent performance curve's training regime that subsumes conventional practice of U-shaped bias-variance risk curves to balance underfitting and overfitting according to empirical risk minimization. The simplicity of the neural network predictors is defined over function classes that contain interpolating functions with regularity or smoothness due to less inductive bias as measured by a function space norm. The interpolating functions with a smaller norm are considered to be simpler. Adversarial cost functions on the neural network predictors in adversarial deep learning settings act as measures of regularization on the inductive bias in game theoretical adversarial deep learning. Here, margin theory is the related work to discover the function classes in adversarial classifiers. Research on the optimality of interpolating predictors is required to extend such function classes in adversarial regressors approximated by multi-label classifiers with vector valued outputs and sum of squared losses at each output. Incorporating such interpolation regimes and their empirical data analytics in adversarial deep learning opens new computational, statistical, and mathematical avenues of research into the optimality properties and utility bounds of deep learning predictors. Li et al. [358] investigate the dimensionality of the parameter space to solve computing problems with neural networks for supervised, reinforcement, and other types of learning. Such results are useful for finding the structure of the objective landscape in adversarial deep learning with compressed representations of the deep neural networks in black-box optimizations. Strumbelj et al. [574] use coalitional game theory to explain individual predictions of classification models. The proposed explanation method is designed to work with any type of classifier. In machine learning, it can be contrasted with model-specific explanation methods such as decision rules and Bayesian networks as well as methods that give explanations in the form of feature contributions in classifier ensembles such as random forests. In deep learning, it can be contrasted with rule extraction methods applied to neural networks to reduce the dependence between end-user requirements (obtained from marketing, medicine, etc.) and underlying machine learning methods. The notion of a prediction difference is proposed between current prediction and expected prediction with respect to the current feature value contribution to the prediction. No assumptions are made on the prior relevance of individual feature values. The changes in a classifier's prediction are decomposed into contributions of individual features using concepts in coalitional game theory. Narayanam et al. [450] propose to discover influential nodes acting as learned features in a social network with Shapley values and cooperative game theory. Shapley values are the solution concepts giving the expected payoff allocations in the coalitional game designs. The problem of information diffusion in social networks is addressed for applications such as viral marketing, sales promotions, and research trends in co-authorship networks for abstract ideas and technical information with computationally efficient algorithms. The target node set selection problem finding influential nodes is formulated as a coverage pattern discovery problem in data mining that models individual decisions influenced by behaviors of immediate neighbors in the social network. Shapley value solution concepts satisfy mathematical properties called linearity, symmetry, and carrier property to discover a fair way of distributing the gains of cooperation among the players in the coalitional game. Shapley values take into account all possible coalitional dynamics and negotiation scenarios among the players. The nodes in social network can be considered to be strategically behaving self-interested individual entities in an organization functioning according to mechanism design in game theory. Then the probabilities of a node being influenced by its neighbors depend on not only the social network communities' structure but also private information the node has about its neighbors. The target node set problem can be used for machine learning applications in marketing, politics, economics, epidemiology, sociology, computer networking, and databases.

In future work, we shall explore dependence between randomization in our adversarial manipulations and optimization in our game formulation. At present, the game theoretical stochastic optima (solving for adversarial data) are determined by the convergence of the adversarial cost function rather than a classification cost function. However, multi-label classification cost functions in a multiplayer strategy space of pure strategies as well as mixed strategies could be another fruitful avenue of research. Assuming a white-box attack scenario on a CNN classifier would mean we could guide the parameter settings in a genetic algorithm and an SA algorithm into application-dependent adversarial data distributions.

An attack scenario with interactions between multiple cooperating adversaries gives rise to coalitional games in the one-leader-multiple-follower style with either single or multiple adversarial objectives. We are also interested in randomization strategies for robust optimization in multiplayer games that can be decomposed into prediction games or Stackelberg games. Here, some of the relevant game theoretical formulations are to be found in literature on evolutionary games, matrix games, robust games, fuzzy games, Markov games, and Bayesian games. The dimensionality of multi-label data in these kinds of games can be tackled by training an adversarial algorithm for dataflow and control-flow parallelization with multiple processing units. Guided search operators in evolutionary learning might lead to attack scenarios with parallelization for stochastic optimization in adversarial step magnitude and direction estimations.

Further, we might also experiment with various classification functions by changing the deep learning architecture or experiment with multi-objective optimization methods by changing the evolutionary operators in the fitness function evaluations of stochastic optimization and constraint-driven games. It is possible that our variational adversaries with Gaussian mixture models could be improved with customized probabilistic models, such as multinomial mixture models and mixture density networks for image data representation. User validation criteria of the generated adversarial data can be represented by deep networks such as the spatial translation network.

We also plan to investigate the more challenging multiplayer game scenarios where adversaries simultaneously attack multiple labels. In this multiplayer adversarial learning problem, we want to simulate manipulations that transform a targeted positive label into any one of many negative labels. The successful attack scenarios in a strategy space of this type would then inform multiplayer games with mixed strategies that have two or more labels as manipulation targets given a single learner. In these scenarios, it is likely that the randomization of strategies and payoffs in the game formulation would affect the weight regularizations and the decision boundaries of the learner.

We can also apply game theory and control theory to optimize the numerical modeling in adversarial deep learning frameworks of iterative attack scenarios and defense optimizations for dynamics detection, characterization, and prediction in feature selection. Class labels and knowledge representations have to be generated for the unknown objects classified as multimodal, multi-view, and multitask predictions. They would lead us onto combining statistical inference in the training procedures of deep neural networks with cost-sensitive classifier design and robust optimization in complex dynamics detection. Custom loss functions in deep learning can be designed to check distributional robustness measures in adversarial feature selection.

To apply probabilistic inference in cybersecurity, we shall design custom loss functions for associative classification with maximum likelihood estimation (MLE). Associative classification methods are used for rule discovery, rule ranking, rule pruning, rule prediction, and rule evaluation in frequent pattern mining. In these methods, a statistically significant frequent pattern is one that is considered both informative and non-redundant according to an interestingness measure. Popular interestingness measures seek to control the rate of false discovery of frequent patterns by counting their frequencies. Common frequency definitions include support, confidence, lift, leverage, conviction, and improvement. In previous research, we observed that the risk of false discovery can be assessed by applying a discriminative learning model to discover the frequent patterns. Minimizing such a discrimination error allows us to derive statistically significant frequent patterns to assess information theoretic loss functions defined over the training data records. We had also generalized interestingness measures of frequent patterns defined over input data sample to conditional expectations estimated over data population in the underlying databases. The conditional expectations determine a convex optimization problem in terms of an incidence matrix of indicator functions relating data records with frequent patterns in MLE modeling. We had then proposed update rules and decision rules to solve such convex optimization problems with iterative scaling (IS) algorithms. Then the computational complexity of IS algorithms is determined by the density of the incidence matrix. In this context, we shall integrate frequent pattern mining with adversarial deep learning to discover condensed representations of the most informative frequent patterns according to information theory. We shall also check conditional inference and variational modeling of the frequent patterns where indicator functions are constrained by fuzzy features. We shall survey the computational tools in multivariate statistics studying systems of probability distributions. Then we can design custom loss functions in deep learning with game theoretical objectives. Previously, we have worked on Granger-causal feature learning in multivariate time series prediction produced by deep regression networks for data mining. They learn the empirical risk of a complex system with custom loss functions. The Granger-causal features in our proposal improve the multivariate regression error with deep learning. At the same time, the explainable understanding of input data distributions is improved with descriptive cause-effect relations which are more informative than correlation coefficients and neural network weights for explaining the regression results. Here, game theoretical payoff functions measure player-driven optimizations that improve training and inference in machine learning and uncertain environments. They also explain the impact of uncertain environments with reference to a distribution of outcomes, and, in the sense of decision-theoretic rationality, payoff functions maximize the expected utility for each player in the game.

4.3.5 Parallel Machines in Reduced Games

Cai et al. [96] discuss the game theoretical equilibria in two-player non-zero sum games with multiplayer generalization. Min-max theorem is proven for a multiplayer polymatrix zero-sum game. Nash equilibrium is found by linear programming. The polymatrix game is defined by a graph whose vertices are players with associated strategies and edges are two-player games. A player's payoff is the sum of all payoffs in games adjacent to it. Zero-sum polymatrix games represent a closed system of payoffs. Equilibrium strategies for the game are max-min strategies representing no-regret play for all players. Oliehoek et al. [473] present asymmetric games for the search in co-evolutionary algorithms that does not require the specification of an evaluation function. In asymmetric games, the current player's strategies are conditioned by the actions taken by previous players. Such co-evolutionary algorithms are useful in algorithmic problems such as game theo-retical machine learning, concept learning, sorting networks, density classification using cellular automata, and function approximation and classification. Complex evaluation cases can be constructed with a search process. High-quality strategies are developed in the course of the search. The solution concept in the search process defines which candidate solutions qualify as optimal solutions and which do not. A game theoretical learning algorithm designs the convergence criteria on expected utility determined by the solution concepts optimized against an intelligent adversary. A Nash equilibrium then specifies mixed (randomized) strategies for each player that have no incentive to deviate given the strategies of other players. So a game theoretical solution to machine learning problems is a recommendation on optimal plays for all players. It leads to multi-agent systems with Nash equilibrium as a solution concept. They can also include Pareto co-evolution to accommodate multiple adversaries with separate objectives. Best response strategies are solved by a partially observable Markov decision process, corresponding to finite extensive form asymmetric games called parallel Nash memory. All possible player beliefs and transitions between them can be generated in the Markov decision process. An alternating maximization or coordinate ascent optimization method solves for the best response strategies.

Bianchi et al. [52] survey algorithmic frameworks called metaheuristics to solve complex optimization problems in game theoretical adversarial deep learning with mathematical formulations for uncertain, stochastic, and dynamic information. Ant colony optimization, evolutionary computation, simulated annealing, and tabu search are all metaheuristics applicable to the stochastic combinatorial optimization problems (SCOPs) in generating adversarial manipulations at every iteration of the adversarial games. In problem-solving with SCOPs, information about the problem data is partially unknown such as the information available with a learner about the specific adversary's strategies. Moreover, SCOPs assume a probability distribution about the knowledge of the problem data such as the adversary type's characterization. SCOPs are solved by dynamic programming. Such metaheuristics combine several heuristics that are either local search algorithms starting from a pre-existent solution/move for the learned features or constructive algorithms that do feature/component construction of a solution for discovering the adversarial manipulations in game theoretical adversarial deep learning. In comparison with heuristics, metaheuristics strike a dynamic stochastic balance between effectively exploiting the search space representing accumulated experience and efficiently exploring new regions of the search space with high-quality solutions. Convergence proofs for metaheuristics are useful to derive analytics insight into the working principles of a computational algorithm. However, they assume infinite computation time, memory space, and sample size to be useful in the implementation of an efficient metaheuristic in practice. Stochastic integer programming, stochastic dynamic programming, simulation optimization, stochastic partitioning methods, progressive hedging, and variable neighborhood search are the research areas in SCOPs. They can be used to extend our research in game theoretical adversarial deep learning to complex real-world simulations that bridge the gap between theory and practice.

Martin [412] introduces a metaheuristic to combine stochastic simulated annealing methods with deterministic local search methods to result in new Markov chains for global optimization. The new metaheuristic is tested on combinatorial optimization (CO) problems such as the traveling salesman and graph partitioning problems having to deal with large data sizes. The iteration of the Markov chain is called chained local optimization that acts as a generalization of the update rules in simulated annealing. It is executed in parallel on a local network of workstations. A distributed memory architecture and a message-passing system run simultaneous Markov chains to produce a population of candidate solutions by performing independent searches for profitable moves. The branching and pruning of Markov chains is shared between the generated populations to duplicate the best candidates at the expense of worst candidates. The parallel search dynamically adapts to give most searches to the fastest processors. Suman et al. [579] review the simulated annealing algorithms for single- and multi-objective optimization problems to obtain optimal solution and Pareto set of optimal solutions, respectively. Pareto simulated annealing is summarized. It creates a sample population of interacting solutions to generate a good approximation to the efficient solution with the concept of neighborhood probabilistically accepting new solutions. Pareto simulated annealing can be used to create efficient solutions to the adversarial manipulations in game theoretical adversarial deep learning. Simulated annealing can be used in the optimization of multiple and conflicting design objectives in multiplayer adversarial games with multimodal and non-smooth cost functions in the adversarial signal processing. Multi-objective simulated annealing algorithms can accommodate constraint handling in practical problem-solving. Moreover, the applications of simulated annealing to hybrid pattern recognition and object classification are also possible. Rajasekaran et al. [503] discuss the concept of simulated annealing as a family of randomized algorithms. Convergence proofs are provided for applying simulated annealing in optimization problems with special graph theoretical properties on the cost function. A nested annealing algorithm is developed to define a search graph corresponding to the given optimization problem. Application-dependent "separability" criterion of the search graph into subgraphs is analyzed to provide tight bounds on the expected behavior of nested annealing. The converged solutions represent a probability state vector of a Markov chain representing the nested annealing algorithm.

Fogel et al. [199] discuss simulated annealing for stochastic optimization in the simulated evolution methods. Simulated evolution is further categorized into genetic algorithms, evolution strategies, and evolutionary programming and reviewed comprehensively. Their implementation on parallel machines and distributed processing architectures is also discussed. Choices between objective functions, generation probability functions, acceptance probability functions, cooling schedules, and search neighborhoods are given with respect to optimization problems in multiple application domains. Henderson et al. [270] discuss the theory of cybernetic optimization and practice of hill-climbing moves in simulated annealing algorithms. Simulated annealing is compared and contrasted with tabu search and genetic algorithms. Ram et al. [505] develop parallel simulated annealing algorithms for complex non-linear optimization problems. Parallel simulated annealing algorithms are categorized into single trial parallelism and multiple trial parallelism. They are also categorized into serial-like algorithms, altered generated algorithms, and asynchronous algorithms based on tradeoffs between cost function accuracy, state generation, parallelism, and communication overhead. Special-purpose computer architectures can be designed to offset computationally involved tradeoffs in annealing algorithms.

For the filtering and estimation, clustering, and classification of the predicted objects of pattern recognition in the spatio-temporal stochastic processes generating adversarial features, we have to formulate deep representation learning for game theoretical adversarial learning. In this context, we can explore adversarial learning theories with reduced games, submodular functions, wavelet analysis, and adversarial training applications with robust object detection, factorization machines, dictionary learning, and granular computing. Here, dictionary learning produces a dictionary of filter elements to reconstruct a highly redundant representation of the training data with a sparse coding model in the data-driven optimization and inference problems for adversarial deep learning. Here, factorization machines are a low-rank approximation of feature engineering a sparse data tensor when most of its predicted elements are unknown. Here, granular computing is useful to create data fusion rules on the feature representations of the training data. It can lead to neuro-fuzzy systems and multi-agent systems in data mining. We can further investigate the transfer of the statistically significant data fusion rules between predictive data representations on the spatial resolution and spectral resolution data distributions of the training manifolds. Here, dictionary learning is a computational machine learning paradigm that can analyze the multimodal feature generation and multivariate optimization problems in prediction tasks.

A better randomization, convergence, and parallelization in the game theoretical optimization algorithm's step magnitudes would generate better stochastic policies in the game theoretical equilibria. Here, Stackelberg games of the optimum adversarial payoff functions would lead to Nash and Stackelberg equilibria and Pareto optima in the game's randomized strategy space. Our research interest in data mining is in predictive modeling with stochastic games and adversarial deep learning. Our data mining methods are then able to accommodate new challenges on the analytic methodologies imposed by big data models, where it is usually impossible to store an entire high-dimensional data stream or to scan it multiple times due to its tremendous volume and changing dynamics to the underlying data distribution over time. Here, parallel algorithms and distributed computing would also yield a significant reduction in the amortized computational cost of adversarial pattern mining on high-dimensional and multidimensional data. The choice of programming models on parallel machines is between data parallelism, task parallelism, and graph parallelism. The implementation detail for distributed data analytics in adversarial deep learning ought to consider the pattern mining development frameworks for the serial data analytics on big data. They include machine learning assumptions on the data model, memory model, programming model, communication model, execution model, and computing model of converting the serial algorithm to parallel algorithm in adversarial deep learning.

A hybrid deep network architecture can be proposed for semantic composition over the input event sequence in deep learning semiotics. Here, we would need to learn distributed representations of the multi-relational data extracted from knowledge bases. We plan to design unsupervised learning models for motif mining with biclustering and evolutionary clustering, multilevel clustering, and model-driven clustering. To create supervised learning with such motifs, we shall focus on compression methods and optimization methods within kernel learning and deep learning. The relevant theory of data mining is in multilevel clustering, multilevel graph partitioning, quasi-clique detection, and dense subgraph discovery. We may scale such game theoretical adversarial deep learning to big data settings with data sampling methods that can address the data dimensionality and data granularity for multiprocessing and embarrassingly parallel batch processing over tensors and graphs. The related research work is in a study of sampling methods such as undersampling, oversampling, uncertainty sampling, reservoir sampling, structural sampling, etc. The big data solutions would involve data engineering operations for caching, sorting, indexing, hashing, encoding, searching, partitioning, sampling, and retrieval in incremental models, sequence models, and ensemble models for cost-sensitive adversarial learning with probabilistic models.

4.4 Stochastic Games in Predictive Modeling

The interaction between an adversary and the classifier has been modeled as a Stackelberg game. Here, adversary's role is not that of a static data generator but an intelligent agent making deliberate data manipulations to evade classifiers. Failure of considering adversarial evasion in classifier design exposes security concerns in fraud detection, computer intrusion detection, web search, spam detection, and phishing detection applications. Re-learning classifier weights is a weak solution to robust classification since evasion attacks are generated at cheaper and faster rate than re-learning.

Li et al. [354] proposed a feature cross-substitution attack to demonstrate objective-driven adversaries exploiting limitations of feature reduction in adversarial settings. Adversary is able to query the classifier according to a fixed query budget and a fixed cost budget. An adversarial evasion model with a sparse regularizer is then presented. Constructing the classifier on feature equivalence classes rather than feature space is proposed as a solution to improve classifier resilience. Another solution proposes bilevel Stackelberg game of interactions between classifier and a collection of adversaries. Stackelberg game is solved by mixed-integer linear programming with constraint generation.

Bianchi et al. [107] presented repeated games for random prediction problems. The problem of sequential prediction is modeled in the framework of Nash equilibrium found in normal form games. Specific min-max theorems are discussed to analyze two-player zero-sum games. A mistake bounds framework is provided to analyze game theoretical learning algorithms. Bruckner [89] proposes prediction games to model the interaction between a learner who builds the predictive model and the adversary who controls the process of data generation. Prediction games framework allows explicit models on game theoretical players' interests, actions, knowledge, and decisions. Then the generalization error of a predictive model is analyzed in terms of the Nash equilibrium by solving non-cooperative two-player static and dynamic Stackelberg games. Stochastic two-player zero-sum games incorporating multiple adversaries were analyzed by Ummels [615]. Cai et al. [713] analyzed polymatrix games that provide multiplayer generalizations to two-player zero-sum games. The corresponding Nash equilibrium strategies may deviate from max-min optimization and are obtained from linear programming solutions.

Zhou et al. [713] surveyed two-player and multiple-player Stackelberg games in adversarial learning algorithms and cybersecurity applications. The interaction between an adversary and a classifier is modeled as one or more of simultaneous games and sequential games where the adversary can be either a leader or a follower in the game. Alpcan et al. [12] presented large-scale strategic games' and reduced games' computation consumption and information limitation on Nash equilibrium solutions. Oliehoek et al. [474] proposed a deep generative adversary with resource-bounded best responses and Nash equilibrium on synthetic data. The generative adversary has a generator network and a discriminator network in a supervised learning problem and operated on discrete data. Specifically, the generator network's loss function depends only the "fake" data, whereas the discriminator network's loss function depends on both "real" data and "fake" data. Both the generator and discriminator participate in a zero-sum strategic-form game where each player's payoff function is defined on a mixed strategy space.

Papernot et al. [482] provided a threat model summarizing various attack scenarios in adversarial learning algorithms. The threats to machine learning models are adversarial manipulations, which are generated during both training process and inference process. In the training stage, adversaries can manipulate the data collection processes by injecting adversarial examples into the training data with intent of modifying learning model's decision boundaries. In the inference stage, adversaries can plan black-box or white-box attacks on learning model's parameters to cause distribution drifts between training data distribution and runtime data distribution. Papernot et al. [482] also proposed no free lunch theorem and probably approximately correct model for adversarial learning. Yang et al. [679] analyze the Nash equilibrium of a differential dynamical system modeling the advanced persistent threat (APT) cyberattack scenario.

Bowling et al. [82] discuss policy learning in multi-agent environments using stochastic games. The rationality and convergence of the learning agents are formulated to design a policy hill-climbing algorithm. The multi-agent learning problem devises learning algorithms for the agent of interest in the presence of other learning agents outside its control. Such a learning is considered to have a moving target for the optimal policy that has to account for changes in other agents' adaptation, while the learning agent is training. Here, stochastic games are a multi-agent extension of Markov decision processes (MDPs) suitable for single-agent learning such as Q-learning. Such stochastic games have utility in adversarial reinforcement learning. They can be improved with ideas from evolutionary game theory such as adjusted replicator dynamics, and randomized weighting algorithms can be introduced into game theoretical adversarial deep learning to redistribute weights with multiplayer games. Bowling et al. [81] develop the learning behaviors of multi-agent systems adapting to non-stationary environments. The relevant techniques for solving stochastic games to find equilibria are given from references in game theory and reinforcement learning research areas. Similarities and differences between the computational algorithms of these research areas are identified. The assumptions on control and limitations on belief of such computational algorithms can be applied into game theoretical adversarial deep learning. Resultant stochastic games are an extension of the simpler general-sum matrix games solved by quadratic programming in game theory. In game theory, they represent the interaction between a learner and its environment to find the equilibrium value of the game formulations but not the equilibrium policies under either physical or rational limitations. In contrast, reinforcement learning does not assume knowledge of the learning environment. The reinforcement learning agents act based only on observations of transitions between learner states and reward functions on actions. The reinforcement learning agent's goal is to find the optimal policies at the game's equilibrium. Finding solution concepts to stochastic games that have opponent-dependent modeling also requires the investigation of generalization and approximation techniques on complex datasets that have implicit assumptions and limitations for adversarial deep learning.

We propose new non-convex best responses in every play of the prediction game solving for the adversarial manipulations. Our bilevel stochastic optimization problem in the prediction game is formulated as a repeated sequential variable-sum two-player Stackelberg game. The optimization problem is solved by an alternating least squares (ALS) search procedure that continuously attacks retrained classifier with adversarial manipulations optimized until Nash equilibrium. The ALS procedure evaluates candidate adversarial manipulations generated by a simulated annealing (SA) procedure for an increase in adversarial payoff function over the targeted class labels. Therefore, the adversarial data generated in the Stackelberg game simulates continuous interactions rather than one-time interactions with the learning processes of the classifier.

4.4.1 Computational Learning Theory Frameworks to Analyze Game Theoretical Learning Algorithms

Johnson et al. [304] conduct an analysis of behavioral measures of trust and trustworthiness with "trust games" and "investment games" in organizations, economy, and society. Increasing trust increases efficiency by lowering costs. Shared willingness due to trustworthy behaviors leads to better economic outcomes per capita. Aggregated trust is found to lead to efficient judicial systems, higher-quality government bureaucracies, lower corruption, and greater financial development. Other models of behavior incorporate fairness preferences into players' utilities. In them, theories of equity lead to predictions on behavioral differences when the endowments are unequal. The trust games must produce a positive rate of return on trust as welfare gain that facilitates further exchange. Trustees respond to every possible behavior from the counterpart to define fair behavior. The counterpart can be a simulated counterpart in adversarial environments. The process of thinking through behavioral implications of every possible outcome changes the players' perception of the game and leads to data-driven decision-making. When the guarantee of anonymity among players is eliminated, behavior is motivated by factors such as individual's concern for their reputation, reciprocating past kind acts, and a fear of retribution. Probability of benefits in future exchanges between players motivates expected payoff from a counterpart player's behavior in addition to trust in the counterpart. Descriptive statistics for trust and trustworthiness are produced following an ordinary least squares regression specification of the trust game payoffs. Outliers and adversarial distributions in such evaluation data significantly bias the parameter estimates. Adversarial manipulation checks ought to verify the adversarial examples to distinguish between simulated and human counterparts to specify the trust game payoffs. Here, adversarial robustness and interaction effects found from game theoretical adversarial deep learning solutions augment the heuristic decision-making strategies and rules of thumb embodied in a culture as strategies for trusting or mistrusting.

Balduzzi et al. [24] present a common language for describing and analyzing game theoretical algorithmics in deep learning. Backpropagation training of deep neural networks is expressed in terms of distributed optimization in game theory, communication protocols to track zeroth-order, first-order, and second-order derivative information. Function semantics and optimization representations are formalized in grammars for games to specify a formal language for the structure of deep learning algorithms. Probabilistic graphical models and factor graphs are used to capture structural features of multivariate distributions and their design and analysis in algorithms for probabilistic inference. Gradient-based optimization is primarily addressed to derive the computational primitives that can shift architecture design focus from low-level algorithm design in neural networks to high-level mechanism design in learning systems. The black-box computational model to analyze the computational complexity of optimization methods is a more abstract view on optimization than the Turing machine model. It specifies a communication protocol that tracks the frequency patterns about queries made by an algorithm to the adversarial/learning optimization objective. Here, zeroth-order black-box optimization methods respond with information about value of function at the query point, while first-order gray-box optimization methods respond with information about gradient information of function. Game theory formulation for the optimization objectives allow non-convex losses that can be formulated as a game at many different scales in the neural network architectures where particular layers of the neural network are solving a convex optimization problem. Structuring rules for the compositionality of adversarial deep learning objectives can be then formalized with the distributed communication protocols and grammars. The resulting feedforward computation is captured in a computation graph data structure that structures queries and responses into query and response graphs, respectively. The communication protocol specifies how data mining information flows through the query and response graphs without specifying players' utilities of the information. Grammars on the distributed communication protocols guarantee that the response graph encodes sufficient information for the players to jointly converge to a game theoretical solution concept for the learning objective function and associated adversarial payoff functions. A grammar can be specified for the players' interactions and error backpropagation in each game to perform a specific data analytics task. The players then jointly encode data mining knowledge about the task. The grammars can also include probabilistic and Bayesian formulations along with methods for unsupervised pre-training. Practicable examples of the grammars are demonstrated for the learned objectives in supervised deep learning models, variational autoencoders and generative adversarial networks for unsupervised learning, and deviator-actor-critic model for deep reinforcement learning.

Hazan et al. [261] discuss regret minimization in repeated games with non-convex loss functions. Such repeated games can be used to design multiplayer games in adversarial deep learning. The notion of a regret in adversarial deep learning is computationally intractable in general. Thus, a formulation for regret is defined for efficient optimization and convergence to an approximate local optimum. Regret minimization in games corresponds to repeated play in which a player accumulates average loss that is proportional to the best response decision in hindsight. Regret is a global optimization criterion chosen by a player over its entire decision set. If the loss function computing the player's payoff subject to other player's actions is convex, then the regret criteria are computationally intractable, and they converge to game theoretical solution concepts such as Nash equilibrium, correlated equilibrium, and coarse correlated equilibrium. A local regret criterion is defined to predict playing points with small gradients on average. An algorithm incurring the sublinear local regret in time has a small time-averaged gradient in expectation for every randomly selected iterate. A notion of time-smoothing captures non-convex online optimization under limited concept drift. By contrast, non-convex continuous optimization algorithms on the players' loss functions focus on finding a local optimum since finding the global optimum is a NP-hard problem. Stochastic second-order methods are used for such non-convex optimization. They converge onto approximately stationary solution concepts in the adversarial deep learning procedures. The local equilibrium is smoothened with respect to past iterates. The smoothening procedure corresponds to form an experience replay in reinforcement learning. The solution concept captures a state of iterated game play where each player examines the past actions played and no player can make deviations to improve the average performance of current play against the opponents' historical play. The learning algorithm is assumed to have access to a noisy stochastic gradient oracle.

Xu et al. [671] investigate the problem of adversarial learning from noise-injected data without assuming a specific adversary type at the learning stages. Information theoretic limits of adversarial robustness called Le Cam type bounds are derived. This work is comparable to other theoretical work in computational learning theory for adversarial learning such as deriving generalization bounds for adversarial learning at test time, robustness certification for statistical inference in adversarial learning, robustly PAC learnability of VC classes, and analysis of the noise injection in neural network training at inference time. The adversary is assumed to have a budget on how much noise is injected into the data. This budget is related to the total variation (TV) distance between the original data distribution and the noise-injected data distribution. TV is a statistical distance that is used in the study of the upper and lower bounds for adversarial robustness in learning problems such as mean estimation, binary classification, and Procrustes analysis. Noise injection methods are restricted to multivariate Gaussian and multivariate uniform noise. An expected risk is estimated in minimax optimization frameworks to derive Le Cam's bound.

Scutari et al. [545] survey optimization methods in communication systems and signal processing. Equilibrium models in cooperative and non-cooperative game theory are used to describe scenarios with interactive decisions in applications such as communications and networking problems, power control and resource sharing in wireless/wired and peer-to-peer networks, cognitive radio systems, distributed routing, flow, and congestion control in communication networks. Variation inequality (VI) theory is utilized as a general class of problems in non-linear analysis of such applications in wireless ad hoc or per-to-peer wired networks, cognitive radio (CR) networks, and multihop communication networks. Then the existence and uniqueness of the game theoretical equilibrium are investigated to devise the convergence properties of iterative distributed algorithms. Such algorithms can also be designed for game theoretical adversarial deep learning with variational adversaries.

Hinrichs et al. [273] discuss transfer learning between game domains so that structural analogy from one learned game speeds up the learning of another related game. Minimal ascension and metamapping are the proposed techniques to transfer analogy matching representations between games with different relational vocabulary. Minimal ascension finds local match hypotheses by exploiting hierarchical relationships between predicates. Metamapping is a generalization of minimal ascension to use all available structural information about predicates in a knowledge base. The game domains range from physics problem-solving to strategy games. Transfer learning is defined as the problem of finding a good analogy representation between the source and target domains and using that knowledge representation to translate symbolic representations of learned knowledge from the source to the target that have very different surface representations. A cognitive theory called structure mapping is used to describe the analogies following human analogical processing and similarity judgments. The mappings include candidate inferences that represent information projected from source to target domains. Non-identical matches between analogies are considered when they are part of a larger relational structure that can be transferred. So structure mapping depends on symbolic, structured representations of the data that include a vocabulary for representing a hierarchy of predicates, set relations, and constraints on types of arguments to predicates. Higher-order predicates such as logical connectives, argument structure, planning, and discourse relationships are assumed to be the same across source and target domains. Game theoretical solution concepts then support qualitative and analogical reasoning on the mappings with compositional strategies in transfer experiments on a finite state machine. The finite state machine then creates a declarative understanding of the most efficient transfer learners at level of actions and effects, threats and hazards, progress toward learning goals, and dynamic analysis of game traces. A static domain analysis with the games leads to path planning and quantity planning in spatial coordinates, ordinal relations, movement operators, and potential influences on these quantities. A static domain analysis produces compositional strategies when source-target domains are not isomorphs. It empirically constraints the search space for automated learning strategies in graph reachability heuristics. By contrast, a dynamic domain analysis verifies the provenance of transferred strategies to replace failed strategies in a new domain with learning goals. A dynamic domain analysis with the games leads to explicit learning goals for knowledge acquisition on the effects of an action, applicability conditions of an action, and decomposition of a goal into subgoals. The dynamic domain analysis operates at a higher-level search space than the state machine representation to drive more efficient exploration. The dynamic domain analysis regresses through the game execution trace to explain an effect and construct a plan to achieve an effect according to preference heuristics. Learned sequences can accommodate unforeseen effects of actions due to adversarial responses where the behavior of adversaries is incompletely known. Initial experiments can then be performed bottom-up to learn action effects and preconditions of actions. Then they can include action-level learning goals to decompose the performance goal of a game to develop a winning strategy and credit assignment with automated reasoning. The improvements made by transfer are characterized by a normalized regret score. A higher regret score indicates that the transfer was beneficial.

Learnability of non-convex optimization landscapes is a topic for future work in game theoretical adversarial deep learning. We can explore the convergence criteria in generalization errors and sampling complexities of the concept classes in game theoretical adversarial deep learning. We can analyze the optimal size of the training data to predict the future behavior of an unknown target function in adversarial deep learning such that the hypothesis function in game theoretical optimization is probably approximately correct. Here, our research into deep generative models and adversarial autoencoders can be extended into a study of the hypothesis functions in generative adversarial learning. Cybersecurity generalization of the generative adversarial learning includes modeling structures in convolutional, conditional, bidirectional, and semi-supervised deep generative models such as GANs and adversarial autoencoders. Interpreting our classes of stochastic optimization problems as the synaptic weights of fuzzy variables leads us to update rules based on fuzzy learning algorithms that create an associative memory in the concept classes. Here, we shall compare our solutions with machine learning baselines such as the inclusion of noise in the optimization procedure, the simplification of the function landscape by increase of the model size, the schemes for derivative-free stochastic optimization, and data resampling in the context of variational learning algorithms.

4.4.2   Game Theoretical Adversarial Deep Learning Algorithms in Information Warfare Applications

Pawlick et al. [487] survey game theory to model defensive deception for cybersecurity and privacy in ubiquitous and wearable computing. A taxonomy of deception is given as perturbation, moving target defense, obfuscation, mixing, honey-x, and attacker engagement. It categorizes the information structures, agents, actions, and duration of deception for its game theory modeling. Deception research is conducted in military applications, psychology, criminology, cybersecurity, economic markets, privacy advocacy, and behavioral sciences. Such deception is commonplace in adversarial or strategic interactions of cybersecurity where one party has information unknown to the other. Attack vectors with such deception have the potential to turn Internet of Things devices into domestic cyber weapons. Cyberattacks can be devised to physically affect critical infrastructure such as power grids, nuclear centrifuges, and water dams. Adversaries obtain information about their targets through reconnaissance where deception counteracts any information asymmetry. Game theory models the deceptive interactions as strategic confrontations of conflict and cooperation between rational agents. Each player in the game of cybersecurity and privacy makes decisions that affect the welfare of the other players. Game theory is able to model the essential, transferable, and universal aspects of defensive deception in cyberspace. One-shot and multiple-interaction games lead to static and dynamic deception, respectively. Deception techniques include impersonation, delays, fakes, camouflage, false excuses, and social engineering. The stages in a malicious deception include design of a cover story, planning, execution, and monitoring. Stackelberg, Nash, and signaling games are the most common game theoretical models with two-player dynamic interactions. Application domains include adversarial machine learning, intrusion detection systems, communications jamming, and airport security.

   Nguyen et al. [462] investigate strategic deception from adversary who has private information in repeatedly interacting with a defender. The sensitive private information with adversary is representative of real-world security domains characterized by imperfect information due to uncertainty about actions and characteristics of opponents. Here, deceptive behaviors can manipulate the outcome of learning to the long-term benefit of a manipulative adversary. The strategic deployment of adversarial deception can be modeled with finitely repeated security games. The defender has incomplete information and underlying uncertainty about the adversary type. At every iteration of the game theoretical interaction between adversary and defender, the defender updates belief about the adversary type based on historical attack data collected at previous iterations. The defender chooses an action to play based in the updated beliefs. The adversary's goal is to optimize an expected utility leading to a perfect Bayesian Nash equilibrium.

Ferguson-Walter et al. [188] discuss how deception in cyber defense balances asymmetric disadvantages by making the adversary's job harder. Cyber deception adds uncertainty about true information by adding misinformation. Cyber deception impacts the decision-making of the adversaries to waste their time, effort, and resources. Cyber deception used by the defender imparts incorrect beliefs to the adversary at every stage of the cyber kill chain in multi-vector multi-stage attacks. Artificial intelligence, computer security, and behavioral science in adaptive or active cyber defenses proactively and dynamically implement predictive defensive strategies without human intervention. Surprise due to unexpected results is an important element to disrupt or delay the attacker's decision processes and actions giving the defender's more time and opportunity to respond and react. Adaptive techniques then detect attacker's response to the cyber deception, to alter the method of deception accordingly. Along with surprise, causing frustration, confusion, and self-doubt are more ways to affect the attacker in cyber deception that exploit the adversary's cognitive biases to craft cognitive overload. In cyber deception research, decoy systems include honeypots and honey-tokens, replay attacks, packet crafting and altered payloads, tar-pitting, and false documents. They create a decoy environment for the adversary with realistic, lightweight virtual systems that appear to be real systems running real services. They are deployed alongside real systems to increase the chances of an adversary being detected and mitigated quickly. They also provide asymmetric advantage to cyber defenders by reducing the chances of a real asset being attacked by distracted adversaries. They also increase the chances of adversaries to reveal themselves by taking additional actions. Autonomous cyber deception systems provide such cyber deception that is adaptive to each adversary type's strategies and preferences in the cyber defense landscape. A cyber deception strategy requires sensors and actuators making decisions on how and when to adapt. Sensors collect behavioral-based post-exploitation adversarial activity such as scanning activity, login attempts, and stolen passwords and deploy decoys such as honey-tokens. Actuators take automated action on a network or a host. Decoy actuators make configuration changes, change IP addresses, open/close ports, add/remove services, spoof the operating system, and create new decoys. Such adaptive cyber defensive systems must consider the co-evolution of multi-step, multi-stage attack/defense situations where defender moves are simulated many steps in advance of the attacker actions. Here, advanced defender goals include preference elicitation about the attacker goals and topological misinformation about incorrect beliefs in the network topology. They can be incorporated into the task of adversarial classification with reinforcement in game theoretical adversarial deep learning with hypergames where the learning algorithm predicts attack preferences. In game theory, intentional deception and misperception utilities are formalized as hypergames where deception is a component of the strategies in play. Hypergames formulate defender goals, observations, subgames, and individual strategies defined in game contexts consisting of an adversary context and a defender context that present player-specific perspectives of the game. Through observation of the attacker, the defender tries to infer the attacker's beliefs over time and apply them in future decision-making. The attacker's beliefs are used to estimate the state of the adversary types as well as attacker's perceived payoffs with knowledge of the game tree and attacker perceptions. The defender then dynamically manipulates the game board with update rules to change its iterative payoffs associated with next possible actions. The decisions made by the defender in an online learning solution alter the actions taken by the attacker, limit the strategies available to the attacker at the next time step, and manipulate the payoffs received by the attacker. Thus, hypergame concepts can investigate attack trees according to defender goals on deception rather than adversarial goals on manipulation where there are resource allocation costs associated with each play.

Cybenko et al. [139] edit a book about adaptation techniques (AT) such as moving target defenses (MTD) to engineer adversarial machine learning systems with randomization for security and resiliency purposes. Adaptive cyber defense (ACD) is categorized into adaptation techniques (AT) and adversarial reasoning (AR) for adversarial learning in operational learning systems. AR combines machine learning, behavioral science, operations research, control theory, and game theory to compute strategies in dynamic, adversarial environments. ACD techniques force the adversaries to re-assess, re-engineer, and re-launch cyberattacks. A game theoretical and control-theoretic analysis for tradeoff analysis of security requirements in ACD presents the adversaries with optimized and dynamically changing attack surfaces. Prototypes and demonstrations of ACD technologies are presented in several real-world scenarios.

Dasgupta et al. [146] conduct a high-quality survey of game theory-based modeling of adversarial learning. A supervised machine learning algorithm's prediction mechanism is summarized. But the ideas are application to other machine learning mechanisms in clustering, ranking, or regression. A taxonomy for adversarial machine learning is characterized in terms of influence, specificity, and security violation dimensions across adversary types. The influence dimension specifies causative and exploratory attacks on learner vulnerabilities to create modified training data and testing data called adversarial data. Adding adversarial data to the learning process of a classification leads to an incorrect classifier that outputs classification errors. Adversarial learning to create secure classifiers is then modeled as a two-player, non-cooperative game. The utility functions of each player reveal the player's preferences over various outcomes of the game expressed in terms of joint actions of all players in the game. The outcome of a game is the strategy selected by each player. The most popular optimization criterion to calculate the outcomes is Nash equilibrium that assumes the outcomes to be best response strategies of rational players. The Nash equilibrium is solved for as a search and optimization problem. In two-player, zero-sum games, the utilities of all players sum to zero at every iteration of the game. In adversarial learning with zero-sum games, the gain in utility for a learner comes at the cost of loss of adversary's utility and vice versa. This observation leads to a minimax theorem for finding the Nash equilibrium in a zero-sum game. The minimax outcome is represented as a constrained optimization problem solved by a linear program. The minimax theorem does not hold for general-sum non-zero sum games. Because the classifier reacts to adversarial manipulations, the strategy selection in adversarial learning is most frequently modeled as a sequential move game rather than a simultaneous move game. In sequential move games, the follower player has information about the strategies selected by the leader player. Such information is used in the optimization of the player's utility functions. However, the leader has to incorporate uncertainty about the follower's strategies leading to Bayesian games. In the normal form Bayesian game, each player has information about utilities of the other competing players. Based on this information, we can calculate the expected utilities conditioned on player types for each player. Security games in cybersecurity are related to Bayesian games for adversarial learning. In security games, the learner is a defender protecting a set of targets from an adversary called the attacker. The defender has to do resource allocation within budget and operational constraints. In general, the learner's utility is calculated on the payoff/value of a learner for correctly classifying the input. Similarly, the adversary's utility is defined as the payoff/value of misclassification of an adversarial input presented to the learner. The learning problem is then formulated as a constrained optimization problem. It is solved as a mixed-integer linear program for the adversary and a robust classification strategy for the learner. Adversarial approaches that avoid reverse engineering black-box classifier's decision boundaries search over an adversarial cost space to determine a minimum set of adversarial examples. Moving target defense extends the resultant learners to employ randomization over multiple classifiers instead of tuning the parameters of a single robust classifier. Adversary can also generate data by selecting, removing, or corrupting features from the input dataset. The learner's objective is to then find an optimal set of features that minimize its loss function. When the learner does not have access to the entire training data, the learning objective becomes an online learning problem. We can then analyze the runtime and sample complexity of online learners pitted against different adversary types with their own adversarial cost functions and adversarial example generation functions. Here, the learner can know about the adversarial cost functions but not its own ground truth or input distribution. Adversarial training of deep neural networks leads to deep learning games. They can be formulated as a repeated zero-sum game. Iterations on repeated plays are then used to adjust the weights of a neural network's edges to converge onto the Nash equilibrium with exponentiated weight and regret matching optimization algorithms. Adversarial robustness of deep learning classifiers can also be improved by adversarial data generators that are used along with adversarial learning procedures. The most common adversarial data generators use perturbation techniques on valid examples, transfer adversarial examples across different learner models, and extend generative adversarial networks. Here, game theory models can be formulated to be informed by modeling and reasoning costs such as cost to solve for Nash equilibrium, cost to maintain game play history, cost to build opponent models from the history of game theoretical interactions, and expenses incurred by the adversary to access legitimate resources. Transfer learning can be combined with adversarial learning in real-world applications to create learning systems on sparse training data that make classification predictions correctly without requiring information-rich data sources. Domain adaptation can be applied to adversarial learning to reliably transfer the robust learners mapped out in the dense source domain to the sparse target domain. The application for combining transfer learning with adversarial learning includes email spam classifiers, social network sentiment analysis tools, and image and sensor data recognition systems on autonomous vehicles.

Hamilton et al. [249] discuss the application in the tactical analysis of information warfare. Game theory algorithms can be developed in military applications to predict future attacks across many possible scenarios and suggest courses of action (COA) in response to the most dangerous possibilities. COA generation techniques can benefit from adversarial learning. Game theoretical frameworks allow detailed analysis of what-if scenarios of chains of events to find exceptions to general rules in cyber-wargaming systems. Such analysis determines the likelihood, method, and cost of scenarios such as intelligence-gathering in attack phase, targeting of the command and control system, data corruption, and denial-of-service attack to prevent the kinetic warfare planning process. Pruning techniques are required to reduce the search space in evaluating complex max-max games so that the most promising node in the game tree is expanded to queue its children for the analysis of the most promising move that is most likely to be predicted in a given real-world scenario. Reinforcement learning techniques can be used to iteratively increase the depth of the game tree and set the corresponding evaluation characteristics to learn which depth best predicts the opponent behavior. Here, the assumption in the design of the defender's evaluation function is that the opponent's evaluation function uses a subset of the heuristics of the defender's evaluation function with changes in optimality weights.

Schlenker et al. [541] introduce a cyber deception game in network security. It is solved with mixed-integer linear program solution and a fast greedy minimax search algorithm. This game theoretical adversarial learning framework for service obfuscation can be used dynamically to create asymmetric information about the true state of a network in addition to static measures of network security such as whitelisting applications, locking permissions, and patching vulnerabilities. Related work is in honeypot selection games, adversary signaling games, and annotated probabilistic logic models on attacker's scan queries. The cyber deception game is a zero-sum Stackelberg game between a network administrator defender and a hacker adversary. Nguyen et al. [463] allocate limited security countermeasures to protect network data from cyberattack scenarios modeled as Bayesian attack graphs.

Multi-stage interactions between a network administrator and cybercriminals are formulated as a security game. Parameterized heuristic strategies are enumerated to exploit the topological structure of attack graphs. Sampling methods are used to overcome the difficulties with computational complexity in predicting opponent actions. In computer security, attack graphs are graphical models that decompose an ontology of complex security scenarios into a taxonomy of simple and quantifiable actions. Attack graphs on the adversary's actions are suitable for designing a moving target defense (MTD) for the defender where proactive tactics are employed to dynamically change the system configurations. Bayesian attack graph formalism models adversarial deep learning problems as simultaneous multi-stage attack graph security game. The vertices in the attack graph represent security conditions of a network system. Edges represent relationships among security conditions. Attack graphs represent the network vulnerabilities in complex security scenarios. The defender protects a set of goal nodes in the attack graph with deployed security countermeasures. Meanwhile, attacker progress selects vertices in attack graph. Security problems are analyzed as equilibrium solutions to dynamic games and stochastic games on the attack graphs with complete/incomplete/imperfect information that is partially observable. Parameterized heuristics estimate the attack value for each vertex based on attack values of neighboring vertices, where attack values correspond to the importance of each vertex in the security game. Attack paths for the attacker are selected by sampling methods. At each time step, the defense strategies are updated by particle filtering to reflect the defender's belief about the outcome of the players' actions in previous time steps. A new defense action is generated from solution concepts of security games based on updated belief and the defender's assumption about the attacker's strategy. The adversarial robustness of the defense strategies depends on uncertainty regarding game states and attacker's strategies. Such complex security games encapsulate a dynamic security environment with uncertainty as a stochastic process over multiple time steps.

Kulkarni et al. [335] discuss planning problems in AI systems. The obfuscation plans are executed in adversarial situations to protect privacy. The adversarial settings include mission planning, military intelligence, reconnaissance, etc. The legible plans are executed in cooperative situations to aid understanding. Obfuscated plans are consistent with at least k goals from a set of decoy goals at the end of the observation sequence. Legible plans are consistent with at most j goals from a set of confounding goals at the end of the observation sequence. Plans are computed from the point of view of a partially informed observer who operates in a belief space. For every action taken by the learning agent and an associated state transition, the observer receives an observation. Related work is in privacy preservation in distributed multi-agent systems, motion planning, and robotics. Goal obfuscation is related to plan recognition literature for noisy action-state observations. "Explainable planning" model's the observing or interacting human's understanding of a planning agent for human-aware multi-model planning.

Zhang et al. [697] survey the intersection of differential privacy and game theory to construct adversarial manipulations in machine learning with mechanism design.

Such adversarial manipulations consider the cost-benefit tradeoffs between privacy violations and security breaches in devising adversarial robustness. Differential privacy limits the expected gain that can be derived for strategic manipulations of the adversarial payoff functions in a security game. Privacy-aware agents in a security game have privacy preferences explicitly formulated in their privacy-aware payoff functions. So they can make tradeoffs between privacy and utility. Mechanism design problems with differential privacy for privacy-aware agents can be combined with the optimization problems in game theory. They include strategy selection, information implication, truthfulness incentivization, privacy cost estimation, private data trading, and game learning. Ye et al. [681] propose a differentially private game theoretical approach to cyber deception. The defender uses differential privacy mechanisms to obfuscate the configurations of systems. The attacker uses Bayesian inference to infer the real configurations of systems. An imperfect information game is used as the cyber deception game with the goal of hiding information about system configurations rather than stopping a cyberattack or identifying the attacker. It can be extended to dynamic security games with multiple defenders and multiple attackers.

Rass et al. [506] investigate matrix games as a risk mitigation tool for advanced persistent threat (APT) defense. APT combines multiple attack vectors such as social engineering or malware from topological vulnerability analysis to result in uncertainty of qualitative expert risk assessments, unknown adversarial incentives, and current system state. Game theoretical adversarial learning optimizes the simultaneous defenses against a stealthy invader using a set of known paths in APT attack. The attack paths are a sequence of vulnerabilities. Graph entropy measures on missed attack paths can measure the uncertainty of network complexity and residual risks from exploits of vulnerabilities that are not yet known to result in attack paths called zero-day exploits. Zero-day exploits are dealt with by a combination of domain knowledge, expert opinion, experience, and information mining, combined with suitable mathematical models of risk acceptance thresholds and loss function distributions in adversarial machine learning. Cyber threat intelligence and domain expertise are fundamental concepts upon which the loss function distributions are measured empirically by human reasoning and experience. Such human reasoning is fuzzy rather than crisp leading to multimodal data distributions. Numerical performance measures for machine learning are insufficient to deal with APT attacks since a lot of reliable statistical data on cybersecurity incidents is not available in real-world applications. Countermeasures against APTs may be identified but not always possible, feasible, or successful. So the defense mechanisms have to assume a worst-case behavior of the attacker that may not fit into a Bayesian or sequential game formulation. The APT mitigation game is discrete time for the defender and continuous time for the attacker. The adversarial data is qualitative fuzzy expert knowledge formulated from a taxonomy or a simulation or both. There is a strong asymmetry between the information known to the attacker and defender. Such an APT mitigation game is modeled as a game of complete information but uncertain payoffs. The uncertain payoffs are probability distributions rather than real numbers. APT mitigation game modeling can be extended to multi-criteria games with optimal tradeoffs between multiple goals that include security requirements such as confidentiality vs. integrity vs. availability, adversarial cost functions in the attack graph about the level of skills required to mount an attack, and ordered set of fixed loss categories that apply to all adversarial and learning goals of interest. Here, the game structure is assumed to follow a stochastic process so that the loss distributions constituting the game structure are stationary distributions of the stochastic process under the chosen convergence criteria.

Huang et al. [286] propose a dynamic game framework for long-term interactions between a stealthy attacker and a proactive defender formulated as a multi-stage game of incomplete information where each player has private information unknown to the other. The players act strategically according to beliefs formed by multi-stage observation and learning. A perfect Bayesian Nash equilibrium is the solution concept computed by an iterative optimization algorithm. The stealthy attacker is an APT attacker who has knowledge of the defenders system architecture, valuable assets, and defense strategies. So APT attacker strategies are tailor-made to invalidate cryptography, firewalls, and intrusion detection systems. APT attackers can disguise as legitimate users in the long term. Multi-stage APT models dividing the attack sequences are classified into attack sequences, or phases are available in the open-source intelligence communities. They include Lockheed-Martin's cyber kill chain, MITRE's ATT&CK, and NSA/CSS technical cyber threat framework. During a reconnaissance phase, the attacker (also called threat actor) collects open-source or internal intelligence to identify valuable targets. Then the attacker escalates privilege to propagate laterally in the cyber network to access confidential information or inflict physical damage. A system defender must incorporate defensive countermeasures across all the phases of APTs with a defense-in-depth strategy. On identifying the utility and strategies of the attackers, game theory provides a quantitative and explainable framework to the system defender to design proactive defense response under uncertainty with better tradeoffs between security and usability. By contrast, rule-based and machine learning-based defense methods cannot deal with uncertainty in the multi-stage impact of defense strategies on both legitimate and adversarial users. Such multi-stage impact is seen in artificial intelligence, economy, and social science where multi-stage interactions occur between multiple agents with incomplete information.

Bohrer et al. [75] apply constructive differential game logic to derive structured proofs in cyber-physical systems (CPS) for safety-critical applications such as robotics, automotives, aviation, spaceflight, medical devices, and power systems. Such formal methods of verification ensure the correctness of learning properties of system models in the implementations of CPS on embedded processors such as in autonomous driving and ground robotics. Here, game theory is used in the analysis of differential equations without closed-form solutions. Game proofs in an adversarial environment then create security warranties for a learning system against different adversary types who violate the system's correctness criteria with manipulation of timing, sensing, control, and physics in hybrid games. Wellman et al. [643] explore causal dependence structure in private information signal patterns on underlying agent states that can act as the epistemic types of adversarial agents. A

Bayesian game is then formulated with the private information. Probabilistic graphical models (PGMs) are used to model the private information. Their dependence structure is able to quantify adversarial agents who reason about their own payoff function values conditioned on the information available on other agents' payoff function values. Bayesian networks are the PGMs used to not only interpret but also generate signal patterns on the private information of players. Thus, PGMs provide a qualitative framework for analyzing the probabilistic dependencies between structural decisions and private signal's game theoretical learning situations. Their graphical structures allow reasoning about the implications of a game situation. Applications are evaluated for prediction markets and auctions that augment the graphical structures with patterns of reasoning available in these domains to suggest generalization of the results in the applicable adversarial deep learning. Jordan et al. [305] conduct an empirical analysis of complex games. The value of empiricism in games lies in the effective exploration of a set of strategies. So generic exploration policies are proposed for strategy exploration in empirical games. They find a best response with minimum regret profile among previously explored strategies. Stochastic best response strategies lead to an effective exploration of the strategy space. So empirical game theoretical analysis (EGTA) can augment expert modeling with empirical sources of knowledge such as high-fidelity data obtained from real-world observations. EGTA games are procedural descriptions of strategic environments. The simulation and search statistics in EGTA can combine with game theoretical solution concepts to characterize the strategic properties of an application domain for adversarial deep learning. An augmented restricted game is defined as a base game to encapsulate EGTA. Additional strategies are generated with reinforcement learning.

Prakash et al. [497] examine the interplay between attack and defense strategies in moving target defense (MTD). Multiple game instances are explored by differences in agent objectives, attack cost, and attack action detectors. Such MTD techniques incorporate probabilistic attack progressions to develop effective policies for deploying and operating machine learning systems in specific adversarial contexts. The behaviors of rational players vary with game theoretical learning features such as system configurations, environmental conditions, agent objectives, and technology characteristics. The systematic simulations in game theoretical learning frameworks can accommodate computational complexities and information uncertainties in learning dynamics of game formulations that are analytically intractable. The adversarial payoff functions in MTD allow tradeoffs between objectives of control and availability. They can incorporate assessments of overall system state as adversarial cost functions. In addition to learning objectives of the adversary and defender, security requirements of the learning system are interpreted as preference patterns of the agents in the MTD game. For example, confidentiality of the learning system is interpreted as defender's strong aversion to allow the attacker to control machine learning servers. Availability is interpreted as the defender's control on a fraction of servers that are not down. A weighting scheme then incorporates tradeoffs between confidentiality and availability in the game formulation. Parameterized families of heuristic strategies are defined by structures and patterns of behavior over time so that they specify the policies of action executing the player's choices among strategies. A restricted game on a selected set of strategies then systematically refines strategy exploration through an iterative process of empirical game analysis. Strategy profiles and validation criteria then emerge according to a game theoretical reasoning process in complex adversarial environments. They can be extended toward sophistication in attacker and defender policies with intent inference, explicit reasoning about threats and counter-threats, and utility models for stochastic downtimes. Roeder et al. [520] propose a method to reduce the shared vulnerabilities between servers called proactive obfuscation. Semantics-preserving code transformations are used to generate diverse executables that bound the number of compromised servers by restarting them periodically. Proactive obfuscation thus makes an adversary's job harder by randomly restarting servers to a fresh state. It is demonstrated in a distributed firewall and a distributed storage based on state machine replication. Costs implicit in proactive obfuscation are evaluated by measuring the system performance. The proposed proactive obfuscation technique can be easily integrated into replica management protocols suitable for adversarial environments. It can incorporate all of address reordering, stack padding, system call reordering, instruction set randomization, heap randomization, and data randomization as defenses against adversarial examples in commercial operating systems. Replica failures are categorized into crashed and compromised replicas. Compromised replicas fall under the control of an adversary. This is called Byzantine failure in the fault-tolerant operating systems literature. The failure model has a compromise threshold that bounds the number of compromised replicas. However, an adversary with access to an obfuscated executable can breach the compromise threshold by generating a customized attack to eventually compromise all replicas. To avoid such an adversarial attack, proactive obfuscation reboots replicas across epochs whose configuration changes over time according to a MTD. Data confidentiality is enforced by storing encrypted data on a server with a different per-server key. Then cryptography techniques can be developed to perform computations on such encrypted data. However, proactive obfuscation cannot defend against all denial-of-service (DoS) attacks that can saturate resources like networks that are not under the control of replicas. To guarantee that the replica refresh happens in a bounded amount of time, some of the operating architectural components are made synchronous by satisfying strong synchronicity properties such as bounded-rate clocks, synchronous processors, timely links, reboot channels, etc. The proactive obfuscation mechanisms are described in a real distributed system to give rise to bounded adversaries evaluating the obfuscation technology.

4.4.3   Game Theoretical Adversarial Deep Learning Algorithms in Cybersecurity Applications

Now, we turn attention to cybersecurity applications of game theoretical adversarial deep learning.

Liang et al. [369] review the game theoretical frameworks for handling network attacks with intrusion detection systems (IDSs) and intrusion prevention systems (IPSs). The application scenarios are categorized as attack-defense analysis and security measurement. The game models are summarized as cooperative games and non-cooperative games. Here, IDSs analyze a cyberattack with methods such as attack signature identification, pattern detection, and statistical analysis. The network administrator acts as the defender in adversarial deep learning. Security measurement reports are created on network security measurements such as evaluation of the confidentiality, integrity, availability, vulnerability, and security risks in the network. Game theory is used in attack-defense analysis of the risk assessment and data-driven decision-making in networking applications with signal game models for predicting actions of the attackers and determining the decisions of the defenders. Based on the number of stages, the game models are classified as static/strategic game that is a one-shot game with imperfect information, dynamic/extensive game with multiple stages and moves that are finite or infinite, and stochastic game according to a transition probability matrix between states where players take actions and receive payoffs. The basic elements of the game theoretical equilibrium to be defined by the adversarial algorithm designer are players, actions, payoff, and strategies. Manshaei et al. [409] organize computer network security into the security of physical and MAC layers, self-organizing networks, intrusion detection systems, anonymity and privacy, economics of network security, and cryptography. The game theoretical equilibrium analysis and security mechanism designs are presented for each security category of the emerging problems in computer networking. The network agents are enumerated as individuals, devices or software, and decision-makers that can act in a cooperative, selfish, or malicious manner. Security decisions based on game theory approaches arrive at security and privacy solutions for limited resource allocation, perceived risk balancing, and underlying incentive mechanism design. Depending on the information about adversary types available to the decision-makers, security games support the formal decision-making, algorithm development, and adversarial machine learning of predicting attacker behavior and interactions between attackers and defenders in terms of action spaces and goals of the decision-makers. The security game formulations can vary between simple deterministic games, complex stochastic games, and limited information games in application focus areas such as jamming and eavesdropping in wireless networks, collaborative intrusion detection systems, cooperative location privacy, tor path selection, cryptography in multi-party computation, revocation in mobile ad hoc networking, and vehicular network security. The security games are then formulated in terms of finite repeated prisoner-dilemma game, Stackelberg leader-follower game, fuzzy game, repeated zero-sum games, stochastic general-sum game, stochastic non-zero sum dynamic game, two-player Stackelberg stochastic game, Bayesian game, coalitional game, variable cost game, incomplete information game, fictitious game, cheap talk game, etc. The equilibrium analysis of the games then provides analytics insight into decisions on issues such as security investment and patch management in complex networking systems. Roy et al. [530] present a cyberspace taxonomy for classifying the game types used in the defense mechanisms of next-generation network security and secure computing. Static games are analyzed with respect to complete imperfect information and incomplete imperfect information. Dynamic games are analyzed with respect to complete perfect information, complete imperfect information, incomplete perfect information, and incomplete imperfect information.

Otrok et al. [477] propose a game theoretical learning model for host-based intrusion detection systems (HIDS) to offset high computation cost in the generation and detection of false alarms for resource-limited systems such as wireless mobile devices. Dynamic, non-cooperative, multi-stage, incomplete information games are formulated for a mobile ad hoc network (MANET) according to a Bayesian probabilistic model and a Dempster-Shafer probabilistic model for the mathematical representation of uncertainty and risk management where the identity of the attacker is unknown. The game solution concepts determine the posterior belief function values of a user to determine misbehavior by decreasing false positives, increasing attacker detection accuracy, and optimizing resource consumption efficiency in HIDS. Perfect Bayesian equilibrium computes a set of strategies that are optimal with respect to the estimated beliefs taken to be probabilities. Once the belief measurement reaches a predefined risk threshold, the HIDS gets to decide whether a user is an attacker or not. The belief measurement is obtained from evidence observed from a data source. A belief fusion algorithm combines belief measurements to generate a final belief of the problem domain. At the cost of extra computational resources, such a final belief measurement is more precise than Bayesian posterior likelihoods. The HIDS game elements are players and type space, strategy space, prior beliefs, utility functions, and HIDS detection rate.

Nguyen et al. [461] discuss a zero-sum Stackelberg security game optimizing a double oracle method on exponentially large action spaces to allocate botnet detection resources in a game theoretical solution for the defense policies. Two botnet data exfiltration scenarios are proposed to represent single and multiple path attack vectors for stealing sensitive network data. Mixed-integer linear programs optimize the defender's and attacker's best response oracles. Greedy heuristics approximate and implement the oracles. L'Huillier et al. [353] utilize dynamic games of incomplete information in phishing fraud detection such as email scams to get private information. A weighted margin support vector machine acts as the adversarial classifier for content-based filtering of phishing. Phishing filtering over data streams of messages is based on online algorithms, generative learning algorithms, and discriminative learning algorithms based in game theoretical adversarial deep learning. Here, phishing can be categorized into deceptive phishing and malware phishing. Deceptive phishing in turn is categorized into social engineering, mimicry, email spoofing, URL hiding, invisible content, and image content. A perfect Bayesian equilibrium is proposed as the solution concept to the adversarial classification signaling game. The players behave according to a notion of sequential rationality where information sets in an extensive-form game determine Bayesian beliefs about the equilibrium strategies defined in terms of joint optimal strategies for each agent as well as beliefs for each agent at each information set at which the agent has to make a move. Then signaling security requirements are imposed on the classifier design that accounts for optimal defense strategies defined by a probability distribution over the classifier's actions in the game. The adversary's actions then maximize a utility function according to the signaling requirements. The adversary's beliefs follow a Bayesian rule. A quadratic program-solver implements an online algorithm for sequential minimal optimization in the weighted margin support vector machine. The phishing corpus is analyzed for structural properties about the body parts of the message, link analysis around IP addresses in the message, programming elements such as HTML, JavaScript forms used in the message, and recommended spam thresholds. Word list frequencies and clustering features representing a phishing strategy are used as the inputs to the adversarial classifier.

Nagurney et al. [447] develop a supply chain network game theory model between retailers and demand markets to maximize expected profits. Optimal product transactions and cybersecurity investment cost functions are recommended with respect to non-linear budget constraints. The consumer preferences are given by demand price functions that show product demands and cybersecurity levels in the supply chain networks. The vulnerabilities of the supply chain network as well as competing retailers are formulated as a variational inequality problem. Nash equilibrium finds optimal expressions for product transactions, security levels, and budget constraints. A sensitivity analysis with adversarial examples quantifies changes in budget, changes in demand price functions, financial damages on product transactions, and reputation costs on cybersecurity investments. Wang et al. [634] present an agent-based spoofing model for price manipulation in financial markets. Here, human traders work through a limit order book that has private information and noisy observations about complex market environment for financial instruments. Game theoretical agents then follow two distinct trading strategies. A non-spoofable zero intelligence (ZO) strategy ignores the order book. It acts as the modeling baseline. A manipulable heuristic belief learning (HBL) exploits the order book to predict price outcomes. HBL is applied to a complex market environment in the full cycle of an order with persistent orders, combined private and fundamental values, noisy observations, stochastic arrivals, and ability to trade multiple units with buy or sell flexibility. A game theoretical analysis on the simulated agent's payoffs is computed across parametrically different environments for market models to measure the effect of spoofing on market performance according to solution concepts found in strategic equilibria. Simple spoofing strategies on trading behavior and market efficiency are shown to mislead traders, distort prices, and reduce total surplus. HBL traders can also benefit from price discovery and social welfare in the game theoretical machine learning. A market mechanism design is proposed to disincentivize manipulation. Then trading strategy variations are proposed to improve the robustness of learning from market information. Thus, adversarial deep learning has the potential to transform financial market landscape (such as foreign exchange and commodity markets) from a human decision ecosystem to an algorithmic trading technology with game theoretical agent-based market models. Automated trading platforms can not only improve market efficiency but also increase market risk and market fluctuations due to manipulative practices around vulnerabilities driven by algorithms. Spoofing is defined as the submission of a large number of spurious buy/sell orders with intent to cancel them before execution, thus corrupting the limit order book's signal on supply and demand. Spoof orders are typically placed outside the current best quotes to mislead investors before any market movement can trigger a trade. Experimental evaluation is around a continuous double auction market model with a single security traded. The market mechanism is designed to have key elements of market microstructure conditions such as fundamental shocks and observation noise. Spoofing the limit order book is interpreted as decision-time attacks on machine learning models to generate adversarial examples with domain constraints on the order streams. Market equilibrium behavior is then specified by game theoretical adversarial deep learning aspects around the market context for balancing the robustness and efficacy of machine learning from order information with cloaking mechanisms. Related work is on adversarial linear regression with multiple learners by Tong et al. [602].

Nisioti et al. [465] present a data-driven decision support framework called DISCLOSE for optimizing forensic investigations of cybersecurity breaches. DISCLOSE maintains a threat intelligence information repository of tactics, techniques, and procedures (TTPs) specifications. Adversarial TTPs are obtained for complex attacks with multiple attack paths from interviewing cybersecurity professionals, MITRE ATT&CK STIX repository, and Common Vulnerability Scoring System (CVSS). Here, game theoretical adversarial deep learning acts as a reasoning hypothesis increases the efficiency of the forensic investigation by decreasing the time and resources for robust reasoning process about the logical links between the uncovered evidence in an objective manner. The game theoretical strategic reasoning can be contrasted with reasoning frameworks in machine learning such as case-based reasoning, ruled-based reasoning, data-driven reasoning, etc. Here, rule-based reasoning is framed from a combination of predefined rules, models, and previous data. Probabilistic relation between available attack actions, findings of a forensic investigation, benefit and cost of each inspection, and budget available to the investigator are considered in the DISCLOSE decision support framework. Liu et al. [383] conduct a systematic survey of security threats in machine learning from the learning theoretic aspects of training/reasoning and testing/inferring phase. Particular emphasis is on the data distributional drifts caused by adversarial samples and subsequent sensitive information violations in statistical machine learning algorithms. The adversarial capability to create adversarial manipulations according to adversarial objectives is qualified by the impact of causative or exploratory security threats, percentage of the training and testing data controlled by the adversary, and extent of features and parameters known to the adversary. Attack types are then categorized as causative attacks, exploratory attacks, integrity attacks, availability attacks, privacy violation attacks, targeted attacks, and indiscriminate attacks.

Current defensive techniques for machine learning are categorized into security assessment mechanisms, countermeasures in the training phase, countermeasures in the testing or inferring phase, data security, and data privacy. They are essential in the design of intelligent systems that learn from massive data with high efficiency, minimum computational cost, and reasonable predictive or classification accuracy.

Xue et al. [674] conduct a survey of security issues in machine learning systems to summarize countermeasure defenses, secure learning techniques, and security evaluation methods. The machine learning security threats and attack models are categorized into training set poisoning, backdoors in the training set, adversarial example attacks, model theft, and recovery of sensitive training data. Adversarial examples are defined to be an intrinsic property of the deep learning models. Model overfitting is then found to have an important influence on recovering sensitive training data by an adversary who can carry out membership inference attacks and model inversion attacks. The threat models, attack approaches, and defense techniques for machine learning systems are systematically analyzed to produce cyber threat intelligence across multiple stages of the cyber kill chain. Adversarial example attacks are found for email spam filtering, Android malware detection, biometric authentication systems, face recognition systems, road sign recognition, cellphone camera recognition, voice control systems, and 3D object attacks. They are contrasted with backdoor attacks and Trojan attacks to create malicious data for the target models. Future research directions are given as attacks under real physical conditions, privacy-preserving machine learning techniques, watermarking-based intellectual property (IP) protection of deep neural networks, remote or lightweight machine learning security techniques, and systematic machine learning security evaluation methods to produce underlying reasons for the attacks and defenses on machine learning. Deep learning attacks can be crafted with deep generative models such as GANs to break a distributed or federated learning framework. Game theoretical adversarial deep learning is categorized as a defense technique to simulate attacks, create robustness strategies, and detect abnormal features in classifier design. It is contrasted with other defense techniques such as data sanitization, input anomaly detection, input pruning and model fine-tuning, adversarial retraining, defensive distillation, gradient masking, and input randomization. It can also be combined with defensive techniques for protecting sensitive data such as cryptography, steganography, distributed machine learning frameworks, trusted platforms, and processors. Security evaluation of machine learning algorithms can also benefit from the training, testing, and validation datasets generated by the game theoretical adversarial deep learning within a design-for-security rather than the design-for-performance paradigm for machine learning. Security evaluation curves can also be created around the performance measures for machine learning and cost functions for adversarial deep learning to characterize the learning system performance, robustness, security, and privacy evaluation metrics calculated in the presence of various adversary types having different attack strengths and knowledge levels.

4.5 Robust Game Theory in Adversarial Learning Games

In a Stackelberg game, adversarial strategies are modeled and solved for the solution rationale and decision-making problem defining the Nash equilibria. The solution space for Nash equilibria is expressed in terms of the necessary and sufficient conditions for game players' convergence criteria [557]. Typical convergence criteria are (i) zero-sum game vs non-zero sum game; (ii) two-player vs multiplayer game; (iii) static game vs evolutionary game; (iv) sequential game vs continuous game; and (v) deterministic game vs stochastic game. Typical players' strategies consider cases where a pair of players (i) do not know each other's performance criteria; (ii) compute each other's strategies at different speeds; (iii) have linear and non-linear payoff functions that may or may not be discontinuous; and (iv) participate in a game with distributed control vs decentralized control. In such games, the Stackelberg strategies and Nash equilibria are analyzed in terms of the structural properties of the coefficient matrices of higher-order matrix-Riccati differential equations.

The optimization of such game theoretical payoff functions presents a complex problem in optimization theory. Such problems are often modeled as decision problems in non-cooperative differential games [86]. The solutions to these problems are presented as Pareto optima, Nash and Stackelberg equilibria, and co-co (cooperative-competitive) solutions for the payoff function.

The Riccati differential equations are also analyzed as differential games in optimal control theory. If the game theoretical players can observe state of the control system, then the Nash equilibrium is computed according to an open-loop solution for the control system. If the game theoretical players cannot consider feedback strategies, then the Nash equilibrium is computed according to a closed-loop solution for the control system. Principles of dynamic programming are used as the computational methods finding the game theoretical optima to the necessary and sufficient conditions for optimal control system.

Furthermore, partial differential state equations of the control system can augment the player's payoff functions to result in stochastic control [9] in game theoretical interactions. Here, the game theoretical equilibria are determined by the necessary and sufficient conditions on the coefficients solving for the Stackelberg Riccati differential, difference, and algebraic equations [206]. The study of such equilibria and their numerical computational methods is the subject of evolutionary and differential game theory [34].

Zhou et al. [710] model multiple types of adversaries in a nested Stackelberg game framework. A single-leader learner has to deal with multiple-follower adversaries. The solution to the game is an optimal mixed strategy for the leader to play in the game. The solution of a two-player Stackelberg equilibrium solution is used as the strategy in a multiplayer Bayesian Stackelberg game. The Stackelberg game is solved as a mixed-integer quadratic programming (MIQP) problem.

Ratliff et al. [507] characterize Nash equilibria in continuous games over non-convex strategy spaces. Sufficient conditions are given for differential Nash equilibria. They require the evaluation of player costs and their derivatives. A dynamical systems viewpoint is taken to analyze the convergence of best response strategies to a stable equilibrium. The results in non-linear programming and optimal control provide first- and second-order necessary and sufficient conditions for local optima assessed as critical points of real-valued functions on training data manifolds. Such continuous games arise in building energy management, pricing of network security, travel-time optimization in transportation networks, and integration of renewables into energy systems. Coupled oscillator models are chosen for illustrating the system properties of continuous games. They have application in power networks, traffic networks, robotics, biological networks, and coordinated motion control. Dianetti et al. [158] investigate the existence of Nash equilibria in monotone-follower stochastic differential games where each player has submodular costs. The monotone-follower problem tracks a stochastic control process to optimize a performance criterion. It has applications in economics and finance, operations research, queuing theory, mathematical biology, aerospace engineering, and insurance mathematics. It can allow explicit feedback strategies to compute equilibria in open-loop and closed-loop strategies in irreversible investment games.

Schuurmans et al. [544] introduce deep learning games. The optimization of supervised deep learning models is expressed as the Nash equilibrium in a game. A bijection is established between the Nash equilibria of a simultaneous move game and KKT points of a directed acyclic neural network in deep learning. Then a step-free regret matching algorithm is proposed for stochastic training to produce sparse supervised learning models in deep learning. Thus, supervised learning is reduced to game playing. A one-shot simultaneous move game is defined for a one-layer learning problem. Regret minimization can also decompose multiplayer games into multiple two-player games. Lippi [373] uses statistical relational learning (SRL) frameworks in the description and the analysis of games. SRL combines first-order logic with probabilistic graphical models to handle uncertainty in data and its representation dependencies. SRL can be used in games such as partial information games, graphical games, and stochastic games. Inference algorithms in SRL such as belief propagation or Markov chain Monte Carlo can be used for opponent modeling, finding Nash equilibria, and discovering Pareto-optimal solutions. SRL produces probabilistic logic clauses to describe the strategies in a game as a high-level, human-interpretable formalism. Games are described as domains of interests, strategies, alliances, rules, relationships, and dependencies among players. Techniques from inductive logic programming can then extract rules from a knowledge base of logic predicates that aid probabilistic reasoning in data-driven decision-making. SRL can also be combined with game theory to learn model structures from data. Some of the SRL methodologies suitable for strategic reasoning in game theory are Causal Probabilistic Time Logic (CPT-L), Logical Markov Decision Programs (LOMDPs), DTProbLog, Infinite Hidden Relational Trust Model (IHRTM), Infinite Relational Models toward trust learning, Relational Reinforcement Learning, Probabilistic Soft Logic, and Independent Choice Logic (ICL). SRL can also handle uncertainty in data to handle game models with incomplete or unknown information. In machine learning, SRL has applications for collective classification such as in link prediction, object classification, and group detection in application domains such as social networks, bioinformatics, chemoinformatics, natural language processing, and the semantic web. Maximum a posteriori (MAP) inference is facilitated by SRL for game theoretical adversarial deep learning with Nash equilibria and Pareto optima in strategic games containing Markov logic. Bector et al. [38] write a text on fuzzy games. It includes fuzzy decision theory and fuzzy mathematical programming that have application in game theoretical adversarial deep learning operating in a fuzzy learning environment. Bonanno et al. [78] discuss the epistemics of game theory. It is useful in defining the rationality and reasoning of adversary types in game theoretical adversarial deep learning. The players' probabilistic beliefs and cardinal preferences can be analyzed both semantically and syntactically in terms of mutual recognition of rationality between them.

Tsipras et al. [609] prove that a tradeoff exists between adversarial robustness and learning performance in the design of robust classifiers. The resulting costs lead to computationally expensive training methods in adversarial learning. Adversarial robustness is defined in terms of low values for expected adversarial loss. Adversarially robust training acts as a data augmentation to regularize the learning model and lead to a better analytics solution. There is a close connection between adversarial robustness and sample complexity of robust learning using generative assumptions on the data. Robust learning models have clean feature interpolations similar to those obtained from deep generative learning. Ye et al. [684] discuss model compression that preserves adversarial robustness with concurrent adversarial training and weight pruning. It can be used for security-critical deep learning scenarios in resource-constrained embedded systems such as mobile phones, IoT devices, personal healthcare wearables, autonomous driving, unmanned aerial systems, etc. Weight pruning exploits sparsity in deep neural networks to prune connection weights without noticeable performance degradation. Adversarially trained model is observed to be less sparse than naturally trained model. Moreover, adversarial training requires more network capacity than to achieve strong adversarial robustness than for correctly classifying benign examples only. ADMM (alternating direction method of multipliers)-based weight pruning is proposed. Brand et al. [83] introduce an iterated matching pennies (IMP) game to analyze adversarial learnability, conventional learnability, and approximability. The "completeness" of learnability is discussed in terms of language identification and statistical consistency in the limit. Any computable prediction method cannot be complete. A Turing machine can learn any computable language. Such a notion of learnability is important in statistics, econometrics, machine learning, inductive inference, and data mining. In this context, game theoretical adversarial deep learning can be used in learnability and approximability problems when players are trying to learn from each other by observations.

4.5.1   Existence and Uniqueness of Game Theoretical Equilibrium Solutions

Nash et al. [455] is the original paper defining equilibrium solution concepts in multiplayer games with pure strategies. Mixed strategies then become probability distributions over pure strategies. Nash et al. [454] discuss non-cooperative game theory without coalitions. Each player acts independently rather than as a coalition without communication or collaboration with other players. The equilibrium solution concepts are then a generalization of those in two-player zero-sum games. Several solution concepts are developed to satisfy the learning hypothesis in game theoretical adversarial deep learning such as with geometrical form solutions and contradiction analysis on equilibrium strategies. Transferability and comparability between adversarial payoff functions are also a line of enquiry to contrast game theoretical equilibrium solutions in real-world applications. Dynamical systems of non-cooperative games can be developed for reducing cooperative games with pre-play negotiations in the cooperative game that become plays in a non-cooperative game to describe all the players' payoffs in an infinite game.

Medanic et al. [418] develop explicit expressions of open-loop multilevel Stackelberg strategies for control in deterministic sequential decision-making problems. Continuous linear systems are solved by quadratic optimization criteria to characterize the Stackelberg controls. Higher-order square-matrix Riccati differential equations are also formulated to characterize the Stackelberg controls with coefficient matrices in a dynamical system used for the statistical inference of their structural properties. The strategies selected in the decision-making sequence for a player are available to the other players after the current play. The dimensionality of the associated dynamical system represents a differential constraint for determining the optimal strategies of next control in the decision-making sequence produced by subsystems in an interconnected learning system.

Freiling et al. [201] study the existence and uniqueness of Stackelberg equilibrium in a two-player differential game with open-loop information structure. Sufficient existence conditions are derived for open-loop equilibrium to solve Riccati matrix differential equations. Time-invariant parameters are discussed to address concept drift in the equilibrium solutions. The equilibrium solutions can be extended with non-cooperative game theory having different hierarchical structures, cost functions, and sample data information patterns in Stackelberg differential games. A linear differential equation describes constraints to the state vector in the game. The payoff functions are constructed to satisfy necessary and sufficient conditions on the solution concepts obtained by solving differential equations.

OReilly et al. [475] study the dynamics of cyber adversaries to harden cyber defenses according to adversarial robustness criteria. The dynamics are formulated as a competitive co-evolutionary system that generates many arms races for harvesting robust solutions. The co-evolutionary process is crafted in the context of network cybersecurity scenarios where the defender leverages artificial intelligence (AI) to gain competitive advantage in an asymmetric adversarial environment. Adversarial AI deploys defensive (worst-case, average-case) tradeoff configurations to anticipate multiple possible adversarial behaviors with reference to their expected impact, goal, strategies, or tactics. The expected impact can be a combination of financial cost, disruption level, or outcome risk. Ranks for the defensive configurations are generated from stochastic search methods to explore the strategy space in simulated competitive engagements of adversaries' behavior. The competitive engagements are between adversarial populations that undergo selection based on performance and variation to adapt. Co-evolutionary logic then results in population-wide adversarial dynamics where adversaries engage and measure their outcomes with reference to other adversaries. Robust defensive configurations are thus formed by co-evolutionary algorithms that help generate diverse behavior. The diversity of behaviors is measured by "solution concepts" of adversarial robustness. There is a fixed budget of computation or time for each adversarial engagement. Modeling-simulation use cases on adversarial threats and defensive models in computer security then support adversarial deep learning emulation with varying model granularity. Such levels of granularity include denial-of-service attacks in a peer-to-peer network, device compromise in an enterprise network, and deceptive defense against internal reconnaissance of an adversary in a software-defined network. The co-evolutionary search algorithm's convergence criteria also facilitate visualizations and comparisons of adversarial behaviors in generative adversarial dynamics. In experiments, the attacker and defender strategies are coevolved in the context of a single, custom, abstract computer network defense simulation. Gaussian process estimation estimates the uncertain adversarial engagements. A recommender technique is used to approximate the adversary's fitness functions. A spatial grid is used to reduce the search space over pairwise engagements of interest. Adversarial engagements are cached to work within a fixed time fitness evaluation budget. The engagement environment supports problem-specific network testbeds, simulators, and models. The behavioral action sequences for attack and defense are expressed with a Backus-Naur form (BNF) grammar that is a context-free grammar representation of adversarial behaviors as data-driven decision-making rules. The BNF grammar communicates adversarial deep learning functionality and enables conversation journeys and model validations in an application domain of discourse. The BNF grammar, engagement environment, and fitness function vary with adversary types. Their modularity and reusability lead to efficient software engineering and problem-solving advantages. The competitive co-evolution fitness functions and solution concepts are dependent on the context of adversarial engagements. The "best" solutions compendium is obtained from a ranking and filtering process on the solution concepts.

Cotter et al. [138] discuss theories of constrained optimization that have application in Neyman-Pearson classification, robust optimization, and fair machine learning. A two-player non-zero sum game is solved to model optimization parameters with non-differentiable constraints on convergence rates and losses counts/proportions of regret minimization. The machine learning fairness problem is formulated as the minimization of empirical loss subject to data-dependent fairness constraints that are not differentiable. A deep neural network with non-convex objective functions is used for modeling the machine learning problems. The constraints are expressed with functions of indicator random variables. The game theoretical equilibria then define stochastic classifiers. Syrgkanis et al. [587] investigate correlated equilibria in multiplayer normal form games embedded into regularized learning algorithms and their black-box reductions. No-regret learning is utilized to make players' decisions. The regret bounds are found in adversarial environments with no-regret algorithms such as multiplicative weights, mirror descent, and follow the regularized/perturbed leader. The no-regret dynamics lead to faster convergence rates for regularized learning algorithms. Their black-box reductions in game theoretical environments preserve the convergence rates while maintaining the regret bounds on adversarial robustness. Results are compared against a simultaneous auction game in terms of utilities, regrets, and convergence to equilibria. The welfare of the game is the result of a variable-sum allocation of payoffs and resource matching corresponding to an unweighted bipartite matching problem.

Many games of interest in adversarial deep learning lie beyond tractable modeling and reasoning. Wellman et al. [642] investigate the gaps between strategic reasoning and game theory. Computational complexity in automated reasoning is shown to be due to number of agents, size of strategy sets and policy spaces, degree of incomplete and imperfect information, and expected payoff computations in a stochastic environment for adversarial learning. Empirical games are introduced as game simulators that perform strategic reasoning through interleaved simulation and game theoretical analysis. The building block for adversarial deep learning is an interaction scenario where payoff information is obtained from data in observations and simulations. Constructing and reasoning about empiric games presents interesting sub-problems in simulation, statistics, search, and game theoretical adversarial deep learning analysis. Empiric game formulations are decomposed into strategy space parametrization over continuous or multidimensional action sets and imperfect information conditioned on observation histories. Strategy space parametrization is done with candidate strategies in baseline or skeletal structures for parametric variations on the game search architecture such as truthful revelation of payoffs, myopic best response strategies, and game tree search in minimax and max-max optimization. Estimation of precise, rigorous, and automated empiric game techniques is recommended to be done with statistical techniques such as Monte Carlo analysis in active learning of strategy choices by adversary types, adjusting for cyber-observable factors with known effects on payoffs, applying control variates to measure demand-adjusted payoffs, hierarchical game reductions to affect computational savings, information theoretic criteria for selecting strategy profiles, and regression in game estimation to generalize payoffs across very large profile spaces given available data. Vorobeychik et al. [623] investigate games with real-valued strategies where payoff information is learned on a sample of strategy profiles. The payoff function learning problem is formulated as a standard regression problem with known structure in a multi-agent environment. Learning performance is measured with respect to relative utility of prescriptive strategies rather than accuracy of payoff functions. The relative utility of strategies is also estimated as the target of supervised learning and as a learning model selector. Thus, game theoretical equilibrium solutions can be determined from a database of game playing experience rather than a specification of strategic interactions in a game. Determining such equilibrium solutions then becomes the target of machine learning applied to games with intractably large or infinite strategy sets defining continuous agents. The equilibrium solutions can be used to represent multi-stage games as one-shot games with strategy sets that are functions of all possible histories of play. Game payoff data is obtained from observations of other agents playing the game and simulations of hypothetical runs of the game. The payoff function approximation task for data mining is then defined as selecting a function from a candidate set to minimize a measure of deviation from a true payoff function representing a black-box or an oracle in adversarial deep learning. Polynomial regression, local regression, and support vector machine regression are used to compute the pure Nash equilibria. The learned functions are initially restricted to finite strategy subsets. Replicator dynamics search for a symmetric mixed equilibrium with an iterative evolutionary algorithm. After a fixed number of iterations, the approximate Nash equilibrium in a payoff matrix over discrete strategy subsets is treated as a learned game. Therefore, regression and discriminative learning methods in supervised learning offer generalization of game theoretical adversarial deep learning to infinite set strategy spaces beyond directly available experience for machine learning. Target functions that support tractable equilibrium calculations can be formulated with deep learning to support "learnability" of adversarial payoff functions according to learning tradeoffs found in various adversarial environments.

Our research into game theoretical adversarial deep learning tradeoffs between the learnability and the robustness of discriminative learning. By "learnability," we mean the ability of the classifier to predict correct labels (without regard to noise), and by robustness, we mean that the prediction is the same with or without noise (without regard to correctness). The tradeoff we observe is that more learnability comes at the price of less robustness and vice versa. The major aim of our research is development of game theoretical adversarial deep learning algorithms applicable to cyberspace security data mining problems. We develop game theoretical payoff functions modeling the decision boundaries of supervised machine learning. They explore the systems theoretic dependence between randomization in adversarial data manipulations and generalizability in black-box learner optimizations with respect to the proposed game theoretical adversarial deep learning. Such robust optimizations study the theories for robustness, fairness, explainability, and transparency in machine learning with prediction games. Here, we develop adversarial learning algorithms for reliability, learnability, efficiency, and complexity in discriminative learning. Resultant game theoretical adversarial deep learning is applied to classification and optimization problems in data analytics.

The optimal results of sample complexity in the game theoretical formulations depend on the optimization methods and target data distributions of the loss functions computed in Nash and Stackelberg equilibria. A better stochastic policy in the game theoretical equilibria would lead to (cooperative-competitive) solutions in (differential dynamical) systems modeling. Here, we can compare the game theoretical adversarial learning solutions with machine learning baselines such as the inclusion of noise in the optimization procedure, the simplification of the function landscape by increase of the model size, the schemes for derivative-free stochastic optimization, and data resampling in the context of variational learning algorithms. We can also explore randomization strategies for robust optimization in multiplayer games that can be decomposed into prediction games or Stackelberg games. They are often modeled as decision problems in non-cooperative differential games.

4.5.2 Optimal Control Theory and Robust Game Theory

Huang et al. [288] describe dynamic games for control system design that is decomposable into cyber, physical, and human layers. Cross-layer design issues give rise to security and resilience challenges in critical infrastructures. Such critical infrastructures are seen in industrial control systems in sectors such as electric power, manufacturing, and transportation. Here, the control system's view of design takes the perspective of sensing, control, and plant dynamics integrated in a feedback loop in the physical layer. The control design techniques such as robust control, adaptive control, and stochastic control deal with information uncertainties, physical disturbances, and adversarial noise in the feedback loop. Adversarial noise is seen in the cyber layer with communication and networking issues between sensors and actuators as well as among multiple distributed agents. By contrast, the human layer is concerned with supervision and management issues such as coordination, operation, planning, and investment. The management issues include social and economic issues, pricing and incentives, and market regulation and risk analysis. In cloud-enabled autonomous systems, service contracts for security services can include incentive-compatible attack-aware cyber insurance policies that can be designed with game theoretical adversarial learning to maximize social welfare and alleviate moral hazard. Adversaries exploit attack surfaces of the control systems to exploit zero-day vulnerabilities in autonomous systems such as self-driving vehicles. Game theory provides frameworks for strategic interaction among components in a complex system to quantify tradeoffs of robustness, security, and resilience in system performance within adversarial environments for control systems. In game theoretical frameworks, secure and resilient control design is viewed as an extension to robust control design. Application focus areas are enumerated as heterogeneous autonomous systems, defensive deception games for industrial control systems, and risk management of cyber-physical networks. The objective of resilient control systems is to have performance guarantees and recovery mechanisms when robustness and security fail due to adversarial attacks and system failures. Here, a robust control system can withstand uncertain parameters and disturbances due to design-for-security machine learning paradigm. The defense mechanisms in robust control system design span cryptography, detection, solution architecture, and communication protocols. The physical systems design is governed by differential-algebraic equations for applications such as multibody robotic systems, power network systems, and water distribution systems. Hence, the learning dynamics can be described with Markov decision processes, difference equations, and partial differential equations in game theoretical adversarial deep learning. The game theory literature can be combined with cognitive, memory, computational, and psychological aspects of the human decision-making process. Here, prospect theory incorporates loss aversion in human decisions and differentiates the perception of losses from the utility of the gains. Attention mechanisms that incorporate limited cognition of the online human decisions can also be incorporated into the game theory. The decentralized ownership of the control system services can provision effective sharing and utilization of the resources of computational, communication, and sensing infrastructures. Then implementation and investment in adversarial deep learning for security then enable high-quality service offerings by mitigating security risks at service levels of control systems. It also prevents the real-time propagation of cyber risks at various socioeconomic scales. Games in autonomous system that consider all such security requirements are designed to achieve the Gestalt Nash equilibrium (GNE). GNE is a game theoretical equilibrium solution concept where no player has an incentive to deviate from the optimal solution. Such solutions are to be found in not only the modular game defined by local agent-agent interactions but also the integrated game defined by the global system-system interactions. It seeks to find a self-adaptability, self-healing, and agile resilience for the heterogeneous autonomous systems faced with multi-stage stealthy attacks such as APTs in adversarial environments.

Dynamic programming principles can be used to efficiently study the convergence properties of the game theoretical optima. In a variational adversary framework, game theoretical modeling can also be used to solve sampling problems in differential privacy mechanisms. The machine learning task is to produce an adversarial sample in the latent space of the variational method according to an implicitly defined distribution that is important for both optimization and classification of the adversarial manipulations in the machine learning. We can then solve it by presenting a framework of deep generative learning and its differential learning scheme in decision problem's non-cooperative differential privacy games. Further, the differential privacy games can be analyzed in terms of optimal control theory. If the game theoretical players can observe state of the control system, then the Nash equilibrium is computed according to an open-loop solution for the control system. If the game theoretical players cannot consider feedback strategies, then the Nash equilibrium is computed according to a closed-loop solution for the control system. Principles of dynamic programming are used as the computational methods finding the game theoretical optima to the necessary and sufficient conditions for optimal control system. Furthermore, partial differential state equations of the control system can augment the player's payoff functions to result in stochastic control in game theoretical interactions. Here, the game theoretical equilibria are determined by the necessary and sufficient conditions on the coefficients solving for the Stackelberg Riccati differential, difference, and algebraic equations of the equilibria. The study of such equilibria and their numerical computational methods is the subject of evolutionary and differential game theory. Then we shall translate such stochastic methods into the language of adversarial learning with variational adversaries. A privacy-centric enhancement of the learning capacity, randomization strategies, and payoff functions in the game formulations would affect the weighting regularizations and the decision boundaries of the machine learning algorithms provided as services. Systems theory motifs from non-linear signal processing and control theory statistics relevant for the adversarial data mining application may also be defined from the domain knowledge. In this context, we propose to explore wavelet decompositions and maximum entropy modeling of the data distributions.

Grunwald et al. [236] develop a decision theory by connecting maximum entropy inference to minimizing worst-case expected loss in zero-sum restricted games between the player's decision-maker and nature. The decision theory is used to derive loss functions that can be used in adversarial deep learning. The maximum entropy distribution defines the decision-maker's minimax strategy. A generalized relative entropy measure is introduced for the decision-theoretic definition of discrepancy and loss function. The generalized relative entropy is comparable to other entropy optimization frameworks such as Renyi entropies and expected Fisher information. Franci et al. [200] typecast the training of generative adversarial networks (GANs) as a variational inequality problem with stochastic Nash equilibrium solution. A stochastic relaxed forward-backward training algorithm is proposed for GANs. Cai et al. [98] conduct a survey of the state of the art in GANs from security and privacy perspective. The game theoretical optimization strategy in GANs is used to generate high-dimensional multimodal probability distributions that have important applications in mathematics and engineering domains. In the GAN-based methods in adversarial deep learning, the generators can be used to not only craft adversarial examples but also design defense mechanisms. In data privacy research, GAN-based methods can be used in image steganography, image anonymization, and image encoding. Variational generative adversarial network (VGAN) and variational autoencoder (VAE) can be built to strike a balance between privacy and utility in synthesized images. In model privacy research, GAN-based methods can be used to protect the learning model privacy anonymization and obfuscation. In application domains of adversarial deep learning, GANs can generate adversarial malware examples with data compression and reconstruction, fake malware generation, and malware detection. They can be used to construct bio-information systems for authentication; financial fraud detection problems in credit card fraud, telecom fraud, and insurance fraud; botnet detection; and network intrusion detection.

The adversarial noise characteristics can be defined with respect to the following notions of noise in future research on game theoretical adversarial deep learning where game theoretical learning models involve evolutionary adversaries, stochastic adversaries, and variational adversaries targeting the misclassification performance of deep neural networks and convolutional neural networks. The extent to which noise on model parameters and training data can benefit the overall quality of the data distributions generated by game theoretical adversarial learning depends on the specific adversarial noise processes and the nature of the generated target distribution.

- Adversarial noise is spam, outlier, discontinuity, and costly
- Adversarial noise is not ground truth, not signal, and non-iid
- Adversarial noise is fake data and false discovery
- Adversarial noise is unexpected prediction and information leak
- Adversarial noise is residual error and unknown object
- Adversarial noise is rare class and sparse structure
- Adversarial noise is complex motif and wrong decision
- Adversarial noise is misclassification example and incorrect regression value
- Adversarial noise is randomized sample and latent variable
- Adversarial noise is due to an underlying stochastic process
- Adversarial noise is statistically insignificant
- Adversarial noise cannot be explained

Ge et al. [213] formulate game design methods for robust quantum control played between the uncertainties (or noises) and the controls in quantum hardware. Lloyd et al. [392] introduce quantum generative adversarial networks where generator and discriminator are equipped with quantum information processors. Romero et al. [523] introduce variational quantum circuit to mimic the target distributions. Such variational circuits for encoding classical information into quantum states are very useful in machine learning applications such as adversarial classification. We can run costly computational learning algorithms or their BLAS subroutines efficiently on a quantum computer. Quantum generalizations of the adversarial deep learning on quantum data distributions would involve quantum sampling, quantum information, and quantum causality modeling to analyze the bias-variance decomposition in adversarial payoff functions applicable into the computational optimization of randomized prediction games. We can derive utility bounds for quantum neural network's deep learning in an empirical risk minimization framework and a mistake bounds framework. We can also define quantum-enhanced learning through interactions in an agent-environment paradigm of the quantum computation to derive separability criteria in the neural computing mechanisms and their generalization error due to quantum measurements. We can develop a theory of sample complexity, formal verification, and fuzzy automata in the adversarial models with reliable guarantees proposed on the quantum generative adversarial learning in quantum neural network's training and optimization. We can create special-purpose quantum information processors such as quantum annealers that are well matched to adversarial deep learning architectures. Hybrid classical-quantum learning schemes would quantify the learnability of the quantum neural networks in non-convex optimization landscapes from the perspective of the generalization error and the estimation error due to quantum measurements. The implementation of trainable unitaries over parameterized quantum circuits can then be analyzed with a no-regret property in the tolerable error of the generated data. Then quantum information processing tasks may be reformulated as discriminative learning, generative learning, and adversarial learning problems with separability criteria to distinguish entanglement for specific quantum states characterized in structured data and computational efficiency. Quantum generalization of generative adversarial networks (GANs) to the quantum mechanical regime include modeling structures in convolutional, conditional, bidirectional, and semi-supervised GANs using quantum circuits. Quantum approaches to generative modeling problems in game theoretical adversarial deep learning may then focus on variational quantum algorithms with Markov chain methods in adversarial training and Bayesian Stackelberg games in adversarial deep learning. We can also characterize the problem of quantum classification in the presence of noise. Then we can study the tradeoff between learnability and robustness of the adversarial machine learning. Efficient quantum information science algorithms with such basis classifiers would help us deal with "big data" in the quantum computers. To derive reliable guarantees on the security evaluation of the quantum neural networks, we can derive generalization errors for the quantum adversarial learning problems with formal verification. A quantum enhancement of these computation procedures in adversarial deep learning can create quantum adversarial machine learning algorithms with inner products of big data, learned row-rank quantum states, unitary transformations as the storing-retrieving problems in data mining, and state/process tomography of quantum measurement learning tasks.

The following adversarial deep learning design tradeoffs must be addressed in future work as notions of benefits and costs incurred for retraining the model and generating an attacker.

- Attacker tradeoff: cost of adapting to the classifier and the benefit from attack
- Defender tradeoff: benefit of a correct attack detection and the cost of a false alarm
- Interaction tradeoff: search space of strategies, payoff functions, costs of participating in the game, relative ranking of each player inferring the decision boundaries, black-box attack scenario where the adversary is unable to observe the classifier's strategies before choosing its strategy
- Equilibrium tradeoff: optimization objectives, misclassification performances, and retraining costs in deep learning
- Utility tradeoff: defender's utility losses in the game are inferior to the utility of the adversary and importance of the costs incurred to generate an attack and to retrain the classifier
- Discrimination tradeoff: more learnability comes at the price of less robustness

To characterize the adversarial data signals in experimental data, we could also estimate the Lyapunov spectra exponents and attractor networks with deep learning models and predictive analytics processes. Here, we can explore the spectral signal processing techniques for (i) describing the complex dynamics in game theoretical solution concepts as modeling errors in multivariate prediction with deep learning, (ii) feature extraction for the machine learning models on the underlying data distribution generating and validating model training, (iii) reconstructing the differential equations as dynamical models of the training data available for adversarial training, and (iv) energy landscape analysis with data distribution schemes and data indexing structures for static and dynamic data that reduce the communication cost and increase the load balancing in distributed memory systems. We would need to create statistical validation criteria for such machine learning with reference to application domain knowledge. In this context, we can explore evaluation metrics in data mining applied to adversarial data modeling in cybersecurity applications.

Chapter 5
Adversarial Defense Mechanisms for Supervised Learning

In this chapter we explore neural network architectures, implementations, cost analysis, and training processes using game theoretical adversarial deep learning. We also define the utility bounds of such deep neural networks within computational learning theories such as empirical risk minimization, mistake bounds frameworks, and no-regret learning. Here mistake bounds framework with no-regret property for online learning provides tolerable error and update rules for training the neural nets on the generated adversarial data. Then cyberspace information processing tasks may be reformulated as discriminative learning, generative learning, and adversarial learning baselines with respect to separability criteria characterizing the structured datasets and computational efficiency for crafting the adversarial loss functions. Proactive defense techniques for each adversarial example are also summarized to construct defense-in-depth environments with adversarial signalling games for mitigating cyberattacks by adaptive adversaries. They can be incorporated into a design-for-security paradigm for machine learning hypotheses to complement the classical design-for-performance paradigm to produce multiple levels of defense against cyberattacks with reference to learning system perspective security goals. We present a vast amount of related literature on the computational optimization algorithmics in defense mechanisms for security requirements in game theoretical adversarial deep learning in a very organized fashion. They can be used for digital forensics, vulnerability identification, impact analysis, risk mitigation, cyber security metrics, data and model development, penetration testing, and semantic interoperability in cybersecurity applications. We point out many applications, limitations of the current methods, promising future directions for game theoretical adversarial deep learning countermeasures development, and technology evaluation in substantial detail. The formalized adversarial deep learning assumptions for robust games can track attack surface generation, capacity, and specificity in safety-critical multitask objectives for adversarial robustness in loss functions design within critical infrastructures protection mechanisms. The resultant algorithmic decision-making clarifies the learning system's capabilities for efficiency, objectivity, and control to a specific audience to enable accuracy, fairness, accountability, availability, integrity, confidentiality, stability, reliability, safety, maintainability, and transparency. In this context, the adversarial deep learning can be formulated according to the principles of composite AI and explainable AI that improve efficiency of supervised learning, reinforcement learning, generative learning, and game theoretical learning with knowledge representations for reasoning about privacy, trust, and security optimization metrics.

Brendel et al. [84] categorize threat models generating adversarial perturbations into (i) gradient-based attacks relying on detailed model information, (ii) score-based attacks relying on confidence scores such as class-conditioned probabilities, (iii) transfer-based attacks relying on substitute models for target models, and (iv) proposed decision-based attacks relying on information about final model decision. Proposed decision-based attacks are called boundary attack and applied to blackbox models for target model.

5.1 Securing Classifiers Against Feature Attacks

Li et al. [354] demonstrate limitations of feature reduction in adversarial settings with objective-driven adversaries. Each adversary is supposed to be able to substitute across similar features in a feature cross-substitution attack. Adversary is also assumed to be able to query classifier according to a fixed query budget and cost budget. An evasion model with sparse regularizer is presented in adversarial setting. Constructing classifier on feature equivalence classes rather than feature space is proposed as a solution to improve classifier resilience to evasion model. Another solution proposes bi-level Stackelberg game of interactions between classifier and a collection of adversaries. Stackelberg game is solved by mixed-integer linear programming with constraint generation. Adversaries' objectives are inferred from (query budget and cost budget) constraint generation converging to local optima on training data.

Globerson et al. [220] analyze classifier robustness with a game theoretical formulation. For a classifier trained on multiple features with varying importance, any single feature is not given too much weight during testing. Adversary is supposed to be able to delete features in testing data that were present in training data. Then a classifier is constructed which is optimal under a worst-case feature deletion scenario. Such a scenario is formulated as a solution to a two-player game between classifier and feature deleter with a minmax objective. Classifier chooses actions that give robust classifier parameters. Feature deleter chooses to delete features that are most harmful to classifier performance. Structure of uncertainty in game convergence is related to existence vs non-existence of a feature. A support vector machine with regularized hinge loss and linear constraints is taken to be the training objective for classifier. Game deletes features that lead to maximum decrease in classifier loss. Cooperative games with Shapley value objectives measuring performance change after deleting a feature are an alternative to the proposed minmax objectives deleting multiple features simultaneously.

Given an evasion attack scenario, Zhang et al. [691] investigate impact of feature reduction on classifier security, if adversary-aware feature selection is not present in classifier training. A smaller feature set is shown to significantly worsen classifier performance under attack which may usually not be the case for a classifier not under attack. Classifier security model is expressed as a regularizer to be optimized and estimated along with classifier's generalization capability during feature selection process. It is implemented as a wrapper-based feature selection method using forward selection and backward elimination of features suitable for both linear and non-linear classifiers with differentiable discriminant functions. Evasion attack scenario is considered an exploratory integrity attack on the testing data fed to a classifier trained on original training data. Optimal evasion strategy is formulated as an optimization problem minimizing the distance between the adversarial examples and the training data such that classifier's discriminant function misclassifies adversarial examples. An adversary-aware feature selection approach maximizes not only the generalization capability of the classifier but also the classifier security against evasion attacks. Here the classifier security is weighted by application-specific constraints and parameters, while the classifier generalization capability is estimated according to the application-dependent discriminant functions and performance measures. Instead of searching for best evasion point by querying classifier with candidate samples of a blackbox search approach, computationally efficient adversarial algorithms are devised to exploit adversary's knowledge of targeted classifier's objective function. They are defined by choices for distance function between adversarial examples and training data and feature representation in classification algorithm. A gradient descent procedure finds gradient steps that reduce distance between adversarial data and training data while projecting current point onto feasible domain of adversarial examples as soon as discriminant function misclassifies it. Initial attack point in gradient descent is set to closest sample that is either classified as legitimate or classified as malicious. Performance of true classifier gracefully decreases against attacks of increasing attack strength determined by upper bound on maximum amount of adversarial modifications and lower bound on misled classifier confidence. A most gracefully degraded classifier is expected to be most secure after retraining on training data as well as adversarial examples. Experiments validating student's t-tests and classification accuracies of feature weight distributions are conducted on TREC 2007 email corpus consisting of legitimate and spam emails. Application-specific constraints on data distributions make it harder for adversary to imitate feature values of legitimate class eventually leading to a low probability of evading detection.

5.2 Adversarial Classification Tasks with Regularizers

Demontis et al. [154] analyze evasion attacks of linear classifiers in a robust optimization framework. Relation between sparsity of feature weights and defense of linear classifiers is investigated to propose a regularizer. Linear classifiers are chosen in adversarial learning algorithm due to their interpretable decisions obtained from the low storage, processing time, and power consumption in mobile and embedded systems. Adversary is supposed to have complete knowledge about target classifier's training data, feature set, and classification algorithm. Adversary's capability of modifying data is given as an application-dependent data constraint. Typically, such data constraints are defined as ℓ_1 and ℓ_1 norms on number of modified features called sparse and dense attacks, respectively. Adversary's attack strategy is formulated as an optimization problem minimizing target classifier's discriminant function for data subject to a distance constraint between adversarial examples and the original data. With an idea of finding sparse and uniform weights, a linear convex combination of ℓ_1 and ℓ_∞ norms is proposed as a robustness regularizer for adversary's attack strategy. Behavior of such regularization against evasion attacks on a support vector machine classifier with hinge loss is then investigated in classification applications for handwritten digit classification, spam filtering, and malware detection. Performance measurement in adversarial settings is done with area under the ROC curve combined with a sparsity and security measures proposed on classifier's weight distributions.

Krause et al. [329] present an information-theoretic objective function to train a discriminative probabilistic classifier called Regularized Information Maximization (RIM). RIM is applied as a clustering framework that accommodates different likelihood functions, balances class separation, and incorporates partial labels for semi-supervised learning. Such discriminative clustering techniques represent the boundaries between clustering categories available in the real-world applications of clustering. They include techniques such as spectral graph partitioning, maximum margin clustering, and neural gas models. Here the unsupervised learning of clustering problems is formalized as a conditional probabilistic model that is suitable for multi-class discriminative clustering. The objective function then maximizes the mutual information between empirical data distribution on the inputs and induced label distribution from the model selection. It is constructed to satisfy mathematical properties for optimization such as decision boundaries should not be located in the input space that is densely populated with data points and clustering configurations in which category labels are evenly distributed across the classes are preferred. Further a regularizing term is introduced to penalize conditional models with complex decision boundaries in the model selection. It depends on the specific choice of the conditional probability distribution being estimated. In multi-class classification problems, prior beliefs about non-uniform class label proportions are encoded as relative entropy terms in RIM's non-convex objective function.

Xu et al. [668] create regularized support vector machines (SVMs) within a robust optimization formulation based in uncertainty sets. Such SVMs have protection to noise and overfitting. They minimize a combination of the training error and a regularization term. The regularization term is typically a tensor norm. It restricts the complexity of the classifier's function class to support generalization performance. It regards the testing data samples as perturbed copies of the training data samples. Therefore bounding such a perturbation reduces the gap between classification errors. Structural risk minimization approach is a regularization technique that minimizes a bound on the generalization error based on the training error and a complexity term. The proposed robust SVM performs a minmax optimization over all possible disturbances between training and testing data samples. Stability of the SVM against a specific perturbation that can be estimated is a related robustness notion that is also studied. The training loss plus the regularization penalty is the regularized loss for training the robust SVM.

Yan et al. [676] propose adversarial margin maximization (AMM) networks having an adversarial perturbation-based regularization of the adversarial learning. A differentiable formulation of the perturbation is backpropagated through the regularized deep nets. Such maximum margin classifiers tend to have better generalization performance due to intra-class compactness and inter-class discriminability. The proposed adversarial defense mechanism is able to generalize to multi-label classifiers so long as a target label is properly chosen for the adversarial perturbation. Zhong et al. [707] embed a margin-based regularization term into the classification objectives of deep neural networks. The regularization term has two steps of optimizations to find potential perturbations in an iterative manner. Large margins in the adversarial classification guarantees the inter-class distance and the intra-class smoothness in the embedding space to improve the robustness of deep nets. A cross-entropy loss function is jointly optimized with a large margin distance constraint acting as the regularization term. Classifier robustness is tested under conditions of feature manipulation and label manipulation.

Alabdulmohsin et al. [7] discuss reverse engineering attacks against classifiers with fixed decision boundaries. Then randomization in the classification due to semidefinite programming in a distribution of classifiers is formulated to mitigate adversarial risks and provide reliable predictions with a high probability. The authors investigate the tradeoffs between the predictive accuracy and variance of the classifier distribution. The reverse engineering attacks proposed are classified under exploratory attack scenarios where the adversary is manipulating testing data distribution. The proposed classification system attempts to make reliable predictions while revealing as little information about the decision boundaries as impossible. The problem learning with a distribution of classifiers is formulated as a convex optimization problem. The defense of the classification system is compared with adversarial classification, kernel matrix correction, ensemble learning, multiple-instance learning, and game theoretical adversarial learning mechanisms. Here exploratory defense strategies are said to cause disinformation about the choice of training data, features, cost function, and learning algorithm. Another exploratory defense strategy is to increase the complexity of the hypothesis space for the adversary without causing overfitting for the classifier. In such a case, randomization strategies would estimate a probability of selecting a class label instead of predicting it as a binary label. The objective of a successful randomization would be to increase the adversary's reverse engineering effort without increasing the classifier's predictive error rate. Furthermore an active learning algorithm is proposed for the adversary to make target queries on the classifier. Here query selection strategies are based on random sampling, selective sampling and uncertainty sampling where the adversary knows that the defender uses a randomized classifier. Once learning is completed by the defender, it is able to mitigate adversarial risks due to the reverse engineering attack by picking a classifier at random from the distributions of classifiers for every query observed from the adversary's side. Linear classifiers are used to build the ensemble of a distribution of classifiers. In the experimental evaluation, accuracy-variance tradeoff curves are created to analyze the Pareto optimality points of the classification system. Every such Pareto-optimal point is a sound strategy for defending the classification system. By drawing classifiers at random from a distribution with large variance, the adversary's computational complexity to carry out the proposed reverse engineering attacks increases significantly at little increase in computational cost for the learning system. Such classification models are suitable for deployment in security-sensitive applications such as spam filtering, intrusion detection, and fraud detection.

Zhang et al. [695] propose an adversarial training to employ least adversarial data for updating the learning model. The adversarial learning objective derives an upper bound for the adversarial risk. The adversarial risk trains a deep neural network using the wrongly predicted adversarial data minimizing loss and correctly predicted adversarial data maximizing loss. Projected gradient descent (PGD) with early stopping is used to create the adversarial data in the training process. Curriculum learning is used in the proposed adversarial training strategy to improve the adversarial robustness of deep neural networks. That is, the deep neural networks initially learn from milder adversarial data and then gradually adapt to stronger adversarial data. Sinha et al. [560] do a theoretical analysis of distributionally robust optimization for adversarial training. The training procedure augments modelling parameters with worst-case perturbations to the training data. It converges to learning models that achieve robustness with small statistical or computational cost relative to empirical risk minimization.

Tsipras et al. [609] study the tradeoffs between standard generalization performance and adversarial robustness to adversarial examples in machine learning. The argument presented is that robust classifiers learn statistically different representations than standard classifiers. The goal of adversarial learning is defined as training models with low expected adversarial loss in the presence of worst-case input perturbations as adversarial examples. Standard classifiers are shown to take advantage of features that are weakly correlated to the class label to achieve standard accuracy. By contrast adversarial manipulations can simulate distribution of the weakly correlated features as if they belong to the wrong class. Thus any standard classifier that aims for high accuracy has to rely on non-robust features that can be arbitrarily manipulated. Furthermore such a tradeoff between standard and adversarial accuracy is inherent to the underlying data distribution itself and is not due to having insufficient samples for training. The adversarial examples generated from perturbing such non-robust features will transfer across all the classifiers that rely on features that are weakly correlated with the correct class label. In finite training data, such brittle features can even arise due to noise. Therefore the adversarial perturbations can be interpreted as invariance properties that a robust model satisfies. Robust training that achieves small loss for all the perturbations can be viewed as a method to embed certain invariances in a standard classification model. In this context, the authors observe that gradients for adversarially trained neural networks align with the perceptually relevant features of the input image. So we can interpret adversarial perturbations as producing salient characteristics of samples belonging to the interpolated target class. Such an explanation cannot be given in standard models where adversarial examples appear as noisy variants of the input image. The interpolated target classes can be represented with deep generative models such as generative adversarial networks and variational autoencoders involving adversarial manipulations into the learned representations. The loss landscape of robust learning models can then be used to smoothly interpolate between classes. Studying the generative assumptions in the data allows us to provide upper bounds on classifier robustness that is able to account for sample complexity of robust learning.

5.3 Adversarial Reinforcement Learning

Reinforcement machine learning is the study of intelligent agents and their actions in a simulated environment such that a notion of cumulative reward is maximized in the interactions between the agent and the environment. Instead of input/output labels required in supervised machine learning, reinforcement learning's focus is to find a balance between exploration and exploitation of patterns. Reinforcement learning can be interpreted as sampling-based methods to solve optimal control problems. The goal of reinforcement learning is to learn a policy that maximizes the expected cumulative reward and minimizes long-term regret. An intelligent agent in reinforcement learning has to randomly select actions without reference to an estimated probability distribution. Associative reinforcement learning tasks combine supervised learning with reinforcement learning. In game theoretical modelling, reinforcement learning can be used to produce error estimates on the optimization with reference to bounded rationality.

Chen et al. [118] review adversarial attacks taxonomy on reinforcement learning. The adversarial examples are classified into implicit adversarial examples that add imperceptible adversarial manipulations to mislead the learner and dominant adversarial examples which add physical world perturbations to change the local information available to reinforcement learning. The adversarial attack scenarios are classified into misclassification attacks to target a neural network performing reinforcement learning and Targeted attacks to target a particular class label in training that is misclassified into the target class label selected by the adversary. The learning model trained according to reinforcement learning policies is called the target agent. Q-Learning is a popular training algorithm for reinforcement learning. It proposed updates to a Q-value representing cumulative reward of the target agent. Through an iterative learning process, the target agent maximizes the Q-value by finding a best path to the goal. It can be represented by utility functions that evaluate strength and weakness of actions in a particular state. Deep Q-Network is a deep learning enhancement to Q-Learning. It gives rise to deep reinforcement learning with deep learning network's loss functions defining the Q-value utilities. The (asynchronous advantage actor-critic) A3C algorithm utilizes the actor-critic framework to improve the training process in deep reinforcement learning. Trust Region Policy Optimization (TRPO) is able to control the changes in reinforcement learning policies from an information-theoretic KL divergence the old and the new policies. The subsequent literature review by Chen et al. [118] shows that the fast gradient sign method (FGSM) can be adapted to reinforcement learning systems and adversarial examples can be crafted for Q-learning paths from the gradient of the maximum Q-value for each point on the path. A policy induction attack is summarized for Deep Q-Networks. Adversarial defense mechanisms are proposed due to adversarial training variants and learning objective regularizations in the adversarial loss functions for deep reinforcement learning. In such attack settings, complete blackbox threat models are quite rare. Variations of adversarial training and regularization terms in the objective function, modifying network structure such as defensive distillation, and deep generative modelling that produces adversarial examples are the most common defense mechanisms. Application domains for such adversarial machine learning include natural language understanding, image understanding, speech recognition, autonomous driving, target-driven visual navigation, game playing, trading systems, recommender systems, dialogue systems, inventory management, and automatic path planning. A survey of game theoretical solution concepts in multi-agent deep reinforcement learning is given by Lu et al. [396].

Dai et al. [141] focus on adversarial attacks that modify the combinatorial structure of data in application domains involving graph data structures. A reinforcement learning-based attack method is proposed to craft an attack policy from the prediction feedback of the target classifier. The target classifier is built with graph neural network models performing graph-level and node-level classification tasks. The family of supervised learning models being analyzed has an application in transductive tasks and inductive tasks. Unlike adversarial attacks on images that are of continuous datasets, the adversarial attacks on graphs have to belong to discrete datasets. Such adversarial manipulations are done by sequentially adding or dropping edges from the graph. The quadratic time complexity of the action space over the graph nodes is addressed with graph decomposition-based techniques. Threat models are classified into (i) white-box attack where the adversary has access to the internals of the target classifier including prediction labels, gradient information, etc., (ii) blackbox attack where only the prediction of the target classifier is available to the adversary, and (iii) restrict blackbox attack where the adversary can do blackbox queries on some of the samples to be able to create adversarial manipulations on the remaining samples. Non-targeted attacks are the focus of the adversarial manipulations. The research can be extended to targeted attacks also. A cross-entropy loss function is used in the classifier training. Graph-level and node-level feature embeddings are used to train the graph neural networks. Graph equivalence indicators are proposed to qualify the classification semantics before and after the adversarial manipulations. A reward function is proposed for the adversary acting as a reinforcement learning agent. A Q-learning algorithm then learns a Markov decision process (MDP) solving a discrete optimization problem with finite horizon. Each adversarial sample that is generated defines such an MDP. To learn a generalizable adversary, the Q-function learning objective in the Q-learning is generalized to transfer over all the adversarial samples and their corresponding MDPs. Further, a blackbox attack method is proposed with a genetic algorithm for zero-order optimization scenarios. The optimization objectives in such zero-order optimization scenarios are solved with derivative-free optimization algorithms. A finite difference method on the function values is used to estimate gradients formed by directional derivatives of the targeted loss function. Convergence criteria for such estimations depend on iteration complexity of the optimization and query complexity of the function evaluation. The unconstrained versions of the derivative-free optimization algorithms such as the alternating direction method of multipliers (ADMM) minimize an empirical average loss function that is non-convex. Bi-level versions of the derivative-free optimization algorithms formulate game theoretical objective that is typically a minmax function in blackbox attacks. It is solved with algorithms such as the zeroth-order stochastic coordinate descent [116]. The computational complexity of these algorithms is addressed by techniques such as dimensionality reduction and importance sampling. The algorithms for game theoretical adversarial deep learning are also comparable to such formulations for the objective function studying adversarial robustness of cost-sensitive classifiers. A regret minimization framework [179] can be used to address computational complexity issues faced by such game theoretical adversaries.

Mandlekar et al. [408] synthesize white-box attacks in deep reinforcement learning policies. Behzadan et al. [41] demonstrate adversarial examples that are transferable across various Deep Q-Networks. The spatiotemporal features of the training process are conjectured to provide defense mechanisms against such adversarial examples. Kos et al. [327] create poisoning attacks over time in deep reinforcement learning. The adversarial examples in image classification settings are compared with adversarial examples in reinforcement learning settings. Learning agent's policy resilience through retraining is also investigated. Ilyas et al. [293] improve blackbox attack scenarios with bandit optimization-based gradient estimation. Pinto et al. [494] train a reinforcement learning agent in the presence of a destabilizing adversary. The adversary applies differences in training and testing conditions as disturbance forces in the reinforcement learning. The policy learning trajectory is then formulated as solution to a two-player zero-sum Markov game. Li et al. [356] discuss operational constraints in the adversarial evasion of security policies. The task of adversarial classification is separated into the task of learning to predict attack preferences and the task of optimizing operational policy that explicitly abides by the operational constraints on the predictor. Then adversary's best response strategies are computed as randomized operational decisions.

Jun et al. [306] propose reward-manipulation attack protocols in online learning with limited feedback. The adversarial objective is to promote or obstruct actions chosen by a stochastic contextual bandit algorithm. Ma et al. [402] propose data poisoning attacks to hijack the behavior of a contextual bandit in an online recommender system. The adversarial data is found by solving a quadratic program with linear constraints. Lin et al. [372] propose adversaries that lure the agent through a preferred sequence of actions to a designated target state. A generative model is used to plan and predict the future states of the agent. Ho et al. [275] propose a generative learning framework to learn imitation learning policies from expert trajectories. The policies are learnt by generative algorithms that bypass learning of the cost functions of the maximum causal entropy in inverse reinforcement learning. Goyal et al. [230] train the generator in generative adversarial networks with a temporal difference (TD) objective rather than gradients of the discriminator. Pfau et al. [492] view generative adversarial networks as actor-critic methods where actor cannot affect the reward. Finn et al. [196] reformulate minmax games in deep generative models as bi-level optimization problems.

Bowling et al. [81] report an analysis of stochastic game theory in multi-agent reinforcement learning. While the actions of a single intelligent agent can be modelled as a Markov decision process that is stationary, multi-agent environments have to model non-stationary data distributions among multiple interacting agents. Here stochastic games would be a natural extension to Markov decision processes that include multiple agents. Such stochastic games would in turn be extensions of matrix games. A stationary strategy can be evaluated in such matrix games only if the other players' strategies are known in advance. Otherwise the matrix games would involve non-stationary environments. Furthermore such games can involve pure or mixed strategies. Two types of matrix games relevant for non-stationary data analytics are collaborative and competitive matrix games categorized according to their payoff functions definitions. Zero-sum games and general-sum games are purely competitive games. Their solutions are expected values of payoff functions found with linear programming and quadratic programming, respectively. Multi-agent reinforcement learning learns stochastic policies that map current state of the multiple agents to a probability distribution over their actions. The stochastic policies can be analyzed with matrix games extended to multiple states involving stochastic games. Each state in a stochastic game can be understood as a matrix game played with joint payoffs of the multiple agents transitioning between states. The equilibria strategies tend to solve computational complex problems requiring randomization, generalization, and approximation techniques in the adversarial machine learning.

Lanctot et al. [345] propose that multi-agent reinforcement learning (MARL) is required to achieve artificial general intelligence. The authors investigate a type of MARL called independent reinforcement learning (InRL) that has agents treat their machine learning experience as non-stationary environments. A learning algorithm is then designed for game theoretical best responses computed for mixtures of policies generated in deep reinforcement learning. Thus game-theoretic modelling is used in the policy selection of reinforcement learning. The algorithmic analytics are empirically benchmarked against related algorithms in the literature such as iterated best response, double oracle, and fictitious play. A machine learning performance measure called joint policy correlation is proposed to reduce overfitting in InRL generalizing from training to execution. The InRL formulation of reinforcement learning treats each learner agent as being oblivious to the remaining agents to be able to treat all of its interactions as belonging to the localized data distributions in non-stationary environments. Such local environments lead to non-stationary and non-Markovian conditions in the convergence criteria on adversarial loss functions derived for several computational algorithms. Then the reinforcement learning policies for the InRL can overfit to the non-stationary environment represented in remaining agent's policies resulting in a subsequent loss in generalization performance. Dynamically reacting to agent's behaviors are addressed in InRL with partial observability in the multi-agent settings. To deal with such sampling dynamics, researchers have to often resort to approximations in the learning algorithms faced with intractable computations. Lanctot et al. [345] use empirical game-theoretic modelling over meta-strategy distributions to compute best responses over a distribution of policies in deep reinforcement learning. A training process with a centralized and empirical payoff table is assumed for distributed and decentralized policy executions. The proposed double oracle algorithm uses deep neural networks as function approximators across game theoretical iterations computing the payoff matrix on approximate best response strategies. Joint policy correlation matrices are calculated to avoid overfitting in the learning process.

Tuyls et al. [612] analyze complex multi-agent interactions with empirical game theoretical analysis. The number of data samples required approximate the underlying game converging to a Nash equilibrium is examined. Each agent is treated as a player with a payoff matrix. First-order dynamical systems in evolutionary game theory formulate the meta-game of complex interactions. Tuyls [611] survey the use of evolutionary game theory in reinforcement learning and multi-agent systems. Kononen [324] constructs learning methods in Markov games for multi-agent reinforcement learning. The particular type of mathematical games proposed is matrix games. The Stackelberg equilibrium concepts in such games are solved by methods of mathematical programming in Markov games. Such Markov games extend Markov decision processes to optimization over multi-state repeated games. The update rules for optimizing the parameters in Q-learning's iteration within online environments are then presented.

Nowé [467] analyzed the optimal policy of an agent operating in a multi-agent reinforcement learning environment with game theory. Here the agent has to contend with a stochastic non-stationary computational environment that varies with the policies of the other agents. So the agents have to discover statistically good solutions for machine learning by either coordinating or competing with other agents. The game theoretical optima found at the Nash equilibrium in such environments are analyzed with respect to computational algorithms for stateless games with Q-learning automata, Markov games with policy gradients, and joint action learning in repeated games. Unlike zero-sum games, such games are general-sum games without special restrictions on the competition between players participating in the game. The solution concepts for such games are found by learning the best response strategies for each player that maximizes the current payoff with respect to current strategies of opponents in the game. Nash equilibrium and regret minimization are the most popular equilibrium concepts for the game theoretical reinforcement learning. It has applications in multi-agent systems. Regret refers to the difference between expected and actual payoffs for an agent. The expected payoff is calculated on various strategies fixed in the game that are either pure or mixed in the search spaces for machine learning. The actual payoff is computed empirically during the game's execution. The accumulated regret is optimized in regret-based learning approaches. Popular algorithms that combine stochastic games with reinforcement learning are Minimax-Q [374], Nash-Q [283], Fictitious Self-Play [267, 268], and counterfactual regret minimization [163].

Song et al. [563] propose imitation learning algorithms multi-agent actor-critic settings. In imitation learning, the agent learns desired behaviors by imitating and expert. The expert optimizes an underlying reward function approximately. The imitating agent learns policies through reinforcement learning. In multi-agent settings, the reward function optima depends on non-stationary environments with multiple optimum solutions. The imitation learning algorithms of a single agent can be extended to multi-agent settings within generative adversarial training frameworks. The authors map imitation learning to a two-player game between a generator and a discriminator. The generator controls the policies of all the distributed agents. The discriminator is a classifier for each agent that distinguishes between agent and expert behavior. The discriminator maps state-action pairs to scores. Discriminators can also incorporate prior information about cooperating and competing agents. To maximize its adversarial reward function, the generator tries to fool the discriminator with synthetic trajectories. Maximum entropy modelling forms the loss function for the maximum likelihood estimation in the proposed imitation learning. Adversarial training is used to incorporate prior knowledge about the multi-agent settings with an indicator function in the augmented reward regularizer within the minmax game for reinforcement learning. A policy gradient algorithm called Kronecker-Factored Trust Region is the optimization algorithm solving for the game theoretical equilibrium concepts. Imitation learning is also called inverse reinforcement learning (IRL).

Multiarmed bandits [79] are a simplified version of reinforcement learning that can benefit from adversarial training. Multiarmed bandit algorithms output an action for the agent without using any information about the state of the environment called context. Contextual bandits [364] extend multiarmed bandits by making output decision conditional on the state of the environment. This allows us to personalize each decision to a situation based on previous observations. The contextual bandit algorithm observes a context, makes a decision, chooses an action from a distribution of alternative actions, and observes an outcome of the decision. A reward function value is associated with every decision. The machine learning goal is to maximize average reward. Unlike supervised learning, contextual bandit algorithms do not have all the reward values for every possible action. In machine learning, contextual bandits have applications in hyperparameter optimization, feature selection, algorithm selection, active learning, collaborative clustering, and reinforcement learning. Adversarial contextual bandits create adversarial manipulations on the contexts and rewards of contextual bandits. The "regret" for a game theoretical player compares the cumulative reward for adversarial contextual bandits to the best reward in the hindsight that is possible for a policy class. Regret bounds can be derived as confidence scores on the solution concepts in game theoretical adversarial learning applied to contextual bandits solving sequential decision-making problems.

Seldin et al. [546] adversarially contaminated stochastic regimes for multiarmed bandits. Multiple control levers are proposed to update learning rate, empirical regret, and adversarial loss. Worst-case performance and regret bounds of randomized algorithms for stochastic bandits in the adversarial regimes are then investigated. House [280] has produced a thesis on game-theoretic approaches to multiarmed bandit scenarios. Here adversary is a rational, competitive controller who reduces the learner's payoffs. An analysis of the plays of the learner and counter plays of the adversary then discovers information about exploration and exploitation in long-term payoffs for a broad class of games. Matrix reconstruction and matrix completion techniques are applied to estimate the long-term payoffs. They take into account non-zero cost of learning that is comparable to opportunity cost in economics. Andersen et al. [16] investigate the capabilities of convolutional neural networks to extract useful features in deep reinforcement learning. Real-time strategy games are chosen as the application domain for short- and long-term planning. A Deep Q-Learning architecture is proposed as the solution.

Auer et al. [21] extend Deep Q-Learning architectures to the study of strategies that can guarantee the expected long-term payoff in multiarmed bandit problems for gamblers or players. A gambler's purpose is described as maximizing the total reward over a sequence of trials where each arm of the bandit has a different distribution of rewards. The adversary controls the generation of rewards associated with each arm at each time step. Adversary has access to unbounded computational power to generate the underlying stochastic process. The performance of the player is measured in terms of regret that is the difference between cumulative reward scored by the player and the total reward scored by the best arm. Such a regret is computed specific to the sequence of payoffs generated by the adversary. A lower bound and upper bound are provided for the computational complexity of the algorithm's regret in a partial information game. Such an adversarial bandit problem can be analyzed as a unknown repeated matrix game. In such a game, the player has no prior knowledge of the adversary. By contrast, the adversary is playing a repeated game against the player with complete knowledge of the game and unbounded computational power. Here value of the game for the player is the best possible expected payoff. A randomized strategy is computed through mathematical programming to achieve such a payoff.

Ilyas et al. [293] integrate blackbox adversarial example generation with bandit optimization involving priors on the distribution of the gradient of the targeted loss function. Such a blackbox threat model can only issue classification queries to the targeted network. By contrast, white-box attacks which exploit full knowledge of the gradient of the targeted loss function to create adversarial examples. Here targeted attacks in adversarial examples induce classification of the target class that is not the original class, while untargeted attacks induce a misclassification in general. To create query-efficient blackbox attacks, a least squares method from signal processing is proposed as the optimal solution to the gradient estimation problem generating adversarial examples. Incorporating data-dependent priors in the blackbox attack leads to query-efficient solutions in comparison to the state of the art. A finite difference method based on least squares regression produces information-theoretical gradient estimates of the targeted loss functions within an iterated projected gradient descent (PGD) attack scenario. The least squares model is solved with a bandit optimization algorithm.

For personalized ranking and attention modelling, Bouneffouf et al. [80] create contextual bandit with restricted context limited to a fixed feature subset accessible by the learner at each iteration. Such features are designed to handle stationary and non-stationary environments. The learning problem is to select the best feature subset so that overall reward is maximized by exploring both the feature space and the arms space. He et al. [266] propose personalized ranking with adversarial objectives for matrix factorization in recommender systems. Adversarial perturbations are crafted on the embedding vectors of users and items recommendations in collaborative filtering. Thus new training methods for personalized ranking can lead to robust recommender models. They can be extended to generic feature-based models like neural factorization machines that support a wide range of recommendation scenarios. Thus personalized ranking with adversarial learning has application in information retrieval tasks such as robust recommendation, text retrieval, web search, question answering, and knowledge graph completion.

5.3.1 Game Theoretical Adversarial Reinforcement Learning

Research into game theoretical adversarial learning can be extended into reinforcement learning since the game theoretical objective functions of adversarial machine learning can be interpreted as bi-level optimization problems [134] solved by actor-critic methods [323] of decision theory. The task of adversarial classification with reinforcement can be separated into the task of learning to predict attack preferences and the task of optimizing operational policy that explicitly abides by the operational constraints on the predictor. Then adversary's best response strategies are computed as randomized operational decisions [716]. To study the theories of robust machine learning, we can develop computational objectives and statistical inference models in randomized prediction games for adversarial algorithms discrimination, learnability, and reliability. We can compare and contrast the blackbox optimizations in game theoretical adversarial learning with multi-agent deep reinforcement learning for model generalizability. Here the research into constrained objective functions for adversarial learning is driven by the adversary's capability and control on training data and validation data taking into account application-specific attack scenarios such as effect on class priors, fraction of samples, and features manipulated by the adversary. Depending on the goal, knowledge, and capability of the adversary, these scenarios are also classified in terms of attack influence, security violation, and attack specificity. Such constrained optimization problems on shallow architectures tend to produce intractable computational algorithms for class estimation and inference of the adversarial cost functions. They necessitate the need for deep learning architectures in the statistical methods solving the optimization problems in adversarial payoff functions. In addition to operation constraints in the security policies, distance and budget constraints in the adversarial cost functions are also a research direction. The model update rules derived from the attack scenarios could impact the convergence of the training process in terms of tradeoffs between learnability and robustness of the proposed discriminative learning. We can characterize the problem of discrimination in the presence of noise in terms of a set of robust points where data encoding is a type of problem-specific error mitigation strategy in cybersecurity classifiers. Then we shall incorporate non-linearities in the classification through representing data with non-linear functions. Such an arrangement would also allow us to explore multiple choices of variational encodings of the learnable decision boundaries. Here, game theoretical payoff functions measure player-driven optimizations that improve training and inference in machine learning and uncertain environments. They also explain the impact of uncertain environments with reference to a distribution of outcomes, and, in the sense of decision-theoretic rationality around decision boundaries, payoff functions maximize the expected utility for each player participating in the game.

Contextual bandits can be combined with game theoretical adversarial learning to analyze multimodal, weakly supervised, noisy, sparse, and multi-structured training datasets found in deep knowledge representation learning over dynamic streams and complex networks. Bias-variance decomposition in the adversarial payoff functions can derive regret bounds and utility bounds for such deep learning networks. Furthermore, user or player feedback can be integrated into machine learning performance measures as validation metrics for personalized recommendation and adversarial ranking. Game theoretical adversarial learning can be used to explore neural network architectures and adversarial cost functions in the training processes implementing the data analytics for such cyber information processing tasks. Here mistake bounds framework with no-regret property for online learning provides the theoretical tools to analyze the tolerable error and update rules for the generated adversarial data. We can also define the utility bounds of neural networks within an empirical risk minimization framework for adversarial learning. Then cyber information processing tasks may be formulated as discriminative learning problems with separability criteria characterized by computational efficiency on structured data. Thus adversarial deep learning can create mistake bounds frameworks in cybersecurity applications. Here randomized prediction games can formulate the learner of robust rank aggregation. We can express the learning robustness, fairness, explainability, and transparency with game theoretical adversarial learning. Attention mechanisms in the deep generative modelling of the variational adversary's best response strategies can simulate and validate the learning environment for contextual bandits. Payoff functions can be proposed for the knowledge representations generated by deep learning networks for the objects in multimodal, multiview, and multitask predictions.

In transfer learning and stochastic optimization over the adversarial examples, deep reinforcement learning has common objectives as game theoretical adversarial deep learning. The reinforcement learning actions are typically expressed as a Markov decision process. It uses dynamic programming techniques in implementation. Sampling problems in adversarial learning can thus focus on resilience enhancements to Markov chain methods. Game theoretical modelling can focus on integrating Bayesian Stackelberg games and Markov Stackelberg games with reinforcement learning. In cybersecurity classifiers, adversarial cost functions can be investigated for reinforcement learning that robustness bounds to adversarial representations. In deep generative learning with Markov decision processes, we can construct resampling dynamics variational autoencoders used in adversarial learning as an alternative to derivative-free stochastic optimization methods in game theoretical modelling of adversaries. The stochastic optimization in game theoretical learning can benefit from the Markov security games. The game theoretical payoff functions over complex systems can benefit from the learning models involving a set of autonomous agents interacting in the shared environment within multi-agent reinforcement learning. Multi-agent environments are inherently non-stationary. The causality and stationarity of the Markov decision processes can be explored within adversarial settings based on principles for statistical inference such as expectation-maximization, minimum description length, maximum likelihood estimation, and empirical risk minimization. They have applications in data mining tasks such as classification, regression, association rule mining, and clustering.

Computational algorithms in evolutionary game theory and numerical methods in differential game theory can augment the game theoretical payoff functions with partial differential state equations of a dynamical system modelling the complex interactions in stochastic control as game theoretical objective functions. Then principles of dynamic programming can be used to study the convergence properties of game theoretical optima. Reliability guarantees can be developed for the solution concepts according to theories of sample complexity, formal verification, and fuzzy automata in the adversarial learning. Variational methods and generative models can represent the adversarial manipulations in the solution concepts for the adversarial losses and feature embeddings in cybersecurity. Proper quantification of the hypothesis set in decision problems of such research leads us into various functional problems, oracular problems, sampling tasks, and optimization problems in the game theoretical adversarial learning. Here we can compare the solutions with machine learning baselines such as the inclusion of noise in the optimization procedure, the simplification of the function landscape by increase of the model size, the schemes for derivative-free stochastic optimization, and data resampling in the context of adversarial learning algorithms. The game theoretical adversarial learning frameworks of iterative attack scenarios and defense optimizations would then be able to apply game theory to the dynamics detection, characterization, and prediction in a dynamical system. The complex dynamics detected would lead us onto adversarial training procedures for the robust optimization of deep neural networks. In cost-sensitive classifier design, we can define custom loss functions to find trends, ranks, changes, and events in the data distributions underlying the dynamic patterns mined from the data.

5.4 Computational Optimization Algorithmics for Game Theoretical Adversarial Learning

In generalized least squares models and generalized linear models for predictive analytics, classification loss functions optimize the class-conditioned data likelihood functions [244, 257] of the targeted deep networks. In this book, the adversarial cost functions regularize such likelihood functions with norms, gradients, and expectations of game theoretical objective functions inferred on the adversarial loss functions. The types of such objective functions determine the types of adversaries participating in prediction games with the classifier. In this book we have proposed adversaries solving for evolutionary objectives and variational objectives in the prediction games. The optimal values for the objectives are searched by evolutionary algorithms such as genetic algorithms, simulated annealing algorithms, and alternating least squares algorithms.

In this section we review additional computational algorithms, stochastic operators, and convergence criteria for computational optimization in deep learning models. Such a study is expected to lead us to better randomization, convergence, and parallelization in computation of the step magnitude and the step direction in our stochastic optimization methods [566]. In designing the iterative update rules of optimization algorithms and fitness functions solving for systems of equations, we are interested in robust optimization, numerical optimization, and non-linear optimization. In addition to game theoretical models, deep learning optimizations of our interest include utility functions found in expectation-maximization algorithms, maximum entropy models, learning classifier systems, deep factorization machines, and probabilistic graphical models.

Fogel [199] categorizes the simulated evolution techniques in stochastic optimization of neural networks. Depending on the facet of natural evolution (i.e., viewed as optimizing problem-solving process), the techniques are called genetic algorithms, evolution strategies, and evolutionary programming. These techniques do not use higher-order statistics of the fitness function to converge onto optimal solutions. These techniques are not as sensitive as gradient-based methods to adversarial perturbations in the fitness function. Pirlot [495] describes the strengths and weaknesses in simulated annealing (SA), Tabu Search (TS), and genetic algorithms (GAs). Ledesma et al. [351] review the procedure to practically implement simulated annealing. Bandyopadhyay et al. [29] use simulated annealing to minimize misclassification rate across decision boundaries in pattern classification. A deterministic annealing algorithm is proposed by Rose [525] to optimize the problems related to clustering, compression, classification, and regression. A hybridization of GA and SA is given by Adler [2]. SA is combined with local search methods into a Markov chain by Martin et al. [413]. Back et al. [22] and Beyer et al. [51] survey developments in evolution strategies (ESs) that allow correlated mutations in GA. Das et al. [145] review all major theoretical studies and algorithm variants of differential evolution (DE) applied to multi-objective, constrained, large-scale, and uncertain optimization problems. Pelikan et al. [489] propose linkage learning across candidate solutions in evolutionary computations.

Zhang et al. [696] survey machine learning problems in an evolutionary computation framework. Goldberg [221] provides more detail on applications of genetic algorithms in machine learning. Michalewicz [425] discusses numerical optimization of the genetic operators to lead to evolutionary programs. Bandaru et al. [27, 28] describe descriptive models and predictive models for data mining in multi-objective optimization datasets. Bertsekas [47] discusses derivative-free stochastic optimization problems. Nemirovski et al. [457] discuss convex-concave stochastic optimization of objective functions given in the form of an expectation integral. Sinha et al. [559] review evolutionary solutions to bi-level optimization problems. Suryan et al. [586] review evolutionary algorithms in inverse optimal control theory that has applications in game theory.

The operation of evolutionary algorithms in constrained environments is analyzed by Eiben [3]. Cantu-Paz [100] provides a survey of parallel constructions in genetic algorithms. Ocenasek et al. [470] survey the designs for parallel estimation of distribution algorithms. Sudholt [159] introduces design and analysis of parallel evolutionary algorithms on multicore CPU architectures. Genetic algorithms have been implemented in embarrassingly parallel programming models such as MapReduce [189, 618]. Whitley et al. [647] give guidelines for debugging and testing evolutionary computations. The no free lunch theorems for optimization [650] apply to the comparisons between optimization criteria of evolutionary computations. Whitley et al. [470] provide a theoretical analysis of the research problems, objective functions, and optimization algorithms in evolutionary computations. Comon et al. [135] propose an enhanced line search (ELS) principle to apply the alternating least squares (ALS) algorithm in iterative optimization of non-linear systems of equations represented by tensor decompositions. A theoretical analysis of simulated annealing (SA) solving for Boltzmann machine and Cauchy machine is given by Tsallis et al. [608].

5.4.1 Game Theoretical Learning

Algorithmic game theory (AGT) [464] is a research area that spans game theory and computer science. It is concerned with the design and analysis of algorithms in strategic environments. Typically the input to the algorithm is distributed among multiple players or agents who have stakes in the algorithm's output. The analysis aspect of AGT applies game theoretical tools such as the best response dynamics in the implementation and analysis of algorithms. The design aspect of AGT is about the computational modelling of the game theoretical properties and algorithmic patterns in the design and improvement of algorithms complexities. Internet-based interactions between computing agents can be modelled with the game theoretical equilibria associated with the data analytics modelling. Computational social choice is a research area that extends the game theoretical models to multi-agent systems that aggregate individual agents' preferences within online mechanisms.

5.4.1.1 Randomization Strategies in Game Theoretical Adversarial Learning

Grunwald et al. [237] show the equivalence between maximum entropy modelling and minimizing worst-case expected loss from an equilibrium theory of zero-sum games for loss functions and decision problems. A generalized relative entropy with regularity conditions is proposed to analyze robust classifiers that minimize divergence between distributions. A minmax theorem is then proposed for Kullback-Leibler divergence between training data and adversarial data distributions treated as a generalized exponential family of distributions. This gives a decision-theoretic interpretation of maximum entropy principle where the adversarial loss function is not only regarded as a logarithmic score. A decision-theoretic definition of discrepancy or relative entropy between probability distributions for training and adversarial data generalizes Bregman divergences to loss functions in machine learning. Maximum entropy modelling is considered to be a version of robust Bayes classifiers.

Cost-sensitive classifiers in machine learning have benefitted from zero-sum game properties in game theory. Adversarial learning algorithms have made improvements on the minmax game formulations to arrive at robust classifiers. Rezek et al. [513] point out the equivalence between inferences drawn on previous observation made in game theory and machine learning. Smooth best responses in fictitious play of repeated games are contrasted with Bayesian inference methods of machine learning integrated over adversarial distributions rather than empirical averages. Then game theory is used in the analysis and design of variational learning algorithms. For clustering a mixture of distributions, the variational learning algorithms exhibit strong convergence properties and update rules. Proposed solutions are closely related to developments in probabilistic graphical models. So probabilistic graphical models can lead to efficient algorithms for calculating the Nash equilibrium in large multiplayer games for supervised machine learning. In general machine learning algorithms design for stationary environments in an idealized academic setting can benefit from a game theoretical analysis of non-stationary scenarios often found in dynamic real-world applications of machine learning techniques.

5.4.1.2 Adversarial Deep Learning in Robust Games

Bowling et al. [82] examine multi-agent reinforcement learning using a framework of stochastic games. Stochastic games are treated as an extension of Markov decision processes to multiple agents. The reinforcement learning of an agent's policy in the presence of other learning agents is analyzed for learning properties called rationality and convergence. To play a part in arriving at the equilibrium solution, the rationality property requires a player to adopt a best response strategy to learn a policy given remaining players have played stationary strategies. The convergence property ensures that all the players participating in the stochastic game eventually end up in a stationary policy conditioned on other players' learning algorithms. If both these properties are satisfied, then all the players are guaranteed to converge to a Nash equilibrium. Each state in a stochastic game is viewed as a matrix game. The game theoretical players transition from one matrix game to another matrix game after receiving payoffs determined by their joint action. The reinforcement learning algorithms considered are single-agent learners, joint action learners, and d minimax-Q. A variable learning rate is used to update the Q-value estimates in policy hill-climbing. It is comparable to randomized weighting algorithms in evolutionary game theory that redistribute weights among mistaken experts.

Stochastic game may be defined as a collection of normal-form games that the agents play repeatedly. It can be represented as a probabilistic automaton in which states are the games and transition labels are joint action-payoff pairs. A repeated game such as the iterated prisoner's dilemma is a stochastic game with only one state. A Markov decision process is a stochastic game with only one player. A deterministic strategy specifies a choice of action for the game theoretical player. A mixed strategy is a probability distribution over deterministic strategies. Nash equilibrium of sequential games has been extended to the solution concept for stochastic games called Markov perfect equilibrium. Stochastic games can be combined with Bayesian games to arrive at a Bayesian Nash equilibrium. Stochastic two-player games on directed graphs are used to model discrete systems operating in an unknown adversarial environment. The discrete system configurations and its adversarial environments are represented as the vertices of the directed graph. The transitions between nodes correspond to joint actions within the discrete system. A path in the directed graph corresponds to an execution of the operational system. A variety of solution concepts such as positional equilibria, stationary equilibria, randomized equilibria, and finite-state equilibria [615] are possible in the stochastic games.

Lippi et al. [373] propose models and algorithms from statistical relational learning (SRL) as tools for the analysis and design of game theoretical modelling in stochastic games. So first-order logic and probabilistic graphical models such as Bayesian networks or Markov networks can represent the uncertainty in games due to dependencies between random variables. Statistical inference algorithms from SRL such as variational methods can find Nash equilibria and Pareto-optimal solutions to game theoretical adversarial learning problems. Here Pareto-optimal equilibrium to the games are a set of strategy profiles for the players where no can increase their payoff without decreasing the payoff of another player. In contrast, Nash equilibrium is reached when the profile chosen by every player in the game is the best response with respect to profiles chosen by the remaining players. Both Pareto-optimal and Nash equilibrium can be extended to multiplayer games. Structure learning algorithms from SRL such as Markov logic networks can produce interpretable probabilistic logic clauses to describe the strategies of an adversary at a high level to humans. Here graphical games apply game theoretical models to combinatorial graphs in machine learning and Monte Carlo tree search can predict the evolution of game theoretical adversarial manipulations. Graphical games consider players as nodes in a graph and edges represent their interactions. So the payoff of a player depends on that of its neighbors rather than all the players in the game. This leads to several local payoff matrices for a player. Logic formalisms in SRL such as inductive logic programming can address knowledge representation learning on games to describe domain of interest in game theory such as strategies, alliances, rules, relationships, and dependencies among players. They can also discover information about the external environment for adversarial learning. Probabilistic reasoning is also useful to deal with missing or incomplete information for decision-making in game theoretical modelling for machine learning. So SRL has application in decision-making scenarios over reinforcement learning and adversary modelling. Markov logic in game theoretical adversarial learning allows us to model adversarial knowledge in terms of logic predicates about evidence (known facts) or query (facts to be inferred). It can be extended to decision-theoretic framework attaching utility functions to first-order clauses in Markov logic decision networks. Expectation-maximization algorithms can be constructed to infer the value of logic predicates. Their relational nature can be exploited to model collective classification algorithms in multiplayer games with interpretable strategies for real-world applications.

Aghassi et al. [4] propose distribution-free robust optimization to contend with payoff uncertainty in incomplete-information games. A robust optimization equilibrium is analyzed for finite games with a bounded polyhedral payoff uncertainty set. Such an equilibrium can be contrasted with non-cooperative, simultaneous-move, one-shot, finite games with complete information leading to a Nash equilibrium. At Nash equilibrium the game theoretical players maximize expected payoff with respect to the probability distributions given by mixed strategy spaces. Such worst-case expected utility models are well-suited for analyzing decision-theoretic situations characterized by uncertainty modelling around the adversarial risk assessments in distributional information available for machine learning as training, testing, and validation datasets. Here sources of uncertainty in the modelling are due to uncertainty in each player payoffs given tuples of actions, uncertainty in players' behaviors, and prior probability distributions around multiple player configurations. To solve incomplete-information games, distribution-free decision criterion of minimax regret is used for the optimization of online learning. The robust game proposed by Aghassi et al. [4] is comparable to such online games. The performance validation criteria for machine learning designed with such game theoretical modelling is then expressible in terms of a player's worst-case expected payoff. The game theoretical equilibria are formulated as dimension-reducing, component-wise projection of the solution set for a system of multilinear equations and inequalities. They can be extended to robust finite games that have additional private information about player's beliefs.

Cohen et al. [133] conduct a multiperturbation Shapley value analysis to estimate usefulness of features in forward selection and backward elimination of feature selection algorithms. The filtered features are able to optimize performance measures over unseen data such as accuracy, error rate, and area under ROC curve. Thus game theoretical modelling of feature selection can do a dimensionality reduction to create feature subsets for enhancing the prediction performance, reducing measurement and storage requirements, reducing training and prediction times, providing better understanding of the underlying data distribution, and producing a data visualization of relevant features. Shapley value of a feature measures its performance in a feature subset. Bounded sets theory is combined with Shapley value estimation to discover an efficient algorithm for extracting robust features in classification problems. Pruning irrelevant features decreases the generalization error of the classifiers. A distribution of feature contributions is used to guide the feature selection algorithms. Adversarial noise can play a major role in manipulating such a distribution to craft low-performing classifiers.

Sun et al. [583] propose a cooperative game theory-based framework to evaluate the discriminatory power of each feature in the context of interrelated features for a feature selection filter. Such a filter can be integrated with any learning algorithm to produce an efficient classifier. A solution for cooperative game constructs a value for each player to create a characteristic function measuring the player's contributions to the game. Conditional mutual information is the reweighting mechanism to evaluate class-dependent relevance of a feature to a feature subset that has been selected previously in the learning algorithm. Banzhaf power index is assigned to each feature based on its marginal contribution to intrinsic correlation properties among features such as causality, interdependence, and independence. Such feature subsets are then used to calculate the proportion of winning coalitions in the payoff function calculation. Dynamic programming is used to implement the cooperative game with reduced time complexity.

Chalkiadakis et al. [110] give a survey of computational algorithms in cooperative game theory. Particular emphasis is placed on efficiently computing solution concepts and compact representations for games. An overview of welfare-maximizing algorithms for game theoretical adversarial learning forming coalitions and bargains is also provided. Combinatorial optimization in machine learning problems can benefit from the discussion on induced subgraph games, minimum cost spanning tree games, and network flow games. Dynamic programming approaches to optimal coalition structure generation are also discussed. They can be adapted to anytime algorithms that produce incrementally better solutions with more time or computational resources.

Garg et al. [211] develop game theoretical modelling for feature clustering. Features are viewed as rational players of a coalitional game and coalitions are interpreted as clusters. Nash stable partition (NSP) is the solution concept from coalitional game theory is used to provide a final clustering configuration of the features. Desirable properties in the clusters can be chosen with reference to the various game theoretical payoff functions. NSP is found by solving an integer linear program (ILP). A hierarchical clustering approach is then proposed to scale the clustering with graph partitioning. All features selected in a cluster are relevant and complementary to each other. To perform feature extraction using the clustering technique, a feature ranking of the feature clusters is also proposed.

Bector et al. [39] review fuzzy mathematical programming in game theoretical modelling. Fuzzy sets can be applied to research areas such as mathematical programming and matrix game theory that occur at the interface of game theory and decision theory. Fuzzy environment can provide generalization to the linear and quadratic programming solving game theoretical objectives in constrained matrix games within two-player non-zero sum games having fuzzy goals. Matrix games with fuzzy payoffs can model multi-objective linear programming problems in adversarial learning. Several solution concepts for such fuzzy matrix games are then described. Fuzziness of the decision function for an adversarial classifier can be modelled with respect to adversarial learning objectives, environments, and constraints. It leads to fuzzy mathematical programming problems in game theoretical adversarial learning. For instance, fuzzy preference relations can be used for knowledge representation learning algorithms over multimodal datasets to eventually solve modality constrained mathematical programming problems formulating the game theoretical models in machine learning. Computational algorithms must be developed to find the optimal solutions for such fuzzy optimization problems in game theoretical adversarial learning.

Perc et al. [490] survey cooperation in evolutionary game theory to solve problems called social dilemmas that represent interaction stochasticity between game theoretical players. An evolution of strategies, promoters of cooperation, and co-evolutionary rules are used to express the emergence of cooperation and defection in evolutionary games. Dynamical interactions between players can be studied with the co-evolutionary rules over complex networks representing interaction network, data population growth, mobility of players, and aging of players. Ficici et al. [193] introduce game theoretical modelling in co-evolutionary memory mechanisms. The collection of salient traits of memory is represented as a mixed strategy. The memory embodies solution of co-evolutionary process obtained at Nash equilibrium. The memory can be subject to resource limitations during training. Memory and drift in co-evolution are interpreted as sampling errors and variational biases in game theoretical modelling. Sensitivities and contingencies around the fitness function evaluation of co-evolution processes can cause a machine learning system to learn, forget, and relearn the memory traits in a cyclic fashion. The solution concept in game theory then represents collection of memory traits belonging to a desired or correct set. The proposed "Nash memory" mechanism accumulates a collection of the traits as best response strategies. Nash equilibrium strategies provide best response solutions expressing the security level of the evolutionary game as a highest expected payoff reached by all the players acting as a collective. This security level is also known as the value of the game. A search heuristic is designed on the co-evolving population that is able to relieve the population of the burden of representing the solution and concentrate on search to improve the solution represented by the memory. Polynomial time algorithms are used to solve a zero-sum game with linear programming. The strategy space for finding Nash memory may be finite or infinite, countable, or uncountable. Herbert et al. [272] propose game theoretical modelling for competitive learning in self-organizing maps (SOM). The focus of the training process in SOM-based clustering is to find a neuron that is most similar to the input vector. The proposed extension GTSOM evaluates the overall quality of the SOM by arriving at a globally optimal position using game theory to propose dynamic and adaptive update rules to the neuron weights that are able to account for density mismatch in clustering problems. The clusters are described in terms of the actual input data and the neurons associated with the data. Game theory is able to rank the neurons to determine the neurons providing greatest increase in SOM quality according to distance from the input vector. Additional quality measures on the neurons can also be introduced to consider related feature maps extracted from the data. Game theoretical strategies are proposed to adjust the learning rate of the SOM such that the input vector will have an increased likelihood to be closer to a different neuron in the next iteration of the training algorithm. A set of game theoretical actions details the clustering neighborhood and density to distinguish or diminish the desired clusters. Training terminates if the SOM has reached a user-defined threshold for the clustering quality preferences.

Schuurmans et al. [544] investigate connections between supervised deep learning methods and game theory. No-regret strategies in game theoretical modelling are found to be effective stochastic training methods for supervised learning problems. Regret matching is proposed as an alternative to gradient descent to efficiently optimize the stochastic performance of supervised deep learning. A supervised learning process over a directed acyclic neural network with differentiable convex activation functions is expressed as a simultaneous move game with simple player actions and utilities. Players choose their actions independent of actions taken by other players. The cumulative regret for each player is defined in terms of their expected utility function. Domain experts and nature can also be accounted for in the mapping of strategies and actions for the learner. A close correspondence is found between convex online learning and two-person zero-sum games. Exponentiated weight algorithm and regret matching are proposed as constrained training algorithms for supervised learning. Training results about the regret bounds, convergence criteria, and global optima of the constrained training algorithms are compared with projected stochastic gradient descent and stochastic gradient descent. The constrained training algorithms are found to be highly competitive in high-dimensional sparse feature spaces in supervised learning networks. Nash equilibrium is guaranteed to be one of the local optima if not the global optima for the deep neural network training. Regret-matching algorithms in evaluation are found to achieve lower misclassification errors than standard deep learning methods. However, the proposed theory does not apply to neural networks with non-smooth activation functions within several hidden layers.

To arrive at the global optima, Oliehoek et al. [472] model generative adversarial networks (GANs) according to finite games in mixed strategies. The proposed solution concept monotonically converges to a resource-bounded Nash equilibrium that is saddle points in mixed strategies. The solution concepts can be made more accurate with additional computational resources for approximate best response computations. The proposed training algorithm for deep generative modelling is able to avoid common problems such as mode collapse, mode degeneration, mode omission, and mode forgetting. The proposed game-theoretic method is called Parallel Nash Memory. It can be exploited to produce improvements in the robust training metrics of classifiers/generator networks performance. The discriminator and the generator models can then be updated according to the best response strategy at each iteration. They can explicitly limit the allowed strategies with finite-state machines. The resulting robust models yield better generative performance at the same total complexity and are closer to a global Nash equilibrium. They can be extended with zero-sum polymatrix games and reduced games with adversarial data guiding the training.

Hsieh et al. [281] also propose training strategies for GANs to discover mixed Nash equilibria. Further sampling methods are proposed to solve the mixed strategy games. The proposed mean-approximation sampling scheme can augment the global optimization frameworks for game theoretical adversarial learning. Specifically, a mean-approximation sampling scheme for bi-affine games is investigated to provision practical training algorithms for GANs. The robust training reformulates the GAN distributions over finite strategies as probability measures over continuous parameter sets. A sampling method called entropic mirror descent estimates such probability measures in a tractable manner. Thus the robust training reformulates the training dynamics of gradient-based algorithms into minmax programs solved with mathematical programming and algorithmic game theory. In the experiments, the stationary optima found by gradient-based algorithms such as SGD, Adam, and RMSProp are found to be not locally or globally minmax optima. This leads to further development in the intuitions of non-convex optimization applied to machine learning validations.

Tembine et al. [595] present an interplay between distributionally robust games and deep generative adversarial networks. A Bregman discrepancy between adversarial and training data distributions is constructed to avoid using a second derivative of the objective function in the optimization algorithm applied to GANs. GANs are formulated as distributionally robust games in adversarial multi-agent settings. The players in the strategic-form game are the neuron units. The plays are the learned weights. The game theoretical objective functions are loss functions obtained from the mismatch between the output and real data measurement. The convergence rate of the proposed deep learning algorithm is derived using a mean estimate. Mean-field learning is seen as a candidate class of algorithms to be investigated for high-dimensional deep learning with games theoretical adversaries acting as decision-makers. f-divergence and Wasserstein metric are used in the experimental evaluation to find the mismatch between generated data and true data. So the hidden layers in a neural network are seen as dynamic interactive environments represented as games. The multimodal output functions in the deep neural networks introduce further difficulties in the game theoretical optimizations of strategic and interdependent parameters in the neural network training algorithms. Misalignment between the updates of the components of neural networks training motivates the need for game-theoretic payoffs in training algorithms such as error backpropagation, stochastic gradient descent, and mean-field or population-based algorithms (such as genetic, swarm, and simulated annealing). The estimation of the expected value of the gradient in the derivative-based methods further requires sampling methods such as Monte Carlo sampling, reinforcement learning, or population-based sampling integrated with continuous action multi-agent adversarial games. Starting from various dimensions of dynamical systems, such a strategic deep learning or deep game-theoretic learning is also useful in addressing hyper-parametrization, curse of dimensionality, and error propagation. The relevant game-theoretic solution concepts for the data-driven model-based strategic deep learning across various threat models include Nash equilibrium, Stackelberg solution, Pareto optima, Berge solution, bargaining solution, and correlated equilibrium.

5.4.1.3 Robust Optimization in Adversarial Learning

Xu et al. [669] regularize support vector machines within a probabilistic robust optimization formulation for classification. The robust optimization minimizes the worst possible empirical error on the true underlying distribution of the training data samples mixed with non-i.i.d. (potentially adversarial) disturbance. The proposed robust optimization offers protection to noise, helps control overfitting, and leads to generalization performance. The regularization terms solve for non-box-type uncertainty sets. A chance-constrained classifier is the outcome of the robust optimization. It is a classifier with probabilistic constraints on misclassification rates. A Bayesian setup selects the regularization coefficients without cross-validation. This research contrasts with classifier regularization bounding the complexity of the function class in a PAC structural risk minimization approach to classification. Robustness is due to a minmax optimization performed over all possible disturbances. The robustness bounds on corrupted samples are able to deal with non-i.i.d. data where training samples and the testing samples are drawn from different distributions, or some adversary manipulates the samples to prevent them from being correctly labelled. Results are compared with robust statistics such as the influence function approach for a regression estimator or a classification algorithm constructed under a small perturbation of the statistics model consisting of non-smooth loss functions. In algorithm design, the proposed robust optimization has the additional advantage of robustifying a learning algorithm when the nature of the perturbation is known a priori or can be well estimated. The statistical consistency proofs on the robust learning in the sample space replace metric entropy, VC dimension, and stability conditions in the feature space for support vector machines with robustness conditions on the expected classification error and regularized loss. Such a view of robust classifiers is able to derive sample complexity bounds for a broad class of algorithms in supervised learning. It forms explicit links between regularization and robustness in pattern classification.

In binary feature spaces, Li et al. [357] represent rational, objective-driven adversaries based on mixed-integer linear programming with constraint generation. An iterative retraining framework is then proposed for adversarial loss minimization in evasion attacks. The resulting game theoretical model is called Stackelberg game multi-adversary model. A new adversarial cost function is proposed to allow feature cross-substitution making a tradeoff between feature selection through sparse regularization and adversarial evasion. The proposed bi-level optimization problem does not require modifications in the learning algorithm. The adversarial risk function on training data models a collection of adversaries. It computes the empirical risk of machine learning in adversarial settings. A non-zero sum Stackelberg equilibrium is found between a single defender (classifier) and multiple followers (evaders) operating within high-cost budgeting constraints. Robustness regularization of the learning algorithm is comparable to robust statistics calculated on data contamination in a worst-case sense for both discrete and continuous features.

Vorobeychik et al. [622] characterize optimal randomization schemes in adversarial classification. The classifier acts as a defender against adversarial reverse engineering and classifier manipulation. In the experiments, the defender's optimal policy is to either randomize uniformly for targeted attacks after ignoring the baseline classification accuracy, or not to randomize at all but choose the better classifier for observed (or inferred) classification correctness and defense against indiscriminate attacks. Such a defense mechanism is of interest in machine learning techniques for cyber (or physical) security such as intrusion detection, spam filtering, and malware generation framed as prediction tasks. In such security domains, the adversary will actively undermine the classifier with evasion and sabotage leading to misclassification patterns and labels. The adversarial classifier can then leverage game theoretical modelling of the learner-attacker interactions, study the algorithmic complexity of the adversarial attack scenarios, and propose randomization-based classifiers. Further an adversarial query-based reverse engineering of efficiently learn the linear classifier used by the defender to solve convex optimization problems in learnable classes is also proposed. It has application in randomization-based cybersecurity domains such as moving target or dynamic defense classification schemes. Here experimental evaluation finds that the better the baseline performance of classifiers, the worse the performance after a targeted attack such as spear phishing. The error rates after targeted attack exploiting misclassifications do not directly depend on the baseline error rate of the classifiers determining the operational security postures.

Hashimoto et al. [255] propose a distributionally robust risk optimization. It minimizes the worst-case risk over all distributions close to the empirical distribution representing training data. The risk mitigation strategy addresses the effect of minority classes in average loss and accuracy calculations called representation disparity. It is observed in face recognition, language identification, dependency parsing, part-of-speech tagging, recommender systems, video captioning, speech recognition, and machine translation. The risk mitigation classifiers tend to achieve fairness in supervised learning over protected labels through constraints calibration into the robust optimization criteria. The distributionally robust risk optimization can accommodate adversarial and high-noise settings to design fair algorithms on unknown latent groups. Minimizing expected risk in machine learning may produce models with very poor performance on worst-case inputs. Uesato et al. [614] define a tractable surrogate objective to the true adversarial risk which tends to be computationally intractable. Optimizing the adversarial risk motivates the study of machine learning model's performance on worst-case inputs. Such an adversarial risk has application in high-stakes situations involving machine learning systems for malware detection, computer vision, robotics, natural language processing, and reinforcement learning.

Wong et al. [652] propose deep ReLU-based classifiers robust against norm-bounded adversarial perturbations on the training data. A robust optimization procedure minimizes the worst-case loss over a convex outer approximation of the set of final-layer activations achieved by norm-bounded perturbation to the input. It is solved with a linear program represented as a deep neural network trained by backpropagation of errors. The class predictions of such robust classifiers are proved to not change within the convex outer bound to the loss function values called "adversarial polytope." Such a worst-case loss analysis of neural networks is valid even for their deep counterparts including representation layers such as convolutional layers. This research is an attempt at deriving tractable robustness bounds for adversarial perturbation regions across the layers in deep networks. It is contrast to research work on combinatorial solvers to verify properties of neural networks. They include satisfiability modulo theories (SMT) solvers and integer programming approaches. However, the state of the art in such verification procedures is too computationally costly to be integrated easily into the current robust training procedures. The data analytics task to solve such convex robust optimization problems is to solve an optimization problem where some of the problem data is unknown but belongs to a bounded set. Provable robustness bounds on the adversarial error and loss of a classifier are derived from the dual solutions of the optimization problem. They can be used in the definition of provable performance metrics measuring robustness and detection of adversarial attacks in custom loss functions evaluated on training, testing and validation datasets.

Sinha et al. [560] propose a distributionally robust optimization problem based on the Wasserstein distance metric. It can be augmented into the adversarial training procedure of machine learning model's parameter updates faced with the worst-case perturbations to the training data. It is able to achieve provable robustness to smooth loss functions with little adversarial cost relative to the empirical risk minimization of the learning loss. It can be used to provide certifying guarantees on computational and statistical performance of adversarial training procedures. Adversarial examples are formed due to a Lagrangian worst-case perturbation of smooth loss functions. The proposed approach to distributional robustness is related to parametric optimization models constrained on moments, support, and directional deviations in training data distribution. It is also related to non-parametric measures for distance between probability distributions such as f-divergence, Kullback-Leibler divergence, and Wasserstein distance.

Rauber et al. [508] create a Python package to generate adversarial perturbations and compare the robustness of machine learning models. The Python package has modules for creating a model on input data, making predictions on output as class probabilities, a misclassification criterion to define adversarial examples, a distance measure on the size of the adversarial perturbations, and an attack algorithm to generate the adversarial perturbation given the input, label, model, and adversarial criterion. Attack algorithms perform hyperparameter tuning to find the minimum perturbation.

5.4.2 Generative Learning

Goodfellow et al. [225] summarize the need for regularization in deep learning. Regularization in deep learning is discussed with reference to underfitting, over-fitting, bias, variance, and generalization to control the computational complexity of machine learning models. Regularized machine learning models perform well on not only the training data but also on new inputs. Regularization terms in the training objective functions are penalties and constraints designed to tradeoff the reduction in the test error with possible increase in train error. Sparse representations, noise robustness, dataset augmentation, adversarial training, semi-supervised learning, multitask learning, and manifold learning are listed as some of the novel regularization techniques to introduce regularization into adversarial learning losses.

Goodfellow et al. [225] also survey the use of analytical optimizations specialized to improve the training procedures in deep learning. They take gradient-based optimization as a comparison baseline in the benchmarking experiments. Their objective is to find the neural network parameters that reduce a cost function involving a performance measure evaluated on training dataset, regularization terms evaluated on training dataset, and adversarial losses evaluated on validation dataset. Here optimization algorithms must contend with parameter initialization strategies, adaptive learning rates during training, and information contained in the second derivatives of the cost function. The goal of an optimized machine learning algorithm can be said to be to minimize the expected generalization error by computing the average training error called empirical risk. The empirical risk minimization tends to overfit to the training dataset. This must be accounted for in the convergence criteria for optimization leading to batch, incremental, stochastic, online, deterministic, and randomized optimization algorithms for deep learning on dynamic data streams. Ill-conditioned problems, local minima, saddle points, exploding gradients, and inexact gradients are listed as some of the theoretical challenges in the optimization algorithms design. Machine learning paradigms such as curriculum learning, generative learning, metric learning, and transfer learning are useful to solve such problems with specialized neural network architectures.

Wang et al. [637] discuss the relation between robustness and optimization of secure deep learning. Adversarial training with projected gradient descent (PGD) attack is chosen as the minmax optimization problem. The inner maximization problem generates adversarial examples by maximizing the classification loss. The outer minimization computes model parameters by minimizing the adversarial loss on adversarial examples. First-order stationary condition (FOSC) having closed-form solution for constrained optimization is proposed as such an adversarial loss. It constructs a dynamic training strategy for robust learning with a gradual increase in the convergence quality of the generated adversarial examples. As a defense mechanism, the adversarial training technique is comparable to moderately robust techniques such as input denoising, gradient regularization, Lipschitz regularization, defensive distillation, model compression, and curriculum adversarial training. The selected PGD attack scenario is comparable to fast gradient sign method (FGSM), Jacobian-based saliency map attack (JSMA), C&W attack, and Frank-Wolfe-based attack. Gradually increasing the computational hardness of adversarial examples is an idea based in the curriculum learning paradigm for machine learning. It leads to a speed up in convergence and improves generalization of deep learning networks. A learning curriculum within a sequential ordering mechanism is designed for adversarial training. The experimental results of the adversarial training are benchmarked against the state-of-the-art attacks on WideResNet.

5.4.2.1 Deep Generative Models for Game Theoretical Adversarial Learning

Kunin et al. [337] study the loss landscape in regularized linear autoencoders (LAE) acting as models for deep representation learning. Autoencoders are trained to minimize the distance between the data and its reconstruction. They learn a subspace spanned by the basis vectors learnt from the training data. LAE is connected with rank-reduced regression models like principal component analysis (PCA). L_2 regularization's effect on orthogonality patterns in the encoder and decoder is investigated. LAE are interpreted as generative processes. Denoising autoencoder and contractive autoencoder are discussed as variants of LAE.

Vincent et al. [621] stack layers of denoising autoencoders in deep neural networks that is able to demonstrate a lower classification error. Higher-level representations of the training data are obtained from the denoising criteria acting as an unsupervised objective for feature detectors. It is able to boost the performance of support vector machines in multi-label classification. The reconstruction errors in the proposed denoising autoencoder can be considered to be an improvement on log-likelihood estimations in stochastic restricted Boltzmann machines utilizing contrastive divergence updates. The infomax principle from independent component analysis is exploited as the denoising criteria maximizing the mutual information between input random variables and higher-level representations. Empirical average of mutual information on training samples is taken as the unbiased estimator for unsupervised learning. The encoder's loss function is expressed as an affine+sigmoid function, while the decoder's loss function is expressed an affine with squared error loss or affine+sigmoid with cross-entropy loss. Minimizing the reconstruction error combines the encoder and decoder loss functions while training the stacked autoencoder. Such a reconstruction error is equivalent to maximizing a lower bound on the mutual information between input and learnt representation. A lower-dimensional learnt representation can be considered as a lossy compressed representation of the input. The learnt representation can be sparse coding representation, dense compressed representation, and variable-size representation that is suitable for extracting useful features in the construction of deep neural network classifiers. Successful unsupervised regularized denoising criteria define and learns the data manifolds. Adversarial examples are likely to be farther from the data manifolds than training examples. A data corruption process can be parameterized into the denoising-based training signals given to the deep denoising autoencoder's learning algorithm.

Kingma et al. [316] introduce stochastic variational inference for efficient learning in directed probabilistic models for autoencoders. An approximate inference model is proposed for i.i.d. datasets leading to intractable posterior distributions in maximum likelihood estimation and maximum a posteriori inference where expectation-maximization algorithms cannot be used. A pattern recognition model in a probabilistic encoder is optimized to perform efficient approximate posterior inference without resorting to expensive sampling methods. It has applications in adversarial learning recognition, denoising, inpainting, representation, and visualization within online, non-stationary settings. The proposed autoencoder mimics hidden random processes underlying the training data distribution to generate artificial variational data that resembles the observed training data. It can be extended toward deep generative architectures, dynamic Bayesian networks, and supervised learning with latent variables and complicated noise distributions.

Variational Inference Alain et al. [8] suggest that autoencoders learn the local manifold structure of the data distribution underlying the training data. So a regularized reconstruction function in autoencoders is able to characterize the shape of the probability density function generating the data as a vector field around a manifold. The autoencoder captures the derivative of the log density with respect to the input as a denoising score matching function. The score matching function arises out of tradeoffs between minimizing reconstruction error and regularizing the autoencoder. The autoencoder training criteria are taken to be a tractable alternative to maximum likelihood estimation. The autoencoder can act as an implicit density model to sample the essence of the target data distribution underlying the training data.

In neural generative models, Mondal et al. [438] hypothesize that the dimensionality of the autoencoder's latent space has affects the quality of generated data. The quality of generated data is compared between autoencoder models and generative adversarial networks. Optimal performance is obtained when dimensionality of the latent space of the autoencoder matches with that of the generative latent space. A Mask Adversarial Auto-Encoder (MaskAAE) is proposed to satisfy such conditions by masking the spurious latent dimensions. Thus deep variational methods can be considered as probabilistic generative models. The latent space representation of data is due to a deterministic or stochastic encoder. The generated data is from a decoder realizing a learnable family of function approximators. The data distribution in the latent space follows a known probability distribution from which sampling is feasible. The algorithmic masking procedure minimizes norm-based reconstruction error and divergence metrics such as JS divergence, KL divergence, or Wasserstein's distance between a masked mixture density prior distribution and the masked encoded latent distribution.

Zhao et al. [701] train deep latent variable models for discrete structures such as text sequences and discretized images in textual style transfer. They are extensions of the Wasserstein autoencoder framework and formalize the autoencoder optimization problem as an optimal transport problem. Different fixed and learned prior distributions from parameterized generators in the adversarially regularized autoencoder can target generative representations in the output space. A transfer learning-based parametric generator is trained to ignore targeted attributes of the input. It can be used for sentiment or style transfer between unaligned source and target domains. Image and sentence manipulations can be done in the latent space via interpolation and vector arithmetic to induce change in the output space. Constructing the style of interpolation requires a combinatorial search. A latent space attribute classifier is introduced to adversarially train the encoder. Such autoencoders accommodate smooth transformations in adversarially regularized continuous latent space to produce complex modifications of generated outputs within the data manifold. An information divergence measure such as the f-divergence or Wasserstein distance minimizes the divergence between learned code distributions of the true and model distributions. The cross-entropy loss in the autoencoder upper bounds the total variational distance between the model/data distributions. Discrete decoders such as recurrent neural networks can be incorporated into the model distributions. Here non-differentiable objective functions are solved by policy gradient methods in reinforcement learning and Gumbel-Softmax distributions to approximate the sampling of discrete data. The autoencoder learning can be interpreted as learning a deep generative model with latent variables so long as the marginalized encoded space is the same as the prior. Adversarial regularization has an impact on discrete encoding, smoothness of encoder, reconstruction in decoder, and output manipulation through prior. The resulting deep latent variable models are sensitive to the training setup and performance measures. Improving their adversarial robustness shall lead to models for complex discrete structures such as documents.

Mescheder et al. [423] unify variational autoencoders (VAEs) and generative adversarial networks (GANs). VAEs are expressed as latent variable models to learn complex probability distributions from training data. An extension called adversarial variational Bayes (AVB) with an interpretable inference model is proposed. It has an auxiliary discriminative network formulating maximum likelihood estimation as a two-player game not unlike the game in GANs. The proposed deep generative model is better than generative models such as Pixel-RNNs, PixelCNNs, real NVP, and

Plug & Play generative networks. In log-likelihood estimation, it has the advantage of GANs to yield generative representations of the training data as well as that of VAEs to yield both a generative model and an inference model. Here a highly expressive inference model combined with a strong decoder allows the VAE to make use of the latent space representations in arriving at the reconstruction error. An adversarial loss in the inference model encourages the aggregated posterior to be close to the prior over the latent variables. Bayesian parameter estimation approximates the posterior distribution as a probabilistic model. It can approximate the variational lower bound for learning a latent variable model minimizing the KL divergence between the training and latent data distributions. The probabilistic model is able to learn multimodal posterior distributions and generate samples for complex datasets. A deep convolutional network is used as the decoder network. The encoder network architecture consisting of a learned basis noise vectors is able to efficiently compute the moments of latent data distribution that is conditioned on the input data distribution. The inference model can represent any family of conditional distributions over the latent variables. The experimental validation is benchmarked against the annealed importance sampling (AIS) method for decoder based generative models.

Blei et al. [72] discuss the utilization of variational inference and optimization in Bayesian statistics for estimating computationally expensive posterior probability densities. Variational methods are found to be faster than sampling methods such as Markov chain Monte Carlo. They measure the information divergence between the approximated data distribution to the posited family of target densities. Here mean-field variational inference is applicable to exponential family models such as maximum entropy models forming the loss functions in machine learning. They can be used in the stochastic optimization of game theoretical adversarial learning. Grunwald et al. [237] show a equivalence theory between maximizing a generalized relative entropy and minimizing worst-case expected loss that is based on zero-sum games between decision-maker and Nature. Robust Bayes acts are found to minimize discrepancy or divergence between distributions maximizing entropy. They are expressed as solutions to minmax theorems on Kullback-Leibler divergence computed for a generalized exponential family of target densities. The minmax theorems are called redundancy-capacity theorems in information theory. Generalized relative entropy is an uncertainty function associated with the loss function for training machine learning models. Additive models for statistical inference that are based on Bregman divergences are special cases of the generalized exponential families. They can be used to derive scoring rules such as Brier score and Bregman score in the decision problems for multi-label classification. A Pythagorean property of Kullback-Leibler divergence leads to an interpretation of minimum relative entropy inference as an information projection operation between adversarial and training data distributions on discrete sample spaces. It can be extended with entropy-related optimization problems based in information theory about moment inequalities and generalized entropy families. Such generalized entropies include Renyi entropies and Fisher information interpreted from a minimax perspective.

Adversarial Autoencoders Bengio et al. [45] discuss denoising and contractive autoencoders for the implicitly learnt density function estimating the underlying data-generating distribution. It can handle both discrete and continuous-valued features with arbitrary corruptions. The reconstruction losses are seen as log-likelihood estimation. Regularization of the reconstruction prevents the autoencoder from learning a simple identity function and instead behaves as a feature learner for supervised learning. In a probabilistic interpretation of autoencoders reconstruction loss, the denoising reconstruction error estimates the energy function for score matching within a Gaussian restricted Boltzmann machine.

Mnih et al. [434] propose a non-iterative approximate inference method to train sigmoid belief networks. It implements efficient exact sampling from the variational posterior in a feedforward network. The training algorithm updates both the neural network model and the inference network by maximizing a variational lower bound on the marginal log-likelihood. Experimental results are shown to be better than a wake-sleep algorithm for stochastic training. Several baselines are explored for variance reduction in the inference network corresponding to a decoder. Such variational objectives can be used to train probabilistic encoders in adversarial learning. They are designed within information-theoretic frameworks such as the minimum description length for encoding non-stationary data distributions.

Adversarial examples lead to an increase in the generalization error and inference time of deep learning networks. Kyatham et al. [341] propose a defense mechanism against adversarial examples based on regularized latent space generative models. It involves an adversarial filter that encodes a quantized latent space from the data a manifold subject to adversarial manipulations. The adversarial filter is not accessible to either than adversaries or the classifier. It has a variational inference mechanism in a regularized, quantized, generative latent space to remap the encoded adversarial data to the true training data manifolds. The adversarial robustness of the decoded data is demonstrated in various attack scenarios involving white-box and blackbox methods. Thus variational autoencoders can be used to explore the feature subspace consisting of adversarial examples. Such feature subspaces can be incorporated into adversarial retraining that is robust to first-order adversaries but is unable to defend against blackbox attacks. Blackbox attacks can also be optimized to circumvent robustness toward obfuscated gradients obtained from an approximation of derivatives in function approximation, reparameterization, and computation of its expectations. The proposed latent space encoder preserves the distance between samples under a metric space transformation from data to latent manifolds. The encoder is used in a quantized generative model that allows a stochastic exploration of a large neighborhood in the latent space. The latent codes are then mapped back to the legitimate data. Thus a decoder can be used to convert adversarial examples into approximate non-adversarial samples. The proposed inference model is called Lipschitz constrained quantized variational autoencoder (LQ-VAE). With a simple binary quantization of the latent space, it can be used an adversarial detector.

Gulrajani et al. [242] present PixelVAE that has an autoregressive decoder based on PixelCNN. PixelVAE is able to learn a useful latent representation for natural image modelling with fine details. PixelVAE can be extended to have multiple stochastic layers to model not only output pixels but also higher-level latent feature maps. Autoregressive conditional likelihoods are explored in the context of data analytics applications such as sentence modelling. The output distributions for the generative and inference networks can be decomposed and factorized over the latent variables to derive a log-likelihood for the reconstructed data that is regularized by a KL divergence of the approximate posterior over latents with an autoregressive prior. The latent representations of the input data are applicable to deep representation learning in semi-supervised classification.

Hou et al. [278] propose a loss function for VAEs that enforces a deep feature consistency preserving the spatial correlation characteristics of the input to give better perceptual quality. The hidden features of a pre-trained deep convolutional neural network (CNN) define a feature perceptual loss for VAE training. Instead of reconstructing pixel-by-pixel measurements, the feature perceptual loss defines a difference between hidden representations of images that have been extracted from a pre-trained deep CNN such as AlexNet, VGGNet, and ImageNet. Latent vectors obtained from such a VAR achieve state-of-the-art performance in facial attribute prediction. The distribution of the latent vectors can be controlled according to a KL divergence from Gaussian random variables. It is combined with a reconstruction loss to train the VAE. Then attribute-conditioned deep VAEs such as deep recurrent attentive writer (DRAW) [232] can be extended to semi-supervised learning with class labels that combines attention mechanism with a sequential variational autoencoding framework. The performance of VAEs can also be improved with discriminative regularization of the reconstruction loss achieved by GAN discriminator on the learned feature representation in VAEs. Feature perceptual loss can be defined by neural style transfer and classification scores on individual features from pre-trained deep CNNs.

Hou et al. [279] extend the deep feature consistent VAE to implement a deep convolutional generative adversarial training mechanism that learns feature embeddings in facial attribute manipulation. A multiview feature extraction strategy is then proposed to extract effective image representations useful in facial attribute prediction tasks. Such a generative model for an image database is useful for generating realistic images from random inputs, compressing the database into the learned parameters of a model, and learning reusable representations of unlabelled data that are applicable into supervised learning tasks such as image classification. The proposed discriminator balances outputs between image reconstruction loss and adversarial loss. The proposed VAE can linearly learn semantic information of facial attributes in a learned latent space. It can extract discriminative facial attribute representations. Images can be transformed between classes by a simple linear combination of their latent vectors. Attribute specific features can be encoded for annotated images to manipulate related attributes of a given image while fixing the remaining attributes. Thus the adversarial training proposed in the VAE can be conditioned on class labels and visual attributes obtained from the data manifold of natural images.

Larsen et al. [347] present an autoencoder that can measure similarities in data space based on learned feature representations. The representations are obtained by combining a variational autoencoder (VAE) with a generative adversarial network (GAN) into an unsupervised generative model. In the reconstructed data distribution, element-wise errors are replaced with feature-wise errors that offer invariance toward image translation. The training results produce latent image representations with disentangled factors of variation. High-level visual features can be modified using vector arithmetic. The VAE decoder and GAN generator share parameters that are trained jointly. Thus generative models can be improved with learned similarity measures included into the reconstruction quality metrics on object classes. At the same time, GANs discriminator can be used to measure sample similarity. The proposed method can also be interpreted as GAN learning complex data distributions with the priors constrained by a VAE.

Tran et al. [605] propose a formulation where reconstructed samples from an autoencoder (AE) are input as "real" samples for the discriminator in a GAN. This affects the convergence criteria of the GAN. Further, a latent data distance constraint is put on the encoder network. It minimizes the distance between latent samples and data samples. A discriminator score distance constraint aligns the distribution of the generated samples with the real data samples. Both the constraints guide the generator of the proposed Dist-GAN to synthesize samples similar to the training data distribution. Thus the adversarial training process in GANs can be combined with AEs to produce samples of a data distribution without explicitly estimating it. The dimensionality reduction in AEs can be used to balance the discriminator and generator capacities leading to convergence issues such as gradient vanishing and mode collapse. The competitive scores produced by the discriminator in a stable Dist-GAN can be used to find multimodal differences between the adversarial and training data distributions. The information divergence measures such as the KL divergence and the JS divergence can be combined with the reconstruction loss of an AE to train an empirical inference model. Here, game theoretical adversarial loss can be interpreted as a regularization term. Coupling the AE with that of the discriminator in GAN allows us to study the convergence conditions of game theoretical adversarial learning from the perspective of computer vision tasks.

Makhzani et al. [404] propose a probabilistic autoencoder called adversarial autoencoder (AAE). It performs variational inference by matching the aggregated posterior of the autoencoder with an arbitrary prior distribution acting as a regularization term. An encoder learns to convert the data distribution to the prior distribution acting as the encoding distribution. The decoder learns a deep generative model that maps an imposed prior to a posterior distribution matching the original data distribution to a decoding distribution. The decoder of the AAE learns a deep generative model such as generative moment matching networks and generative adversarial networks. Recognition networks can predict posterior decoding distributions over latent variables. The autoencoder is trained with a reconstruction error criterion between the model distribution and a data distribution. It is combined with an adversarial training criterion that discriminatively predicts whether a generated sample arises from the hidden code of an autoencoder or from a sampled distribution specified by the user. The adversarial training procedure consists of a reconstruction phase for training the autoencoder followed by a regularization phase for smoothing the adversarial network. The reconstruction phase updates the encoder and the decoder to minimize the reconstruction error of inputs. The regularization phase updates discriminative network to distinguish between true samples generated using prior and generated samples that are the hidden codes computed by the autoencoder. Then the generator is updated to confuse the discriminative network. The generator of the adversarial network is also the encoder of the autoencoder. After training, the decoder of the autoencoder defines a generative model that maps an imposed prior to the data distribution. The encoder can be one of a deterministic function, a stochastic distribution such as the Gaussian posterior, and a universal approximator of the posterior that combines both training and adversarial data distributions. A re-parametrization trick is used in the back-propagation of error through the encoder of a stochastic distribution. In case of a universal approximator of the posterior, the adversarial training procedure is interpreted as an efficient method of sampling from the aggregated posterior. The imposed prior can be a complicated distribution in a high-dimensional space such as the swiss roll distribution without an explicit functional form for the distribution. The reconstruction phase of the adversarial training can also incorporate class label mixtures information to better shape the distribution of the hidden code. Here, a semi-supervised classifier minimizes the cross-entropy cost calculated on conditional posteriors estimated for each labelled mini-batch. AAE designs demonstrate that deep generative models can be adversarially trained with not only sampling methods such as restricted Boltzmann machines but also variational methods such as importance weighted autoencoders. The proposed AAE is shown to have applications in semi-supervised classification, unsupervised clustering, dimensionality reduction, and data visualization.

Scutari et al. [545] analyze game theoretical modelling as a set of coupled convex optimization problems in applied mathematics. Such convex optimization problems are widely studied in signal processing for the design of single-user and multiuser communication systems. Here, cooperative and non-cooperative game theory approaches can be used to model the equilibria in communications and networking problems. Such optimizations can also be generalized to variation inequality problems in non-linear analysis. Thus signal processing can be used in the study of the existence and uniqueness of the Nash equilibrium in game theoretical adversarial learning. Further, iterative distributed computational algorithms can be designed to study the convergence properties and equilibrium programming of the game theoretical modelling. The related adversarial learning applications also have relevance in signal processing and communication applications such as resource sharing in multihop communication networks, cognitive radio networks, wireless ad hoc networks, and per-to-peer wired networks.

Gidel et al. [217] explore variational inequality framework as a saddle point optimization method for designing adversarial training. GANs training is extended to include variational inequalities averaging and extrapolation. In mathematical programming, variational inequality problems generalize the stationary conditions for two-player games. At stationary points the directional derivative of cost function is non-negative in any feasible direction for the optimization. They can be generalized to continuous vector fields. The variational inequality problem finds an optimal set on the vector fields. The game theoretical modelling in deep generative modelling can be explored within the variational inequality framework to produce stochastic variational inequalities with bounded constraints and regret minimization in online learning. Here non-zero games are the GANs learning objectives. Variational inequalities can be leveraged in various practical optimization algorithms. Harker et al. [252] review finite-dimensional variational inequality problems in game theory especially for non-linear models. Solving for equilibrium models is a topic called equilibrium programming in non-linear optimization. They can be used to produce numerical computational methods to study the convergence properties of game-theoretic equilibria. Sensitivity and stability analysis of the equilibria to changes in model parameters is an important part of the existence and uniqueness of the solution. The resultant numerical modelling can be integrated into a game theoretical adversarial learning to optimize the dynamics modelling and computation in iterative attack scenarios and defense mechanisms. Daniele [143] recontextualizes dynamics modelling as evolutionary variational inequalities within dynamic networks evolving over time. The dynamics modelling has applications in finance, economics, computer science, and mathematics.

Distributional Smoothing Features Vincent et al. [620] extend unsupervised pre-training to unsupervised learning of representations such that the learned representations are robust to partial corruption of the input pattern. Deep generative models are then created by stacking denoising autoencoders for manifold learning. A higher-level representation of observed patterns is produced by optimizing a local unsupervised learning criterion. Global training criteria are then proposed for optimizing the performance appropriate to the task at hand. The unsupervised representations act as an initialization for the optimization algorithms that are able to avoid poor solutions. Restricted Boltzmann machines trained by contrastive divergence and various autoencoders are found to benefit from such a training process. An information-theoretic perspective is then provided for analyzing the robust autoencoders that efficiently model complex data distributions and demonstrate superior generalization performance on dependencies in the data distributions characterizing the observed input. The proposed denoising procedure is comparable to training dataset augmentation with adversarial patterns. But the denoising procedure does not use any prior knowledge about the image topology and class labels for supervised learning. To deal with corruption due to noise that is adversarial or otherwise, the denoising procedure does not produce smooth functions for regularization but learns the robustness information in variational inference over large, non-additive, destruction of information. A reconstruction cross-entropy is the training objective. It maximizes a lower bound on the mutual information between training loss and adversarial loss. However, deep directed graphical models continue to pose optimization challenges in deep generative modelling especially for learning high-level concepts from multimodal inputs.

Zhao et al. [705] propose deep generative models that can learn from feature hierarchies in supervised learning tasks. Multiple layers of latent variables are trained with variational methods. Unlike discriminative methods that learn invariant and local feature hierarchies, the proposed variational methods learn interpretable hierarchical features preserving information on natural image datasets. The learnt representations can be generalized to adversarially trained models that support statistical inference. The hidden layers of latent variables are characterized in two designs. The first design recursively stacks generative models assuming that the bottom layer alone contains information to reconstruct the data distribution and the information does not depend on the specific family of distributions used to define the hierarchy. The second design focuses on single-layer latent variable models in which high-level features are positioned to certain parts of the latent code and low-level features to others. This approach is called variational ladder autoencoder. It maximizes a marginal log-likelihood over the training dataset. The likelihood is complex and intractable for generative models. The marginalization is due to the latent variables of the autoencoder. Following a variational inference model, an evidence lower bound (ELBO) involving Kullback-Leibler divergence is optimized as a solution for the intractable marginal likelihood optimization. Such an inference is shown to produce learned structured representations that are better than assuming a Markov independence structure in the latent variables to factorize the inference distribution according to an autoregressive hierarchical variational autoencoder.

Sønderby et al. [562] propose a ladder variational autoencoder for unsupervised learning of feature representations. It recursively corrects the generative distribution with a data-dependent approximate likelihood. A predictive log-likelihood provides lower bound to the bottom-up inference in layered variational autoencoders. It can also be used in the design of a deep distributed hierarchy of latent variables in inference and generative learning models. The hierarchies of conditional stochastic variables in such VAEs are interpreted as a computationally efficient representation of factorized models. They approximate a variational approximate posterior lower bounding the intractable true posterior. It is estimated by dependency structure modelling between bottom-up likelihood inference and top-down generative information modelling in deep learning. Such a parameterization of the VAEs allows interaction between the bottom-up and top-down signals like in the variational ladder autoencoder. The generative performance of the variational distributions is compared with VAE baselines such as variational Gaussian processes, normalizing flows, importance weighted autoencoders, and auxiliary deep generative models. The KL divergence bounding the log-likelihood training criterion is approximated using Monte Carlo sampling. A stochastic backpropagation algorithm is used to optimize the generative and inference parameters. In the VAE inference, each stochastic layer is specified as a fully factorized Gaussian distribution. Variational regularization terms are introduced into the loss function for generative log-likelihood distribution estimators. This model can also accommodate explicit parameter sharing between inference and generative distributions to produce recursive variational distributions with attention mechanisms such as in the deep recurrent attentive writer (DRAW) [232]. In game theoretical adversarial learning, such attention mechanisms create best response strategies for the adversary as randomized operational decisions while the cost-sensitive classifier learns representations for multimodal, multiview, and multitask distributions.

Zhou et al. [708] propose a deep autoencoder to distinguish between high-quality reconstructed data and outliers. It is able find random anomalies as well as structured corruptions with unsupervised anomaly detection algorithms. It is an extension of denoising autoencoders and maximum correntropy autoencoders where the reconstruction cost is a noise-resistant entropy. By defining a non-linear projection to a low-dimensional hidden layer, the proposed robust autoencoder is a non-linear version of robust principal component analysis. It produces a non-linear representation of the data suitable for producing lower reconstruction error rates on complicated input distributions. An alternating direction method of multipliers is the optimization algorithm used to train the autoencoder. Such robust autoencoders can be used to detect cyberattacks in network data. Lin [371] provides an overview of rank aggregation methods. They act as stochastic search methods to combine different optimization criteria in stationary distributions. Distance measures are used to aggregate ranked lists. The orders of elements in an optimal list are specified in a probability matrix parameterized by cross-entropy Monte Carlo information divergence criteria between training and adversarial distributions. Gregor et al. [234] introduce deep autoregressive networks to learn hierarchies of distributed representations from data. A parameter estimation algorithm based on minimum description length (MDL) maximizes a variational lower bound on the log-likelihood estimated on the training data. The encoder's representation plays the role of a variational distribution that is concise and irredundant from an information-theoretic point of view. Autoregressive structure in the latent variables captures dependencies between activation units of the same layer.

In the multivariate statistics literature studying systems of probability distributions, copulas model multivariate distributions. Copulas construct joint distributions with different dependence structures such as tail dependency modelled as marginal distributions. Vine copulas allow arbitrary density estimation. Entropy-based information-theoretic measures such as the mutual information can be contrasted with copula to quantify the multivariate dependencies between features involved in multiple regression over joint data distributions. Tagasovska et al. [591] introduce vine copula autoencoder to estimate the multivariate distribution of the encoded data. A generative model combines the estimated distribution with a decoder. As an implicit generative model, vine copulas do not impose as many restrictions as variational methods on training in the latent space. They do not make explicit distributional assumptions on the decoder of the data generative process. They act as a flexible tool for constructing features in high-dimensional multivariate distributions. New data can be constructed by decoding the random samples generated by the vine copula. Selection of copula families allows flexibility in modelling and exploration of parameter values in the autoencoders design using adversarial training mechanisms.

Wieczorek et al. [648] apply a copula transformation in the latent space of an autoencoder to construct sparse representations of the features. Such representations of data extract compact, sparse, interpretable features in machine learning. The sparse features are combined with deep information bottleneck principle in variational inference to derive information-theoretic limits on deep learning networks efficiency. Variational lower bounds are derived on the information bottleneck optimization problem formulated as mutual information between adversarial and training data distributions. It involves entropy term on discrete features, differential entropy term on continuous features, and marginal copula entropy term on the latent features. Copula augmentation of variational autoencoders is proposed to provide resilience to adversarial attacks due to a positive influence on the convergence rates of the autoencoder.

Hua et al. [284] develop reduced-rank estimators and filters for subspace computation. The proposed alternating power (AP) method for computing reduced ranks is computationally more efficient than existing methods in the literature. Such a rank reduction is shown to have application in a multivariate system with a large number of sources and receivers where the internal structure and interference of multipath signals is represented with a reduced-rank channel matrix. Such systems implicitly require to reduce the model complexity to offset computational load. Thus reduced-rank estimation and filtering are useful in a variety of signal processing applications requiring data/model reduction, robustness against adversarial noise and modelling errors, and high computational efficiency. Here adversarial deep learning in reduced-rank estimation can be contrasted with the more conventional methods as a computationally efficient representation learning procedure for rank estimation such as eigenvalue decomposition (EVD), singular value decomposition (SVD), and subspace decomposition (SSD) techniques. Furthermore, the proposed AP method for optimization is an alternative to the gradient searching methods used in the optimization of adversarial learning. It extends the iterative quadratic minimum distance (IQMD) approach to optimization of the loss functions in adversarial deep learning.

Luedtke et al. [397] construct adversarial Monte Carlo meta-learning (AMC) for computationally intensive statistical procedures in frequentist and Bayesian approaches that require optimizing maximum likelihood estimators and sampling from an intractable probability distribution, respectively. Here statistical problems are formulated as two-player games in which Nature adversarially selects a distribution for a statistician to answer scientific question using data drawn from this distribution. Optimal solutions are found by players' strategies parameterized by deep neural networks. The worst case for sampling complexity in the data-generating mechanisms is found when the performance of the statistical procedure is least desirable. Such sampling complexity problems are solved by minimax optimization procedures that are statistically equivalent to Bayes procedures derived from a least favorable prior on a quantity of interest that is most difficult to compute. To establish rates of convergence and performance guarantees on such least favorable priors, automation methods are designed over a restricted class of priors prespecified on a finite set of distributions in statistical decision problems. The proposed AMC can be used to incorporate adversarial strategies in the tuning, selection, and optimization of supervised learning procedures. The adversarial data-generating mechanism can be constructed from a statistical model. Such a statistical framework for adversarial learning is illustrated in three classes of statistical problems: point estimation, prediction, and confidence region construction. A minimax risk is optimized on the class of possible learning procedures. In general, such an optimization is non-deterministic polynomial time (NP) hard. A variety of adversarial strategies are hypothesized to deal with such computational complexities in the learning procedures by numerical optimization. One such strategy iteratively improves on the maximal risk of the statistical procedure. Nested minimax algorithms to numerically construct a minmax procedure are another strategy. Another strategy uses alternating algorithms to hybridize the nested minimax and maximin algorithms. Therefore optimal statistical procedures for data mining can be constructed with adversarial deep learning especially when existing statistical procedures tend to fail.

Romano et al. [521] analyze the stability of deep-learning classification machines like CNNs. They find links between stability of the classification to noise and the underlying structure of the signal. Such links are quantified in terms of dictionary learning of sparse representations of data. Thus the research areas of sparse representation learning and dictionary learning can be can be used to analyze the sensitivity of regressors and robustness of classifiers to adversarial perturbations. A robustness bound on the energy of the noise is found to be a function of the sparsity of the signal and its characteristics expressed as weights of a dictionary representation. Parseval networks are then found to be an empirical regularization to improve the classification stability. Sparse solutions and incoherent dictionaries/filters on the incoming signals are proposed as the solutions to construct robust neural networks on the adversarial noise. Guo et al. [243] reveal relationships between sparsity of deep classifiers and their adversarial robustness. Higher sparsity is found to imply better robustness in non-linear deep neural networks. Sparse classifiers are not only computationally efficient but also theoretically attractive. They can be used in the design of defense mechanisms in adversarial deep learning such as adversarial training, knowledge distillation, detecting and rejecting, gradient masking, and randomization. Here inefficiency leads to redundancy in the deep classifier designs with network pruning and weight tensors regularization.

Kreutz-Delgado et al. [330] develop data-driven learning of domain-specific dictionaries for maximum likelihood and maximum a posteriori estimation. As a generalization of vector quantization, the dictionary elements are interpreted as concepts, features, or words representing the events encountered and signals generated in the adversarial environment. Experimental evaluation shows that the proposed representation learning algorithms based on underdetermined system solvers perform better than independent component analysis (ICA) methods. Moreover the dictionaries result in both higher compression (fewer bits per pixel) and higher accuracy (lower mean square error). The environmentally meaningful dictionaries are obtained physically or biologically by maximizing the mutual information between the set of these vectors and the signals generated by the environment. A minimal spanning set of linearly independent vectors or dictionaries represents the measured signals of interest with noise reduction and data compression. Matching a source signal to a sparse dictionary can also be understood as maximum entropy modelling of its statistical structure. The resulting dictionary estimates are then termed as approximate maximum likelihood estimates of the source signal. Adaptive filtering literature for the current dictionary estimate can also be used to track the sensitivity of learning to the adversarial noise with data-driven corrections. The use of learned dictionaries is also compared with the use of predefined wavelet dictionaries to recreate the observed sensor signals with separability and factorizability in the data distributions for discriminative-generative modelling in game theoretical adversarial deep learning. Applications are found for the resultant multimodal loss functions, multiview cost functions, and multitask objective functions in biomedical imaging, geophysical seismic sounding, and multitarget tracking.

Zou et al. [718] sparse principal component analysis (SPCA) use the lasso to produce modified principal components with sparse loadings. SPCA is formulated as a regression optimization framework with computationally efficient algorithms on multivariate data. Regression criteria identifying important variables rather than simple thresholding on explained variance are used to derive the leading principal components. Without sparsity constraints, the method reduces to PCA. Sprechmann et al. [568] create a clustering framework with dictionary learning and sparse coding. The representative points for clustering are modelled in terms of data distributions represented in one dictionary for each cluster. Thus the entire clustering configuration is modelled as a union of learned low dimensional subspaces and their data points. Learned dictionaries make the unsupervised clustering framework suitable for processing large datasets in a robust manner. An EM-like iterative optimization algorithm is designed to separate the clusters into the dictionaries. The dictionaries are also used in a new measurement of representation quality that combines sparse coding, dictionary learning, and spectral clustering for both hard and soft clustering.

5.4.2.2 Mathematical Programming in Game Theoretical Adversarial Learning

Evolutionary algorithms (EA) have been used in stochastic optimization to generate rule-based data mining models with attribute interactions [694]. The EA-based stochastic search and optimization algorithms are evolutionary programming (EP), evolutionary strategies (ES), genetic algorithms (GA), differential evolution (DE), estimation of distribution algorithm (EDA) and swarm intelligence (SI) algorithms [258, 641].

In our adversarial algorithm, the search and optimization algorithm is either a genetic algorithm or a simulated annealing algorithm. The adversarial data samples are generated by the selection, crossover, mutation search operators in the genetic algorithm and the annealing search operator in the simulated annealing algorithm. By using probabilistic hill-climbing algorithms over Markov chains in multivariate models, the current search operators can be extended to define explicit probabilistic distributions performing a complex neighborhood search for the candidate solutions [10].

Harada et al. [251] analyze the advances in parallel genetic algorithms (PGAs). PGAs can be used as optimization algorithms when the target goal function is non-derivable, non-continuous, and ill-defined and does not have any analytical expression. They can incorporate high-dimensionality search space, customized operators for the application, complex datasets in the search algorithm, and nonlinear restrictions on the optimization objective. Here they can profit from parallelization and distributed processing platforms such as multiprocessors, GPUs, FPGAs, clusters, grids, and clouds by saving on the search and optimization saving on function calls and numerical computations. The optimization API to implement PGAs can be categorized into parallel computing, distributed computing, MPI, and CUDA. Such implementations run on uniprocessors, parallel computers, and workstation networks. They enable the development of the state-of-the-art optimization algorithms for single-objective, multi-objective, and parallel algorithms in an object-oriented architecture. PGAs solve problems in real-world applications such as data mining, path finding, road traffic, land-use planning, nanoscience, electronics, building structure, and power systems. PGAs are useful for feature selection, hyperparameter optimization, and feature engineering in data mining. They lead to applications in big data analytics, deep learning, computational intelligence, and data provenance with adversarial machine learning. The active areas for research in PGAs are scalability to high-dimensional datasets, robustness of the optimization results to changes in the algorithms' parameters due to uncertainties in the data and dynamic learning environments, evaluation of multi-objective functions to efficiently construct diverse and high-quality solutions in multicriteria decision-making, analysis of algorithmic tradeoffs such as usability/efficiency in designing the search, parallel algorithms and learning metrics in big data solutions, data processing and algorithmic analysis in PGAs on fog/edge computing devices and services, PGAs for high-performance computing that combines exact/approximate algorithms for synchronous/asynchronous communication policies, and microservices architectures building complex solutions with PGAs acting as web services provisioning validated optimization.

The most popular evolutionary algorithms for machine learning optimization are Stochastic hill-climbing, simulated annealing, and genetic algorithms. Goldberg [222] discuss the use of genetic algorithms in stochastic optimization of machine learning. Evolutionary mechanisms are simulated in a computer with data populations containing solution characteristics that are evolved over generations of such populations training a machine learning model in an environment of objective functions for optimizing the populations. It is an iterative optimization algorithm where each individual solution is characterized by a fitness function value. It will converge to a solution if the population and its learning objectives are well-defined. Here genetic algorithms work on a population of many possible solutions simultaneously. They require to compute the fitness function values without needing auxiliary information such as derivatives of the objective function. They then use probabilistic update rules to evolve randomization into the candidate solutions. Here deep learning can be used to represent the training data as solution populations for genetic algorithm. Extensions of the genetic algorithms to multi-objective optimization result in Pareto-optimal solutions. The concept of optimization in the genetic algorithms can be expanded to select not only the modelling parameters but also the fitness function and optimization technique as part of the adversarial machine learning problem.

Michalewicz [426] surveys the evolutionary programming techniques to incorporate problem-specific knowledge as specialized operators in genetic algorithms. They lead to evolution programs that are probabilistic algorithms extending the principles of genetic algorithms. The specialized operators can be used for numerical optimization, model tuning, constrained search, strategy learning, and multimodal optimization in game theoretical adversarial learning. Here deep learning networks can go beyond binary encoding of the populations to represent features for machine learning in fuzzy, numerical, computational operators for evolution programs. The players associated with particular strategies in game theoretical modelling can be represented as the population in evolution programs. The adversarial payoff functions can then act as the fitness functions evaluating individual solutions to be selected for the next generation. Better strategies can be constructed by mating players across generations. Representations of the strategies can be randomized with genetic operators. A player's regret minimization is determined by the average of payoffs it receives over all the games it plays. In this manner evolution programs can be used to solve multi-label multiplayer games in supervised adversarial learning with simultaneous optimization of multiple objectives in real-world decision-making problems. Symbolic empirical learning is a research area in evolutionary programming that can induce classification rules for supervised learning. In contrast to such symbolic classifier systems that maintain explicit knowledge in a high-level descriptive language, statistical models represent knowledge as a set of examples and statistics associated with them and connectionist models represent knowledge among the weights assigned to neural network connections. The symbolic empirical learning applied to a classifier system has to define rule-based systems such as a detector-effector system to encode-decode training data to a genetic representation of solutions, a message system on inputs to the genetic algorithm, a rule system producing a population of classifiers, a credit system on evolving solutions across generations, and a genetic procedure to generate populations for the various rule-based systems. Here evolution programs can be used to model the behavior of a game theoretical attack scenario in supervised adversarial learning. Problem-specific feature representations and specialized operators for evolution programs can apply evolutionary algorithms in finite-state machines for numerical optimization, machine learning, iterated games, optimal control, signal processing, cognitive modelling, engineering design, system integration, and robotics. Strategic oscillation is a constrained optimization approach that is applicable to combinatorial and non-linear optimization problems solved with evolution programs. It attaches a feasibility/infeasibility context to cost-sensitive design of neighborhood search and stochastic optimization in evolution programs. The configuration of rule-based systems for selecting a region to be traversed and the direction of traversal are determined by the ability to approach and cross the feasibility frontier from different directions. Retracing a prior trajectory is avoided by mechanisms of memory and probability. A constructive process for reaching the feasibility frontier is accompanied by a destructive process for dismantling its structure resulting in a strategic oscillation around the boundary. Such strategic oscillations can be used to guide the increase in adversarial payoff functions around classifier boundaries around with a search procedure probing the depths of associated regions. Problem constraints on such search can bound and penalize the search with a constraint set on vector-valued functions. Tradeoffs between different degrees of violation of the component constraints can be allowed according to their feature importance scores. Such problems are called constraint satisfaction problems in evolution programs and are comparable to constraint programming techniques in mathematical optimization. Therefore game theoretical adversarial deep learning can benefit from evolutionary techniques for function optimization with self-adapting systems incorporating control parameters into solution vectors, co-evolutionary systems where evolutionary processes are connected across populations, polyploid structures incorporating memory of non-stationary environments into individual solutions, and massively parallel programming models embedding evolutionary computation.

McCune et al. [417] present a survey of vertex-centric programming model in distributed processing frameworks for complex networks. It consists of inter-dependent components to compute iterative graph algorithms at scale. Thus we can evaluate the sensitivity of adversarial loss functions with respect to the connectivity structure discovery, representation, visualization, and evaluation of the game theoretical modelling on complex networks. In the context of adversarial machine learning over graph pattern mining dynamics, we can explore functional programming constructs suitable for distributed processing such as MapReduce and bulk synchronous parallel. The choice of programming models is between data parallelism, task parallelism, and graph parallelism. Haller et al. [247] discuss the challenges of implementing parallel and distributed machine learning with functional programming abstractions. The implementation detail for distributed data analytics ought to consider machine learning assumptions implicit in the data model, memory model, programming model, communication model, execution model, and the computing model of the parallel and serial algorithms. The relevant features learning methods include samples, trees, clusters, wavelets, kernels, splines, nets, filters, wrappers and factors in data series, sequences, graphs, and networks. The game theoretical modelling will require to learn dense substructures, rare classes, and condensed patterns over transactional, sequential, and graph datasets where random process generating training data may not be the same as that governing testing data. Miller et al. [430] discuss parallel programming models tailor-made for machine learning implemented in the Scala programming language. They would have to support distributed graph processing, provide parallel bulk operations on generic collections, and create a parallel domain-specific language for machine learning on heterogeneous hardware platforms. Scala language's features to architect and distribute parallel run time systems for machine learning are also covered. For game theoretical modelling, we would have to design unsupervised learning mechanisms with motif mining models such as biclustering and evolutionary clustering, multilevel clustering and model-driven clustering. To create supervised adversarial learning models with such motifs, we can focus on compression methods and optimization methods within kernel learning and deep learning. The relevant theory of data mining is in multilevel clustering, multilevel graph partitioning, quasi-clique detection and dense subgraph discovery. Data indexing structures for dynamic data would also reduce the communication cost and increase the load balancing in such distributed memory systems.

Mohamadi et al. [436] construct a fuzzy classification system with simulated annealing. The discovered knowledge is in the form of if-then prediction rules of a symbolic knowledge representation. They can be evaluated for several statistical significance criteria such as the degree of confidence in the prediction, classification accuracy rate on unknown-class instances, and interpretability of the approximate reasoning method of fuzzy systems. Any tailored membership functions can be developed in the fuzzy classification system for a given pattern classification problem. The simulated annealing does a global search of the classification problem to escape local optimum. A genetic algorithm needs polynomial time on average. Beyer et al. [50] conduct a complexity analysis of evolutionary algorithms in continuous and discrete search spaces. Such a theoretical approach to design can help us understand and teach evolutionary algorithms as probabilistic optimization methods in computational intelligence. A first analysis is around a performance measure called progress velocity. It is the average distance in the search space traveled in the useful direction per function evaluation. Self-adaptation and an associated success probability of the mutation strength consider the objective function as a blackbox for optimization. In a blackbox algorithm, all the calculations are free, and only the sampling is charged. Finally the statistical goodness of the solution found by evolutionary algorithms depends on knowledge or ignorance of the problem characteristics represented as machine learning features for optimization. To account for such design issues, a complexity analysis predicts the behavior of evolutionary algorithms after a dynamical system. The concept of convergence order in optimization theory provides bounds to the fitness noise and evolutionary dynamics. As randomized algorithms we can associate a success probability of reaching the optima to evolutionary algorithms. Given a probability distribution of the inputs, the randomization is lower bounded for the worst-case expected optimization time. In practice they evolve approximate solutions under hardware restrictions. In this sense evolutionary algorithms can be designed as amelioration techniques.

Xue et al. [672] survey the state-of-the-art on evolutionary computation as a global search technique for feature selection in a large search space. Such a feature selection has application in several machine learning tasks such as classification, clustering, regression, and prediction. Genetic algorithms, particle swarm optimization, and ant colony optimization are the most popular evolutionary computation methods in feature selection. They can be integrated and embedded into classifier learning as embedded approaches to feature selection. Then genetic programming acts as an optimization technique for machine learning. Learning classifier systems are able to benefit from the embedded feature selection. Here feature interactions to target concept are evaluated with optimal feature subsets evaluated with evolutionary computation. Evolutionary algorithms have a role to play in the search for feature subsets as well as their evaluation criteria where the objective is to maximize the classification accuracy while minimizing the number of features. Therefore feature selection with evolutionary methods can be treated as a multi-objective problem that must find a set of non-dominated tradeoff solutions. They do not need to make assumptions about the search space such as whether it is linearly or non-linearly separable and differentiable. Their population-based mechanisms can produce multiple solutions in a single run that can be parallelized. But there is a need to increase the stability of the evolutionary algorithms that tend to select different features from different runs. This design issue also increases the computational complexity of evolutionary algorithms on real-world tasks with a large number of features. The performance evaluation measures for evolutionary computing in machine learning are sourced from information theory, correlation measures, distance measures, fuzzy set theory, and rough set theory. They lead to applications in image and signal processing, face recognition, human action recognition, speaker recognition, handwritten digit recognition, personal identification, biomarker detection, disease diagnosis, email spam detection, network security, language learning, and power system optimization.

Suman et al. [579] review optimization algorithms based on simulated annealing for single and multi-objective optimization problems. A probability calculation to build the annealing schedule is discussed across various algorithms. The annealing schedules can be used to obtain a Pareto set of solutions for multi-objective optimization problems. A study of the computational results and performance environment of simulated annealing can suggest improvements to the annealing schedules. Simulated annealing takes less time than genetic algorithm because it finds optimal solutions by point-by-point iteration rather than search over a population of individuals. It can be considered as a randomized heuristic approach to combinatorial optimization problems such as the travelling salesman problem. It can efficiently accommodate multiple and conflicting design objectives in multi-objective optimization problems such as integrated circuits layout. Gradient- and Hessian-based methods are ineffective in signal processing applications involving optimization problems with multimodal and non-smooth loss functions. The adaptive simulated annealing is an optimization tool in such non-linear optimization problems. It can be applied to not only optimization problems but also in object classification and pattern recognition where distance metrics can be the objective functions. Simulated annealing can be combined with genetic algorithms to provide efficient solutions exploring the neighborhood of simulated annealing in multicriteria problems where genetic algorithms adjust the parameters tuned for each objective in each iteration. Such genetic algorithms can model the sample population of interacting solutions while the simulated annealing accepts feasible solutions with some probability determined by an annealing schedule.

Deb [149] discusses the challenges in multi-objective optimization especially when the objectives are in conflict with one another. Then they give rise to tradeoff optimal solutions with or without optimization constraints called Pareto-optimal solutions. Evolutionary multi-objective optimization is the research area studying such problems. Unlike gradient-based methods, evolutionary multi-objective optimization does not require any derivative information to find the optimal solution. It can solve multimodal problems and normalize decision variables with an evolving population utilizing the minimum and maximum values of objective and constraint functions. It can incorporate both stochastic and deterministic operators that tend to converge to desired solutions with high probability. Such operators include selection, crossover, mutation, and elite preservation. The use of a data population in the search mechanism of the evolutionary optimization is implicitly amenable to embarrassingly parallel programming over different regions of the search space. It can solve real-world optimization problems involving non-differentiable objectives and discontinuous constraints, non-linear solutions, discreteness, scale, randomization in the computation, and uncertainty in the decision. A mathematical concept called partial ordering defines the non-dominating Pareto-optimal solutions in evolutionary multi-objective optimization. The convergence criteria of evolutionary multi-objective optimization can be combined with mathematical optimization techniques to produce dynamic optimizers. Such evolutionary multi-objective optimization algorithms are explainable with respect to an application such as spacecraft trajectory design. They are evaluated with performance measures on the Pareto-optimal front such as error ratio, distance from reference set, hypervolume, coverage, R-metrics, etc. Evolutionary multi-objective optimization algorithms can deal with stochastiticies in problem parameters, decision variables, feature dimensions, and convergence properties with a probabilistic scoring of the objective and constraint function values finding imprecise solutions in uncertain environments. Such procedures are called stochastic programming methods leading to robustness frontier in the optimal solutions. It is practically solved with bi-level optimization formulations in many areas of science and engineering.

Kelley [313] does a mathematical analysis of the necessary and sufficient conditions in iterative optimization. The optimization algorithms for noisy objectives and bounded constraints is summarized. Sra et al. [570] discuss the role of optimization methods in machine learning. Stochastic gradient descent methods are summarized for non-smooth convex large-scale optimization. Regret minimization methods are proposed to select, learn, and combine features to optimize loss functions in machine learning. The need for approximate optimization and its asymptotic analysis is given for large-scale machine learning. Finally the relationship of robustness learning and generalization error and its role in robust optimization with adversarial learning is presented. Online optimization and bandit optimization are proposed as the methods to deal with adversarial noise and label noise in supervised learning.

Koziel et al. [328] review the research area called computational optimization. Computational optimization models and algorithms try to make optimal use of available resources to maximize the profit, output, performance, and efficiency while minimizing the cost and energy consumption. Search algorithms are the practical tools to reach the optimal solutions in computational optimization. They have to cope with uncertainty in real-world systems with robust designs for the objective functions in the computational optimization. Convex optimization techniques that are widely used in machine learning are special cases of computational optimization. Satisfactory designs for robustness have to create optimization methodologies that can make do with limited computational resources and analytically intractable objectives. Such optimization methodologies consist of model, optimizer, and simulator components. Mathematical or numerical model is a representation of the real-world problem. Optimizer is the algorithm finding optimal solutions. In the search processes, optimizer generates and searches for new solutions from a known solution. Evaluator or simulator is the computational tool that is efficient in the utilization of the overall computing time and cost. It is typically involved in the evaluation of objective function values. The no free lunch theorems for machine learning and optimization state that there is no possibility of a single universal model, optimizer, and simulator being applicable to all the variety of optimization problems. Here optimization algorithms and their improvements can be categorized into derivative-based methods or derivative-free methods, trajectory-based or population-based methods, deterministic or stochastic methods, memoryless or history-based methods, and local or global methods.

Derivative-free optimization algorithms are benchmarked with trajectory plots. Moré et al. [442] propose data profiles as a benchmarking tool to analyze the performance of derivative-free optimization solvers when there is a limited amount of computational budget for the benchmarking problems. They can be combined with convergence criteria to evaluate decreases in the objective function values with expensive function evaluations in smooth, noisy, and piecewise-smooth problems. Performance profiles evaluate solver performance for different levels of discriminative accuracy. The dominant computational cost is due to number of function evaluations per iteration. Performance profiles and data profiles are cumulative distribution functions comparing different solvers. Unlike performance profiles, data profiles express the computational budget to reach a given reduction in function value in terms of simplex gradients for all the solvers. The data plots complement the relative performance measures of performance plots with computational budgets. Kyrola et al. [342] propose a parallel coordinate descent algorithm for minimizing L_1 regularized losses called Shotgun. An empirical study of Shotgun is performed in Lasso and sparse logistic regression problems. It proves to be a scalable optimization method.

Oliehoek et al. [473] present the game-theoretic solution concepts to guarantee progress in co-evolutionary algorithms. Co-evolutionary algorithms are an approach to evolutionary computation that searches for optimal solutions to test-based problems without the need to specify a fitness function. In game theoretical adversarial learning, co-evolutionary algorithms can analyze the desired solution concept maximizing expected utility in learning in games, concept learning, function approximation and classification, and density classification using cellular automata. Pareto-co-evolution associates each test with a separate objective where the set of non-dominated solutions is the specified solution concept. In multi-agent systems, Nash equilibrium is the solution concept specified in two-player games. It recommends a randomized mixed strategy for each player participating in the game. A Parallel Nash Memory is presented by Oliehoek et al. [473] to analyze the solution concept in asymmetric games. It recommends a best response strategy from a partially observable Markov decision process constructed for finite extensive form games. The extensive form representation shows a tree representation of the game theoretical interactions in an application. A co-evolutionary algorithm is used not only as a search heuristic but also as a test of the memory mechanism in Parallel Nash Memory. It is able to identify the best response strategies. The Markov decision process is then solved using dynamic programming techniques such as value iteration. Then the Parallel Nash Memory procedure reduces to coordinate ascent or alternating maximization. Cai et al. [97] propose a multiplayer generalization of zero-sum minimax games to zero-sum polymatrix games. A polymatrix game is defined by a graph where the vertices are the players and the edges are two-player games. Given a strategy profile for all the players, the payoff for each vertex is the sum of the payoffs of all the games in its adjacency list. The payoffs for all the players add up to zero. Different game theoretical equilibria assign different payoffs to players in zero-sum polymatrix games. No-regret learning algorithms are used to find the Nash equilibrium in zero-sum polymatrix games. Bertsekas et al. [48] provide numerical methods for parallel and distributed computation in game theoretical modelling. Dynamic Programming, Markov decision processes, and stochastic optimization algorithms can be used to design asynchronous iterative methods in game theoretical adversarial learning. Bisseling et al. [70] explain the bulk synchronous parallel model and its message-passing interface for embarrassingly parallel programming in the scientific computations for game theoretical adversarial deep learning. The computational optimization cost of parallel programming with low-rank tensor approximations is expressed as computation cost, communication cost, and synchronization cost.

Research into computational algorithms for optimization creates numerical methods with best possible characterization of the machine learning features in the solutions and then reduces an estimation of the modelling errors for the complexity classes designing the optimal solutions. The amount of computational work involved in realizing the algorithm depends on the information in the data type under consideration. It comprises not only the computational work involved in obtaining the information on initial data but also the amount of work involved in processing the information in a machine learning model. Here game theoretical adversarial learning analyzes the stability and robustness of a machine learning algorithm in relation to the principal terms of the estimation error of computation. The genetic algorithms in the game theoretical modelling can be combined with optimization techniques like simulated annealing utilizing both line search and trust region methods to craft the adversarial manipulations. In a study of the convergence properties of the game theoretical optima, the genetic algorithms can also be replaced with derivative-free stochastic optimization algorithms such as pattern search, multilevel coordinate search, and differential evolution. Numerical computational methods in evolutionary and differential game theory can augment the adversarial payoff functions with partial differential state equations of a dynamical system to result in stochastic control in the game theoretical interactions. Stackelberg Riccati differential, difference, and algebraic equations of the game theoretical equilibria can be modelled as the attack scenarios of adversarial learning with variational and generative adversaries. Mathematical optimization under uncertainty can be the view taken as a defense mechanism for the machine learning that is made robust by including optimization algorithms such as stochastic programming, non-linear programming, fuzzy programming, adaptive robust optimization, and data-driven robust optimization in its adversarial training procedures. A privacy-centric enhancement of the learning capacity, randomization strategies, and payoff functions in the game theoretical formulations of classifiers would affect the reweighting regularizations and corresponding decision boundaries of the machine learning algorithms provisioned as cloud services.

5.4.2.3   Low-Rank Approximations in Game Theoretical Adversarial Learning

An adversary can explore the signal filtering, detection, and estimation in tensors to express the machine learning robustness, fairness, explainability, and transparency. Here tensor representations of the training data distributions in deep learning networks explore the structure and context underlying data with learning and optimization theories based on tensors algebra sensitivities of the loss functions in machine learning. Tensor can be understood as a multidimensional array. Each direction in a tensor is called a mode. The number of features in a mode is called dimension. Rank of a tensor is the total number of covariant indices of a tensor. Rank is the minimal number of modes in a tensor. Rank is independent of the number of dimensions of the feature space underlying the tensor. Rank of a tensor is also called order or degree of the tensor. In various applications, tensors are decomposed into lower-order tensors using abstract algebra.

From the perspective of supervised machine learning, the tensor algebra can be based in computational learning theories of machine learning models and data mining tasks. In game theoretical adversarial learning, the applications of tensor decompositions are of interest in the study of the bias-variance tradeoffs in the adversarial payoff functions for mathematical optimization. We can attempt to explain the tensor decompositions in the adversarial manipulations to learn about the effects of algorithmic bias in deep learning. Subsequently robust optimization theories can be proposed for randomization-based adversarial deep learning. Such deep learning theories would also have application in the data mining tasks such as novelty detection and feature extraction. Here factorization machines are a low-rank approximation of the feature engineering in a sparse data tensor when most of its predicted elements are unknown. Here granular computing is useful to create data fusion rules on the feature representations of the training data. It can lead to neuro-fuzzy systems and multi-agent systems in data mining.

We can further investigate the transfer of the statistically significant data fusion rules between predictive data representations on the spatial resolution and spectral resolution data distributions of the training manifolds. Complex structure temporal data in cybersecurity can also be represented as dynamic multidimensional graphs for positive unlabelled learning. Such graphs can be interpreted as both a complex network and a complex tensor in data mining. They require the use of distributed big data processing for graph mining and deep learning. Here we can do graph data mining in terms of graph sampling, graph partitioning, graph compression, graph clustering, and graph search. We may scale the machine learning with data sampling methods that can address the data dimensionality and data granularity for multiprocessing and embarrassingly parallel batch processing over tensors and graphs. The related work is in a study of sampling methods such as undersampling, oversampling, uncertainty sampling, reservoir sampling, structural sampling, etc. The big data solutions would involve data engineering operations for caching, sorting, indexing, hashing, encoding, searching, partitioning, sampling and retrieval in incremental models, sequence models, and ensemble models for cost-sensitive learning with graphical models. For the Sensitivity analysis on big data, we can analyze the prediction validation metrics that tune the deep neural network parameters according to misclassification trends in structural datasets. Common validation metrics include confusion matrix, precision-recall curve, ROC curve, lift curve, and kappa statistic. Here we find literature on sequence learning and discriminative learning for modelling the feature extractions and regression residuals. For deep representation learning of the such data distributions, we can decompose the historical data into recent, frequent, and supervised patterns. Here we can experiment with discretization methods such as sliding windows, dynamic time warping and time frequency methods like wavelets, and shapelets. We may then treat data distributions as 1D vector or 2D tensors in deep learning to extend the collaborative filtering on end-user feedback into data cubes acting as data structures for distance metric learning.

We can also define synopsis data structures on tensors and graphs to derive the machine learning features. The synopsis data structures would aid similarity search and metric learning in complex network analysis. In this context we can explore the causality and stationarity of Markov chains with expectation-maximization and minimum description length principles for statistical inference. The analytics results are applicable in data mining tasks such as clustering, classification, and association analysis. We can extend them into feature learning for structured prediction, change detection, event mining, and pattern mining with deep learning. Here the learnt features can be one of sampled features, constructed features, extracted features, inferred features, and predictive features. In terms of the modelling parameter estimation, regularization parameters would do dimensionality reduction, while learning parameters do predictive classification and regression. Combining all these parameters in a data mining model would allow us to do sensitivity analysis of the model for different data samples. The error minimization over various types of parameters can be modelled as loss functions in classification models and cost functions in optimization models for game theoretical adversarial deep learning. The relevant deep neural networks include feature-based models and memory based models. The choice between deep neural nets for data mining is determined by statistical hypothesis testing methods in data analytics methods. Such methods include maximum likelihood estimation, sequential hypothesis tests, shift invariant methods, support vector machines, and tensor decomposition methods.

Grasedyck et al. [231] produce a literature review of low-rank tensor approximation techniques in scientific computing. A particular emphasis is put on tensors induced by the discretization of multivariate functions representing the solution to high-dimensional partial differential equation. Higher-order tensors suffer from the curse of dimensionality. So they have to be approximated with a compression scheme such as the tensor decompositions in low-rank tensor techniques. Such techniques have several applications such as in the approximation solutions of multidimensional integrals, multidimensional convolution, partial differential equations, Schrodinger equations, stochastic automata networks, computational finance, multivariate regression, wavelet analysis, and adversarial deep learning. Some of the popular low-rank tensor decompositions to improve the robustness of adversarial learning and efficiency of deep learning are CP decomposition, Tucker decomposition, tensor train decomposition, and tensor networks. The computational algorithms finding the decompositions include iterative methods combined with truncation, optimization-based algorithms, discretization algorithms, dynamical algorithms, successive rank-1 approximation, and blackbox approximation. They can be used to modify, improve, and study the convergence of the alternating least squares search and optimization procedure in the adversarial deep learning with variational adversaries. Thus they can produce low cost adversarial payoff functions for sparse attack scenarios. In this context, we can derive robust classification models in the game theoretical adversarial learning frameworks. We can conduct a study of the existing adversarial cost functions with respect to robustness bounds and privacy budgets in the sparse representation learning models for adversarial learning. Here we can also formulate data mining extensions of my adversarial learning into web mining, time series analysis, cyber-physical systems autonomous navigation and its manipulation, multimedia pattern recognition, and network security analytics. Such game theoretical modelling is useful in the adversarial deep learning over multi-modal, weakly supervised, noisy, sparse, linked, streaming, and multi-structured datasets. We can apply resultant sampling dynamics into the privacy-preserving data mining and fuzzy signal processing of noisy, sparse, soft matching patterns as feature embeddings in cybersecurity. The cybersecurity solutions can be provisioned as cloud services proposing security orchestrations in service-oriented architectures. The relevant machine learning paradigms include incremental learning, online learning, reinforcement learning, and utility learning on stream data. The related work is in data stream mining with class and cost distribution information for features, anomalies, novelties, changes, and communities in the stream.

Nouy [466] provides a survey of low-rank tensor methods to approximate functions expressed as two-order tensors for vector-valued functions, or higher-order tensors for multivariate functions. The low-rank approximations in vector-valued functions are computed by projection methods based on samples of the function or on equations satisfied by the function. In multivariate functions, the low-rank approximations correspond to model order reduction methods. They include reduced basis, proper orthogonal decomposition, Krylov subspace, balanced truncation methods, and proper generalized decomposition. Such models have application in sensitivity analysis, uncertainty quantification, and non-linear optimization in game theoretical adversarial learning. Model order reduction methods can act as sparse approximation methods selecting a dictionary of functions that exploit prior information on adversarial manipulations on low-rank manifolds. Depending on the computational complexity of these methods in dealing with the curse of dimensionality, there have been evolved several notions of ranks in the low-rank approximations of the multivariate functions applicable to machine learning. The low-rank approximations can be obtained by tensor completion methods that reconstruct the tensor by the minimization of a least squares loss function. Their dual approaches can produce game theoretical regularizations of the rank minimization problems. A challenging question on computational complexity of such approaches is the number of samples required for a stable reconstruction of the low-rank approximations. Low-rank truncation methods can systematically limit the storage and computational complexity in the algebraic operations. They require a solution of optimization problems on a low-dimensional manifold with greedy constructions of the low-rank approximations. The resulting adversarial algorithms can be analyzed as inexact versions incorporating data perturbations in the machine learning. Characterizing the game theoretical adversarial learning in such approximation classes yields a class of adversarial loss functions with algebraic or exponential convergence rates. Here dictionary learning produces a dictionary of filter elements to reconstruct a highly redundant representation of the adversarial data distribution with a sparse coding models in the data-driven optimization & inference problems. As a computational machine learning paradigm, dictionary learning can analyze the multimodal feature generation and multivariate optimization problems. To characterize the data signals in experimental data, we could also estimate the Lyapunov spectra exponents and attractor networks with deep learning models and predictive analytics processes. We can explore the spectral signal processing techniques for describing the complex dynamics in game theoretical interactions as features extracted on the underlying data distribution generating and validating the adversarial manipulations. Further, we can reconstruct the differential equations underlying game theoretical models as dynamical systems of the training data distributions. An optimization landscape analysis of the data distributions with tensor indexing structures on static and dynamic data can reduce the communication cost and increase the load balancing in distributed memory systems for embarrassingly parallel processing of the game theoretical adversarial deep learning. The iterative updates to the low-rank approximations can be obtained from tradeoffs between learnability and robustness of supervised deep learning. We can characterize the cybersecurity problems of discrimination in the presence of adversarial noise in terms of a set of robust points where data representations showcase a type of problem-specific error mitigation mechanism in the classifier design. Such an arrangement would also allow for exploring multiple choices of variational encodings of the learnable decision boundaries in game theoretical modelling.

Filisbino et al. [195] model multidimensional image databases with tensor decomposition. Ranked tensor components act as a dimensionality reduction technique. They can be used to estimate the covariance structure of a database with a concurrent subspace analysis. They can also compute the discriminant weights of separating hyperplanes in it through a discriminant principal component analysis.

Such non-linear dimensionality reduction generalizes adversarial machine learning-based in linear dimensionality reduction techniques such as principal component analysis (PCA), linear discriminant analysis (LDA), and multidimensional scaling (MDS) solving for a linear optimization criterion. They are classified as subspace learning methods in machine learning. A tensor representation for images can be proposed with subspace learning methods such as singular value decomposition method (SVD), concurrent subspace analysis (CSA), multilinear independent components analysis (MICA), multilinear principal component analysis (MPCA), tensor discriminant analysis (TDA), and tensor rank-one decomposition. Such image representations have application in face and gait recognition, digital number recognition, signal processing, content analysis, and anomaly detection in data mining. The analytics task is to identify the most discriminant "directions" in the tensor analysis applied to a particular classification task. This is a feature ranking method in a projected subspace for classification that identifies the most discriminant "directions" rather than the highest variance features in the data samples. The machine learning models checks the alignment of the ranked tensor principal components with separating hyperplane directions determined by the corresponding discriminant weights. Kernel methods such as support vector machines can create the hyperplane directions.

Srebro et al. [571] approximate a target matrix with a weighted low-rank matrix. An expectation-maximization (EM) procedure parameterizes the approximation that may not have a closed-form solution. The weighted low-rank matrix is used in training a linear factor model, a logistic regression, and a mixture-of-Gaussians noise model. Singular value decomposition (SVD) is one such approximation where the Frobenius norm to the target matrix is minimized. The weighting of the approximation is influenced by adversarial noise leading to a better reconstruction of the underlying probabilistic structure and statistical distribution in the data. The weights can also arise out of constraints on the approximation encoded as features of varying importance. They can be also due to the noise variance and algorithmic bias in the training data. Here game theoretical modelling can be used to optimize the approximation and weighting when the noise model associated with the matrix elements are unknown. Its results can be benchmarked against the comparable alternating-optimization methods. The alternating-optimization methods view the weighted low-rank approximation problem as a maximum-likelihood problem with missing values. The target matrix weights are mapped to a 0/1 configuration where observed elements have weight 1 and missing elements have weight 0. The weighted cost of a matrix is equivalent to the log-likelihood of the observed elements. An EM algorithm updates a parameter matrix in the expectation step to maximize the expected log-likelihood of a data matrix where the missing values are imputed according to a distribution imposed by the current estimate of the log-likelihood. In the maximization step, the data matrix is reestimated as a data-driven weighted low-rank approximation. Such a probabilistic system can be extended to several target matrices in an EM learning framework. The maximum likelihood is then estimated on a low-rank approximation of their average if the target matrices can be fully observed. If some of the target matrices are not fully observed, the EM algorithm can be used to fill in the missing values in the target matrices that are in turn estimated as a low-rank approximation. The iterative updates to the target and weight matrix can be based on variational bounds on estimating the log-likelihood. Therefore we can mix weighted low-rank approximation iterations and variational bound iterations while still ensuring convergence for both.

Tsourakakis [610] improve the Tucker decomposition to analyze multi-aspect data and extract latent factors. A new sampling algorithm computes the decompositions in tensor streams where the tensor does not fit in the available memory. The Tucker decomposition is formulated as a non-linear optimization problem. It is solved with a computationally expensive alternating least squares (ALS) optimization algorithm. The ALS procedure is sped up with randomized algorithms that select columns according to a biased probability distribution for tensor decompositions. They can be interpreted as generalizations of low-rank approximation methods. Further the randomized algorithm is amenable to embarrassingly parallel processing on tensor streams. Such low-rank approximations represent statistically significant portions of the training data obtained from real-world processes. They have application in data mining tasks such as network anomaly detection. Here outliers are detected relative to the subspace spanned by the principal components in the training data.

Zou et al. [717] propose sparse principal component analysis (SPCA) where an elastic net produces modified principal components with sparse loadings. Principal component analysis is conducted as a regression-type optimization problem. Such a SPCA has applications in handwritten zip code classification, human face recognition, gene expression data analysis, and multivariate data analysis. Richtarik et al. [517] benchmark eight different optimization formulations for SPCA and their efficient parallel implementations on multicore, GPU, and cluster. The robust formulations use objective functions that are functions of the covariance matrix. An alternating maximization method is the optimization algorithm. It measures data variance using L_1 and L_2 norm. Anandkumar et al. [14] propose robust decomposition of a tensor into low-rank and sparse components. The proposed method does a gradient ascent on a regularized variational form of the eigenvector problem. The regularized objective satisfies convexity and smoothness properties for optimization. Empirical moments in probabilistic are represented as higher-order moment tensors to be decomposed. Then corruptions on the moments are assumed to occur due to adversarial manipulations or systematic bias in estimating the moments. The experimental results are compared with robust matrix PCA on flattened tensor and matrix slices of the tensor. They have applications in image and video denoising, multitask learning, and robust learning of latent variable models. Romano et al. [522] analyze the robustness of a classifier to adversarial perturbations by using the theory of sparse representations. Bounds are derived on the performance of the adversarial learner's properties and structure in regression and classification. The bounds are shown to be a function of the sparsity of the signal and the characteristics of the filters/dictionaries/weights on the incoming signals. They unveil the data model governing the sensitivity to adversarial attacks. Adversarial regularization mechanism based on sparse solutions and incoherent dictionaries is proposed to improve the stability of the robust learner dealing with adversarial noise. The relation of the intrinsic properties of the signal to the success of the classification task is explored as a generative model. The stability of the classification model is studied in both binary- and multi-class settings.

Kreutz-Delgado et al. [331] develop data-driven algorithms for domain-specific dictionary learning. They perform maximum likelihood and maximum a posteriori estimation. Priors are obtained from sparse representations of environmental signals matched with a dictionary as concepts, features, and words. In experimental evaluation the proposed dictionary learning has better performance in signal-to-noise ratios than independent component analysis methods. Images encoded with a dictionary have higher compression (fewer bits per pixel) and higher accuracy (lower mean square error). The dictionary provides succinct sparse representation for most statistically representative signal vectors in the data-generating environment. The statistical structure in the generated signals spanning a learning environment is represented with a set of basis vectors spanning a lower-dimensional manifold of meaningful signals in a dictionary. The dictionary learning maximizes the mutual information between the basis vectors and the generated signals. Projecting the signals onto the dictionary results in noise reduction and data compression. The tensor decomposition problem in dictionary learning is to produce low-rank approximations completing the dictionary. The signal representation problem as an entropy minimization elaborates the statistical structure in data distributions. It can also be viewed as a generalization of vector quantization. Stochastic generative models can be developed in deep learning to solve such problems. A combination of expectation-maximization and variational approximation techniques can also be used in the dictionary learning.

Luedtke et al. [398] propose adversarial Monte Carlo meta-learning to construct optimal statistical estimation procedures in problems like point estimation and interval estimation. A two-player game is formulated between Nature and a statistician. Neural network parameters are repeatedly updated across the game interactions to arrive at a representation of the finite observed samples in numerical experiments. Thus adversarial learning can be incorporated into frequentist and Bayesian approaches of measuring the machine learning performance. In frequentist approaches adversarial learning can solve for the worst-case performance of maximum likelihood estimators expressed as a minimaxity optimization criterion. In Bayesian approaches adversarial learning can approximate posterior probability distributions where minimax optimization derives Bayes procedures from least favorable mixtures of priors. Here maximum empirical risk of a statistical procedure can be determined from its least favorable distribution. Minimax adversarial learning algorithms iteratively update such risks to improve of machine learning models. New statistical procedures can be constructed for data mining tasks in a cost-effective manner using deep adversarial learning. For instance, Zhou et al. [711] present a sparse relevance vector machine ensemble for adversarial learning. During model training, it is able to model adversarial attacks with kernel parameters. A concept drift in the directions of kernel parameters minimizes the likelihood of positive (malicious) data points. It is used in the learning of weights in a relevance vector machine. Here game theoretical modelling can be said to be solving a constrained optimization problem. Such optimization can be contrasted with non-game-theoretic methods making assumptions about the distribution of the adversarially corrupted data, available computing resources, and adversary's knowledge of the targeted machine learning model. Here relevance vector machine (RVM) ensemble acts as a sparse linearly parameterized model for adversarial learning. RVM has a prior over the weights to be estimated expressed as a set of hyperparameters associated with the weights. Training data points associated with non-zero weights are called relevance vectors. Yin et al. [688] limit the cost of constructing adversarial manipulations with sparse feature attacks in a non-zero sum game with budgeted adversaries. The non-zero sum game solves a robust regression problem.

Gemulla et al. [214] factor large matrices in an iterative stochastic optimization algorithm extending gradient descent. The low-rank approximation is produced by minimizing a loss function that measures the difference between original input matrix and product of the factors returned by the factorization algorithm. A stratum loss is defined on the loss computed on each stratum that expresses the input matrix as a union of pieces. The convergence criteria are studied with reference to stochastic approximation theory and regenerative process theory. The gradient descent variant is specialized to a matrix factorization algorithm that can be fully distributed and run on web-scale datasets. Thus low-rank matrix factorization is very useful in big data analytics involving massive datasets on the Internet. Such analytics tasks discover and quantify the interactions between two given entities in "dyadic data" found in applications such as topic detection, keyword search, and news personalization. The training loss can be regularized with several factorization methods suitable for the emerging distributed processing platforms. He et al. [265] propose neural factorization machines for categorical predictors with highly sparse binary features. NFM model the feature interactions representing non-linear and complex structure in real-world data. Deep neural networks are able to model the higher-order feature interactions as low-rank tensors. They are able to augment and subsume combinatorial features combining multiple predictor variables in machine learning feature engineering. The deep learning models are able to generalize to unseen feature combinations by embedding high-dimensional sparse features into a low-dimensional latent space. The NFMs have application as embedding methods for sparse data prediction in online advertising, microblog retrieval, and open relation extraction. They can learn non-linear feature interactions by embedding the latent feature vectors into various deep neural network architectures constructed to improve learning and generalization ability. Thus they are better than linear models to learn feature interactions such as higher-Order FM and Exponential Machines. In classification, regression, and ranking tasks, they can regularize loss functions such as hinge loss, log loss, pairwise personalized ranking loss, and contrastive max-margin loss. Therefore factorization machines are suitable for modelling high cardinality and sparsely observed adversarial data distributions. They can represent datasets found in text analysis and recommender systems with a low-rank approximation of a matrix or a tensor. They enable a variety of business analytics tasks involving sparse data such as recommendation and prediction. He et al. [266] propose adversarial personalized ranking (APR) to enhance the robustness of a recommender model. APR enhances the feature ranking methods used in top-k recommendation with adversarial training. Bayesian personalized ranking (BPR) is taken as the learner participating in a minimax game with an adversary who crafts adversarial perturbations on model parameters to maximize the BPR objective function. Adversarial perturbations are obtained from embedding vectors of users and items contributing to collaborative filtering. Adversarial training is able to improve the generalization error of personalized ranking in robust recommender models. The top-k recommendation lists are evaluated with performance measures such as hit ratio (HR), normalized discounted cumulative gain (NDCG). The statistical significance testing in personalized ranking lists for multimedia recommendation is performed with one-sample paired t-test. Making a recommender model resistant to adversarial examples results in a robust and stable predictive function improving the generalization performance in information retrieval. APR can be combined with NFMs to support recommendation scenarios such as cold-start, context-aware, session-based recommendation. It has application in information retrieval tasks such as text retrieval, web search, question answering, and knowledge graph completion.

5.4.2.4 Relative Distribution Methods in Adversarial Deep Learning

In computational learning theory, distributional learning theory is a framework for learning distributions from samples. It can be exploited in game theoretical adversarial deep learning for designing approximation algorithms targeting machine learning models. We summarize relevant ideas in distance metric learning and deep metric learning.

Goldberger et al. [223] propose a learned distance metric used within a stochastic neighbor selection rule in nearest neighbor methods for classification. It is a low-rank representation of the data that is able to reduce the storage and search costs in forming the nearest neighbors. The leave-one-out performance is the evaluation measure optimized on the training dataset. The distance metric produces a distance matrix on training dataset that is symmetric positive semidefinite matrix used in the calculation of a Mahalanobis distance. It estimates a transformation of the input space where nearest neighbor classifications performs well. The stochastic neighbor selection rule gives soft assignment of neighbors in a supervised learning objective function. Maximizing the supervised learning objective function is equivalent to minimizing the L_1 norm between the true class distribution in the underlying data and the stochastic class distribution induced on the training dataset. Maximizing the objective corresponds to error free classification of the entire training dataset. The proposed low-rank distance metric is comparable to dimensionality reduction techniques like factor analysis, principal components analysis, independent components analysis, linear discriminant analysis, and relevant components analysis. It solves a constrained optimization problem without making parametric assumptions about structure of class distributions and decision boundaries.

Chopra et al. [128] construct a trainable similarity metric for recognition and verification applications. The similarity metric learns a function to map input patterns into target space such that L_1 norm in the target space approximates the semantics distance in the input space. The mapping function is architected as a convolutional neural network that is robust to geometric distortions. A discriminative loss function minimizes the similarity metric for a face database with high variability in pose, lighting, expression, position, and artificial occlusions. The loss function is derived from energy-based models (EBMs). In comparison to generative models, EBMs do not need to estimate normalized probability distributions over the input space. Such approaches to recognition tasks are suitable for datasets where the number of categories is large and the number of samples per category is small.

Xing et al. [666] propose a distance metric learning problem over (dis)similar relationships side information in data points. The distance metric learning is framed as a convex optimization problem with efficient solutions. The learned metric is trained over the full feature space of the inputs rather than a feature embedding derived from the training dataset. So it generalizes more easily to previously unseen data. Experimental evaluation is carried out on variants of K-means such as constrained K-means, K-means + metric, and constrained K-means + metric.

Ye et al. [682] propose instance specific distance metric learning in nearest neighbor methods. It assigns multiple metrics to different localities in the training data. The proposed Instance Specific METric Subspace (ISMETS) spans the metric space in a generative manner. It induces a metric subspace for each instance by inferring the expectation over the metric bases in a Bayesian manner. The statistical inference is done according to a variational Bayes framework. The posterior demonstrates advantages of interpretability, effectiveness, and robustness. In multimodal data analytics, such a distance metric learning is comparable to constrained convex programming, and information-theoretical approaches such as maximum entropy modelling. It can predict distance metrics for unseen test instances inductively as well as transductively. It can incorporate parallelization techniques and approximation tricks.

Shen et al. [553] propose a boosting-based technique for learning a quadratic Mahalanobis distance metric. Semidefinite programming solution is given to the boosting. It expresses positive semidefinite matrices as a linear combination of trace-one rank-one matrices. They act as weak learners within an efficient and scalable boosting-based learning process. The proposed semidefinite programming can incorporate various types of constraints for rank aggregation in classification and regression loss functions. Such a distance metric learning is closely related to subspace methods like principal component analysis, linear discriminant analysis, locality preserving projection, and relevant component analysis. They can be interpreted as projections of data from input space to a lower-dimensional output space while preserving the neighborhood structure of the training dataset in an information-theoretical sense. Here supervised distance metric learning utilizes side information presented as constraints on the optimization problem. A sparse greedy approximation algorithm solves the optimization problem in an AdaBoost-like optimization procedure for semidefinite programming.

Sriperumbudur et al. [572] analyze integral probability metrics (IPMs) as measurable functions of distance between two probability distributions. IPMs a generalization of popular distance metrics such as KL divergence, Φ-divergences, Hellinger divergences, Renyi divergences, Kantorovich metric, Fortet-Mourier metric, Stein discrepancies, Lipschitz distance, total variation distance, Fisher distance, and kernel distance. Their empirical estimators are useful in machine learning to compute the distance between training and adversarial data distributions. In binary classification IPMs are applicable to the empirical risk and smoothing optimization between class-conditional distributions. Thus badness of a statistical fit to the training dataset can be measured by probability divergence measures such as IPMs. It has applications for model selection in classifier design and density estimation in adversarial attack scenario. It has implications for the convergence criteria of game theoretical adversarial learning in particular and generative adversarial learning in general. An appropriate choice of the probability divergence measure gives a statistical significance test statistic on alternative hypothesis for the adversarial training, an efficient loss function to target in the adversarial learning, and the convergence behavior for game theoretical modelling. In this context, the mathematics around "distance," "metric," and "divergence" between adversarial datasets and training datasets is of interest to model relative distributions obeying the triangle inequality in game theoretical adversarial learning.

Liu et al. [380] survey transfer metric learning to analyze multimodal data in multimedia applications where the target domains are in classification and searching tasks for data analytics. In contrast to transfer metric learning algorithms, distance metric learning algorithms rely on the label information in the target domain for model training. Transfer metric learning can deal with limited label information with multiview learning. The multimodal feature representations for prediction with transfer learning have application in multimedia such as sentiment analysis, opinion mining, deception detection, Internet fraud detection, and online product searching. The goal of transfer learning is improving the learning performance for tasks/domains of interest by applying knowledge/skills learnt from related tasks/domains. Here transfer metric learning allows knowledge transfer with distance estimation for both linear and non-linear target metrics to guide multimodal classification and multimedia search applications in the target domains. Few labelled samples are used in combination with large amounts of unlabelled datasets in the multimodal classification loss functions. Further a ranking based loss function analysis is conducted for the multimedia search applications. SIFT features such as visual words, wavelet texture, and textual tags are derived as the multimodal features. The divergence minimization for distance computation on multiple domains is categorized as representation-based divergence minimization, distance-based divergence minimization, and Kernel-based divergence minimization. The divergence minimization problems are solved with optimization methods such as canonical correlation maximization, Burg matrix divergence minimization, Bregman divergence minimization, log-determinant divergence minimization, and Von Neumann divergence minimization.

Bellet et al. [44] survey the utility of distance metric learning in machine learning, pattern recognition, and data mining. Metric learning is a research area that automatically learns the distance metrics from data. Supervised Mahalanobis distance metric learning is a baseline for comparison with the learnt metrics. Variants of metric learning algorithms include those for non-linear metric learning, similarity learning, edit distance learning, local metric learning, multitask metric learning, and semi-supervised metric learning. In the context of adversarial learning, metric learning allows us to derive generalization guarantees to the machine learning model's performance. Kulis et al. [334] provide another survey of tuning a learned distance metric to a particular task in data analytics in a supervised manner. Supervised metric learning is based on labelling information regarding the distances of the transformed data. It is of special interest in scaling the data analytics to high-dimensional feature spaces in computer vision, image retrieval, face recognition, pose estimation, text analysis, music analysis, program analysis, and multimedia. Metric learning has extensions in non-linear regression, feature ranking, dimensionality reduction, database indexing, and domain adaptation. Deep learning networks have an important role to play in the development of metric learning methods.

Hoffer et al. [277] propose a triplet network deep learning model to learn useful representations by distance comparisons. It is applied in the learning of a ranking in image information retrieval. The similarity function is induced by a norm metric embedding for multi-class-labelled dataset. A deep network is the embedding function. It finds the L_2 distance between inputs of two labels and the embedded representation of a third label input acting as a reference label. The neural network architecture allows this analytics task to be expressed as a two-class classification problem where the objective of the loss function is to learn a metric embedding that measures the proximity to the reference label. A back-propagation algorithm updates this learning model. The model learns comparative measures rather than class labels between labelled data distributions. This learning mechanism can be leverages to classify new data sources with unknown labels.

Chen et al. [120] propose a discriminative metric-based generative adversarial networks (DMGANs) that use probability-based methods for generating real-like samples in image synthesis tasks. A generator is trained to generate realistic samples by reducing the distance between real and generated samples. The discriminator acts as a feature extractor that is learning a discriminative loss constrained by an identity-preserving loss. The discriminative loss maximizes the distance between real and fake samples in the feature space. The identity-preserving loss calculates distance between samples and their centers. The centers are updated during the GAN training. It maps the generated samples into a latent feature space used to label the samples. Thus DMGAN recovers the implicit distribution of the real data. It learns representative features in a transformed space. The proposed identity-preserving loss can be contrasted with triplet loss and contrastive loss that learn intra-class variations by constraining the distance between their samples. Thus GANs can be improved from the perspective of deep metric learning. Such GANs have applications in image generation, image super-resolution, image-to-image translation, object detection, and face recognition. By deriving back-propagation signals through a competitive process, GANs do not require intractable probabilistic computations unlike deep Boltzmann machines and generative stochastic networks.

Nowozin et al. [468] interpret GANs as generative neural samplers where probabilistic models implement the sampling. Such probabilistic models produce a sample from a random input vector where the probability distribution is defined by the neural network weights. The GANs can produce samples but cannot compute their likelihoods. From the perspective of estimating likelihoods, the proposed f-GAN generalizes adversarial training methods in GANs to a variational divergence estimation process. f-GAN uses a f-divergence to train the generative neural samplers. The f-divergence can be replaced with various choices of divergence functions resulting in changes to the training complexity and the quality of the obtained generative models. A decision threshold is used to classify the generator samples. The proposed variational divergence minimization can perform sampling, estimation, and likelihood evaluation with GANs. It is comparable to the combination of mixture density networks with recurrent neural networks to yield generative models of handwritten text. It improves existing probabilistic models for deep learning such as real-valued neural autoregressive density estimator, diffusion probabilistic models, and noise contrastive estimation. It can be combined with VAEs for efficient inference. It can extend optimization objectives such as the kernel maximum mean discrepancy with total variation metric, the Wasserstein distance, and the Kolmogorov distance.

Fedus et al. [184] view GAN equilibrium as Nash equilibria rather than divergence minimization between the training distribution and the model distribution. So a game theoretical modelling of the GAN equilibrium is shown to improve minimax GANs in terms of sample quality and diversity. Adversarial cost functions are combined with the minmax objective of the game as non-saturating regularization functions so that generated samples are produced with a high probability of being real. A gradient penalty on data manifold analyzed from the perspective of regret minimization is chosen as the non-saturating regularization objective. A no-regret algorithm approximates the discriminator in GAN to be linear around the data manifold. The trajectory to the Nash equilibrium is does not correspond to gradually minimizing the information divergence. Instead the GAN training dynamics optimize different distance metrics regularized by adversarial cost functions. Therefore we can measure information divergence between minimal representations of training data and adversarial data feature embeddings with deep metric learning-based adversarial cost functions. We may also enforce a prior distribution on the latent factors for coherent data generation in generative learning.

Bojanowski et al. [76] introduce Generative Latent Optimization (GLO) to train deep convolutional generators using reconstruction losses. GLO is an alternative to the adversarial optimization scheme in GANs. GLO allows linear interpolations in the noise space into semantic interpolations in the image space, allows linear arithmetic in the noise space, and predicts target images from learnable noise vectors. In the experimental evaluation, GLO is compared with principal component analysis (PCA), variational autoencoders (VAE), and GANs. The mode collapse in GANs is investigated with a reconstruction criterion.

Bauso et al. [36] formulate distributionally robust games using f-divergence in multiplayer games between training distribution and adversarial distribution scenarios. Each player has to contend with a worst-case distribution called the adversarial distribution. Bregman learning algorithms speed up the computation of robust equilibria. The adversarial learning scenarios are selected by nature assumed to be a virtual player solving a non-convex non-concave objective function. A triality theory is proposed for the dimensionality reduction of the robust game. A swarm algorithm estimates the expected gradient solving for adversarial manipulations.

Kamath et al. [307] study the loss functions in the problem of distribution approximations in statistical learning where a distribution is approximated from its samples. In compression applications the Kullback-Leibler divergence is recommended as the relevant loss function. In classification applications the L_1 and L_2 losses are recommended as the relevant loss function. In generative learning the f-divergences are recommended as the relevant loss function. Here the minmax cumulative loss for a given loss function and the optimal estimator achieving has practical importance in training machine learning models. Sugiyama et al. [576, 577] discuss the approximation of two probability distributions from their samples. This is a problem with implications for statistics, information theory, and machine learning. Kullback-Leibler divergence of maximum likelihood estimation models is compared by the authors with Pearson divergence, L^2-distance for efficiency, robustness, and stability. Here proper distances must satisfy the triangle inequality that is an extension of the Pythagorean theorem to various geometric metric spaces. They must not be sensitive to outliers. They must not be numerically unstable. They must have a relative density ratio function that is bounded and computationally efficient. The authors survey several data analytics applications utilizing the divergence measures such as change-point detection, salient object detection, and class balance estimation in several data mining tasks such as feature extraction, clustering, independent component analysis, causal feature learning, independent component analysis, and canonical dependency analysis. Direct divergence approximation in combination with dimensionality reduction is said to be a better strategy in experiments rather than naive density estimation of distributions from samples. The difference between such statistical distances and information divergences is their effect on the convergence criteria in the sequences of learned probability distributions estimated by generative models and variational methods. The divergences being optimized are typically discontinuous with respect to the generator's parameters. So novel ways for practically estimating the infimum and supremum of the relative density ratio function are to be devised in adversarial deep learning-based on metric geometry, applied probability, and statistics.

5.5 Defense Mechanisms in Adversarial Machine Learning

Zhang et al. [690] propose defense mechanisms in adversarial data manipulations at test time. Such evasion attacks obfuscate the content of spam emails and exploit code embedded in malware samples and network packets. Classifier security is found to worsen with feature selection. So security properties of the feature selection are investigated against evasion attacks. A wrapper-based implementation is proposed to incorporate the adversarial manipulation strategies in spam and malware detection with adversary-aware feature selection in classifiers with both linear and non-linear discriminant functions. In security-sensitive data mining tasks, selecting the relevant subset of features improves classifier's generalization performance, reduces computational complexity of learning, and allows better understanding of the modelling detail. During the feature selection process, classifier security is modelled as a regularization term to be optimized along with the classifier's generalization capability. The distance between manipulated sample and legitimate sample and constraints on the classifier and feature representations is used to develop efficient adversarial algorithms in blackbox attack settings. Security evaluation of the adversarial classifier is conducted against the attacks of increasing strength. It is correlated with a figure of merit called hardness of evasion. Here L_1 norm promotes sparsity in the adversarial manipulations in contrast to L_2 norm. Countermeasures for evasion attacks explicitly incorporate knowledge of the adversarial manipulations into learning algorithms. They include game theoretical adversarial learning algorithms, probabilistic models of the hypothesized attack strategy, combination of weaker classifiers in multiple classifier systems, and data sanitization based on robust statistics.

Biggio et al. [55] conduct a security evaluation of support vector machines (SVMs) incorporated in real-world security systems. They are involved in an arms race in security application domains such as malware detection, intrusion detection, and spam filtering with increasing complexity and exposure. Thus machine learning patterns must be incorporated into the security applications to complement traditional signature-based detection on unfiltered samples and unpopular attacks. The attack patterns are categorized as poisoning attacks that mislead the learning algorithm, evasion attacks that evade detection at deployment time, and privacy breaches that gain information about the modelling details. Here adversaries manipulate data to exploit vulnerabilities in learning algorithms that make stationarity assumptions in performance evaluation-based techniques like cross-validation, bootstrapping, and empirical risk minimization. Adversary-aware designs of SVMs are designed as the countermeasure techniques. A differential privacy framework is proposed as a countermeasure for privacy attacks. A survey of the arms race between adversary and classifier is detailed in terms of the machine learning features being exploited in image spam classifiers and outlier detectors in computer networks. In this context, adversarial learning problems can be considered as a proactive arms race where the classifier anticipates the adversaries' moves. Security evaluation of the adversarial learning solutions is conducted with application-dependent criteria represented within the hypothesized attack scenarios. Attack impact is evaluated in terms of bounded loss functions on labelled datasets that act as aggregated statistics of sensitive data.

Biggio et al. [53] view poisoning attacks as a type of outliers in training data. Weighted bagging ensembles are then proposed as countermeasures against poisoning attacks. Thus the problem of designing robust classifiers is formulated in terms of mitigating outlier samples in training data by reducing the variance component of estimation or classification or regression error. Thus robust statistics can reduce the effect of poisoning attacks in training data. Cybersecurity applications are shown in spam filtering and intrusion detection. The intrusion detection is focused on web applications in security-critical environments like medical, financial, military, and administrative systems. The objective of the adversary submitting malicious queries is to access confidential information or cause a denial of service. Biggio et al. [61] design robust classifiers by generating a data distribution for adversarial classification tasks from a maximum likelihood estimation model. Cybersecurity applications are in biometric identity verification and spam filtering. The class labels for supervised learning are malicious (M) or legitimate (L) to classify the user as accessing a computer system as "genuine" (L) or "impostor" (M). Spam detection baselines for a naive Bayes text classifier are good word insertion (GWI) and bad word obfuscation (BWO) against text-based spam filters. Countermeasures modify classification algorithms in their training phase. The baselines in biometric traits are spoof attacks against multimodal biometric systems for identity verification. They are considered to be exploratory integrity attacks. Performance is evaluated using the receiver operating characteristic (ROC) curve, which shows the percentage of accepted genuine users (genuine acceptance rate, GAR) as a function of the percentage of accepted impostors (false acceptance rate, FAR), for all values of the decision threshold.

Dekel et al. [151] present robust classifiers that approximate the learning problem with linear programming that is analyzed to provide statistical risk bounds on the divergence between training and classification data distributions. The statistical learning in a perceptron then deals with the online learning variant of the problem. A L_∞ regularization scheme is used to balance sparsity and density in the classifier learning susceptible to adversarial feature-corrupting noise. Minimizing empirical risk is formulated as a combinatorial optimization problem. The online classifier is restricted to a hyper-cube to control its complexity. Test instances are corrupted by a greedy adversary. Computational tradeoffs are seen on the robustness of the classifiers training on sparse and dense data. Xu et al. [669] demonstrate equivalence between regularized support vector machines (SVMs) and robust optimization formulations. Robustness is said to be the reason for generalization performance in SVMs for a class of non-boxed type uncertainty sets. Robust optimization theory is used to motivate the construction of regularization terms in machine learning for non-i.i.d learning settings. Testing samples are considered to a perturbation of training samples. Such formulations of SVMs are based on chance-constrained classifiers. In minimizing an upper bound on the expected classification error, they are mathematically equivalent to minmax formulations of the optimization problem in game theoretical modelling. A robust optimization view of SVMs can derive sample complexity bounds for a broad class of classification algorithms. However, the robustness in feature space that is guaranteed by the regularization process does not guarantee robustness in the observation space due to "non-smooth" feature mappings in certain kernels.

Demontis et al. [155] link the developments in robust optimization with sparsity, regularization, and security of linear classifiers. The linear classifiers are used in embedded systems and mobile devices for their interpretability of decisions, low processing time, and small memory requirements. The sparsity of feature weights is found to have a desirable effect on not only the processing cost but also the security of the linear classifiers. Robust optimization is shown to have an effect on classifier regularization where evasion attacks are considered as a form of adversarial noise. Thus the problem of adversarial machine learning is to select the optimal regularizer against different types of adversarial noise. The adversarial cost of modifying the data is expressed in terms of L_1 norm yielding a sparse attack that is proportional to the e distance between the original and modified sample in Euclidean space. The attack strategy is to minimize the classifier's discriminant function so that a malicious sample is classified as a legitimate sample with high confidence. The robust optimization problem is defined in terms of the bounded perturbations of the training data and the associated uncertainty set including L_1 balls. The learning problem is to minimize the discriminative loss for a two-class classification problem under worst-case, bounded perturbations of the training data. The proposed regularizer is shown to tradeoff feature sparsity with computational cost of the security evaluation. Cybersecurity applications are shown for handwritten digit classification, spam filtering, and PDF malware detection.

Feng et al. [187] propose a robust logistic regression algorithm. It is robust to adversarial outliers in a corrupted covariate matrix. A simple linear programming procedure learns the logistic regression parameters in binary classification problems. It is compared with an iterative reweighted method for optimizing the logistic regression. The adversarial outliers are arbitrary, unbounded, and not from any specific distribution. They skew the parameter estimation in logistic regression to decrease its performance. The resultant regression curve is far away from the ground truth. The labelled predictions on inliers are wrong. The loss functions in logistic regression are 0-1 loss, hinge loss, exponential loss and logistic loss. Instead of likelihood inference, robust estimators and their regression parameters can be proposed by robustly estimating the linear correlation statistics such as the covariate matrix. Theoretical bounds can be derived by empirical and population risks bounds on the logistic regression. The proposed robust estimator scales to large problems contain corrupted training samples in a computationally efficient manner.

Barreno et al. [32] give a taxonomy of attacks as well as defenses on machine learning algorithms and systems. Machine learning models offer benefits by being trained on novel differences between normal (known good) and attack (known bad) data distributions. The hypothesis space or function class for such supervised machine learning models consist of lookup tables, linear functions, polynomials, Boolean functions, and neural networks. The learning theoretic tradeoffs are between explanation and generalization. They have applications in spam email filtering, fault detection, intrusion detection, virus detection, web services, agent systems, and cluster monitoring that have to contend with dynamically changing data patterns. More complicated learning algorithms train with continuous streams of unlabelled points in an online learning paradigm for semi-supervised learning. The feature space for constructing the decision boundaries between normal and attack data points is a metric space on distances between points. Regularization is proposed as the defense mechanism in causative attacks, while randomization is recommended in exploratory attacks. Smoothing the learner's solution removes the complexity exploitable by an adversary. Targeted attacks are more sensitive to variations in the decision boundary. Preprocessing on prior distributions can encode domain knowledge in baselines for learner estimation. Randomization in the positioning of the decision boundary is suggested as a defense mechanism in targeted attacks. Publicly available digital watermarks verification algorithms must also deal with the sensitivity of the targeted attacks. A large number of misclassified data points are indicative of causative attacks. Causative attacks can be mitigated with a test dataset consisting of well-known intrusions. Exploratory attacks are characterized by sudden large clusters near the decision boundary. They can be detected by running a clustering algorithm on the classifier's training dataset. Detecting such attacks gives the learner information about the adversary's capabilities that can be used in defense mechanisms. Game theoretical models such as deception games formalize such information as adversarial data manipulations constructed by each player. They involve partial information for each player and its influence on information seen by other players. Such information is encoded as probability distributions and discretization states in adversarial payoff functions where a cost is associated for changing features in attack points for the adversary and measuring each feature in the data for the learner. In more complicated games, the learner can confuse the adversary's estimates of the learner's states. The goal of the learner is to permit "honeypot" intrusions to trick the adversary and prevent it from learning the decision boundary. In such a case, the roles of the learner and adversary are reversed. The cost of countermeasures is said to depend on the impact of legitimate data on the learning process. A learner including prior information loses adaptability to new data. At the same time a learner that accommodates information from the training data becomes more vulnerable to attack. Thus we have to consider factors on security and secrecy of the decision boundary in the learning process for retraining. It includes tradeoff between the amount of training data for the learner in training and the secrecy of the resultant learner in deployment. Relationship between multilevel retraining and adversary's domain knowledge is an open problem for research. We can produce information-theoretic bounds on the information gained by an adversary by observing the behavior of the learner on particular data points. Depending on the classification details of the learner in realistic settings, it may be possible to attack confidence limits with the strength of its predictions. Adaptive weighting mechanisms in game theory such as aggregating algorithm and weighted majority algorithm can combine advice from a set of experts to predict a sequence of game theoretical interactions that have a learning performance comparable to the best expert in adversarially chosen sequences. Control systems are an alternative to game theory applicable to search oriented expert systems in military command and control.

Biggio et al. [62] conduct a survey of complex systems for pattern recognition in adversarial settings. Here adversaries can devise attacks to exploit either preprocessing steps such as parsing errors or complicated vulnerabilities in learning algorithms such as denial of service, missing detection, and malicious samples or events. Then reactive and proactive security paradigms can be exploited by the learner to improve its security by design. The system analysis and design components for pattern recognition is centered around data collection of training data and its ground truth, preprocessing to extract structural components, feature extraction on parsed samples, feature selection with or without human supervision, learning algorithm to build a classifier from a labelled dataset, and a decision rule to assign labels to an input test sample based on a thresholding strategy on the classifier's score. The components can be deployed at different physical locations so that an adversary can target the communication channels requiring remote authentication and security protocols for human supervision. An attack surface can be constructed for all these operational vulnerabilities. It is useful for creating statistical hypotheses on the adversary's goal and knowledge of the target system and its capabilities to manipulate data causing system failure. The feedback on classifier's decisions can improve the adversary's knowledge on how the pattern recognition systems are implemented, where they are deployed, and when they operate. Thus the weakest security link of pattern recognition systems is not always the learning or classification component. Learning with such invariances is essential to a minimax approach with high computational complexity in game theoretical adversarial deep learning. It has applications in user authentication, computer vision and forensics, sentiment analysis, and market segmentation.

Barreno et al. [30] present a taxonomy of attacks on machine learning systems. It can be used to structure the costs for the adversary and the learner in building secure learning systems resilient to attacks. The learner's analysis of errors assumes a binary classification setting. Its extension to multi-label settings is not straightforward. In retraining procedures, the classifier interleaves training with evaluation. Such a retraining can be analyzed within (regularized) empirical risk minimization frameworks. Empirical risk is calculated as the expected loss of a loss function approximating the true cost. The regularization of empirical risk prevents overfitting to training data with notions of hypothesis complexity on non-stationary data distributions. The threat model posed by the adversary is expressed in terms of attacker goal/incentives and attacker capabilities. The choices made by the adversary and the learner are presented as domain-specific strategies with associated cost function assessing them. For example, the learner model maybe a support vector machine with a chosen kernel, loss, regularization, and cross-validation plan in the learning hypothesis. The adversary then chooses a statistical procedure to produce a data distribution on which to evaluate and validate the learning hypothesis. The statistical procedure may also treat the learner as an oracle that provides labels to query instances in probing attacks. With probing, the adversary may find high-cost data points for the learner. Here one-shot games minimize adversarial cost when each move happens, while iterated games minimize total accumulated cost found by playing a game that repeats several times. The authors summarize such costs and their practical considerations in several game theoretical models for causative availability attacks and exploratory integrity attacks. Their defense mechanisms in adversarial classifiers change the likelihood function of the learner so that it can measure each feature at a different known cost. The adversary then plays optimally against the original cost-sensitive classifier. Here the research area of robust statistics can compare the candidate procedures to design procedures for achieving robust learners. It can be used to develop an information theory for secure learning systems that can measure the information leakage in terms of number of bits. It can also quantify the empirical risk associated with side channel attacks on the leaked information.

5.5.1 Defense Mechanisms in Adversarial Deep Learning

To create robust machine learning in malware detection, Tong et al. [601] identify conserved features that cannot be modified without compromising malicious functionality. They are used to construct a successful defense against a realizable evasion attack. Machine learning robustness is then generalized to multiple realizable attacks to do model hardening with a feature space accounting for a series of realizable attacks in robust optimization. A collection of feature extractors is designed to compute numerical vector values and associated object labels for features from corresponding input entities. Depending on the assumptions about the learning algorithm and the adversarial model, evasion defense is classified into game-theoretic reasoning, robust optimization, and iterative adversarial retraining. Generalizability of evasion defenses is evaluated over feature space models of evasion attacks that are realizable. Structure-based PDF classifiers on binary features of structural properties in PDF files as well as content-based PDF classifiers on PDF metadata and content are used to distinguish between benign and malicious instances. Realizable evasion attacks are crafted with EvadeML that has blackbox access to the classifier, mimicry attack that manipulates a malicious PDF file using content injection to resemble benign PDF file, MalGAN to generate malware examples, reverse mimicry attack to inject malicious payloads into target benign files, and custom attack to replace entries in attack PDF files with hexadecimal representations that obfuscate tags for code execution in PDF. Iterative adversarial retraining is selected as the defense mechanism to produce a robust classifier. Chaowei et al. [111] leverage spatial context information in semantic segmentation to detect adversarial examples even when dealing with a strong adaptive adversary. The hypothesis for the defense mechanism is that adversarial examples in different machine learning tasks contain unique statistical properties that provide in-depth understanding of the potential defensive mechanisms. In semantic segmentation tasks, this translates to giving prediction labels to each pixel in an image subject to contextual information in its spatial neighborhood. Ground truth adversarial targets are then defined in a real-world autonomous driving video dataset. Adversarial examples are found to be not transferable between the detection strategies with deep learning among variety of segmentation tasks/scenarios.

He et al. [264] conclude that an ensembling defense combining multiple weak defenses does not create a strong defense to a variety of adversarial examples crafted by an adaptive adversary. Feiman et al. [185] propose to detect adversarial examples from density estimates on the feature space of the last hidden layer. Bayesian uncertainty estimates are also used to detect adversarial samples in low-confidence regions of the input space. By contrast, Raghunathan et al. [501] produce robustness certificates for a neural network whose defense mechanism is based on regularization and adversarial training. The certificates ensure error due to adversarial attack is bounded by a certain value for a variety of adversarial examples. Here, adversarial training is said to minimize a lower bound on the worst-case loss due to which it cannot generalize to new attacks designed to mislead an optimizer. The certificate on the adversarial loss is a semidefinite relaxation on the optimizer that can be computed efficiently. It is contrasted with upper bounds on the adversarial loss due to spectral and Frobenius norm. Related work is found in the control theory literature on verifying robustness of dynamical systems. Lyapunov functions can be used to model the evolution over time of the activation values in a neural network as a time-varying dynamical system so that adversarial loss bounds can be understood in terms of stability proofs on the trajectory of this system. Certification methods on stability and performance of model families in machine learning systems can also benefit from safety verification and controller synthesis procedures around robust data representations used in robotics for critical infrastructures. Miyato et al. [433] propose a new regularization method for adversarial training without overfitting. A virtual adversarial loss is defined on the robustness of the conditional label distribution around each input data point. The regularization term is interpreted as a prior distribution about the a priori knowledge or belief about the learning model. The specific belief taken from the laws of physics is that the class-conditional posteriors of the machine learning system are smooth with respect to the spatial and/or temporal inputs. A local distributional smoothness of output distribution with respect to the input distribution is defined to be the divergence-based distributional robustness of the model against virtual adversarial direction. Virtual adversarial direction is interpreted as the most anisotropic direction giving a "virtual" label to an unlabelled data point. Resultant adversarial noise regularization improves the generalization performance in semi-supervised tasks of image classification.

Papernot et al. [484] introduce defensive distillation to defend deep neural networks against adversarial samples. It is a training procedure for deep nets using knowledge transferred from a different deep net. The motivation for distillation is to reduce the computational complexity of deep learning architectures by transferring knowledge from larger to smaller architectures so that deep learning can be deployed on resource-constrained cyber-physical devices. Defensive distillation applies this idea to extract knowledge from a deep neural network for improving its resilience. The knowledge transfer is used to reduce the amplitudes of the deep net gradients exploited by the adversaries. Thus models trained with defensive distillation are less sensitive to adversarial samples. As a security countermeasure, it leads to smoother classifier models with improved generalizability properties. Defensive distillation leads to two folds during training called direction sensitivity estimation and perturbation selection where adversarial goal is assumed to be misclassifying samples from a specific source class into a distinct target class. The transferred knowledge consists of not only the weight parameters learnt by the deep net but also the encoded class probability vectors produced by the network during training. Soft class probabilities are better than hard class labels because they hold relative information about entropy of classes in addition to each sample's correct class. Such information on class-conditional probabilities can be used to guide the convergence of the deep net to an optimal modelling solution that enhances classification robustness. To deal with optimization attacks with new objectives and optimizers, Papernot et al. [478] extend the folds in Papernot et al. [484] to add an outlier class to mitigate adversarial examples and provide uncertainty estimates in neural networks through stochastic inference. By transferring both knowledge and uncertainty, the extended defensive distillation does not need the defender to generate adversarial examples according to heuristics.

Tramer et al. [603] introduce ensemble adversarial training to augment the training data with adversarial perturbations transferred from other pre-trained models. Including blackbox attacks in such adversarial perturbations significantly improves the transferability of the adversarial examples. Such a defense mechanism is useful in the costlier multistep attacks. Fast gradient sign method (FGSM) and its variants such as single-step least-likely class method (Step-LL) and iterative attack (I-FGSM or Iter-LL) are used to create adversarial examples. Both white-box and blackbox adversaries are used to evaluate the robustness gains in defense strategies. Thus adversarial training is improved by decoupling adversarial examples generation from the model training. At the same time, interactive adversaries are also proposed to include queries on the target model's prediction function in their attack. Wu et al. [655] propose highly confident near neighbor framework to combine prediction confidence information and nearest neighbor search to reinforce adversarial robustness. Meng et al. [422] propose MagNet framework for the defense mechanism. It includes separate detector networks and a reformer network to detect the adversarial examples. The detector networks are autoencoders to learn the data manifold of normal examples without assuming any particular stochastic process for generating them. They are trained according to a reconstruction loss criterion that approximates the distance between input and manifold of normal examples. The reformer network is another autoencoder that moves adversarial examples toward the data manifold of normal examples to correctly classify them. Based on cryptography ideas, defense via diversity is advocated to randomly pick one out of several defenses at run time in a gray-box attack. Carlini et al. [105] are then able to construct transferable adversarial examples for MagNet and adversarial perturbation elimination GAN (APE-GAN). Based on distance metrics, Carlini et al. [106] also succeed at constructing adversarial examples for defensively distilled networks.

Metzen et al. [424] augment deep neural networks with a detector network. It does binary classification between genuine data and adversarial data to detect a specific adversary type. It can act as a method for hardening detectors against dynamic adversaries. Cisse et al. [131] introduce Parseval networks for empirical and theoretical analysis of the robustness of predictions made by deep nets subject to adversarial perturbations. They act as a regularization method with orthonormality constraints for reducing the effect adversarial manipulations. Similarly, Gu et al. [239] propose a Deep Contractive Network (DCN) acting as a smoothness penalty on adversarial training. DCN is an extension of contractive autoencoder (CAE) that has the ability to remove adversarial noise. Thus ideas from ideas from denoising autoencoder (DAE), contractive autoencoder (CAE), and marginalized denoising autoencoder (mDAE) provide a strong framework for adversarially training deep neural networks with a robustness criteria tuned toward human perception. By contrast, Kos et al. [326] create adversarial examples in the latent space for deep generative models such as variational autoencoders (VAEs) and generative adversarial networks (GANs). Xiao et al. [660] propose AdvGAN to generate adversarial examples with conditional adversarial networks in semi-white-box and blackbox attack scenarios. Jin et al. [303] propose APE-GAN to defend against adversarial examples in white-box attack scenarios. The generator alters adversarial perturbations with tiny changes to input examples. The discriminator is optimized to separate clean examples and reconstructed examples without adversarial perturbations. A loss function is invented to make adversarial examples consistent with original images data manifold. APE-GAN can be combined with other defense mechanisms such as adversarial retraining.

Assuming the hypothesis that adversarial examples lie in the low probability regions of the training distribution, Song et al. [565] design PixelDefend to move maliciously perturbed images back to the distribution seen in the training data. A generative model computes probabilities of all training images. Such a probability density is used to rank the adversarial examples created by a variety of attacking methods. A constrained optimization problem that is intractable is formulated to purify the adversarial examples. It is approximated with a greedy decoding procedure. Results are compared with other defense mechanisms in the literature such as adversarial training, label smoothing, and feature squeezing. Bojanowski et al. [77] introduce a Generative Latent Optimization (GLO) framework to train generators using reconstruction losses. It is useful in interpolating between training samples and adversarial examples. It also permits linear arithmetic between noise vectors in the latent space to study interpolations of adversarial examples without the need for an adversarial game between the generator and the discriminator. The generator then translates the linear interpolations in the noise space into semantic interpolations in the image space. The learnable noise space is able to disentangle the non-linear factors of variation of image space into linear statistics. Kyatham et al. [341] incorporate adversarial perturbations to a regularized and quantized generative latent space to then map it to the true data manifold. A defense mechanism based on generative autoencoders then is able to circumvent disadvantages of related defense mechanisms such as approximation of derivatives in adversarial training and reparameterization of expectations in adversarial filtering. The latent encoder preserves distances in a metric space on the latent and the data manifolds. It allows stochastic exploration of the latent neighborhood of a known distribution. Multiple decoders are used to easily explore a data sample in the latent space and remap it back to a data point in the legitimate data. The latent space exploration can be conducted with variational inference performed by learned hierarchical latent representations of the data such as in ladder variational autoencoders [561] and Mask Adversarial Auto-Encoder [438].

Fawzi et al. [181] provide a theoretical framework for analyzing the robustness of classifiers subject to adversarial perturbations. Upper bounds for robustness are established for linear and quadratic classifiers. Robustness is expressed as a distinguishability measure between the classes. For linear classifiers it is the distance between means of the classes. For quadratic classifiers it is the distance between the matrices of second order moments of the classes. Robustness bounds for the classifiers are established independent of the learning algorithms and defense mechanisms. De Silva et al. [148] propose an attack-cost-aware adversarial learning (CAL) countermeasure to design attack-resilient classifiers. The attack cost structure information is obtained from vulnerability analysis of a machine learning system. CAL framework projects potentially falsified test instances onto space of legitimate feature vectors with an attack cost function acting as the distance metric. The projection operator can be interpreted as a generalized likelihood ratio test. CAL framework is applicable to any classification technique. Insua et al. [519] provide an adversarial risk analysis for adversarial classification that can be considered to be an alternative to game-theoretic frameworks. The attack scenarios are restricted to exploratory attacks and integrity violation attacks. A Bayesian approach to adversarial classification is taken to propose generative classifiers. A frequentist approach to adversarial classification is taken to propose discriminative classifiers. Expected utilities associated with the adversary's worst consequences are the optimization criteria. Generative models of samples in the adversarial data distribution lead to computational difficulties on high-dimensional data. So adversarial examples are algorithmically sampled from regions of high adversarial loss with a noise term to account for the defender uncertainty over attacker model. The attacker uncertainty over defender model is accounted by scalable Bayesian approaches to deep learning. In general, application-specific assumptions are reduced to a minimum while learning the adversarial utilities and probabilities in a Bayesian paradigm. Such adversarial risk analysis allows us to combine Bayesian methods with game theoretical adversarial deep learning.

Schmidt et al. [542] study the information-theoretic sample complexity of adversarially robust learning independent of the training algorithm or the model family. Due to statistical nature of deep learning, adversarial examples are said to provably occur in every learning approach. A lower bound is established on the hardness of robustness in deep classifiers that correspond to a restricted adversary applying worst-case distribution shifts. The adversary is not adaptive to the classifier settings. Thus a clear gap can be demonstrated between robust and standard generalization for the hypothesis classes and distributional classes in adversarial machine learning.

As a result defense mechanisms must be tailor-made for a particular adversary type and a specific training dataset. Adding prior information on the robustness tradeoffs into the model architecture can help create robust classifiers. Wong et al. [653] address robustness gaps between real-world perturbations and datasets typical to adversarial defenses with learnable perturbation sets. A conditional generator defines the perturbation sets over a constrained region of the latent space. The conditional generator is a conditional variational autoencoder. It can generate perturbations at different complexities and scales starting from baseline image transformations. As a threat model, learning perturbation sets with quantitative metrics is empirically and certifiably robust to adversarial manipulations, variations, and corruptions. Seshia et al. [548] argue for the need of semantic and context specifications of machine learning systems in resource-constrained environments. System-level semantic specifications about the adversarial manipulations can be used to produce not only the misclassified labels but also semantic information on system-level implications. Such a semantic adversarial approach is useful for adversarial learning applications in embedded systems involving Internet of Things (IoT) devices and cyber-physical control systems (CPCS). Then the components of adversarial robustness around system-level specifications in the training algorithm can be expressed as semantic modification space, semantic loss functions for training, and semantic data set augmentation. Probabilistic programming languages can be used to guide the semantic adversarial learning by representing distributional assumptions regarding data generation, inference, and verification. Algorithmic methods can be used in the design and analysis of AML/A2I-based learning systems. Formal specification of deep learning models and machine learning systems can also benefit from exploring tradeoffs between semantic robustness and resource-efficient implementation in error-resilient system design.

Rouhani et al. [529] propose an automated framework DeepFense for the efficient and safe execution of deep learning in critical and time-sensitive applications such as unmanned vehicles, drones, and video surveillance systems. DeepFense leverages modular redundancies in hardware/software/algorithm co-design to achieve just-in-time performance in resource-constrained settings. Online adversarial sample detection is evaluated on FPGAs and GPUs. Each modular redundancy learns the probability density function of typical data points and associated rare/risky regions with dictionary learning. In addition to machine learning performance validation, the system performance is customized toward latency, energy consumption, and memory footprint around the underlying hardware resource provisioning. Learnability tradeoffs are found between not only system performance and adversarial robustness but also resource limitation and model reliability of the machine learning system. Robustness of the adversarial deep learning ought to confirm with the user-defined and/or hardware-specific optimization constraints. FPGAs are used to provide fine-grained parallelism and just-in-time response in the adversarial defense mechanisms. Deep learning benchmarks are then showcased against the state-of-the-art adversarial attacks. A Markov chain of defender modules is used to mitigate adaptive adversary attacks. DeepFense is presented as an unsupervised learning method for smoothing the decision boundaries to remove the adversarial noise variables. It is shown to improve the robustness of the deep learning models by learning the adversarial data density in the latent space due to adaptive attacks on the existing online defense mechanisms. Ghafouri et al. [216] propose supervised regression as a defense mechanism to detect sensor reading manipulations in cyberphysical systems (CPS). The interaction between CPS defender and attacker is modelled as a Stackelberg game where the defender chooses approximately optimal decision thresholds using supervised regression and adversarial anomaly detection to increase the machine learning system's resilience. Such interactions can be used to develop heuristic algorithms for resilient detectors with regression-based modelling in sensor networks. The resultant resilient detectors can be used to specify strong constraints on the feasible sensor manipulations by leveraging relationships among measurements from multiple sensors.

Taran et al. [594] propose a new defense mechanism based on second Kerckhoffs's cryptographic principle. It leads to a gray-box attack scenario where the adversary has access to the classification predictions, training/testing data, and class labels for machine learning but not the corresponding cryptographic secret key encrypting the knowledge of the defense mechanism parameters. The secret key imposes a preprocessing encoder block that can be implemented as a dataindependent transformation in various ways due to which the adversary is not able to decrypt the parameters of a classifier's defense mechanism in a reasonable amount of time within the available modern computational means. The proposed cryptographic defense mechanism can be integrated with defense via retraining, defense via detection and rejection, defense via input preprocessing, and defense via regeneration. Thus integrating asymmetric cryptography with adversarial learning leads to an information advantage of the defender/learner over attacker/adversary. The entropy of the secret key is higher than the entropy of the adversarial signal. Its data transformation is non-differentiable. To further protect the defense mechanism, the classifier system's architecture is assumed to be not accessible to the adversary. This leads to the design of learning protocols with cryptographic principles in pattern recognition systems deployed on protected servers or special devices or chips for adversarial learning applications such as digital watermarking, cryptanalysis, digital forensics, steganalysis, and device identification. Xu et al. [671] investigate the information-theoretic limits of adversarial learning. It has applications in solution domains such as computer vision, video surveillance, natural language processing, voice recognition, and cybersecurity. It is also applicable to learning problems such as classification, regression, feature embeddings (in words and nodes), and generative models. The adversary is supposed to have an attack budget on the adversarial noise that can be injected at learning time. The attack budget is expressed as a statistical distance called the total variation distance (TVD) between the original data distribution and the noise-injected data distribution. Related work on the statistical limits of adversarial robustness includes generalization bounds for adversarial learning, robustness certification for inference, robustly PAC learnability of VC classes, and analysis of the effect of injecting noise in the network at inference time.

Jha et al. [297] create satisfiability modulo theories (SMT) solvers with a combination of oracle-guided learning from examples and constraint-based synthesis from components in a machine learning library. Such an automatic synthesis of programs for program deobfuscation is useful in the formal verification of adversarial learning. A validation oracle checks whether the machine learning program is correct or not based on adversarial learning security requirements. It has connections to optimization procedures in computational learning theory and bit-manipulating programs. In a non-stationarity adversarial environment, Lowe et al. [395] explore deep reinforcement learning methods for multi-agent domains. Actor-critic methods can be adapted for adversarial learning to learn policies around game theoretical interactions in adversarial deep learning over complex multi-agent coordination. They solve for robust multi-agent policies in cooperative and competitive attack scenarios from emergent behavior and complexity in co-evolving agents. Thus reinforcement learning is applicable to adversarial learning environments with multiple adversaries.

Li et al. [361] create robust malware detectors for adversarial examples on Android malware. A combination of a variational autoencoder (VAE) and a multi-layer perceptron (MLP) is used to design a novel loss function that disentangles the features of different malware classes. The feature space of Android malware is represented in a discrete fashion. The proposed defense mechanism computes a similarity metric between benign and malicious examples while preserving malicious functionality. The final classification model simultaneously does malware detection and adversarial example defense. Hassan et al. [256] address trust-boundary protection to allow user access privilege in Industrial Internet of Things (IIoT) environments. Adversaries can use model skewing techniques to generate adversarial examples on the attack surface in the IIoT network. A downsampler-encoder-based cooperative data generator is used to create the adversarial examples in IIoT devices. Such IIoT devices include IoT devices such as sensors, programmable logic controllers, actuators, intelligent electronic devices, and cyber-physical systems (CPS) in industrial operations. CPS include subsystems and processes for design, infrastructure, monitoring and control, scheduling, and maintaining the value chain of data analytics for precise control of physical processes, autonomous management of industrial system collaboration, less expensive production data collection, and intelligent processing in real time. The vulnerabilities and threats of such industrial protocols, networks, systems, and services are open to exploitation by adversaries. They are further exacerbated by existing security loopholes in conventional IT systems. Here defense mechanisms in adversarial deep learning are used to uphold security objectives of IIoT data such as confidentiality, integrity, and availability. Further applications of adversarial deep learning are given by Abusnaina et al. [1] and Martins et al. [414]. Abusnaina et al. [1] analyze IoT malware detection with control flow graph (CFG)-based features. A graph embedding and augmentation method is used to generate and embed adversarial examples into training data of IoT software. CFG features allow the exploration of IoT malware through graph theory and machine learning. Martins et al. [414] analyze the generation and detection of adversarial examples in intrusion and malware detection scenarios.

For the generation of adversarial examples, machine learning algorithms are categorized into symbolists such as decision tree, connectionists such as neural network, evolutionaries such as genetic algorithms, Bayesians such as naive Bayes, analogizers such as k-nearest neighbors. Adversarial defenses for malware and intrusion detection are given as adversarial training, gradient hiding, defensive distillation, feature squeezing, transferability block, universal perturbation defense method, and MagNet autoencoders.

5.5.2 Explainable Artificial Intelligence in Adversarial Deep Learning

Tan et al. [592] discuss attention maps in computer vision tasks. A geometric prior on the spatial context for a pixel is modelled as a novel self-attention module. It does not require the computationally expensive positional encoding of content-driven attention maps constructed with queries and keys. The self-attention training concept is applicable to not only computer vision tasks but also natural language processing tasks. In image recognition tasks, it is categorized into channel attention and spatial attention. Sen et al. [547] conduct a quantitative assessment of human versus computational attention mechanisms in text classification tasks. They are contrasted on overlap in word selections, distribution over lexical categories, and context-dependency of sentiment polarity. The attention mechanisms are useful for interpretability about the modelling details such as model debugging, architecture selection in natural language processing (NLP) tasks such as language modelling, machine translation, document classification, and question answering. They create explainable attention scores for the model predictions that can be linked with the feature importance measures on dimensionality reduction. Human attention is measured from the perspectives of measures for behavioral similarity, lexical (grammatical) similarity, and context-dependency sentiment polarity. Resultant attention maps are compared with attention-based recurrent neural networks (RNNs). Bidirectional RNNs with attention mechanisms are found to be similar to human attention according to the human attention measures. An attention map is defined as a vector with sequence of words associated with positions in the text. Neural networks can produce the attention maps by computing either probability distributions or bitwise operations on the word sequences. The NLP prediction tasks become more difficult on long text as the accuracy and similarity scores of the models decrease. Lin et al. [370] create RankGAN to generate natural language descriptions of human-written and machine-written sentences. The discriminator does a relative ranking of the text to help create a better generator. Such relative ranking information can benefit from rank aggregation methods used in the distributional smoothing of adversarial learning features.

The attention maps in deep learning can be contrasted with the feature maps as described by Thaller et al. [596] for analyzing the design patterns in recurrent software development problems. Feature maps are software representations based on microstructures that are human- and machine-comprehensible. A vector space over micro-structures in a feature map can be defined as the high-dimensional feature space for detecting instances of design patterns in source code with machine learning. Thus machine learning-based pattern descriptions can be used to solve high-level object-oriented (OO) architectural problems around creation, structure, or behavior of classes and objects. The semantics in pattern descriptions contains the name, intent, motivation applicable to structures, participants, and collaborations in the source code. They are used to make design decisions and documentation rationales during software product development. Retrieving such encoded information with design pattern detection (DPD) is useful in the redevelopment and maintenance of software products. DPDs find structures and dependencies in the source code to produce abstract semantics graph (ASG) highlighting the algorithms and their moving parts for improving the system performance. Burnap et al. [94] develop self-organizing feature maps (SOFM) to distinguish between malicious and trusted portable executable software samples. The machine learning features are created on bytes and packets in the footprint left behind by a computer system during execution over CPU, RAM, swap, and network. Unlike features derived from API calls, such execution features cannot be obfuscated easily in APT style attacks. SOFMs capture topographic neighborhoods in the data separated by fuzzy boundaries between machine activity classes. The SOFMs are able to address the plasticity-stability dilemma for a learning system that needs to adapt to environment while maintaining the efficacy of stable function. Utilizing topographical neighborhoods as fuzzy feature sets in machine classification algorithms improves the generalization behavior of the learning algorithms on unseen samples in malicious payload such as polymorphic malware. SOFMs can also be used for data visualization and exploration in security operation centers. Dotter et al. [164] try to attribute the adversarially perturbed inputs to particular attack methods in an attempt to expose the attack algorithm, model architecture, and hyperparameters used in the attack over a supervised learning framework. Cyber attribution indicators are obtained for tradecraft and malware tactics, techniques, and procedures (TTPs) that leave behind particular identifying signals and signatures. Such attribution of attacks can be used alongside other cyber indicators of tradecraft such as intent and infrastructure. Here adversarial deep learning techniques in attribution classifier design can automatically reverse engineer the tool-chains for adversarial attribution behind cyberattacks such as deepfakes, multimedia falsification, adversarial machine learning attacks, and information deception attacks. The attack attribution on the adversarial dataset is expressed as attack algorithm attribution, hyperparameter attribution, model attribution, and norm attribution.

Samek et al. [538] develop sensitivity analysis methods for visualizing, explaining, and interpreting deep learning models to increase the transparency of their predictions. Interpretability and explainability of trustworthy artificial intelligence applications is an emerging discipline in machine learning that computes the sensitivity of the prediction with respect to changes in the input. Deep learning models act as a blackbox system by default. There is an urgent need to understand the learnings of a model and explain its individual predictions to advance machine learning models beyond neural networks. Such methods for explainable artificial intelligence are required in machine learning systems for the verification of the system's decision-making, improvement of the system architectures, knowledge transfer of the learning of the system to a human user, and compliance of algorithmic decisions to privacy regulation. Thus the relation between generalizability, compactness, and explainability of the learned representations in adversarial deep learning is an active area of research. Ancona et al. [15] use Shapley values from cooperative game theory to assign relevance scores in attribution methods. They quantify the "relevance" or "contribution" of each input feature in a given input sample. The target output in a classification task is chosen to be the prediction with the highest output probability that is associated with the parts of the input most relevant for the prediction. The relevance scores also contain information to assess the input for evidence that supports or rejects a predicted class label. The attribution methods can also be subject to adversarial attacks without reliable quantitative metrics based in ground truth to evaluate the explanations. Here Shapley values act as a self-evident property of the explanations designed for stronger theoretical guarantees on their reliability. Shapley values can be assigned to attributes such that certain desirable axioms are satisfied on the completeness, symmetry, linearity, continuity, and implementation invariance of the attribution methods. Choras et al. [129] discuss the lack of fairness and explainability in the state-of-the-art algorithms for machine learning and artificial intelligence in several application domains that use deep learning capabilities to solve detection or prediction tasks. Here the security frameworks in adversarial machine learning can introduce disinformation to mislead the deep learning results. Fairness in artificial intelligence is then concerned about ethical and legal frameworks around the disinformation that can be maliciously spread in the society at large. The algorithmic bias resulting from the bias of human operators providing data with misrepresentations and discriminations leads to unfairness in artificial intelligence. Here there is a need to create training datasets without skewed samples, tainted examples, and limited features leading to sensitive biased attributes in the training algorithm and subsequent sample size disparity in the classification algorithm. So machine learning fairness is to be defined according to notions of unawareness, group fairness, and counterfactual fairness in the mathematical formulations of adversarial deep learning. Here the counterfactuals due to adversarial machine learning can be modelled as causal graphs explaining the predictions of supervised deep learning. In this context, game theoretical adversarial deep learning procedures provide a statistical framework for optimizing the tradeoffs between accuracy and fairness measures on the machine learning system performance. They can construct fair classifiers with reference to a sequence of cost-sensitive classification problems providing randomized classifiers with the lowest empirical error within the desired optimization constraints. Arrieta et al. [17] survey the literature on explainable AI (XAI) and provide a taxonomy on recent contributions in deep learning. It leads onto the broader concept of responsible artificial intelligence around methodologies for the large-scale implementation of artificial intelligence in real-world organizations with fairness, explainability, and accountability built into the artificial intelligence for every regulated industry in each economic activity sectors. Interpretability as a design driver in machine learning supports impartiality in decision-making, facilitates the provision of learnable robustness, and acts as an insurance on the underlying truthful causality existing in the model reasoning. Samek et al. [537] provide another review of XAI in deep neural networks.

Ribeiro et al. [515] learn a local interpretable model around a classifier's predictions. It explains individual predictions as the solutions to a submodular optimization problem. The utility of such explanations is validated in the experiments assessing trust in machine learning blackboxes by understanding the reasons behind the predictions. A local interpretable model-agnostic explanations (LIME) framework is presented to the problems of "trusting a prediction" to take action based on it, "trusting the model" to behave in reasonable ways when deployed in the real world. Interpretable representations for textual and visual artifacts are produced as explanation tensors for each input instance such that domain- and task-specific interpretability criteria are accommodated. LIME has applications in recommendation systems for speech, video, and medical domains to design human-in-the-loop machine learning systems. Hartl et al. [254] introduce feature sensitivity measure called adversarial robustness score (ARS) for sequential network flow data in intrusion detection systems (IDS). It is useful as a feature importance measure used in the generation of adversarial samples for recurrent neural networks (RNNs). ARS can be used alongside accuracy to evaluate security-sensitive machine learning systems. It improves upon explainability methods such as partial dependence plots (PDPs) for sequential data. Proposed defense mechanisms use ARS to leave out the manipulable features, reduce the attack surface, and harden the resulting IDS. Melis et al. [421] evaluate trust in Android malware detectors as they transition from performing well on benchmark data to being deployed in an operating environment. A gradient-based approach identifies the most influential local features to increase accuracy without losing interpretability of decisions. The explanations can provide insights into vulnerabilities of any blackbox machine-learning model used for malware detection. Demetrio et al. [153] provide feature attribution to each decision made for the classification of malware binaries. The explanations are then used to generate adversarial malware binaries that are better than the state-of-the-art attack algorithms against deep learning algorithms that provide highly non-linear decision functions. Contributions of each feature to the label of a data point are calculated with respect to baselines that create ground truth for the modelling. Adversarial perturbations then increase the contributions computed for the modelling output on the modified features in the baselines. Sensitivity axioms are created for the baselines to guide the training algorithm of back-propagating errors through the neural network. Integrated gradients are used to explain the classification results. However, the explainable models continue to be vulnerable to adversarial manipulations. Marino et al. [411] generate explanations for misclassifications in data-driven intrusion detection systems. The explanations provide reasonings behind the misclassification and match them with expert knowledge. The explanations are applicable to any classifier that has gradients. They can be used in digital forensics and vulnerability assessment of the underlying machine learning system. Such XAI makes use of data visualizations and natural language descriptions to explain the reasoning for the decisions made by the machine learning systems. The reasoning can be understood by a human and be used for simplifying the knowledge discovery process in data. It can also be used to produce debugging diagnostics on the machine learning system. Explanations are assumed to be the minimum modifications required to correctly classify the misclassified samples. The adversarial manipulations are used to visualize the learning features that are responsible for misclassification. Misclassifications are frequently found to occur between samples with conflicting data characteristics.

Liu et al. [382] investigate model interpretation to support an adversarial detection framework explaining predictions in the target machine learning model. Adversarial training is then used to improve the robustness of the detectors on adversarial samples. Feature manipulation costs are estimated to categorize adversary types. Existing detection frameworks are categorized into feature engineering methods that are vulnerable to adaptive adversaries, game theoretical interactions between detectors and adversaries where the modelling specifics vary with the machine learning classifier architectures, and deep neural network defenses such as adversarial training, defensive distillation, and feature squeezing. Misclassified data points are seeded from evasion-prone samples likely to shift across the decision boundary. Adversarial attacks are constructed on perturbation directions based on model interpretation of input data instances classified as benign or malicious. Lundberg et al. [399] propose a game theoretical framework called SHAP (SHapley Additive exPlanations) to study the tradeoffs between accuracy and interpretability in deep learning outputs. SHAP computes additive feature importance measure for each prediction as Shapley regression values. Sampling approximation is made in the computation of the Shapley values. Shapley value estimation methods are augmented with feature attribution methods satisfying desirable properties on the explanations such as local accuracy matching explanation model with the original model, missingness to disallow missing features to have any impact, and consistency on input's attribution with respect to changes in the model state due to other inputs. Then cooperative game theory is used to mathematically prove do not violate accuracy and interpretability requirements where Shapley values act as the conditional expectation functions of feature importance in the original model. The conditional expectation functions are approximated with model-specific methods such as Shapley sampling values, Kernel SHAP, Max SHAP, and Deep SHAP. Model-agnostic approximations are obtained from a quantitative input influence method that is a sampling approximation of a permutation version of the classic Shapley value equations. Joint estimation of SHAP values with regression provides better sample complexity/efficiency than direct use of classical Shapley equations. Thus game theoretical explanations of the adversarial deep learning provide avenues to create new explanation model classes.

Beyazit et al. [49] propose interpretable representations learned by a deep generative model by extracting independent marginals as well as causality entanglement features in the training data. A training regularizer then penalizes disagreement between the extracted feature interactions and a given dependency structure in the training data. The regularizer imposes structural constraints on the latent space of feature interactions to give better than state-of-the-art generalization performance. The feature interactions use a Bayesian network to calculate the maximum likelihood parameters measuring the disagreement between latent space and training space. Mutual information maximization in InfoGAN extracts the visually meaningful features and their manipulations. The dependency structure model's the relationship between observed and salient features of the data. The dependency structure acts as an additional learning constraint on the training of InfoGAN. A likelihood function for the generator measures the probability of the training data given the best data generator model. The feedforward pass of the InfoGAN is seen as a mapping from the space of the observed variables to a decision. The objective function for the data-generating distribution produces data instances that fit mean squared error (MSE) for linear Gaussian models. A structural loss function acts as the regularizer of InfoGAN training. Optimal graph structures can be designed in the latent space to explore salient features. Such interpretable representations can be utilized in transfer learning, zero-shot learning and reinforcement learning. Molnar [437] surveys the model-agnostic methods for interpreting blackbox models in deep learning. They include feature importance, accumulated local effects, Shapley values, and LIME. The results of the interpretation methods include feature summary statistic, feature summary visualization, learned weights, counterfactual explanations, and white boxes. Typically the interpretation methods for deep neural networks are model-specific and restricted to specific model classes. Model-agnostic methods for interpretation of machine learning techniques in general include partial dependence plots, accumulated local effect plots, feature interaction (H-statistic), functional decomposition, permutation feature importance, and global surrogate models. Neural network interpretation is expressed in terms of learned features, pixel attribution (saliency maps), influential instances, counterfactual explanations, and adversarial examples.

Bitton et al. [71] conduct a threat analysis of machine learning production systems. The threat model enumerates machine learning assets, potential adversaries, adversarial objectives, learning goals, and attack scenarios in learning systems. A scoring system is designed for various adversarial attacks. It uses an analytic hierarchy process (AHP) for ranking attack attributes of cybersecurity experts. Then an attack graph generation framework called MulVAL is developed as a logical attack graph to incorporate the effects of cyberattacks in machine learning production systems for several use cases in cybersecurity, fraud detection, financial trading, personalized marketing, resource optimization, healthcare, and autonomous vehicles. Misleading critical decisions made around these use cases has a statistically significant impact on contingency planning, business continuity, revenue streams, and even human lives. In addition to bugs in the machine learning systems, they must also contend with logical vulnerabilities in the underlying ML algorithms. Adversaries can exploit such bugs and vulnerabilities as attack scenarios for adversarial machine learning. Therefore machine learning systems must be equipped with tactical and strategic tools to analyze, detect, protect, and respond to cyberattacks. Such tools have been developed as frameworks and libraries like CleverHans adversarial examples library, Adversarial Robustness Toolbox, Foolbox toolbox, SecML library, and MLsploit. Currently they implement algorithms to generate and discriminate adversarial examples. But they ought to be extended to quantify the risk machine learning systems, conduct cybersecurity threats modelling in specific deployments and target environments for machine learning algorithms, and quantify different attributes of the attack technique such as attacker model, attack impact, and attack performance. Here the characteristics of the machine learning production pipeline can be expressed as elements of data, deployment, delivery, and orchestration to create threat analysis ontology for asset, vulnerability, attacker, capability, impact, threat, and attack technique. The MulVAL framework analyzes logical attack graphs to automatically extract information from formal vulnerability databases and network scanning tools. It enumerates all possible attack paths in a polynomial time on new and emerging attack scenarios. MulVAL is useful in the design of risk assessment and countermeasure planning algorithms validated with explicit interaction rules and predicates for attack modelling in the Datalog programming language. Elitzur et al. [171] analyze cyber threat intelligence (CTI) on previous attacks for attack reconstruction in tools on unobserved attack patterns that can augment alert correlations and data visualizations for cybersecurity analysts studying the attack hypotheses in the digital forensics of adversarial machine learning with cyber kill chains. An Attack Hypothesis Generator (AHG) constructs a knowledge graph on the threat intelligence to generate attack hypotheses in a security information and event management (SIEM). Here CTI is categorized into strategic threat intelligence, operational threat intelligence, tactical threat intelligence, and technical threat intelligence. They are used to construct knowledge graph to support adversarial reasoning with graph mining features on topological similarity, correlation, and frequent patterns. Executing Semantic Web Rule Languages on the knowledge graphs can be used in the data-driven analytics of logic-based deductive inference rules. Link prediction and collaborative filtering in knowledge graphs can improve the attack hypothesis generation with attack scenarios that are likely to occur. Matern et al. [416] create visual artifacts that can be used in statistical forensics tools to expose adversarial manipulations in Deepfakes. The adversarial goal in automatic video generation is to create a malicious manipulation to convey a semantic message within a video that is not originally intended in the training material. Here image forensics search physical or statistical image artifacts to form statistical fingerprints, validate noise priors, and learn specific manipulation traces on the residuals of an image to detect adversarial manipulations. The proposed visual artifacts are categorized into computer vision problems such as global consistency, illumination estimation, and geometry estimation. Kamath et al. [307] address a theoretical question in statistical learning on how a distribution can be approximated with its samples. Smooth loss measures are proposed for distribution approximations. For compression and investment applications, the relevant loss is Kullback-Leibler (KL) divergence. For classification it is L_1, L_2, Hellinger, chi-squared, softmax losses. For adversarial learning, the least worst-case loss for a game theoretical optimal estimator for adversarial deep learning is minmax loss. For online learning in resource-constrained environments, the loss is minmax cumulative loss based on statistics and information theory to minimize losses over successive estimates.

Katzir et al. [311] quantify the adversarial resilience of machine learning systems with formal methods applicable to multisensory fusion systems. A model robustness (MRB) score is proposed for evaluating the adversarial resilience to control resilience vs accuracy tradeoffs in dynamic malware classification. An adversary-aware feature selection aims to find feature subsets for which the adversary's budget is insufficient to create adversarial manipulations, classifier generalization is maximized, and training dimensionality is minimized. Then the MRB is used as the resilient feature selection criteria. An experimental evaluation is then conducted on feature manipulation costs for the adversary to target resilient and non-resilient features of adversary resilient classifiers in cyber defense systems with multisensor fusion. Sadeghi et al. [534] survey the intersection of computational intelligence and machine learning in autonomous vehicles, assistive robots, and biometric systems. Here the misclassifications due to adversarial attacks result in erroneous decisions and unreliable operations. Adversarial machine learning systems can be categorized in a fine-grained manner according to the input dataset, the ML architecture, the adversary's specifications, the attack generation methodology, and the defense strategy. Cho et al. [127] propose security and dependability metrics as key metrics for building trustworthy machine learning systems in multi-domain environment spanning hardware, software, network, human factors, and physical environments. The trustworthiness metric framework supports ontology-based framework for trust, resilience, and agility. It can be used in vulnerability assessment, computational red teaming, and measurement of trustworthy systems. The trustworthy metrics (or measurements) can be used in the validation of adversarial machine learning for objectivity based on certainty, efficiency based on quantification, and control based on feedback. They act as data attributes about the quality of a system such as usability, manageability, functionality, performance, dependability, adaptability, security, and cost. They can incorporate security requirements such as availability, integrity, confidentiality, reliability, availability, integrity, safety, and maintainability. Data provenance techniques can also be included with the trustworthy metrics to evaluate trustworthy information sharing in socio-technical systems and cyber sensing. Definitions of data provenance can be used to attest to the data quality assertions. They connect reliability and reproducibility of data analytics applications with data origin and ownership, modelling validation, and justification of unexpected results.

Ye et al. [683] create instance specific distance learning methods suitable for different local optima on the adversarial algorithms designed for statistical properties in the true data distribution. The proposed ISMETS (Instance Specific METric Subspace) spans the whole metric space for distance learning in a generative manner. It learns the metric subspace for each instance by inferring expectations of distributions in variational inference over metric bases according to a Bayesian paradigm for induction and transduction. The metric subspaces are useful for understanding the interpretability and robustness of the results in adversarial deep learning with latent allocation variables incorporating side information. Parallel programming techniques and numerical approximation methods can also be incorporated into the metric learning framework to extend it to high-dimensional datasets. Such distance metric learning algorithms can be further used to constrain the optimization costs in adversarial payoff functions to solve multi-objective, constrained, large-scale, and uncertain optimization problems for adversarial deep learning. Sugiyama et al. [578] discuss the importance of computing divergence approximators between probability distributions types from their samples in machine learning, information theory, and statistics. The divergence estimators have data mining applications on data analytics distributions such as change-point detection, class-balance estimation, feature selection and extraction, clustering, object matching, independent component analysis, and causal direction estimation. The divergence is estimated in a computationally efficient manner without approximating the underlying probability distributions. While Kullback-Leibler divergence is the most popular of such divergence approximators, other approximators such as Pearson divergence and L^2-distance measures are also useful in machine learning due to their stability and robustness properties. The divergence measures can be called a distance for metric learning when they satisfy the mathematical properties of non-negativity, non-degeneracy, symmetry, and triangle inequality. In adversarial generative learning, we wish to achieve convergence to an approximation of the target distributions with deep learning. Hence statistical distance measures and relative distribution methods represent a suitable measure to evaluate the generalization performance of the target distribution. Tzeng et al. [613] apply adversarial learning methods to domain adaptation to understand domain shifts due to dataset/algorithmic biases. Thus adversarial deep learning can be used to generate complex samples across diverse domains. Generalization performance of the adversarial deep learning can be improved by minimizing the divergence between training, testing, and validation domains with suitably designed adversarial losses. Thus adversarial adaptation generalizes prior approaches to domain adaptation. Such an adversarial adaptation called Adversarial Discriminative Domain Adaptation (ADDA) is proposed by Tzeng et al. [613]. ADDA can be used to represent the source and target domains in a common feature space. It can also be used to reconstruct target domain from source representations. Here generalized adversarial adaptation minimizes an approximate domain discrepancy in the adversarial objective for the learning algorithm. We can also measure the information divergence between minimal representations of training data and adversarial data feature embeddings with deep metric learning-based adversarial cost functions for domain adaptation. We may also enforce a prior distribution on the latent factors for coherent data generation in supervised deep learning.

Hayes et al. [259] apply adversarial training for image synthesis in steganographic algorithms expressed as discriminative learning tasks constructing robust steganalyzers. Steganography is concerned with hiding information by embedding it within a non-secret medium. Both steganography and cryptography provide privacy-preserving methods for secret communication. A steganography message is encrypted with cryptography methods before embedding it in the non-secret medium such as a cover message with texts and images. The embedded message is statistically no different from a random string. A steganographic message is then decoded to reveal the ciphertext of the message. The ciphertext is then decrypted with a cryptographic key. Steganographic algorithms then seek to minimize perturbations in the embedding medium. The proposed discriminative learning task embeds the secret message in a cover message with an algorithm to generate a steganographic image. The adversary learns weaknesses in the embedding algorithm to distinguish cover images from steganographic images. Thus adversarial training in steganalysis techniques is used to model the cover distribution correctly. Modesitt et al. [435] combine cryptography with adversarial deep learning for applications in cryptanalysis and encryption. Deep neural networks perform symmetric encryption in an adversarial environment. They play cryptographic games with an adversary to detect cryptographically insecure communication based on ciphertext indistinguishability. Neural Steganography is then provided to create steganographic algorithms in the presence of adversarial networks. Krause et al. [329] learn a probabilistic discriminative classifier called Regularized Information Maximization (RIM) from an unlabelled and partially labelled dataset. RIM has an information-theoretic objective function to balance class separation, class balance, and classifier complexity in different class-conditional likelihood functions. RIM can also be interpreted as discriminative clustering algorithms to represent the boundaries between categories. Existing discriminative clustering algorithms such as spectral graph partitioning and maximum margin clustering are not probabilistic models like RIM. RIM maximizes the mutual information between empirical distribution on the inputs and induced label distribution regularized by a complexity penalty. The regularization term penalizes complex decision boundaries to yield sensible clustering solutions. Relative entropy is used to accommodate prior beliefs on label distribution in multi-class classification problems for semi-supervised learning as a cross-entropy regularization term. RIM leads to efficient, scalable optimization procedures for automatic model selection determining the number of clusters. The clustering results are compared with ground truth labels on the dataset categories with an adjusted Rand index (ARI) comparing statistical inference clusters with the ground truth labels. Resulting semi-supervised methods are found to significantly improve the classification performance of supervised baselines when the number of labelled examples is small.

Chapter 6
Physical World Adversarial Attacks on Images and Texts

During the past decades, deep neural networks (DNNs) have shown great success in a wide range of applications, including image classification in the computer vision (CV) domain [263, 282, 558] and text recognition in the natural language processing (NLP) field [157, 276]. However, recent researches have shown that DNNs are immensely brittle toward adversarial examples primarily in the image domain [228, 589]. For example, Goodfellow et al. [228] demonstrated that adding nearly zero noises to a panda image can mislead the GoogLeNet to incorrect label (gibbon) with high confidence (99.3%). This phenomenon raises great concern about DNNs security implementation and attracts much attention in the CV community since 2014. In the literature, numerous approaches have been proposed to generate adversarial examples to attack DNNs (aka, the attack branch) and design corresponding mechanisms to defense these potential attacks (aka, the defense branch). In this chapter, we focus on the adversarial attack direction to craft high-quality adversarial examples in both the CV domain and the NLP domain.

6.1 Adversarial Attacks on Images

Adversarial attack is an effective strategy to investigate the properties of DNNs and promote their security and integrity applications. Adversarial attack on images aims to generate adversarial examples by adding subtle pixel perturbations to the clean images so that the well-trained deep learning model makes wrong predictions [5]. In image classification, Szegedy et al. [589] first revealed an intriguing weakness that DNNs' input-output mappings are extremely discontinuous—a human imperceptible perturbation is enough to cause the neural network to make misclassification (Fig. 6.1). Even worse, the same perturbation on the image can fool multiple DNNs although they have different network architectures. This result implies the current

© The Author(s), under exclusive license to Springer Nature Switzerland AG 2023
A. Sreevallabh Chivukula et al., *Adversarial Machine Learning*,
https://doi.org/10.1007/978-3-030-99772-4_6

Fig. 6.1 Successful adversarial examples from [589] to mislead AlexNet [332]. The perturbations are almost imperceptible by human vision system, but the AlexNet predicts the adversarial examples as "ostrich, struthio, camelus" from top to bottom

Original   Perturbation   Adversarial

DNNs are highly unstable toward adversarial attacks and attracted great interest in the CV community.

Based on [589], a number of approaches for image adversarial attacks have been proposed, such as gradient-based attack [161, 228, 338, 441, 658], score-based attack [260, 292, 452], decision-based attack [85, 113, 114, 360, 543], and transformation-based attack [115, 175, 630, 662]. Most of these attack strategies compute perturbations for each single image by using existing dataset. Compared with single image attack, crafting universal perturbation for a group of images belonging to the same class is more challenging [440]. Additionally, most of existing attack mechanisms are evaluated on public datasets rather than the physical world environment, where the latter setting is more complex. In this character, we introduce a novel image-agnostic attack module to generate natural perturbations for traffic sign attack. This attack module can generate a universal perturbation for a group of road signs, which is feasible for real-world implementation. Empirical results on both public datasets and physical world pictures demonstrate that the method outperforms baselines in terms of attack success rate and perturbation cost. By using the soft attention module, it generates more natural perturbations, which look like tree shadows by human drivers.

In this section, we review four kinds of adversarial attack methods on images, i.e., gradient-based attack (6.1.1), score-based attack (6.1.2), decision-based attack (6.1.3), and transformation-based attack (6.1.4).

6.1.1 Gradient-Based Attack

Gradient-based attack [161, 228, 338, 441, 658] seeks for the most sensitive perturbing direction for an input data according to the gradient of loss function. Goodfellow et al. [228] proposed the well-known fast gradient sign method (FGSM), which determines the perturbation direction (increase or decrease) for each pixel by leveraging the gradient of the loss function. They argued that the vulnerability of the neural networks is due to the linear nature instead of non-linearity or overfitting. To achieve efficiency, FGSM is designed for learning perturbations via a single gradient step. Although this procedure accelerates the adversarial training, it often fails to find the minimal perturbation and results in high perturbation cost [104].

Kurakin et al. [338] refined the FGSM by repeating the gradient step many times with a smaller step size in each iteration. This iterative FGSM (I-FGSM) misleads the classifier in a higher rate with relatively smaller perturbations. Kurakin et al. also shown that the proposed I-FGSM can mislead the target classifier even for the physical world systems. Specifically, they printed the generated adversarial example on papers and taken their photos with cell phone camera. The reported results elaborate that a large fraction of these photos are incorrectly classified by an ImageNet Inception classifier [588]. The DeepFool method [441] further reduces the perturbations strength by iteratively searching for the distance between a clean input to its closest classification hyperplane. However, the greedy optimization strategies in both I-FGSM and DeepFool are easily leading to a local optimum.

Dong et al. [161] designed the momentum I-FGSM (MI-FGSM), which employs a velocity vector to memorize all the previous gradients during iterations to escape from poor local maximum. Besides the white-box attack, Dong et al. also explored the blackbox attack by improving the transferability of adversarial examples. To improve the transferability, they studied momentum iterative methods for attacking an ensemble of models instead of only one model. The theoretical foundation is that if the generated adversarial example can fool all the ensemble models, it is more likely to achieve success attack on an unknown model, as the transferability is the fact that different machine learning models learn similar decision boundaries around a data point.

Recently, Xiang et al. [658] embedded the FGSM into the gray-box attack scheme, where the victim network structure is inaccessible but can be derived by the side-channel attack (SCA). Specifically, the SCA is a technique that derives internal knowledge via hardware side-channel information, such as time/power consumption and electromagnetic radiation. Although SCA cannot exactly reveal the parameter weights or loss function, it can derive the basic network structure. Therefore, it is more practical than a white-box attack, as the network structure is usually unknown, yet superior to the blackbox model where no information is available.

6.1.2 Score-Based Attack

Score-based attack [260, 292, 452] relies on the output scores (e.g., predicted probability) instead of the gradient information in constructing adversarial perturbations, without access of either model architecture and model weights. Narodytska et al. [452] applied the confidence score to guide a greedy local search method, which finds a few pixels (even single pixel) that are most helpful in generating perturbations. It adopts the "top-k misclassification" criteria, which means the search procedure will stop until it pushes the correct label out of the top-k scores. One shortcoming for single pixel attack is that the perturbed pixel may outside of the expected range.

Hayes and Danezis [260] trained an attacker neural network to learn perturbations, which then used to attack another blackbox target network. The attacker model is trained to minimize the difference between the original input image and the output adversary image, where the output image can mislead the target model. To achieve this, they defined the loss function by combining the output confidence scores of both networks, i.e., the reconstruction loss and misclassification loss. The reconstruction loss measures the distance between the input and output of the attacker model to ensure the adversarial output looks similar with the clean input. The misclassification loss is defined according to the type of attack (targeted or untargeted) to make high-attack success rate.

Ilyas et al. [292] considered three more realistic scenarios than typical blackbox settings, including (1) the query-limited setting, (2) partial information setting, and (3) label-only setting. Specifically, the query-limited setting means the attacker has limited number of queries to the classifier, the partial information setting indicates that the adversary only know the top-k probabilities, and the label-only setting denotes the attacker only has access to the top-k labels but does not know their probabilities. For the query-limited setting, the authors employed the natural evolution strategy (NES) to estimate the gradient and generate adversarial examples. To solve the query-limited setting, the authors started from an instance of the target class instead of the original input, so the top-k class will be appeared in the prediction results. For the label-only setting, they further defined the Monte Carlo approximation to estimate the proxy score of softmax probability.

Based on [292], Zhao et al. [704] proposed a zeroth-order natural gradient descent (ZO-NGD) algorithm to perform adversarial attacks. Specifically, it multiplies the natural gradient with the Fisher information matrix (FIM) to optimize the probabilistic models. Then it incorporates FIM with the second-order natural gradient descent (NGD) to achieve high query efficiency.

6.1.3 Decision-Based Attack

Decision-based attack [85, 113, 114, 360, 543] requires only the model classification decision (i.e., the top-1 class label) and frees the need of either model gradient or their output scores. One typical work is the boundary attack [85], which starts with an adversarial point, i.e., an image selected from the target class. Then it reduces the noise by implementing the random walk along the decision boundary while staying adversarial. This method adds minimal perturbations (in terms of L_2-distance) compared with gradient-based methods and requires almost no hyperparameter to tune. However, it needs much more iterations to deliver the final adversarial example due to the slow convergence.

Different from boundary attack that minimize perturbations in terms of the L_2-norm, Schott et al. [543] proposed a novel decision-based attack, i.e., pointwise attack, that reduces noises by minimizing the L_0-norm. It firstly initializes the starting point with salt-pepper noise or Gaussian noise until the image is misclassified. Then it repeatedly resets each perturbed pixel to clean image while making sure the noisy image still adversarial. This procedure goes on until there is no pixel can be reset anymore.

Chen and Jordan [113] developed the boundary attack [85] and proposed an unbiased estimation of the gradient direction at the decision boundary using binary search. They analyze the estimation error when the sample is not exactly lying at the boundary and named their method as Boundary Attack ++. Compare with boundary attack, Boundary Attack ++ not only reduces the number of model queries but also able to switch between L_2 and L_∞ distance by designing two clip operators.

In [114], Chen et al. employed the binary information of the decision boundary to estimate the gradient direction and presented the decision-based HopSkipJumpAttack (HSJA). This method is designed for both targeted or untargeted attack by minimizing the distance of L_2 or L_∞. Specifically, HSJA is an iterative algorithm, where each iteration contains three steps: the gradient direction estimation, the geometrical step-size search, and a binary method for boundary search. This method achieved competitive results by attacking popular defense mechanisms, while its query efficiency needs improvement.

Li et al. [360] pointed out that the large number of query iterations for boundary-based attack is due to the high dimensional input (e.g., image). Thereby, three subspace optimization methods (i.e., spatial subspace, frequency subspace and principle component subspace) are explored in their Query-Efficient Boundary-Based Blackbox Attack (QEBA) for perturbation sampling. In particular, the spatial subspace leverages linear interpolation to reduce the image into a low-dimensional space. The second frequency subspace is obtained by discrete cosine transformation (DCT), while the third one selects major components with principle component analysis (PCA).

6.1.4 Transformation-Based Attack

Finally, transformation-based attack [115, 175, 630, 662] crafts adversarial images by shifting pixels' spatial location instead of directly modifying their value. For example, Xiao et al. [662] proposed the spatially transformed adversarial (stAdv) method, which measures the magnitude of perturbations via local geometry distortion instead of the L_p-norm. The reason is that the spatial transformation on an image often leads to large L_p loss, but such perturbations are visually imperceptible to human and hard to be defend. For each pixel, its spatial location can be moved to four-pixel neighbors, i.e., top-left, top-right, bottom-left, and bottom-right. The stAdv constructs an objective function to minimize the local distortion and solve this minimizing problem with the L-BFGS optimizer [379].

Engstrom et al. [175] also found that simply rotating or translating a natural image is enough to fool a deep vision model. To simultaneously perform the translation and rotation, the author defines three parameters where two parameters for translation and one angle parameter to control the rotation. Then they designed three distinct ways to optimize these parameters, including the first-order method, the grid search, and the worst-of-k selection. The first-order method needs full knowledge of the classifier to compute the gradient of loss function, while the second and third strategies can perform under blackbox settings.

Wang et al. [630] investigated the effect of image spatial transformation on the image-to-image (Im2Im) translation task, which is more sophisticated than pure classification problem. They revealed that the geometrical image transformation (i.e., translation, rotation, and scale) in the input domain can cause incorrect color map of Im2Im framework in the target domain. Different from the previous works that depend only on the spatial transformation,

Chen et al. [115] integrated linear spatial transformation (i.e., affine transformation) with color transformation and proposed a two-phase combination attack. Except the affine transformation, the authors defined the color transformation as the change of illumination, because these adjustments do not change the semantic information of an image. Besides, since the L_p-norm is inappropriate for measuring the adversarial quality in transformation attack, the authors employed the structural similarity index (SSI) [638] to measure the perceptual quality. These adversary models can be potentially applied to protect social users' interaction for influence learning [95, 362].

Based on attacker's knowledge, these methods can be divided into white-box attack, blackbox attack and gray-box attack. Specifically, white-box attack assumes attackers know everything about the victim model (e.g., architecture, parameters, training method, and data), blackbox attack assumes the adversary only knows the output of the model (prediction label or probability) given an input, and gray-box attack means the scenario where the hacker knows part of information (e.g., the network structure) and the rest (e.g., parameters) is missing. Based on attacker's specificity, these methods fall into targeted attack where the model outputs a user-

Table 6.1 Summary of the properties for different attacking methods. The properties are Targeted attack, Untargeted attack, White-box attack, Blackbox attack and Gray-box attack

Attacking methods	Properties				
	Targeted	Untargeted	White	Black	Gray
FGSM [228]	✓	✓	✓		
I-FGSM [338]	✓	✓	✓		
DeepFool [441]		✓	✓		
MI-FGSM [161]	✓	✓	✓	✓	
Xiang et al. [658]	✓				✓
Narodytska et al. [452]	Top-k misclass		✓		
Hayes and Danezis [260]	✓	✓		✓	
Ilyas et al. [292]	✓			✓	
Zhao et al. [704]		✓	✓		
Boundary Attack [85]	✓	✓		✓	
Pointwise attack [543]		✓		✓	
Boundary Attack ++ [113]	✓	✓		✓	
HSJA [114]	✓	✓		✓	
QEBA [360]	✓			✓	
stAdv [662]	✓		✓		
Engstrom et al. [175]		✓		✓	
Wang et al. [630]		✓		✓	
Chen et al. [115]	✓		✓		

specified label, or untargeted attack where the model is misled to any label other than the correct label. A summary is provided in Table 6.1.

6.2 Adversarial Attacks on Texts

Compared with adversarial image attack, the vulnerability of deep learning models in text recognition is greatly underestimated. There are some difficulties in crafting text adversarial samples. Firstly, the output of a text attack system should meet various natural properties, such as lexical correctness, syntactic correctness, and semantic similarity. These properties make sure the human prediction will not change after the adversarial attack. Secondly, the words in text sequences are discrete tokens instead of continuous pixel values in image space. Therefore, it is infeasible to directly compute the model gradient with respect to every word. A direct roundabout method is mapping the sentences into continuous word embedding space [483], but it cannot ensure that words closed in the embedding space are syntactically coherence to readers [13]. Thirdly, making small perturbations on many pixels may still yield a meaningful image from the view of human perception. However, any small changes, even a single word, on text document can make a sentence meaningless.

The first attempt of text attack can be traced back to 2016, when Papernot et al. [483] investigating the robustness of recurrent neural networks (RNNs) in processing sequential data. In this work [483], Papernot et al. proved that the RNNs can be 100% fooled by averagely changing 9 words in a 71-word movie review for sentiment analysis task. Since 2016, several lines of works have been proposed to generate adversarial text examples, including the character-level attack [42, 169, 209], word-level attack [13, 302, 333, 483, 509], and sentence-level attack [300, 625]. Table 6.2 elaborates three adversarial examples generated by different attack strategies. Specifically, character-level attack generates adversarial texts by deleting, inserting, or swapping characters. However, these character-level modifications lead to misspelled words, which can be easily detected by spell check machines. Sentence-level attack concatenates an adversarial sentence before or after the original texts to confuse deep architecture models, but they usually lead to dramatic semantic changes and generate human incomprehensible sentences. To address these drawbacks, most recent studies have focused on the word-level attack, which replaces the original word with another carefully selected one. However,

Table 6.2 Three successful adversarial text examples generated by the character-level attack, sentence-level attack, and word-level attack strategies

Character-level attack modifies input character from "$p \rightarrow B$" [169].
Original: Chancellor Gordon Brown has sought to quell speculation over who should run the Labour Party and turned the attack on the opposition Conservatives.
Adversarial: Chancellor Gordon Brown has sought to quell speculation over who should run the Labour Party and turned the attack on the oBposition Conservatives.
Sentence-level attack adds one sentence at the end of the input [300].
Original: Peyton Manning became the first quarterback ever to lead two different teams to multiple Super Bowls. He is also the oldest quarterback ever to play in a Super Bowl at age 39. The past record was held by John Elway, who led the Broncos to victory in Super Bowl XXXIII at age 38 and is currently Denver's Executive Vice President of Football Operations and General Manager.
Adversarial: Peyton Manning became the first quarterback ever to lead two different teams to multiple Super Bowls. He is also the oldest quarterback ever to play in a Super Bowl at age 39. The past record was held by John Elway, who led the Broncos to victory in Super Bowl XXXIII at age 38 and is currently Denver's Executive Vice President of Football Operations and General Manager. Quarterback Jeff Dean had jersey number 37 in Champ Bowl XXXIV.
Word-level attack replaces input word from "$funny \rightarrow laughable$" [509].
Original: Ah man this movie was funny as hell, yet strange. I like how they kept the shakespearian language in this movie, it just felt ironic because of how idiotic the movie really was. this movie has got to be one of troma's best movies. highly recommended for some senseless fun!
Adversarial: Ah man this movie was laughable as hell, yet strange. I like how they kept the shakespearian language in this movie, it just felt ironic because of how idiotic the movie really was. this movie has got to be one of troma's best movies. highly recommended for some senseless fun!

existing word substitution strategies are far from perfect in achieving high-attack success rate and low substitution rate.

In this section, we review the related text attack methods, including character-level attack (6.2.1), sentence-level attack (6.2.2), word-level attack (6.2.3), and multilevel attack (6.2.4).

6.2.1 Character-Level Attack

Firstly, character-level attack [42, 169, 170, 209, 218] generates adversarial text by deleting, inserting or swapping characters. Belinkov and Bisk [42] devised four types of synthetic noise: (1) swap two adjacent characters but exclude the first and last letters (e.g., *noise* → *nosie*), (2) randomize the order of all the letters in a word except for the first and last (e.g., *noise* → *nisoe*), (3) fully random a word including the first and last characters (e.g., *noise* → *iones*), and (4) keyboard typo that randomly replace one letter in each word with an adjacent key (e.g., *noise* → *noide*). These strategies can mislead the neural machine translation (NMT) models in a large degree. However, they modify every word of an input sentence as they can, which leads to a high perturbation loss. For example, the "swap" of two letters is applied to all words with length ≥ 4, as it does not alter the first and last letters.

To reduce the distortion degree, Ebrahimi *et al.* [169] proposed HotFlip, which represents every character as a one-hot vector and proposes two character operations, i.e., the character insertion and character deletion. Specifically, HotFlip estimates the best character change (aka, atomic flip operation) by computing directional derivatives with respect to one-hot vector representation. Then it employs a beam search to find a sequential of manipulations that can perform well together to confuse a well-trained classifier. Besides, the HotFlip sets the upper bond of character flips as 20% for each training sample to restrict the manipulations.

To minimize the edit distance and reduce the distortion degree, Gao et al. [209] designed a blackbox DeepWordBug and made the text perturbations only on those highest important words. Specifically, it evaluates the word importance score by directly removing words one by one and comparing the prediction changes. The DeepWordBug modifies words by following four character operations, including (1) replace a letter in the word with a random letters, (2) delete a random character in the word, (3) insert a random letter in the word, and (4) swap two adjacent letters in the word. They defines the edit distance as the Levenshtein distance, so the edit distance for (1), (2), and (3) is 1, but this distance for (4) is 2.

Gil et al. [218] exhibited that the HotFlip method that designed under the white-box setting can be applied to performing blackbox attack via an efficient distillation. This white-to-black procedure contains three steps: firstly, train a source text classification model and a target blackbox model; secondly, craft adversarial examples by attack the source model with HotFlip under white-box; and, thirdly, train an attacker to generate new adversarial examples to attack the black box target model. The attacker is trained using the $(input, output)$ pairs with a carefully designed cross-entropy loss function, where the $input$ denotes the original input word and the $output$ is the modifications made in the second step.

Eger et al. [170] proposed Visual Perturber (VIPER) algorithm to replace characters with their visually similar symbols, which is commonly used in Internet slang (e.g., n00b) and toxic comment (e.g., !d10t), etc. The advantages of visual attack include the needless of any linguistic knowledge beyond the character level and the less damaging to human perception and understanding. The visually similar symbol candidates are selected from three character embedding space, including the image-based character embedding space (ICES), description-based character embedding space (DCES), and easy character embedding space (ECES). The ECES achieves the maximal effect on the target model by appending symbol below or above a character (e.g., $c \rightarrow \hat{c}$), but these perturbations need manual selection.

However, one common drawback for character-level attacks is that they breaks the lexical constraint and leads to misspelled word, which can be easily detected and removed by a spell-check machine installed before the classifier.

6.2.2 Sentence-Level Attack

Sentence-level attack [250, 300, 348, 564, 625, 632] concatenates an adversarial sentence before or more commonly after the clean input text to confuse deep architecture models. For example, Jia and Liang [300] appended a compatible sentence to the end of paragraph to fool reading comprehension models (RCM). The adversarial sentence looks similar to the original question by combining altered question and fake answers, aiming to mislead RCM into wrong answer location. Nevertheless, this strategy requires a lot of human intervention and cannot be fully automated, e.g., it relies on about 50 manually defined rules to ensure the adversarial sentence in a declarative form.

Wallace et al. [625] sought for the universal adversarial triggers, i.e., input-agnostic sequences, which causes a specific target prediction when it is concatenated to any input from the same dataset. The universal sequence is randomly initialized and iteratively updated to increase the likelihood of the target prediction using token replacement gradient as HotFlip, while this method fails to guarantee a semantically meaningful output to human perception and often generates irregular text (e.g., "zoning tapping fiennes").

Recently, Song et al. [564] proposed the Natural Universal Trigger Search (NUTS) to craft fluent trigger that carries semantic meanings. The NUTS employs a pre-trained adversarially regularized autoencoder (ARAE) to generate triggers and adopts a gradient-based search to maximize the loss function of the classification system. During optimization, multiple independent noise vectors (256 vectors in their experiment) are firstly initialized. Then those optimized candidate triggers are re-ranked according to both of the classifier accuracy and the naturalness.

Wang et al. [632] proposed Controlled Adversarial Text Generation (CATGen) model that generated adversarial sentence by changing a controllable attribute of the input sentence. To be specific, the CATGen contains two main modules, i.e., an encoder-decoder framework for text generation and an attribute classifier. The encoder and decoder are both RNNs to learn a copy an input sentence. The attribute classifier is trained on an auxiliary dataset, aiming to learn controllable attributes (e.g., category, gender, domain) that are irrelevant to the task-label (e.g., positive, negative). For example, by changing the attribute from "Kitchen" to "Phone," the input sentence "amazing **knife**, used for my **edc** for a long time, only **switched** because i got tired of the same old **knife** (Pos.)" becomes "amazing **case**. used for my **iphone5** for a long time, only **problem** because i got tired of the same old **kindle** (Neg.)."

Except for the classification task, Han et al. [250] investigated the adversarial attack for the structured prediction tasks in NLP and proposed a sequence-to-sequence (seq2seq) sentence generator. Different from the classification task, one special challenge for the structured prediction models is the structured output of the prediction model is more sensitive to small perturbations in the input sentence. For example, shifting only one word of the sentence "I am a writer" to "I fire a writer" makes the dependency parser delivering different parse tree. To solve this problem, the seq2seq generator is trained by reinforcement learning and taking the parse tree as one term of the reward function. Then it can be used to produce adversarial sentences directly given an input sentence without access the victim model, i.e., acting as an online attacker.

Le et al. [348] explored the robustness of neural fake news detection models and proposed the Malcom framework to generate adversarial comments. Fake news are usually consist of a title, content, comments, and replies, where the title and content are unchangeable if the attacker is not the publisher. However, an adversary can make any malicious comments for the published article. As a part of input, the adversary comment can mislead the same detector without the ownership of the target article. To ensure the adversary comment is relevant to the article, Malcom train a conditional text generator together with a STYLE module and an ATTACK module by designing an objective function under white-box. This white-box attack can also be transferred to some unknown fake news classifiers under blackbox settings.

Additionally, the sentence-level attack usually appears in other NLP tasks, such as natural machine translation (NMT) [296] and question answering (QA) [207]. However, as these methods manipulate text document on sentence level, they usually lead to high perturbation cost and significant semantic changes.

6.2.3 Word-Level Attack

Word-level attack [13, 212, 302, 359, 365, 483, 509, 689] replaces original input words with carefully picked words. The core problems are (1) how to select proper candidate words and (2) how to determine the word substitution order. Incipiently, Papernot et al. [483] projected words into a 128-dimension embedding space and leveraged the Jacobian matrix to evaluates input-output interaction. However, a small perturbation in the embedding space may lead to totally irrelevant words since there is no hard guarantee that words close in the embedding space are semantically similar. Therefore, subsequent studies focused on synonym substitution strategy that search synonyms from the GloVe embedding space, existing thesaurus (e.g., WordNet and HowNet), or BERT masked language model (MLM).

By using GloVe, Alzantot et al. [13] designed a population-based genetic algorithm (GA) to imitate the natural selection. The optimization procedure starts from the initial generation by a set of distinct word modifications. In every next generation, crossover, and mutation are employed for population evolving and candidate optimization. Particularly, the crossover takes more than one parent solution to produce one child solution, and the mutation is designed for increasing the diversity of population members. Jin et al. [302] presented TextFooler, which collected substitution candidates from GloVe embedding space. Different from the GA, TextFooler determines the word substitution order by calculating the word importance score (WIS). Specifically, the WIS is defined as the reduction of the true label probability and the increase of the wrong label score by iteratively deleting each input word. However, the GloVe embedding usually fails to distinguish antonyms from synonyms. For example, the nearest neighbors for *expensive* in GloVe space are {*pricey, cheaper, costly*}, where *cheaper* is its antonym. Therefore, Glove-based algorithms have to use a counter-fitting method to postprocess adversary's vectors to ensure the semantic constraint [444].

Compared with GloVe, utilizing well-organized linguistic thesaurus, e.g., synonym-based WordNet [429] and sememe-based HowNet [162], is more straightforward way. Specifically, the WordNet [429] is large lexical dataset of English, in which nouns, verbs, adjectives, and adverbs are grouped into sets of cognitive synonyms (synsets). HowNet [162] annotates words by their sememes, where the sememe is a minimum unit of semantic meaning in linguistics. Ren et al. [509] sought synonyms for each input word from the WordNet synsets and determined the replacement priority of the input words by calculating the probability weighted word saliency (PWWS). Then they sequentially substitute each word with the best candidate following the PWWS descending order until find a successful adversarial sample. Zang et al. [689] manifested that the sememe-based HowNet can provide more substitute words than WordNet and proposed the particle swarm optimization (PSO) to determine which group of words should be attacked. In PSO, each sentence is treated as a particle in a search space, and each dimension of the particle corresponds to a word. Therefore, a successful adversarial example can be found by gradually optimizing the particle's location.

Some recent studies utilized BERT masked language model (MLM) to generate contextual perturbations, such as BERT-Attack [365] and BERT-based adversarial examples (BAE) [212]. The pre-trained BERT MLM can ensure the predicted token fit in the sentence well but unable to preserve the semantic similarity. For example, in the sentence "the food was [MASK]," predicting the [MASK] as *good* or *bad* is equally fluent but resulting in opposite sentiment label. Besides, both of BERT-Attack and BAE adopt a static word replacement order guided by the word importance score (WIS), leading to redundancy word substitution. The difference lies in that Garg and Ramakrishnan [212] defined the WIS as probability decrease of the correct label after deleting a word, while Li et al. [365] replaced each of the original words by a dummy symbol [MASK].

In addition, Li et al. [359] presented the ContextuaLized AdversaRial Example (CLARE) model to generate fluent adversarial output via a mask-then-infill procedure. Instead of using the BERT MLM, the CLARE employs the pre-trained RoBERTa [390] MLM to provide the contextualized infilling words. The CLARE adopts three text perturbations, i.e., replace, insert, and merge, which are replace an input token, insert a new token, and merge a bigram. For each input word, CLARE will try all these three perturbations and select the one that minimizes the gold label's probability.

6.2.4 Multilevel Attack

Multilevel attack combines at least two of the above three attack strategies to create adversarial text [363, 368, 626]. Unlike the single strategy, multilevel attack algorithms are relatively more complicated and computationally expensive [633]. For example, Liang et al. [368] presented to dress up text input on both character-level and word-level via three strategies, i.e., insertion, modification, and removal. These strategies are applied on those hot characters and hot words (i.e., classification-important items) that identified by leveraging the cost gradient. Besides, they proposed a natural language watermarking technique to improve the readability and utility of the adversarial text, e.g., inserting semantically empty phrases. It is worth mentioning that using a single strategy (e.g., removal) is often insufficient to fool a classifier and combining three strategies is essential to crafting subtle adversarial samples. However, there lacks a clear optimization principle about how to combine these strategies.

Li et al. [363] proposed the TextBugger that modified the benign text on both word-level and character-level. Specifically, it defines five kinds of bug perturbation methods, including (1) insert a space into the word, (2) delete a random character of the word except the first and last character, (3) swap two adjacent letters of a word, (4) replace characters with visually similar characters, and (5) replace a word with its k-nearest neighbors in the GloVe embedding space. For each input word, it selects the best bug from these five strategies as the one that reduces the ground truth probability the most. The final adversarial output is crafted by iteratively repeating this procedure on every input word.

Wang et al. [626] presented a tree-based attack framework T3 that perturbed text on both word-level (T3(WORD)) and sentence-level (T3(SENT)). The core component of T3 is a pre-trained tree-based autoencoder, which can convert the discrete text space into a continuous semantic embedding space. This solves the

Table 6.3 Summary of the properties for different text attacking methods. The properties are Targeted attack, Untargeted attack, White-box attack, and Black-box attack

Attacking methods	Properties			
	Targeted	Untargeted	White	Black
Belinkov and Bisk [42]		✓		✓
HotFlip [169]		✓	✓	
DeepWordBug [209]		✓		✓
Gil et al. [218]		✓	✓	✓
VIPER [170]		✓		✓
Jia and Liang [300]		✓		✓
Wallace et al. [625]	✓		✓	
NUTS [564]		✓	✓	
CATGen et al. [632]		✓	✓	
Han et al. [250]		✓		✓
Malcom [348]	✓		✓	✓
Papernot et al. [483]		✓	✓	
Alzantot et al. [13]	✓			✓
TextFooler [302]		✓		✓
PWWS [509]		✓		✓
PSO [689]	✓			✓
BERT-Attack [365]		✓		✓
BAE [212]		✓		✓
CLARE [359]		✓		✓
Liang et al. [368]	✓		✓	✓
TextBugger [363]		✓	✓	✓
T3 [626]	✓		✓	

discrete input challenge so that the gradient-based optimization method can be used to find an adversarial embeddings. Finally, the adversarial embeddings can be mapped back to the adversarial text by a tree-based decoder with a set of tree grammar rules. The high-attack success rate is achieved by a sequence of iterations.

Similar to image attack, the typical properties of these text attack methods are summarized in Table 6.3. As we can see from Table 6.3 that most of existing text attack methods are designed for untargeted attack.

6.3 Spam Filtering

6.3.1 Text Spam

Email spam filtering has been analyzed as a lazy learning problem in concept drifts [152]. Kazemian et al. [312] compare machine learning techniques to detect malicious web pages. Adversarial examples in reading comprehension systems are analyzed by Jia et al. [301]. Chen et al. [117] discuss adversarial examples in machine-learning classifiers for malware detection. Miyato et al. [432] discuss adversarial training with adversarial examples on word embeddings in a recurrent neural network. Dasgupta et al. [147] adversarial attack scenarios in text classification for sentiment analysis on social media sites. Cheng et al. [121] craft adversarial examples for sequence-to-sequence (seq2seq) models.

Our method is not specific to any particular data source. We experiment with image databases, text databases, and time series databases.

6.3.2 Image Spam

The image spam detection problem is a part of content-based filtering of multimedia data in adversarial environments. Such multimedia data is often produced on the Internet communities and mobile networks. According to the survey by Attar et al. [20], image spam is created by embedding spam text message into images. The adversarial objective is to prevent text recognition by optical character recognition software. Keyword detection, text categorization, image classification, and near duplicate detection are the existing techniques for image spam detection. In applying these techniques to adversarial learning, the underlying assumption is that the text in legitimate images (and corresponding features discriminating between spam images and legitimate images) is unlikely to be obfuscated with adversarial features.

The adversarial features can also be built on the rationale of content-based image retrieval where search for either spam images or legitimate images is driven by a set of low-level features found in query images. In such methods, the distance between a query image and templates in database is computed for each feature space and compared to a threshold to decide whether an image is a spam image or a legitimate image. Thus, the generalization capability of the adversarial learning algorithms over image spam strongly depends on choice of proper features for adversarial data manipulation. In the existing literature, the choice of features depends on assumptions about properties which best discriminate between spam images and legitimate images. The most commonly used features include text obfuscation, text area, low-level image properties (like color, texture, etc.), image similarity, image regions similarity, and image metadata. The relevant features are then selected based on results concerning classification accuracy, true positive rate, false positive rate, precision, and recall. The most common classifiers include support vector machines, decision trees, maximum entropy models, and Bayesian networks.

6.3.3 Biometric Spam

Biometrics is an area of research where security is a major issue. Security in biometrics is determined by the vulnerability of pattern classification methods. Biggio et al. [64] investigate attacks and defenses for adversarial learning in adaptive biometrics systems. The attacks in an adaptive biometrics system pertain to either the recognition of biometrics or the changes of biometric traits over time. To effectively deal with these attacks, the stored biometric templates ought to match the claimed identities submitted during verification.

The attack points found during the process of matching biometrics identity are categorized by Biggio et al. [64] as sensor input, feature extraction, template database, matching algorithm, template update, scoring rule, and scoring thresholds. In adaptive biometrics additional attack points include template theft and malware infection disregarding intrinsic failures. These attacks are further classified into attacks on sensors, interfaces and channels connecting modules, processing modules and algorithms, and template databases.

Following attacks are seen in adaptive biometric systems:

- **Spoofing** attacks fabricate a fake biometric trait to impersonate an enrolled client.
- **Replay** attacks stage stolen biometrics as features in the matching algorithm.
- **Hill-climbing** attacks affect the communication channels by iteratively sending perturbed data to the matching algorithm and retaining data that gives maximum matching score. The iterations in attack continue until convergence of the optimization method used by the adversary.
- **Malware infection** attacks exploit well-known software and hardware vulnerabilities through hacking techniques and programming practices.
- **Template theft** attacks target improperly protected template databases that are not encrypted.

Biggio et al. [64] then go onto characterize attacks in biometric systems according to the security framework discussed by Vidyadhari et al. [619]. A spoofing attack scenario, a poisoning attack scenario, and an evasion attack scenario are discussed as a motivation for adversarial learning algorithms in secure-by-design biometric systems. Pattern matching algorithms in secure-by-design biometric systems are recommended to be designed ground up according to the considerations in statistical databases. Such considerations include learning with invariances, error tolerance in PAC learning, and online learning with game theory.

Chapter 7
Adversarial Perturbation for Privacy Preservation

While adversarial examples (AEs) or adversarial perturbations (APs) are usually treated as a security risk up to date, they can also serve as privacy protection tools when facing deep learning-based privacy attacks. This chapter will first introduce a privacy model for visual data, one of the most important types of data in deep learning applications. Then we will discuss AP-based privacy protection mechanisms that incorporate different levels of privacy. While the research on this topic is still in its infancy stage, this chapter will overview the state-of-the-art works and shed light on future research.

7.1 Adversarial Perturbation for Privacy Preservation

Due to their unprecedented accuracy, deep learning methods have become the basis of new AI-based services on the Internet in big data era. Meanwhile, it raises obvious privacy issues. The deep learning-assisted privacy attack can extract sensitive personal information not only from the text but also from unstructured data such as images and videos. This prompts us to revisit the privacy challenges in a big data era with various intelligent technologies emerging [375]. In particular, the emerging deep learning technique can "automatically collect and process millions of photos or videos to extract private/sensitive information from social networks." Therefore, thoroughly investigating the privacy problem in the context of deep learning is an urgent need.

Although most of the existing research work considered adversarial examples (AEs) or adversarial perturbations (APs) as attack methods that threaten the system security, AP can also serve as a privacy protection tool when facing the deep learning-based privacy attacks. The fundamental idea of AP is to generate a small but intentional worst-case disturbance to an original image, which misleads CNN-based recognition models without causing a significant difference perceptible to human eyes. Therefore, it is feasible to design AP-based privacy protection mechanisms against privacy attacks.

There has been some recent work that uses adversarial perturbations as a method for image privacy protection [376, 502]. Liu *et al.* [391] proposed an algorithm that is against automatic detection using adversarial examples based on the "Faster RCNN framework." Oh et al. [471] set up a game theoretical framework and studied the effectiveness of adversarial image perturbations for privacy protection. Shafahi et al. [549] presented an optimization-based method for crafting poison images, in which just one single poison image could control classifier behavior. Jia et al. [298] proposed a two-phase framework called AttriGuard to defend against attribute inference attacks launched by a classifier. Liu et al. [377] investigated schemes for using adversarial examples in ML systems so that they cannot identify the sensitive information from images. Li et al. [366] proposed to use adversarial perturbation for face de-identification. Komkov and Petiushko [322] showed that carefully computed adversarial stickers on a hat could reduce its wearer's likelihood of being recognized. Zhu et al. [715] introduced a new "polytope attack" in which poison images were designed to surround the targeted image in the feature space. Xue et al. [673] proposed to use adversarial perturbation to protect multiple private objects in street view images. Friedrich et al. [204] proposed a privacy-preserving shareable representation of medical texts for a de-identification classifier. Fawkes [551] helped users wearing imperceptible "cloaks" to their own photos before releasing them. When used to train facial recognition models, these "cloaked" images produce functional models that consistently cause normal images of the user to be misidentified.

As almost all existing AP-based privacy protection research focus on visual data, especially image data, the discussion in this chapter will also be conducted in the context of images and videos. We will first briefly define privacy model in visual data and then introduce three different groups of AP-based privacy protection mechanisms.

7.1.1 Visual Data Privacy Model

Before we start to discuss the privacy protection methods, it is important to first clarify and model image and video privacy. As defined in GDPR [176], privacy is defined as something that are related to personal identities. In this sense, a single-level privacy model is not always necessary, nor is it enough for an image or video. For example, a street view image containing an individual's face is private as a whole, but it also contains much non-private information. In this case, using image-level privacy may be too strong for practical use. If we are able to ensure the face is anonymous, the whole image can be used as part of the street view service. Therefore, it is more general to use a multilevel visual privacy model. The idea is to define a three-level privacy model as follows:

- File-level privacy: an image or a video.
- Object-level privacy: faces, people, car, etc.
- Feature-level privacy: identity, appearance, pose, etc.

From the first to third level, the model changes from a coarse-grained one to a fine-grained one. Based on this multilevel privacy model, we can divide existing AP-based into three groups and discuss them in next subsection, respectively.

7.1.2 Privacy Protection Mechanisms Using Adversarial Perturbations

7.1.2.1 File-Level Privacy Protection

For file-level privacy protection, we aim to mislead the deep learning tool to a wrong image class. We consider the scenario of social networks [376]. In more detail, users post images on social network platforms. Suppose an attacker collects images through a crawler and use DNNs to mine sensitive information. Figure 7.1 shows an example of such system architecture. When a user shares an image on social

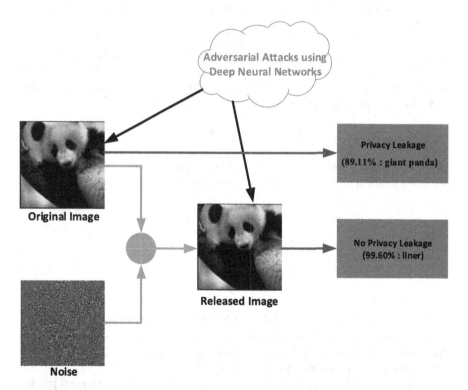

Fig. 7.1 An example of the system architecture for AP-based file-level privacy protection

networks without any preprocessing on the original image, an adversary equipped with DNNs can automatically obtain useful information from this image (i.e., this is a giant panda with high confidence, indicating a likely event of visiting a zoo). Other sensitive information such as the user's activity, location or even name can be detected by similar powerful deep learning models. In order to prevent the privacy leakage, we will add adversarial perturbation to the original image, so the released image can mislead the DNN models to get the wrong information. Meanwhile, we hope to keep the noise as small as possible so that it has a minor impact on the image quality and user experience.

We can define this file-level privacy protection problem as a optimization problem whose target is to minimize the probability of the perturbed image being correctly classified by the attacker, i.e.,

$$P1: \min \Pr(class_p = class_{\mathbf{X}}|o),$$

where o is the observation, $class_p$ is the predicted class of the adversary, and $class_{\mathbf{X}}$ is the true class of the original image $\mathbf{X}$.

The output of $P1$ will be a number between 0 and 1, where "0" means completely private and "1" indicates no privacy.

There are many different methods to generate the noise for the adversarial example, among which the most widely used one is the fast gradient sign method (FGSM).

Let θ be the parameters of a model, $\mathbf{X}$ the input to the model, y the targets associated with $\mathbf{X}$ (we can randomly pick up a class that we want to mislead the deep learning model), and $J(\theta; \mathbf{X}; y)$ be the cost function (output) used to train the neural network [228]. The cost function can be linearized around the current value of θ, obtaining an optimal max-norm constrained perturbation of

$$\eta = \epsilon \text{sign}(\nabla_{\mathbf{X}} J(\theta; \mathbf{X}; y)),$$

where ϵ is a small scalar which keeps the noise imperceptible to human eyes and $\nabla_{\mathbf{X}}$ is the gradient of the cost function J with regard to the input image $\mathbf{X}$,

$$\nabla_{\mathbf{X}} J(\theta; \mathbf{X}; y) = \frac{\partial J}{\partial \mathbf{X}}.$$

And the release image is generated by

$$\mathbf{X}' = \eta + \mathbf{X}.$$

Figure 7.2 gives an example of the result of the file-level privacy protection. The deep learning model has high confidence (92.42%) to classify the original image as "minibus." And when we add a small noise using FGSM, it will be misclassified as a "washbasin" with even higher confidence (99.37%).

Existing research results show that AP-based methods can achieve good privacy protection against the deep learning tools at the cost of adding a small amount

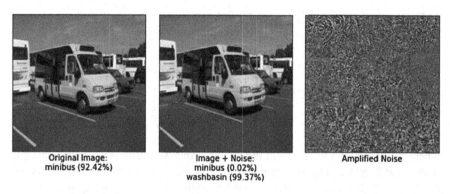

Original Image:
minibus (92.42%)

Image + Noise:
minibus (0.02%)
washbasin (99.37%)

Amplified Noise

Fig. 7.2 An example of the result of the file-level privacy protection (the colors of noises are amplified by normalization otherwise they would be hard to see)

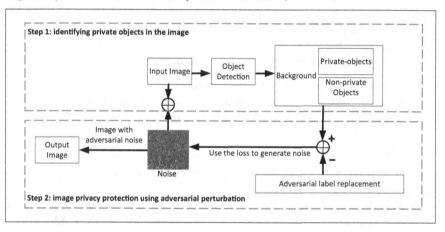

Fig. 7.3 Framework of AP-based object-level privacy protection algorithm

of noise that is imperceptible to human eyes [376]. And the effectiveness of the proposed method is especially good with images of complex structures and textures.

7.1.2.2 Object-Level Privacy Protection

File-level privacy protection is suitable for simple images that contain only one major object. In practice, there are generally multiple objects in a given image, especially for social network images. And some of the objects are privacy-sensitive, while others might be privacy-insensitive. In this case, we can use an object-level privacy protection framework to solve the problem [673].

As shown in Fig. 7.3, the framework can consist of two major steps: (i) identifying private objects in the image and (ii) image privacy protection using adversarial perturbation.

For the first step, a DNN-based object detector can be used. If we have an input image $\mathbf{X}$, the output of the object detection module is represented as

$$
C(\mathbf{X}) = \begin{pmatrix} x_1 & y_1 & w_1 & h_1 & c_1 \\ x_2 & y_2 & w_2 & h_2 & c_2 \\ \vdots & \vdots & \vdots & \vdots & \vdots \\ x_n & y_n & w_n & h_n & c_n \end{pmatrix},
$$

where x_i, y_i, w_i, and h_i represent the up left corner x-coordinate, y-coordinate and width, and height of anchors, respectively. i is the index of the regions of interest (ROI) ($i = 1, 2, \ldots, n$), which is equivalent to the number of objects in the image. c_j is the class label (e.g., cat, dog, face).

It is worth noting that many object detectors such as Faster RCNN [510] treat background as a class, i.e., c_{bg}. *threshold* is used to deal with the unrecognizable area that may appear. If the probability of all classes is less than *threshold*, it is recognized as the background.

Then we define what are private objects according to GDPR:

- Personal identity—license plate, phone number, address, etc.
- Biometrics—face, calendar data, fingerprints, retinal scans, photos, etc.
- Electronic records—cookies, IP locations, mobile device IDs, social network activity records

According to this definition, all classes in the object detection output are divided into two subsets: $\mathbf{C}_{private}$ is the set of private classes, and $\mathbf{C}_{non-private}$ includes non-private classes.

Then in the second step, a small adversarial perturbation δX targeting on private objects is applied to generate the privacy-free image $\mathbf{X}^{pr} = \mathbf{X} + \delta X$, so that only non-private information can be detected when passing $\mathbf{X}^{pr}$ through an object detector, i.e.,

$$
C(\mathbf{X}^{pr}) = \begin{pmatrix} x_1 & y_1 & w_1 & h_1 & c_1^{pr} \\ x_2 & y_2 & w_2 & h_2 & c_2^{pr} \\ \vdots & \vdots & \vdots & \vdots & \vdots \\ x_n & y_n & w_n & h_n & c_n^{pr} \end{pmatrix},
$$

where $\forall c_j \in \mathbf{C}_{private} : c_j^{pr} = c_{bg}$.

Based on the above-described framework, our target is to fool the network by changing the class of the private objects to background, while the non-private objects are recognized as their original classes. Meanwhile, the added noise δX should be small so that it is imperceptible for humans. Hence, the problem can be formulated as follows:

$$
\arg\min_{\delta X} \|\delta X\|_2
$$

$$\text{s.t.: } \forall c_j \in \mathbf{C}_{private} : c_j^{pr} = c_{bg}$$

$$\forall c_j \in \mathbf{C}_{non\text{-}private} : c_j^{pr} = c_j$$

An AP-based image privacy protection algorithm can be used to solve the above problem. As shown in Fig. 7.3, the object detector finds all objects in the image at the beginning. Then, we replace the label of the private objects with the background and use the corresponding loss function to calculate the gradient. Then the noise is updated according to the gradient. Finally, the perturbed image is generated, in which all privacy objects are treated as background by the object detector.

The key part of the algorithm is to trick the classification loss ($\mathcal{L}_{cls}$) so as to mislead the object detector recognizing the privacy objects to background, as shown in Eq. (7.1):

$$\mathcal{L}_{cls} = \frac{1}{n} \sum_i En(p_i, p_i^*) + \lambda \left\| \mathbf{X} - \mathbf{X}^{pr} \right\|_2, \tag{7.1}$$

where $p_i = [p_{i1}, \ldots, p_{im}]$ is the probability of the content of an anchor being recognized as each class. p_i^* is one-hot encoded ($p_i^* = [0, 0, \ldots, 1, \ldots, 0, 0]$), in which 1 appears in the position where we set the class as the correct class. p_i^* will be generated according to ground truth label if the object is non-private, while it will be changed to the background if the object is private. n is the total number of objects in the image so that the entropy will be averaged over all anchors. Next, we can use $\mathcal{L}_{cls}$ to generate the perturbation, using the fast gradient sign method (FGSM) [228].

Using the targeted FGSM, the perturbation can be calculated in the direction of the gradient:

$$\delta X = -\epsilon \text{sign}(\nabla_{\mathbf{X}} \mathcal{L}_{cls}) = -\epsilon \text{sign}(\frac{\mathcal{L}_{cls}}{\partial \mathbf{X}}),$$

where ϵ is the step parameter that scales the noise. Therefore, the generated image will be:

$$\mathbf{X}^{pr} = \mathbf{X} + \delta X = \mathbf{X} - \epsilon \text{sign}(\frac{\mathcal{L}_{cls}}{\partial \mathbf{X}})$$

7.1.2.3 Feature-Level Privacy Protection

In some other cases, we only need to change certain features in image or video, using the human imperceptible adversarial perturbation. A typical example is to change the person's identity (against the face recognition system) in the image while keeping the appearance visually unchanged.

A face recognition system is a technology that is capable of recognizing or authenticating a person from an image or a video frame. With recent advanced

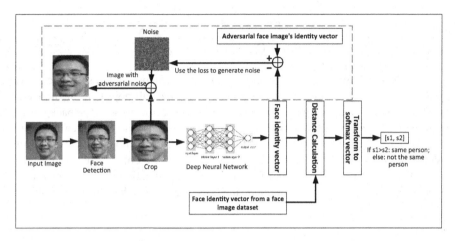

Fig. 7.4 Illustration of a typical face recognition system and the process of generating adversarial image perturbation

deep learning neural networks, the accuracy of artificial intelligence-based face recognition systems has begun to surpass human accuracy in some benchmark tests. As a result, they are beginning to see a wider range of uses in many applications, such as access control and security monitoring.

Figure 7.4 depicts a typical face recognition system. When an input image is received, it first detects the position of the face and crops the face to the size that is aligned with the system settings. The DNN is used to calculate a face embedding (a numerical vector representing the facial features) from the face image. Then the system can calculate the distance between the embedding of the input face and any given embedding from the system database. The distance is converted to a vector containing two soft values that indicate the face recognition result: if the first value is greater than the second one, then the two embeddings are from images of the same person. Otherwise, they are the images of two different persons.

In a sense, the face recognition system is similar to the person in performing the task of recognizing another person: the person compares the new image with their memory. If the image looks close to someone in their memory, they reckon it as the same person. The only difference is how DNN and humans measure the "distance" between images.

From the privacy protection perspective, we aim to add noise to the original image so that the face recognition system cannot identify the person correctly. In more details, based on the privacy protection successful rate metric, the proposed image privacy protection problem can be formulated as:

$$P2: \max \ \Pr(ID_{\mathbf{X'}} \neq ID_{\mathbf{X}}), \tag{7.2}$$

where $ID_{\mathbf{X}}$ is the identity of the original image and $ID_{\mathbf{X'}}$ is the identity of the image with perturbation.

The adversarial perturbation can be generated with FGSM algorithm or a more powerful method, i.e., the multistep variant FGSM^N, which is essentially projected gradient descent (PGD) on the negative loss function [338].

In PGD, the FGSM will be repeated for N times or until the absolute value of noise reaches a predefined upper bound, i.e.,

$$\mathbf{X}'_0 = \mathbf{X}$$
$$\mathbf{X}'_n = \mathbf{X}'_{n-1} + \epsilon \operatorname{sign}(\nabla_{\mathbf{X}} J(\theta; \mathbf{X}'_{n-1}; y))$$
$$= \mathbf{X}'_{n-1} + \eta_{n-1}, 1 \leq n \leq N.$$

An illustration of the process of is shown in Fig. 7.4. First, a different person was specifically or randomly selected. Then the embedding vector of this adversarial face will be calculated and used as the value of y. The image with adversarial perturbation is generated by the PGD algorithm and finally tested using the face recognition system.

7.1.3 Discussion and Future Works

Although AP-based methods have shown superb effectiveness of privacy protection even at imperceptible noise level, there are currently two major issues with this group of methods: (1) these methods depend highly upon the accessibility to target systems, so can only be guaranteed for target-specific recognizers (i.e., requiring white-box knowledge), and (2) the transferability of adversarial perturbation, i.e., its effectiveness on alternative unknown models are not as good as against the target model.

To solve the above issues, some papers [287, 295] have transferred the calculation of noise direction from the output layer to the intermediate layer of the model. This can avoid the differences between models, thereby increasing transferability. Pidhorskyi paper [493] studied the potential of adding adversarial perturbations on feature level of images. As different DNN models have similar outputs in the feature levels, it will also increase the transferability.

From the privacy protection perspective, there are some other mechanisms. For example, there are some researchers who start to use GAN to generate content to replace the sensitive information in the images [101, 581, 645, 706]. Sun et al. [581] proposed GAN-based head inpainting to remove the original identity. Additionally, there recently have been a few attempts to combine the DP notion with image privacy. Fan [178] proposed an ϵ-differential private method in the pixel level of the image. However, making image pixels indistinguishable does not make much sense in practice, and the quality of the generated image is quite low. It will be an interesting topic to compare the different privacy protection mechanisms. Finally, after the first stage of image privacy protection, research on video privacy protection has also started [644]. As directly applying existing image privacy protection methods to videos will introduce high computational complexity and big latency, designing more effective video privacy protection mechanisms is also promising research directions.

Correction to: Adversarial Machine Learning

Attack Surfaces, Defence Mechanisms, Learning Theories in Artificial Intelligence

Aneesh Sreevallabh Chivukula, Xinghao Yang, Bo Liu,
Wei Liu, and Wanlei Zhou

Correction to:
A. Sreevallabh Chivukula et al., *Adversarial Machine*
Learning, **https://doi.org/10.1007/978-3-030-99772-4**

The book was inadvertently published with wrong title and affiliation in the FM. This has been updated in the book.

The updated original version for this book can be found at
https://doi.org/10.1007/978-3-030-99772-4

References

1. A. ABUSNAINA, A. KHORMALI, H. ALASMARY, J. PARK, A. ANWAR, AND A. MOHAISEN, *Adversarial learning attacks on graph-based iot malware detection systems*, in 2019 IEEE 39th International Conference on Distributed Computing Systems (ICDCS), 2019, pp. 1296–1305.
2. D. ADLER, *Genetic algorithms and simulated annealing: a marriage proposal*, in IEEE International Conference on Neural Networks, March 1993, pp. 1104–1109 vol.2.
3. E. A.E., *Evolutionary algorithms and constraint satisfaction: Definitions, survey, methodology, and research directions*, in Kallel L., Naudts B., Rogers A. (eds) Theoretical Aspects of Evolutionary Computing., Springer, Berlin, Heidelberg, 2001.
4. M. AGHASSI AND D. BERTSIMAS, *Robust game theory*, Math. Program., 107 (2006), pp. 231–273.
5. N. AKHTAR AND A. MIAN, *Threat of adversarial attacks on deep learning in computer vision: A survey*, Ieee Access, 6 (2018), pp. 14410–14430.
6. N. AKHTAR AND A. S. MIAN, *Threat of adversarial attacks on deep learning in computer vision: A survey*, IEEE Access, 6 (2018), pp. 14410–14430.
7. I. M. ALABDULMOHSIN, X. GAO, AND X. ZHANG, *Adding robustness to support vector machines against adversarial reverse engineering*, in Proceedings of the 23rd ACM International Conference on Conference on Information and Knowledge Management, CIKM '14, New York, NY, USA, 2014, Association for Computing Machinery, pp. 231–240.
8. G. ALAIN AND Y. BENGIO, *What regularized auto-encoders learn from the data-generating distribution*, J. Mach. Learn. Res., 15 (2014).
9. J. V. ALAIN BENSOUSSAN, JENS FREHSE, *Nash and stackelberg differential games*, Chinese Annals of Mathematics, Series B, 33 (2012), pp. 317–332.
10. E. ALBA AND M. TOMASSINI, *Parallelism and evolutionary algorithms*, IEEE Transactions on Evolutionary Computation, 6 (2002), pp. 443–462.
11. T. ALPCAN, B. I. P. RUBINSTEIN, AND C. LECKIE, *Large-scale strategic games and adversarial machine learning*, in 2016 IEEE 55th Conference on Decision and Control, CDC, IEEE, Dec 2016, pp. 4420–4426.
12. T. ALPCAN, B. I. P. RUBINSTEIN, AND C. LECKIE, *Large-scale strategic games and adversarial machine learning*, in 2016 IEEE 55th Conference on Decision and Control (CDC), 2016.
13. M. ALZANTOT, Y. SHARMA, A. ELGOHARY, B.-J. HO, M. SRIVASTAVA, AND K.-W. CHANG, *Generating natural language adversarial examples*, Proceedings of the 2018 conference on Empirical Methods in Natural Language Processing, (2018), pp. 2890–2896.

14. A. ANANDKUMAR, P. JAIN, Y. SHI, AND U. N. NIRANJAN, *Tensor vs. matrix methods: Robust tensor decomposition under block sparse perturbations*, in Proceedings of the 19th International Conference on Artificial Intelligence and Statistics, A. Gretton and C. C. Robert, eds., vol. 51 of Proceedings of Machine Learning Research, Cadiz, Spain, 09–11 May 2016, PMLR, pp. 268–276.

15. M. ANCONA, C. ÖZTIRELI, AND M. H. GROSS, *Explaining deep neural networks with a polynomial time algorithm for shapley value approximation*, in Proceedings of the 36th International Conference on Machine Learning, ICML 2019, 9-15 June 2019, Long Beach, California, USA, 2019, pp. 272–281.

16. P. ANDERSEN, M. GOODWIN, AND O. GRANMO, *Deep RTS: A game environment for deep reinforcement learning in real-time strategy games*, in 2018 IEEE Conference on Computational Intelligence and Games, CIG 2018, Maastricht, The Netherlands, August 14-17, 2018, IEEE, 2018, pp. 1–8.

17. A. B. ARRIETA, N. D. RODRÍGUEZ, J. D. SER, A. BENNETOT, S. TABIK, A. BARBADO, S. GARCÍA, S. GIL-LOPEZ, D. MOLINA, R. BENJAMINS, R. CHATILA, AND F. HERRERA, *Explainable artificial intelligence (XAI): concepts, taxonomies, opportunities and challenges toward responsible AI*, Inf. Fusion, 58 (2020), pp. 82–115.

18. K. ASIF, W. XING, S. BEHPOUR, AND B. D. ZIEBART, *Adversarial cost-sensitive classification*, in Proceedings of the Thirty-First Conference on Uncertainty in Artificial Intelligence, UAI'15, Arlington, Virginia, USA, 2015, AUAI Press, pp. 92–101.

19. A. ATHALYE, L. ENGSTROM, A. ILYAS, AND K. KWOK, *Synthesizing robust adversarial examples*, in Proceedings of the 35th International Conference on Machine Learning, J. Dy and A. Krause, eds., vol. 80 of Proceedings of Machine Learning Research, PMLR, 10–15 Jul 2018, pp. 284–293.

20. A. ATTAR, R. M. RAD, AND R. E. ATANI, *A survey of image spamming and filtering techniques*, Artificial Intelligence Review, 40 (2013), pp. 71–105.

21. P. AUER, N. CESA-BIANCHI, Y. FREUND, AND R. SCHAPIRE, *Gambling in a rigged casino: The adversarial multi-armed bandit problem*, in Proceedings of IEEE 36th Annual Foundations of Computer Science, 1995, pp. 322–331.

22. T. BACK, F. HOFFMEISTER, AND H.-P. SCHWEFEL, *A survey of evolution strategies*, in Proceedings of the Fourth International Conference on Genetic Algorithms, Morgan Kaufmann, 1991, pp. 2–9.

23. D. BAEHRENS, T. SCHROETER, S. HARMELING, M. KAWANABE, K. HANSEN, AND K.-R. MÜLLER, *How to explain individual classification decisions*, J. Mach. Learn. Res., 11 (2010), pp. 1803–1831.

24. D. BALDUZZI, *Grammars for games: A gradient-based, game-theoretic framework for optimization in deep learning*, Frontiers Robotics AI, 2 (2016), p. 39.

25. S. BALUJA AND I. FISCHER, *Learning to attack: Adversarial transformation networks*, in Proceedings of the Thirty-Second AAAI Conference on Artificial Intelligence, 2018.

26. ——, *Learning to attack: Adversarial transformation networks*, in Proceedings of AAAI-2018, 2018.

27. S. BANDARU, A. H. C. NG, AND K. DEB, *Data mining methods for knowledge discovery in multi-objective optimization: Part A - survey*, Expert Syst. Appl., 70 (2017), pp. 139–159.

28. ——, *Data mining methods for knowledge discovery in multi-objective optimization: Part B - new developments and applications*, Expert Syst. Appl., 70 (2017), pp. 119–138.

29. S. BANDYOPADHYAY, S. K. PAL, AND C. MURTHY, *Simulated annealing based pattern classification*, Information Sciences, 109 (1998), pp. 165–184.

30. M. BARRENO, B. NELSON, A. D. JOSEPH, AND J. D. TYGAR, *The security of machine learning*, Mach. Learn., 81 (2010), p. 121–148.

31. M. BARRENO, B. NELSON, R. SEARS, A. D. JOSEPH, AND J. D. TYGAR, *Can machine learning be secure?*, in Proceedings of the 2006 ACM Symposium on Information, Computer and Communications Security, ASIACCS '06, New York, NY, USA, 2006, ACM, pp. 16–25.

32. ——, *Can machine learning be secure?*, in Proceedings of the 2006 ACM Symposium on Information, Computer and Communications Security, ASIACCS '06, New York, NY, USA, 2006, Association for Computing Machinery, p. 16–25.

33. A. BARTH, B. I. RUBINSTEIN, M. SUNDARARAJAN, J. C. MITCHELL, D. SONG, AND P. L. BARTLETT, *A learning-based approach to reactive security*, International Conference on Financial Cryptography and Data Security, (2010), pp. 192–206.

34. T. BASAR AND J. MOON, *Riccati equations in nash and stackelberg differential and dynamic games*, IFAC-PapersOnLine, 50 (2017), pp. 9547–9554. 20th IFAC World Congress.

35. O. BASTANI, Y. IOANNOU, L. LAMPROPOULOS, D. VYTINIOTIS, A. V. NORI, AND A. CRIMINISI, *Measuring neural net robustness with constraints*, in Proceedings of the 30th International Conference on Neural Information Processing Systems, NIPS, Red Hook, NY, USA, 2016, Curran Associates Inc., pp. 2621–2629.

36. D. BAUSO, J. GAO, AND H. TEMBINE, *Distributionally robust games: F-divergence and learning*, in Proceedings of the 11th EAI International Conference on Performance Evaluation Methodologies and Tools, VALUETOOLS 2017, New York, NY, USA, 2017, Association for Computing Machinery, p. 148–155.

37. A. BEAR AND F. CUSHMAN, *Loss functions modulate the optimal bias-variance trade-off*, in CogSci, cognitivesciencesociety.org, 2020.

38. C. BECTOR AND S. CHANDRA, *Fuzzy Mathematical Programming and Fuzzy Matrix Games*, vol. 169, 01 2005.

39. C. R. BECTOR AND S. CHANDRA, *Fuzzy Mathematical Programming and Fuzzy Matrix Games (Studies in Fuzziness and Soft Computing)*, Springer-Verlag, Berlin, Heidelberg, 2005.

40. E. BEGOLI AND J. HOREY, *Design principles for effective knowledge discovery from big data*, in 2012 Joint Working IEEE/IFIP Conference on Software Architecture and European Conference on Software Architecture, 2012, pp. 215–218.

41. V. BEHZADAN AND A. MUNIR, *Vulnerability of deep reinforcement learning to policy induction attacks*, in Machine Learning and Data Mining in Pattern Recognition - 13th International Conference, MLDM 2017, New York, NY, USA, July 15-20, 2017, Proceedings, 2017, pp. 262–275.

42. Y. BELINKOV AND Y. BISK, *Synthetic and natural noise both break neural machine translation*, in International Conference on Learning Representations, 2018.

43. M. BELKIN, D. J. HSU, S. MA, AND S. MANDAL, *Reconciling modern machine learning practice and the classical bias-variance trade-off*, Proceedings of the National Academy of Sciences, 116 (2019), pp. 15849–15854.

44. A. BELLET, A. HABRARD, AND M. SEBBAN, *A Survey on Metric Learning for Feature Vectors and Structured Data*, research report, Laboratoire Hubert Curien UMR 5516, 2013.

45. Y. BENGIO, L. YAO, G. ALAIN, AND P. VINCENT, *Generalized denoising auto-encoders as generative models*, in Advances in Neural Information Processing Systems, C. J. C. Burges, L. Bottou, M. Welling, Z. Ghahramani, and K. Q. Weinberger, eds., vol. 26, Curran Associates, Inc., 2013.

46. D. BERTHELOT, T. SCHUMM, AND L. METZ, *BEGAN: boundary equilibrium generative adversarial networks*, CoRR, abs/1703.10717 (2017).

47. D. P. BERTSEKAS, *Stochastic optimization problems with nondifferentiable cost functionals*, J. OPTIM. THEORY APPL, 12 (1973), pp. 218–231.

48. D. P. BERTSEKAS AND J. N. TSITSIKLIS, *Parallel and Distributed Computation: Numerical Methods*, Prentice-Hall, Inc., USA, 1989.

49. E. BEYAZIT, D. TUNCEL, X. YUAN, N. TZENG, AND X. WU, *Learning interpretable representations with informative entanglements*, in IJCAI, ijcai.org, 2020, pp. 1970–1976.

50. H. BEYER, H. SCHWEFEL, AND I. WEGENER, *How to analyse evolutionary algorithms*, Theor. Comput. Sci., 287 (2002), pp. 101–130.

51. H.-G. BEYER AND H.-P. SCHWEFEL, *Evolution strategies - A comprehensive introduction*, Natural Computing, 1 (2002), pp. 3–52.

52. L. BIANCHI, M. DORIGO, L. M. GAMBARDELLA, AND W. J. GUTJAHR, *A survey on meta-heuristics for stochastic combinatorial optimization*, Natural Computing: An International Journal, 8 (2009).

53. B. BIGGIO, I. CORONA, G. FUMERA, G. GIACINTO, AND F. ROLI, *Bagging classifiers for fighting poisoning attacks in adversarial classification tasks*, in Proceedings of the 10th

International Conference on Multiple Classifier Systems, MCS'11, Berlin, Heidelberg, 2011, Springer-Verlag.

54. B. BIGGIO, I. CORONA, D. MAIORCA, B. NELSON, N. ŠRNDIĆ, P. LASKOV, G. GIACINTO, AND F. ROLI, *Evasion attacks against machine learning at test time*, in Machine Learning and Knowledge Discovery in Databases, H. Blockeel, K. Kersting, S. Nijssen, and F. Železný, eds., Berlin, Heidelberg, 2013, Springer Berlin Heidelberg, pp. 387–402.

55. B. BIGGIO, I. CORONA, B. NELSON, B. I. P. RUBINSTEIN, D. MAIORCA, G. FUMERA, G. GIACINTO, AND F. ROLI, *Security evaluation of support vector machines in adversarial environments*, CoRR, abs/1401.7727 (2014).

56. B. BIGGIO, G. FUMERA, I. PILLAI, AND F. ROLI, *A survey and experimental evaluation of image spam filtering techniques*, Pattern Recogn. Lett., 32 (2011), pp. 1436–1446.

57. B. BIGGIO, G. FUMERA, AND F. ROLI, *Adversarial pattern classification using multiple classifiers and randomisation*, in Structural, Syntactic, and Statistical Pattern Recognition, N. da Vitoria Lobo, T. Kasparis, F. Roli, J. T. Kwok, M. Georgiopoulos, G. C. Anagnostopoulos, and M. Loog, eds., Berlin, Heidelberg, 2008, Springer Berlin Heidelberg, pp. 500–509.

58. ——, *Multiple classifier systems for adversarial classification tasks*, in Multiple Classifier Systems, J. A. Benediktsson, J. Kittler, and F. Roli, eds., Berlin, Heidelberg, 2009, Springer Berlin Heidelberg, pp. 132–141.

59. B. BIGGIO, G. FUMERA, AND F. ROLI, *Multiple classifier systems for robust classifier design in adversarial environments*, Journal of Machine Learning and Cybernetics, 1 (2010), p. 27–41.

60. B. BIGGIO, G. FUMERA, AND F. ROLI, *Multiple classifier systems for robust classifier design in adversarial environments*, International Journal of Machine Learning and Cybernetics, 1 (2010), pp. 27–41.

61. B. BIGGIO, G. FUMERA, AND F. ROLI, *Design of robust classifiers for adversarial environments*, in SMC, IEEE, 2011, pp. 977–982.

62. ——, *Pattern recognition systems under attack: Design issues and research challenges*, Int. J. Pattern Recognit. Artif. Intell., 28 (2014).

63. B. BIGGIO, G. FUMERA, AND F. ROLI, *Security evaluation of pattern classifiers under attack*, IEEE transactions on knowledge and data engineering, 26 (2014), pp. 984–996.

64. B. BIGGIO, G. FUMERA, P. RUSSU, L. DIDACI, AND F. ROLI, *Adversarial biometric recognition: A review on biometric system security from the adversarial machine learning perspective*, IEEE Signal Processing Magazine, 32 (2015), pp. 31–41.

65. B. BIGGIO, B. NELSON, AND P. LASKOV, *Poisoning attacks against support vector machines*, (2012), pp. 1467–1474.

66. ——, *Poisoning attacks against support vector machines*, in Proceedings of the 29th International Coference on International Conference on Machine Learning, ICML'12, USA, 2012, Omnipress, pp. 1467–1474.

67. B. BIGGIO, I. PILLAI, S. ROTA BULO, D. ARIU, M. PELILLO, AND F. ROLI, *Is data clustering in adversarial settings secure?*, in Proceedings of the 2013 ACM Workshop on Artificial Intelligence and Security, AISec '13, New York, NY, USA, 2013, ACM, pp. 87–98.

68. B. BIGGIO AND F. ROLI, *Wild patterns: Ten years after the rise of adversarial machine learning*, in Proceedings of the 2018 ACM SIGSAC Conference on Computer and Communications Security, CCS '18, New York, NY, USA, 2018, ACM, pp. 2154–2156.

69. C. M. BISHOP, *Pattern Recognition and Machine Learning (Information Science and Statistics)*, Springer-Verlag, Berlin, Heidelberg, 2006.

70. R. H. BISSELING, *Parallel Scientific Computation: A Structured Approach Using BSP and MPI*, Oxford University Press, Inc., USA, 2004.

71. R. BITTON, N. MAMAN, I. SINGH, S. MOMIYAMA, Y. ELOVICI, AND A. SHABTAI, *A framework for evaluating the cybersecurity risk of real world, machine learning production systems*, CoRR, abs/2107.01806 (2021).

72. D. M. BLEI, A. KUCUKELBIR, AND J. D. MCAULIFFE, *Variational inference: A review for statisticians*, Journal of the American Statistical Association, 112 (2017), pp. 859–877.

73. M. BLONDEL, A. FUJINO, N. UEDA, AND M. ISHIHATA, *Higher-order factorization machines*, in Proceedings of the 30th International Conference on Neural Information Processing Systems, NIPS'16, Red Hook, NY, USA, 2016, Curran Associates Inc., p. 3359–3367.

74. A. BLUM, J. MORGENSTERN, A. SHARMA, AND A. SMITH, *Privacy-preserving public information for sequential games*, in Proceedings of the 2015 Conference on Innovations in Theoretical Computer Science, ITCS '15, New York, NY, USA, 2015, Association for Computing Machinery.

75. B. BOHRER AND A. PLATZER, *Structured proofs for adversarial cyber-physical systems*, ACM Trans. Embed. Comput. Syst., 20 (2021).

76. P. BOJANOWSKI, A. JOULIN, D. LOPEZ-PAS, AND A. SZLAM, *Optimizing the latent space of generative networks*, in Proceedings of the 35th International Conference on Machine Learning, J. Dy and A. Krause, eds., vol. 80 of Proceedings of Machine Learning Research, PMLR, 10–15 Jul 2018, pp. 600–609.

77. P. BOJANOWSKI, A. JOULIN, D. LOPEZ-PAZ, AND A. SZLAM, *Optimizing the latent space of generative networks*, in International Conference on Machine Learning, 2018, pp. 599–608.

78. G. BONANNO, *Epistemic foundations of game theory*, Working Papers 106, University of California, Davis, Department of Economics, June 2014.

79. D. BOUNEFFOUF AND I. RISH, *A survey on practical applications of multi-armed and contextual bandits*, ArXiv, abs/1904.10040 (2019).

80. D. BOUNEFFOUF, I. RISH, G. CECCHI, AND R. FERAUD, *Context attentive bandits: Contextual bandit with restricted context*, in Proceedings of the Twenty-Sixth International Joint Conference on Artificial Intelligence, IJCAI-17, 2017, pp. 1468–1475.

81. M. BOWLING AND M. VELOSO, *An analysis of stochastic game theory for multiagent reinforcement learning*, Technical report CMU-CS-00-165, Computer Science Department, Carnegie Mellon University, 2000.

82. M. BOWLING AND M. VELOSO, *Rational and convergent learning in stochastic games*, in Proceedings of the 17th International Joint Conference on Artificial Intelligence - Volume 2, IJCAI'01, San Francisco, CA, USA, 2001, Morgan Kaufmann Publishers Inc.

83. M. BRAND AND D. L. DOWE, *The imp game: Learnability, approximability and adversarial learning beyond σ_1^0*, J. Log. Comput., 27 (2017), pp. 2171–2192.

84. W. BRENDEL, J. RAUBER, AND M. BETHGE, *Decision-based adversarial attacks: Reliable attacks against black-box machine learning models*, in International Conference on Learning Representations, 2018.

85. W. BRENDEL, J. RAUBER, AND M. BETHGE, *Decision-based adversarial attacks: Reliable attacks against black-box machine learning models*, in International Conference on Learning Representations, 2018.

86. A. BRESSAN, *Noncooperative differential games*, Milan Journal of Mathematics, 79 (2011), pp. 357–427.

87. T. BROWN, D. MANE, A. ROY, M. ABADI, AND J. GILMER, *Adversarial patch*, 2017.

88. C. BROWNE, E. J. POWLEY, D. WHITEHOUSE, S. M. LUCAS, P. I. COWLING, P. ROHLFSHAGEN, S. TAVENER, D. P. LIEBANA, S. SAMOTHRAKIS, AND S. COLTON, *A survey of monte carlo tree search methods*, IEEE Trans. Comput. Intellig. and AI in Games, 4 (2012), pp. 1–43.

89. M. BRÜCKNER, *Prediction games: machine learning in the presence of an adversary*, PhD thesis, University of Potsdam, 2012.

90. M. BRÜCKNER, C. KANZOW, AND T. SCHEFFER, *Static prediction games for adversarial learning problems*, J. Mach. Learn. Res., (2012).

91. M. BRUCKNER AND T. SCHEFFER, *Stackelberg games for adversarial prediction problems*, in Proceedings of the 17th ACM SIGKDD International Conference on Knowledge Discovery and Data Mining, KDD '11, New York, NY, USA, 2011, Association for Computing Machinery, p. 547–555.

92. A. BUJA, W. STUETZLE, AND Y. SHEN, *Loss functions for binary class probability estimation and classification: Structure and applications*, 2005.

93. S. BULO AND M. PELILLO, *A game-theoretic approach to hypergraph clustering*, in Advances in Neural Information Processing Systems, Y. Bengio, D. Schuurmans, J. Lafferty, C. Williams, and A. Culotta, eds., vol. 22, Curran Associates, Inc., 2009.

94. P. BURNAP, R. FRENCH, F. TURNER, AND K. JONES, *Malware classification using self organising feature maps and machine activity data*, Computers & Security, 73 (2018), pp. 399–410.

95. T. CAI, J. LI, A. S. MIAN, T. SELLIS, J. X. YU, ET AL., *Target-aware holistic influence maximization in spatial social networks*, IEEE Transactions on Knowledge and Data Engineering, (2020).

96. Y. CAI, O. CANDOGAN, C. DASKALAKIS, AND C. PAPADIMITRIOU, *Zero-sum polymatrix games: A generalization of minmax*, Mathematics of Operations Research, 41 (2016), pp. 648–655.

97. Y. CAI, O. CANDOGAN, C. DASKALAKIS, AND C. PAPADIMITRIOU, *Zero-sum polymatrix games: A generalization of minmax*, Math. Oper. Res., 41 (2016), pp. 648–655.

98. Z. CAI, Z. XIONG, H. XU, P. WANG, W. LI, AND Y. PAN, *Generative adversarial networks: A survey toward private and secure applications*, ACM Comput. Surv., 54 (2021).

99. C. F. CAMERER, T.-H. HO, AND J. K. CHONG, *Behavioural Game Theory: Thinking, Learning and Teaching*, in Advances in Understanding Strategic Behaviour, S. Huck, ed., Palgrave Macmillan Books, Palgrave Macmillan, 2004, ch. 8, pp. 120–180.

100. E. CANTU-PAZ, *A survey of parallel genetic algorithms*, CALCULATEURS PARALLELES, 10 (1998).

101. J. CAO, B. LIU, Y. WEN, R. XIE, AND L. SONG, *Personalized and invertible face de-identification by disentangled identity information manipulation*, in 2021 IEEE/CVF International Conference on Computer Vision ICCV 2021, Oct 2021, pp. 269–272.

102. N. CARLINI AND D. WAGNER, *Adversarial examples are not easily detected: Bypassing ten detection methods*, in Proceedings of the 10th ACM Workshop on Artificial Intelligence and Security, AISec '17, New York, NY, USA, 2017, ACM, pp. 3–14.

103. N. CARLINI AND D. WAGNER, *Towards evaluating the robustness of neural networks*, in 2017 IEEE Symposium on Security and Privacy (SP), 2017, pp. 39–57.

104. N. CARLINI AND D. WAGNER, *Towards evaluating the robustness of neural networks*, in 2017 IEEE Symposium on Security and Privacy (SP), 2017, pp. 39–57.

105. N. CARLINI AND D. A. WAGNER, *Magnet and 'efficient defenses against adversarial attacks' are not robust to adversarial examples*, CoRR, abs/1711.08478 (2017).

106. ——, *Towards evaluating the robustness of neural networks*, in IEEE Symposium on Security and Privacy, IEEE Computer Society, 2017, pp. 39–57.

107. N. CESA-BIANCHI AND G. LUGOSI, *Prediction and Playing Games*, Cambridge University Press, 2006.

108. ——, *Prediction, Learning, and Games*, Cambridge University Press, USA, 2006.

109. G. CHALKIADAKIS, E. ELKIND, AND M. WOOLDRIDGE, *Computational aspects of cooperative game theory*, vol. 5, 10 2011.

110. ——, *Computational Aspects of Cooperative Game Theory (Synthesis Lectures on Artificial Inetlligence and Machine Learning)*, Morgan & Claypool Publishers, 1st ed., 2011.

111. B. L. F. Y. J. Y. M. L. CHAOWEI XIAO, DUIZHI DENG AND D. SONG, *Characterizing adversarial examples based on spatial consistency information for semantic segmentation*, in ECCV, 2018.

112. A. CHATTOPADHYAY, P. MANUPRIYA, A. SARKAR, AND V. N. BALASUBRAMANIAN, *Neural network attributions: A causal perspective*, in Proceedings of the 36th International Conference on Machine Learning, ICML 2019, 9-15 June 2019, Long Beach, California, USA, 2019, pp. 981–990.

113. J. CHEN AND M. I. JORDAN, *Boundary attack++: Query-efficient decision-based adversarial attack*, arXiv preprint arXiv:1904.02144, (2019).

114. J. CHEN, M. I. JORDAN, AND M. J. WAINWRIGHT, *Hopskipjumpattack: A query-efficient decision-based attack*, in 2020 IEEE Symposium on Security and Privacy (SP), 2020, pp. 1277–1294.

115. J. CHEN, D. WANG, AND H. CHEN, *Explore the transformation space for adversarial images*, in Proceedings of the Tenth ACM Conference on Data and Application Security and Privacy, 2020, pp. 109–120.

116. P.-Y. CHEN, H. ZHANG, Y. SHARMA, J. YI, AND C.-J. HSIEH, *Zoo: Zeroth order optimization based black-box attacks to deep neural networks without training substitute models*, in Proceedings of the 10th ACM Workshop on Artificial Intelligence and Security, AISec '17, New York, NY, USA, 2017, Association for Computing Machinery.

117. S. CHEN, M. XUE, L. FAN, S. HAO, L. XU, H. ZHU, AND B. LI, *Automated poisoning attacks and defenses in malware detection systems: An adversarial machine learning approach*, Computers and Security, 73 (2018), pp. 326–344.

118. T. CHEN, J. LIU, Y. XIANG, W. NIU, E. TONG, AND Z. HAN, *Adversarial attack and defense in reinforcement learning-from AI security view*, Cybersecur., 2 (2019), p. 11.

119. X. CHEN, Y. DUAN, R. HOUTHOOFT, J. SCHULMAN, I. SUTSKEVER, AND P. ABBEEL, *Infogan: Interpretable representation learning by information maximizing generative adversarial nets*, in Advances in Neural Information Processing Systems 29, D. D. Lee, M. Sugiyama, U. V. Luxburg, I. Guyon, and R. Garnett, eds., Curran Associates, Inc., 2016, pp. 2172–2180.

120. Z. CHEN, C. WANG, H. WU, K. SHANG, AND J. WANG, *Dmgan: Discriminative metric-based generative adversarial networks*, Knowl. Based Syst., 192 (2020), p. 105370.

121. M. CHENG, J. YI, H. ZHANG, P. CHEN, AND C. HSIEH, *Seq2sick: Evaluating the robustness of sequence-to-sequence models with adversarial examples*, CoRR, abs/1803.01128 (2018).

122. T. CHIN, C. ZHANG, AND D. MARCULESCU, *Improving the adversarial robustness of transfer learning via noisy feature distillation*, CoRR, abs/2002.02998 (2020).

123. A. CHIVUKULA AND W. LIU, *Adversarial deep learning models with multiple adversaries*, IEEE Transactions on Knowledge and Data Engineering, 31 (2019), pp. 1066–1079.

124. A. CHIVUKULA, X. YANG, W. LIU, T. ZHU, AND W. ZHOU, *Game theoretical adversarial deep learning with variational adversaries*, IEEE Transactions on Knowledge and Data Engineering, (2020), pp. 1–1.

125. A. S. CHIVUKULA AND W. LIU, *Adversarial deep learning models with multiple adversaries*, IEEE Transactions on Knowledge and Data Engineering, 31 (2019), pp. 1066–1079.

126. A. S. CHIVUKULA, X. YANG, W. LIU, T. ZHU, AND W. ZHOU, *Game theoretical adversarial deep learning with variational adversaries*, IEEE Transactions on Knowledge and Data Engineering, 33 (2021), pp. 3568–3581.

127. J.-H. CHO, P. M. HURLEY, AND S. XU, *Metrics and measurement of trustworthy systems*, in MILCOM 2016 - 2016 IEEE Military Communications Conference, 2016, pp. 1237–1242.

128. S. CHOPRA, R. HADSELL, AND Y. LECUN, *Learning a similarity metric discriminatively, with application to face verification*, in 2005 IEEE Computer Society Conference on Computer Vision and Pattern Recognition (CVPR'05), vol. 1, 2005, pp. 539–546 vol. 1.

129. M. CHORAS, M. PAWLICKI, D. PUCHALSKI, AND R. KOZIK, *Machine learning - the results are not the only thing that matters! what about security, explainability and fairness?*, in ICCS (4), vol. 12140 of Lecture Notes in Computer Science, Springer, 2020, pp. 615–628.

130. H. CHRISTOPHER FREY AND S. R. PATIL, *Identification and review of sensitivity analysis methods*, Risk Analysis, 22 (2002), pp. 553–578.

131. M. CISSE, P. BOJANOWSKI, E. GRAVE, Y. DAUPHIN, AND N. USUNIER, *Parseval networks: Improving robustness to adversarial examples*, in Proceedings of the 34th International Conference on Machine Learning, D. Precup and Y. W. Teh, eds., vol. 70 of Proceedings of Machine Learning Research, PMLR, 06–11 Aug 2017, pp. 854–863.

132. S. COHEN, G. DROR, AND E. RUPPIN, *Feature selection via coalitional game theory*, Neural Comput., 19 (2007), p. 1939–1961.

133. ——, *Feature selection via coalitional game theory*, Neural Comput., 19 (2007).

134. B. COLSON, P. MARCOTTE, AND G. SAVARD, *An overview of bilevel optimization*, 2007.

135. P. COMON, X. LUCIANI, AND A. L. F. DE ALMEIDA, *Tensor decompositions, alternating least squares and other tales*, Journal of Chemometrics, 23 (2009), pp. 393–405.

136. I. CORONA, G. GIACINTO, AND F. ROLI, *Adversarial attacks against intrusion detection systems: Taxonomy, solutions and open issues*, Inf. Sci., 239 (2013), pp. 201–225.

137. P. CORTEZ AND M. J. EMBRECHTS, *Using sensitivity analysis and visualization techniques to open black box data mining models*, Inf. Sci., 225 (2013), p. 1–17.

138. A. COTTER, H. JIANG, AND K. SRIDHARAN, *Two-player games for efficient non-convex constrained optimization*, in ALT, vol. 98 of Proceedings of Machine Learning Research, PMLR, 2019, pp. 300–332.

139. G. CYBENKO, S. JAJODIA, M. P. WELLMAN, AND P. LIU, *Adversarial and uncertain reasoning for adaptive cyber defense: Building the scientific foundation*, in ICISS, vol. 8880 of Lecture Notes in Computer Science, Springer, 2014, pp. 1–8.

140. G. DAI, J. XIE, AND Y. FANG, *Metric-based generative adversarial network*, in Proceedings of the 2017 ACM on Multimedia Conference, MM '17, New York, NY, USA, 2017, ACM, pp. 672–680.

141. H. DAI, H. LI, T. TIAN, X. HUANG, L. WANG, J. ZHU, AND L. SONG, *Adversarial attack on graph structured data*, in Proceedings of the 35th International Conference on Machine Learning, J. Dy and A. Krause, eds., vol. 80 of Proceedings of Machine Learning Research, PMLR, 10–15 Jul 2018, pp. 1115–1124.

142. N. DALVI, P. DOMINGOS, MAUSAM, S. SANGHAI, AND D. VERMA, *Adversarial classification*, in Proceedings of the Tenth ACM SIGKDD International Conference on Knowledge Discovery and Data Mining, KDD '04, New York, NY, USA, 2004, ACM, pp. 99–108.

143. P. DANIELE, *Dynamic networks and evolutionary variational inequalities / Patrizia Daniele.*, New dimensions in networks, Edward Elgar Pub., Cheltenham, UK ;, 2006.

144. A. DAS AND P. RAD, *Opportunities and challenges in explainable artificial intelligence (XAI): A survey*, CoRR, abs/2006.11371 (2020).

145. S. DAS AND P. N. SUGANTHAN, *Differential evolution: A survey of the state-of-the-art*, IEEE Transactions on Evolutionary Computation, 15 (2011), pp. 4–31.

146. P. DASGUPTA AND J. B. COLLINS, *A survey of game theoretic approaches for adversarial machine learning in cybersecurity tasks*, AI Mag., 40 (2019), pp. 31–43.

147. P. DASGUPTA, J. B. COLLINS, AND A. BUHMAN, *Gray-box techniques for adversarial text generation*, in Proceedings of the AAAI Symposium on Adversary-Aware Learning Techniques and Trends in Cybersecurity (ALEC 2018) co-located with the Association for the Advancement of Artificial Intelligence 2018 Fall Symposium Series (AAAI-FSS 2018), Arlington, Virginia, USA, October 18-20, 2018., 2018, pp. 17–23.

148. S. DE SILVA, J. KIM, AND R. RAICH, *Cost aware adversarial learning*, in ICASSP 2020 - 2020 IEEE International Conference on Acoustics, Speech and Signal Processing (ICASSP), 2020, pp. 3587–3591.

149. K. DEB, *Multi-Objective Optimization Using Evolutionary Algorithms*, John Wiley & Sons, Inc., USA, 2001.

150. K. DEB AND D. SAXENA, *On finding pareto-optimal solutions through dimensionality reduction for certain large-dimensional multi-objective optimization problems*, IEEE Congress on Evolutionary Computation, (2005).

151. O. DEKEL, O. SHAMIR, AND L. XIAO, *Learning to classify with missing and corrupted features*, Machine Learning Journal, (2009).

152. S. J. DELANY, P. CUNNINGHAM, A. TSYMBAL, AND L. COYLE, *A case-based technique for tracking concept drift in spam filtering*, Knowl.-Based Syst., 18 (2005), pp. 187–195.

153. L. DEMETRIO, B. BIGGIO, G. LAGORIO, F. ROLI, AND A. ARMANDO, *Explaining vulnerabilities of deep learning to adversarial malware binaries*, in Proceedings of the Third Italian Conference on Cyber Security, Pisa, Italy, February 13-15, 2019, 2019.

154. A. DEMONTIS, P. RUSSU, B. BIGGIO, G. FUMERA, AND F. ROLI, *On security and sparsity of linear classifiers for adversarial settings*, in Joint IAPR Int'l Workshop on Structural, Syntactic, and Statistical Pattern Recognition, vol. 10029 of LNCS, Merida, Mexico, 2016, Springer International Publishing, Springer International Publishing, pp. 322–332.

155. A. DEMONTIS, P. RUSSU, B. BIGGIO, G. FUMERA, AND F. ROLI, *On security and sparsity of linear classifiers for adversarial settings*, in Structural, Syntactic, and Statistical Pattern Recognition, A. Robles-Kelly, M. Loog, B. Biggio, F. Escolano, and R. Wilson, eds., Cham, 2016, Springer International Publishing, pp. 322–332.

156. L. DENG, *Three classes of deep learning architectures and their applications: A tutorial survey*, APSIPA Transactions on Signal and Information Processing, (2012).

157. J. DEVLIN, M.-W. CHANG, K. LEE, AND K. TOUTANOVA, *Bert: Pre-training of deep bidirectional transformers for language understanding*, arXiv preprint arXiv:1810.04805, (2018).

158. J. DIANETTI AND G. FERRARI, *Nonzero-sum submodular monotone-follower games: Existence and approximation of nash equilibria*, SIAM J. Control. Optim., 58 (2020), pp. 1257–1288.

159. S. DIRK, *Parallel evolutionary algorithms*, Springer Handbooks., (2015).

160. P. DOMINGOS, *A unified bias-variance decomposition and its applications*, in In Proc. 17th International Conf. on Machine Learning, Morgan Kaufmann, 2000, pp. 231–238.

161. Y. DONG, F. LIAO, T. PANG, H. SU, J. ZHU, X. HU, AND J. LI, *Boosting adversarial attacks with momentum*, in Proceedings of the IEEE conference on computer vision and pattern recognition, June 2018, pp. 9185–9193.

162. Z. DONG AND Q. DONG, *Hownet and the computation of meaning*, World Scientific, 2006.

163. R. D'ORAZIO, D. MORRILL, J. R. WRIGHT, AND M. BOWLING, *Alternative function approximation parameterizations for solving games: An analysis of undefined-regression counterfactual regret minimization*, in Proceedings of the 19th International Conference on Autonomous Agents and MultiAgent Systems, AAMAS '20, Richland, SC, 2020, International Foundation for Autonomous Agents and Multiagent Systems.

164. M. DOTTER, S. XIE, K. MANVILLE, J. HARGUESS, C. BUSHO, AND M. RODRIGUEZ, *Adversarial attack attribution: Discovering attributable signals in adversarial ML attacks*, CoRR, abs/2101.02899 (2021).

165. L. DRITSOULA, P. LOISEAU, AND J. MUSACCHIO, *A game-theoretical approach for finding optimal strategies in an intruder classification game*, in CDC, IEEE, 2012, pp. 7744–7751.

166. R. O. DUDA, P. E. HART, AND D. G. STORK, *Pattern Classification (2Nd Edition)*, Wiley-Interscience, 2000.

167. E. DUESTERWALD, A. MURTHI, G. VENKATARAMAN, M. SINN, AND D. VIJAYKEERTHY, *Exploring the hyperparameter landscape of adversarial robustness*, Safe Machine Learning workshop at ICLR, (2019).

168. J. EBRAHIMI, D. LOWD, AND D. DOU, *On adversarial examples for character-level neural machine translation*, in Proceedings of the 27th International Conference on Computational Linguistics, COLING 2018, Santa Fe, New Mexico, USA, August 20-26, 2018, 2018, pp. 653–663.

169. J. EBRAHIMI, A. RAO, D. LOWD, AND D. DOU, *Hotflip: White-box adversarial examples for text classification*, in Proceedings of the 56th Annual Meeting of the Association for Computational Linguistics, 2018, pp. 31–36.

170. S. EGER, G. G. ŞAHIN, A. RÜCKLÉ, J.-U. LEE, C. SCHULZ, M. MESGAR, K. SWARNKAR, E. SIMPSON, AND I. GUREVYCH, *Text processing like humans do: Visually attacking and shielding NLP systems*, in Proceedings of the 2019 Conference of the North American Chapter of the Association for Computational Linguistics: Human Language Technologies, Volume 1 (Long and Short Papers), Minneapolis, Minnesota, June 2019, Association for Computational Linguistics, pp. 1634–1647.

171. A. ELITZUR, R. PUZIS, AND P. ZILBERMAN, *Attack hypothesis generation*, in 2019 European Intelligence and Security Informatics Conference (EISIC), 2019, pp. 40–47.

172. G. ELSAYED, S. SHANKAR, B. CHEUNG, N. PAPERNOT, A. KURAKIN, I. GOODFELLOW, AND J. SOHL-DICKSTEIN, *Adversarial examples that fool both computer vision and time-limited humans*, in Advances in Neural Information Processing Systems, S. Bengio, H. Wallach, H. Larochelle, K. Grauman, N. Cesa-Bianchi, and R. Garnett, eds., vol. 31, Curran Associates, Inc., 2018.

173. A. ENGELBRECHT, *Sensitivity analysis for decision boundaries*, Neural Processing Letters, 10 (2004), pp. 253–266.

174. A. P. ENGELBRECHT, *Sensitivity analysis for decision boundaries*, Neural Process. Lett., 10 (1999), pp. 253–266.

175. L. ENGSTROM, B. TRAN, D. TSIPRAS, L. SCHMIDT, AND A. MADRY, *Exploring the landscape of spatial robustness*, in Proceedings of the 36th International Conference on Machine Learning, 2019, pp. 1802–1811.

176. EU, *The eu general data protection regulation*, 2019.

177. K. EYKHOLT, I. EVTIMOV, E. FERNANDES, B. LI, A. RAHMATI, C. XIAO, A. PRAKASH, T. KOHNO, AND D. SONG, *Robust physical-world attacks on deep learning visual classification*, in 2018 IEEE/CVF Conference on Computer Vision and Pattern Recognition, June 2018, pp. 1625–1634.

178. L. FAN, *Image pixelization with differential privacy*, in IFIP Annual Conference on Data and Applications Security and Privacy, Springer, 2018, pp. 148–162.

179. G. FARINA, C. KROER, AND T. SANDHOLM, *Regret minimization in behaviorally-constrained zero-sum games*, in Proceedings of the 34th International Conference on Machine Learning, D. Precup and Y. W. Teh, eds., vol. 70 of Proceedings of Machine Learning Research, PMLR, 06–11 Aug 2017, pp. 1107–1116.

180. T. FAWCETT, *Roc graphs: Notes and practical considerations for researchers*, (2007).

181. A. FAWZI, O. FAWZI, AND P. FROSSARD, *Analysis of classifiers' robustness to adversarial perturbations*, Mach. Learn., 107 (2018), pp. 481–508.

182. U. FAYYAD, G. PIATETSKY-SHAPIRO, AND P. SMYTH, *The kdd process for extracting useful knowledge from volumes of data*, Commun. ACM, 39 (1996), pp. 27–34.

183. ——, *Knowledge discovery and data mining: Towards a unifying framework*, in Proceedings of the Second International Conference on Knowledge Discovery and Data Mining, KDD'96, AAAI Press, 1996, p. 82–88.

184. W. FEDUS, M. ROSCA, B. LAKSHMINARAYANAN, A. M. DAI, S. MOHAMED, AND I. J. GOODFELLOW, *Many paths to equilibrium: Gans do not need to decrease a divergence at every step*, in 6th International Conference on Learning Representations, ICLR 2018, Vancouver, BC, Canada, April 30 - May 3, 2018, Conference Track Proceedings, OpenReview.net, 2018.

185. R. FEINMAN, R. R. CURTIN, S. SHINTRE, AND A. B. GARDNER, *Detecting adversarial samples from artifacts*, in International Conference on Machine Learning, 2017.

186. J. FENG, H. XU, S. MANNOR, AND S. YAN, *Robust logistic regression and classification*, in Proceedings of the 27th International Conference on Neural Information Processing Systems - Volume 1, NIPS'14, Cambridge, MA, USA, 2014, MIT Press, pp. 253–261.

187. ——, *Robust logistic regression and classification*, in Advances in Neural Information Processing Systems, Z. Ghahramani, M. Welling, C. Cortes, N. Lawrence, and K. Q. Weinberger, eds., vol. 27, Curran Associates, Inc., 2014.

188. K. FERGUSON-WALTER, S. FUGATE, J. MAUGER, AND M. MAJOR, *Game theory for adaptive defensive cyber deception*, in Proceedings of the 6th Annual Symposium on Hot Topics in the Science of Security, HotSoS '19, New York, NY, USA, 2019, Association for Computing Machinery.

189. F. FERRUCCI, P. SALZA, AND F. SARRO, *Using hadoop mapreduce for parallel genetic algorithms: A comparison of the global, grid and island models*, Evolutionary Computation, 26 (2018), pp. 535–567.

190. S. FICICI, O. MELNIK, AND J. POLLACK, *A game-theoretic and dynamical-systems analysis of selection methods in coevolution*, IEEE Transactions on Evolutionary Computation, 9 (2005), pp. 580–602.

191. S. G. FICICI, *A game-theoretic investigation of selection methods in two-population coevolution*, in Proceedings of the 8th Annual Conference on Genetic and Evolutionary Computation, GECCO '06, New York, NY, USA, 2006, Association for Computing Machinery.

192. S. G. FICICI AND J. B. POLLACK, *A game-theoretic approach to the simple coevolutionary algorithm*, in PPSN, vol. 1917 of Lecture Notes in Computer Science, Springer, 2000, pp. 467–476.

193. ——, *A game-theoretic memory mechanism for coevolution*, in Genetic and Evolutionary Computation - GECCO 2003, Genetic and Evolutionary Computation Conference, Chicago, IL, USA, July 12-16, 2003. Proceedings, Part I, E. Cantú-Paz, J. A. Foster, K. Deb, L. Davis,

R. Roy, U. O'Reilly, H. Beyer, R. K. Standish, G. Kendall, S. W. Wilson, M. Harman, J. Wegener, D. Dasgupta, M. A. Potter, A. C. Schultz, K. A. Dowsland, N. Jonoska, and J. F. Miller, eds., vol. 2723 of Lecture Notes in Computer Science, Springer, 2003, pp. 286–297.

194. G. FIDEL, R. BITTON, AND A. SHABTAI, *When explainability meets adversarial learning: Detecting adversarial examples using SHAP signatures*, CoRR, abs/1909.03418 (2019).

195. T. A. FILISBINO, G. A. GIRALDI, AND C. E. THOMAZ, *Ranking methods for tensor components analysis and their application to face images*, in 2013 XXVI Conference on Graphics, Patterns and Images, 2013, pp. 312–319.

196. C. FINN, P. F. CHRISTIANO, P. ABBEEL, AND S. LEVINE, *A connection between generative adversarial networks, inverse reinforcement learning, and energy-based models*, CoRR, abs/1611.03852 (2016).

197. P. A. FLACH, *The geometry of ROC space: Understanding machine learning metrics through ROC isometrics*, in Machine Learning, Proceedings of the Twentieth International Conference (ICML 2003), August 21-24, 2003, Washington, DC, USA, T. Fawcett and N. Mishra, eds., AAAI Press, 2003, pp. 194–201.

198. W. FLESHMAN, E. RAFF, R. ZAK, M. MCLEAN, AND C. NICHOLAS, *Static malware detection & subterfuge: Quantifying the robustness of machine learning and current antivirus*, in 13th International Conference on Malicious and Unwanted Software, MALWARE 2018, Nantucket, MA, USA, October 22-24, 2018, 2018, pp. 3–12.

199. D. FOGEL, *An introduction to simulated evolutionary optimization*, IEEE Transactions on Neural Networks, 5 (1994), pp. 3–14.

200. B. FRANCI AND S. GRAMMATICO, *A game-theoretic approach for generative adversarial networks*, in CDC, IEEE, 2020, pp. 1646–1651.

201. G. FREILING, G. JANK, AND S. R. LEE, *Existence and uniqueness of open-loop stackelberg equilibria in linear-quadratic differential games*, J. Optim. Theory Appl., 110 (2001), p. 515–544.

202. A. A. FREITAS, *A review of evolutionary algorithms for data mining*, in Data Mining and Knowledge Discovery Handbook, Springer, 2010, pp. 371–400.

203. Y. FREUND AND R. E. SCHAPIRE, *Game theory, on-line prediction and boosting*, in Proceedings of the Ninth Annual Conference on Computational Learning Theory, COLT '96, New York, NY, USA, 1996, Association for Computing Machinery, p. 325–332.

204. M. FRIEDRICH, A. KÖHN, G. WIEDEMANN, AND C. BIEMANN, *Adversarial learning of privacy-preserving text representations for de-identification of medical records*, in Proceedings of the 57th Annual Meeting of the Association for Computational Linguistics (ACL'20), 2020, pp. 5829–5839.

205. N. FROSST AND G. E. HINTON, *Distilling a neural network into a soft decision tree*, in Proceedings of the First International Workshop on Comprehensibility and Explanation in AI and ML 2017 co-located with 16th International Conference of the Italian Association for Artificial Intelligence (AI*IA 2017), Bari, Italy, November 16th and 17th, 2017, 2017.

206. S. R. L. G. FREILING, G. JANK, *Existence and uniqueness of open-loop stackelberg equilibria in linear-quadratic differential games*, Journal of Optimization Theory and Applications, 110 (2001), pp. 515–544.

207. W. C. GAN AND H. T. NG, *Improving the robustness of question answering systems to question paraphrasing*, in Proceedings of the 57th Annual Meeting of the Association for Computational Linguistics, 2019, pp. 6065–6075.

208. Z. GAN, L. CHEN, W. WANG, Y. PU, Y. ZHANG, H. LIU, C. LI, AND L. CARIN, *Triangle generative adversarial networks*, in NIPS, 2017, pp. 5253–5262.

209. J. GAO, J. LANCHANTIN, M. L. SOFFA, AND Y. QI, *Black-box generation of adversarial text sequences to evade deep learning classifiers*, in IEEE SPW, 2018, pp. 50–56.

210. D. GARG, S. SELLAMANICKAM, AND S. SHEVADE, *A game theoretic approach for feature clustering and its application to feature selection*, 05 2011, pp. 13–25.

211. D. GARG, S. SELLAMANICKAM, AND S. K. SHEVADE, *A game theoretic approach for feature clustering and its application to feature selection*, in Advances in Knowledge Discovery and Data Mining - 15th Pacific-Asia Conference, PAKDD 2011, Shenzhen, China, May 24-27,

2011, Proceedings, Part I, J. Z. HUANG, L. CAO, and J. SRIVASTAVA, eds., vol. 6634 of Lecture Notes in Computer Science, Springer, 2011, pp. 13–25.

212. S. GARG AND G. RAMAKRISHNAN, *Bae: Bert-based adversarial examples for text classification*, arXiv preprint arXiv:2004.01970, (2020).

213. X. GE, H. DING, H. RABITZ, AND R.-B. WU, *Robust quantum control in games: An adversarial learning approach*, Phys. Rev. A, 101 (2020), p. 052317.

214. R. GEMULLA, E. NIJKAMP, P. J. HAAS, AND Y. SISMANIS, *Large-scale matrix factorization with distributed stochastic gradient descent*, in Proceedings of the 17th ACM SIGKDD International Conference on Knowledge Discovery and Data Mining, KDD '11, New York, NY, USA, 2011, Association for Computing Machinery.

215. A. GHAFOURI, Y. VOROBEYCHIK, AND X. KOUTSOUKOS, *Adversarial regression for detecting attacks in cyber-physical systems*, in Proceedings of the 27th International Joint Conference on Artificial Intelligence, IJCAI'18, AAAI Press, 2018, p. 3769–3775.

216. ——, *Adversarial regression for detecting attacks in cyber-physical systems*, in Proceedings of the 27th International Joint Conference on Artificial Intelligence, IJCAI'18, AAAI Press, 2018.

217. G. GIDEL, H. BERARD, G. VIGNOUD, P. VINCENT, AND S. LACOSTE-JULIEN, *A variational inequality perspective on generative adversarial networks*, in 7th International Conference on Learning Representations, ICLR 2019, New Orleans, LA, USA, May 6-9, 2019, OpenReview.net, 2019.

218. Y. GIL, Y. CHAI, O. GORODISSKY, AND J. BERANT, *White-to-black: Efficient distillation of black-box adversarial attacks*, arXiv preprint arXiv:1904.02405, (2019).

219. J. GILMER, R. P. ADAMS, I. J. GOODFELLOW, D. ANDERSEN, AND G. E. DAHL, *Motivating the rules of the game for adversarial example research*, CoRR, abs/1807.06732 (2018).

220. A. GLOBERSON AND S. ROWEIS, *Nightmare at test time: Robust learning by feature deletion*, in Proceedings of the 23rd International Conference on Machine Learning, ICML '06, New York, NY, USA, 2006, ACM, pp. 353–360.

221. D. E. GOLDBERG, *Genetic Algorithms in Search, Optimization and Machine Learning*, Addison-Wesley Longman Publishing Co., Inc., Boston, MA, USA, 1st ed., 1989.

222. ——, *Genetic Algorithms in Search, Optimization and Machine Learning*, Addison-Wesley Longman Publishing Co., Inc., USA, 1st ed., 1989.

223. J. GOLDBERGER, S. ROWEIS, G. HINTON, AND R. SALAKHUTDINOV, *Neighbourhood components analysis*, in Proceedings of the 17th International Conference on Neural Information Processing Systems, NIPS'04, Cambridge, MA, USA, 2004, MIT Press.

224. A. GOLDSTEIN, A. KAPELNER, J. BLEICH, AND E. PITKIN, *Peeking inside the black box: Visualizing statistical learning with plots of individual conditional expectation*, Journal of Computational and Graphical Statistics, 24 (2013), pp. 44–65.

225. I. GOODFELLOW, Y. BENGIO, AND A. COURVILLE, *Deep Learning*, MIT Press, 2016. http://www.deeplearningbook.org.

226. I. GOODFELLOW, J. POUGET-ABADIE, M. MIRZA, B. XU, D. WARDE-FARLEY, S. OZAIR, A. COURVILLE, AND Y. BENGIO, *Generative adversarial nets*, in Advances in neural information processing systems (NIPS), 2014, pp. 2672–2680.

227. I. GOODFELLOW, J. SHLENS, AND C. SZEGEDY, *Explaining and harnessing adversarial examples*, in Proceedings of International Conference on Learning Representations, 2015.

228. I. J. GOODFELLOW, J. SHLENS, AND C. SZEGEDY, *Explaining and harnessing adversarial examples*, arXiv preprint arXiv:1412.6572, (2014).

229. S. GORE AND V. GOVINDARAJU, *Feature selection using cooperative game theory and relief algorithm*, in Knowledge, Information and Creativity Support Systems: Recent Trends, Advances and Solutions - Selected Papers from KICSS'2013 - 8th International Conference on Knowledge, Information, and Creativity Support Systems, November 7-9, 2013, Kraków, Poland, A. M. J. Skulimowski and J. Kacprzyk, eds., vol. 364 of Advances in Intelligent Systems and Computing, Springer, 2013, pp. 401–412.

230. A. GOYAL, N. R. KE, A. LAMB, R. D. HJELM, C. PAL, J. PINEAU, AND Y. BENGIO, *Actual: Actor-critic under adversarial learning*, CoRR, abs/1711.04755 (2017).

231. L. Grasedyck, D. Kressner, and C. Tobler, *A literature survey of low-rank tensor approximation techniques*, GAMM-Mitteilungen, (2013), pp. 53–78.

232. K. Gregor, I. Danihelka, A. Graves, D. Rezende, and D. Wierstra, *Draw: A recurrent neural network for image generation*, in Proceedings of the 32nd International Conference on Machine Learning, F. Bach and D. Blei, eds., vol. 37 of Proceedings of Machine Learning Research, Lille, France, 07–09 Jul 2015, PMLR, pp. 1462–1471.

233. K. Gregor, I. Danihelka, A. Graves, D. J. Rezende, and D. Wierstra, *DRAW: A recurrent neural network for image generation*, in Proceedings of the 32nd International Conference on Machine Learning, ICML 2015, Lille, France, 6-11 July 2015, 2015, pp. 1462–1471.

234. K. Gregor, I. Danihelka, A. Mnih, C. Blundell, and D. Wierstra, *Deep autoregressive networks*, in Proceedings of the 31st International Conference on Machine Learning, E. P. Xing and T. Jebara, eds., vol. 32 of Proceedings of Machine Learning Research, Bejing, China, 22–24 Jun 2014, PMLR, pp. 1242–1250.

235. K. Grosse, N. Papernot, P. Manoharan, M. Backes, and P. D. McDaniel, *Adversarial examples for malware detection*, in Computer Security - ESORICS 2017 - 22nd European Symposium on Research in Computer Security, Oslo, Norway, September 11-15, 2017, Proceedings, Part II, 2017, pp. 62–79.

236. P. D. Grunwald and A. P. Dawid, *Game theory, maximum entropy, minimum discrepancy and robust Bayesian decision theory*, The Annals of Statistics, 32 (2004), pp. 1367–1433.

237. ——, *Game theory, maximum entropy, minimum discrepancy and robust bayesian decision theory*, THE ANNALS OF STATISTICS, 32 (2004), p. 2004.

238. S. Gu and L. Rigazio, *Towards deep neural network architectures robust to adversarial examples*, (2015).

239. ——, *Towards deep neural network architectures robust to adversarial examples*, in ICLR (Workshop), 2015.

240. R. Guidotti, A. Monreale, S. Ruggieri, F. Turini, F. Giannotti, and D. Pedreschi, *A survey of methods for explaining black box models*, ACM Comput. Surv., 51 (2018).

241. I. Gulrajani, F. Ahmed, M. Arjovsky, V. Dumoulin, and A. C. Courville, *Improved training of wasserstein gans*, in Advances in Neural Information Processing Systems 30, I. Guyon, U. V. Luxburg, S. Bengio, H. Wallach, R. Fergus, S. Vishwanathan, and R. Garnett, eds., Curran Associates, Inc., 2017, pp. 5767–5777.

242. I. Gulrajani, K. Kumar, F. Ahmed, A. A. Taïga, F. Visin, D. Vázquez, and A. C. Courville, *Pixelvae: A latent variable model for natural images*, in 5th International Conference on Learning Representations, ICLR 2017, Toulon, France, April 24-26, 2017, Conference Track Proceedings, OpenReview.net, 2017.

243. Y. Guo, C. Zhang, C. Zhang, and Y. Chen, *Sparse dnns with improved adversarial robustness*, in Advances in Neural Information Processing Systems, S. Bengio, H. Wallach, H. Larochelle, K. Grauman, N. Cesa-Bianchi, and R. Garnett, eds., vol. 31, Curran Associates, Inc., 2018.

244. M. R. Gupta and Y. Chen, *Theory and use of the em algorithm*, Found. Trends Signal Process., 4 (2011), pp. 223–296.

245. S. Gurumurthy, R. K. Sarvadevabhatla, and R. V. Babu, *Deligan: Generative adversarial networks for diverse and limited data*, in CVPR, IEEE Computer Society, 2017, pp. 4941–4949.

246. D. Ha and D. Eck, *A neural representation of sketch drawings*, in ICLR 2018.

247. P. Haller and H. Miller, *Parallelizing machine learning- functionally: A framework and abstractions for parallel graph processing*, CA, USA, 2011, Stanford.

248. J. Halpern, *Computer science and game theory: A brief survey*, Palgrave Dictionary of Economics, (2007).

249. S. N. Hamilton and W. L. Miller, *The role of game theory in information warfare*, 2002.

250. W. Han, L. Zhang, Y. Jiang, and K. Tu, *Adversarial attack and defense of structured prediction models*, arXiv preprint arXiv:2010.01610, (2020).

251. T. HARADA AND E. ALBA, *Parallel genetic algorithms: A useful survey*, ACM Comput. Surv., 53 (2020).

252. P. T. HARKER AND J.-S. PANG, *Finite-dimensional variational inequality and nonlinear complementarity problems: A survey of theory, algorithms and applications*, Math. Program., 48 (1990).

253. S. HART AND A. MAS-COLELL, *A general class of adaptive strategies.*, J. Econ. Theory, 98 (2001), pp. 26–54.

254. A. HARTL, M. BACHL, J. FABINI, AND T. ZSEBY, *Explainability and adversarial robustness for rnns*, in BigDataService, IEEE, 2020, pp. 148–156.

255. T. B. HASHIMOTO, M. SRIVASTAVA, H. NAMKOONG, AND P. LIANG, *Fairness without demographics in repeated loss minimization*, in Proceedings of the 35th International Conference on Machine Learning, ICML 2018, Stockholmsmässan, Stockholm, Sweden, July 10-15, 2018, J. G. Dy and A. Krause, eds., vol. 80 of Proceedings of Machine Learning Research, PMLR, 2018, pp. 1934–1943.

256. M. M. HASSAN, M. R. HASSAN, S. HUDA, AND V. H. C. DE ALBUQUERQUE, *A robust deep-learning-enabled trust-boundary protection for adversarial industrial iot environment*, IEEE Internet of Things Journal, 8 (2021), pp. 9611–9621.

257. T. HASTIE, R. TIBSHIRANI, AND J. FRIEDMAN, *The elements of statistical learning – data mining, inference, and prediction*.

258. M. HAUSCHILD AND M. PELIKAN, *An introduction and survey of estimation of distribution algorithms*, Swarm and Evolutionary Computation, 1 (2011), pp. 111–128.

259. J. HAYES AND G. DANEZIS, *Generating steganographic images via adversarial training*, in NIPS, 2017, pp. 1954–1963.

260. J. HAYES AND G. DANEZIS, *Machine learning as an adversarial service: Learning black-box adversarial examples*, arXiv preprint arXiv:1708.05207, 2 (2017).

261. E. HAZAN, K. SINGH, AND C. ZHANG, *Efficient regret minimization in non-convex games*, in Proceedings of the 34th International Conference on Machine Learning - Volume 70, ICML'17, JMLR.org, 2017.

262. D. HE, W. CHEN, L. WANG, AND T.-Y. LIU, *A game- heoretic machine learning approach for revenue maximization in sponsored search*, in Proceedings of the Twenty-Third International Joint Conference on Artificial Intelligence, IJCAI '13, AAAI Press, 2013.

263. K. HE, X. ZHANG, S. REN, AND J. SUN, *Deep residual learning for image recognition*, in Proceedings of the IEEE conference on computer vision and pattern recognition, 2016, pp. 770–778.

264. W. HE, J. WEI, X. CHEN, N. CARLINI, AND D. SONG, *Adversarial example defenses: Ensembles of weak defenses are not strong*, in Proceedings of the 11th USENIX Conference on Offensive Technologies, WOOT'17, USA, 2017, USENIX Association, p. 15.

265. X. HE AND T.-S. CHUA, *Neural factorization machines for sparse predictive analytics*, Proceedings of the 40th International ACM SIGIR Conference on Research and Development in Information Retrieval, (2017).

266. X. HE, Z. HE, X. DU, AND T.-S. CHUA, *Adversarial personalized ranking for recommendation*, in The 41st International ACM SIGIR Conference on Research & Development in Information Retrieval, SIGIR '18, New York, NY, USA, 2018, Association for Computing Machinery, p. 355–364.

267. J. HEINRICH, M. LANCTOT, AND D. SILVER, *Fictitious self-play in extensive-form games*, in Proceedings of the 32nd International Conference on Machine Learning, F. Bach and D. Blei, eds., vol. 37 of Proceedings of Machine Learning Research, Lille, France, 07–09 Jul 2015, PMLR, pp. 805–813.

268. J. HEINRICH AND D. SILVER, *Deep reinforcement learning from self-play in imperfect-information games*, ArXiv, abs/1603.01121 (2016).

269. J. C. HELTON AND F. J. DAVIS, *Sampling-based methods for uncertainty and sensitivity analysis.*, 2000.

270. D. HENDERSON, S. JACOBSON, AND A. JOHNSON, *The Theory and Practice of Simulated Annealing*, 04 2006, pp. 287–319.

271. J. HERBERT AND J. YAO, *A game-theoretic approach to competitive learning in self-organizing maps*, vol. 3610, 08 2005, pp. 129–138.
272. J. HERBERT AND J. YAO, *A game-theoretic approach to competitive learning in self-organizing maps*, in Advances in Natural Computation, L. Wang, K. Chen, and Y. S. Ong, eds., Berlin, Heidelberg, 2005, Springer Berlin Heidelberg, pp. 129–138.
273. T. HINRICHS AND K. D. FORBUS, *Transfer learning through analogy in games*, AI Magazine, 32 (2011), p. 70.
274. D. R. HJELM, A. P. JACOB, T. CHE, K. CHO, AND Y. BENGIO, *Boundary-seeking generative adversarial networks*.
275. J. HO AND S. ERMON, *Generative adversarial imitation learning*, in Advances in Neural Information Processing Systems 29: Annual Conference on Neural Information Processing Systems 2016, December 5-10, 2016, Barcelona, Spain, 2016, pp. 4565–4573.
276. S. HOCHREITER AND J. SCHMIDHUBER, *Long short-term memory*, Neural computation, 9 (1997), pp. 1735–1780.
277. E. HOFFER AND N. AILON, *Deep metric learning using triplet network*, in Similarity-Based Pattern Recognition, A. Feragen, M. Pelillo, and M. Loog, eds., Cham, 2015, Springer International Publishing, pp. 84–92.
278. X. HOU, L. SHEN, K. SUN, AND G. QIU, *Deep feature consistent variational autoencoder*, in 2017 IEEE Winter Conference on Applications of Computer Vision, WACV 2017, Santa Rosa, CA, USA, March 24-31, 2017, IEEE Computer Society, 2017, pp. 1133–1141.
279. X. HOU, K. SUN, L. SHEN, AND G. QIU, *Improving variational autoencoder with deep feature consistent and generative adversarial training*, Neurocomputing, 341 (2019), pp. 183–194.
280. J. T. HOUSE, *Game-theoretic approaches for adversarial multi-armed bandit scenarios*, ProQuest Dissertations Publishing, (2012).
281. Y.-P. HSIEH, C. LIU, AND V. CEVHER, *Finding mixed Nash equilibria of generative adversarial networks*, in Proceedings of the 36th International Conference on Machine Learning, K. Chaudhuri and R. Salakhutdinov, eds., vol. 97 of Proceedings of Machine Learning Research, PMLR, 09–15 Jun 2019, pp. 2810–2819.
282. J. HU, L. SHEN, AND G. SUN, *Squeeze-and-excitation networks*, in Proceedings of the IEEE conference on computer vision and pattern recognition, 2018, pp. 7132–7141.
283. J. HU AND M. P. WELLMAN, *Nash q-learning for general-sum stochastic games*, J. Mach. Learn. Res., 4 (2003), pp. 1039–1069.
284. Y. HUA, M. NIKPOUR, AND P. STOICA, *Optimal reduced-rank estimation and filtering*, IEEE Transactions on Signal Processing, 49 (2001), pp. 457–469.
285. L. HUANG, A. D. JOSEPH, B. NELSON, B. I. RUBINSTEIN, AND J. TYGAR, *Adversarial machine learning*, in Proceedings of the 4th ACM workshop on Security and artificial intelligence, ACM, 2011, pp. 43–58.
286. L. HUANG AND Q. ZHU, *A dynamic games approach to proactive defense strategies against advanced persistent threats in cyber-physical systems*, Computers & Security, 89 (2019), p. 101660.
287. Q. HUANG, I. KATSMAN, H. HE, Z. GU, S. BELONGIE, AND S.-N. LIM, *Enhancing adversarial example transferability with an intermediate level attack*, in Proceedings of the IEEE International Conference on Computer Vision, 2019, pp. 4733–4742.
288. Y. HUANG, J. CHEN, L. HUANG, AND Q. ZHU, *Dynamic games for secure and resilient control system design*, National Science Review, 7 (2020), pp. 1125–1141.
289. C. L. L. J. H. G. HUANG CH., LEE TH., *Adversarial attacks on sdn-based deep learning ids system*, in In: Kim K., Kim H. (eds) Mobile and Wireless Technology 2018. ICMWT 2018. Lecture Notes in Electrical Engineering, vol. 513, Springer, Singapore.
290. A. IGNATIEV, N. NARODYTSKA, AND J. MARQUES-SILVA, *Abduction-based explanations for machine learning models*, in The Thirty-Third AAAI Conference on Artificial Intelligence, AAAI 2019, The Thirty-First Innovative Applications of Artificial Intelligence Conference, IAAI 2019, The Ninth AAAI Symposium on Educational Advances in Artificial Intelligence, EAAI 2019, Honolulu, Hawaii, USA, January 27 - February 1, 2019, 2019, pp. 1511–1519.

291. A. IGNATIEV, N. NARODYTSKA, AND J. MARQUES-SILVA, *On relating explanations and adversarial examples*, in Advances in Neural Information Processing Systems 32, H. Wallach, H. Larochelle, A. Beygelzimer, F. d'Alché-Buc, E. Fox, and R. Garnett, eds., Curran Associates, Inc., 2019, pp. 15857–15867.

292. A. ILYAS, L. ENGSTROM, A. ATHALYE, J. LIN, A. ATHALYE, L. ENGSTROM, A. ILYAS, AND K. KWOK, *Black-box adversarial attacks with limited queries and information*, in Proceedings of the 35th International Conference on Machine Learning,{ICML} 2018, 2018.

293. A. ILYAS, L. ENGSTROM, AND A. MADRY, *Prior convictions: Black-box adversarial attacks with bandits and priors*, in 7th International Conference on Learning Representations, ICLR 2019, New Orleans, LA, USA, May 6-9, 2019, 2019.

294. A. ILYAS, S. SANTURKAR, D. TSIPRAS, L. ENGSTROM, B. TRAN, AND A. MADRY, *Adversarial examples are not bugs, they are features*, in Advances in Neural Information Processing Systems 32, H. Wallach, H. Larochelle, A. Beygelzimer, F. d'Alché-Buc, E. Fox, and R. Garnett, eds., Curran Associates, Inc., 2019, pp. 125–136.

295. N. INKAWHICH, W. WEN, H. H. LI, AND Y. CHEN, *Feature space perturbations yield more transferable adversarial examples*, in Proceedings of the IEEE Conference on Computer Vision and Pattern Recognition, 2019, pp. 7066–7074.

296. M. IYYER, J. WIETING, K. GIMPEL, AND L. ZETTLEMOYER, *Adversarial example generation with syntactically controlled paraphrase networks*, CoRR, abs/1804.06059 (2018).

297. S. JHA, S. GULWANI, S. A. SESHIA, AND A. TIWARI, *Oracle-guided component-based program synthesis*, ICSE '10, New York, NY, USA, 2010, Association for Computing Machinery.

298. J. JIA AND N. Z. GONG, *AttriGuard: A practical defense against attribute inference attacks via adversarial machine learning*, in Proceedings of the 27th USENIX Security Symposium (USENIX'18), 2018, pp. 513–529.

299. R. JIA, I. C. KONSTANTAKOPOULOS, B. LI, AND C. SPANOS, *Poisoning attacks on data-driven utility learning in games*, in 2018 Annual American Control Conference (ACC), 2018, pp. 5774–5780.

300. R. JIA AND P. LIANG, *Adversarial examples for evaluating reading comprehension systems*, in Proceedings of the 2017 Conference on Empirical Methods in Natural Language Processing, 2017, pp. 2021–2031.

301. R. JIA AND P. LIANG, *Adversarial examples for evaluating reading comprehension systems*, in Proceedings of the 2017 Conference on Empirical Methods in Natural Language Processing, EMNLP 2017, Copenhagen, Denmark, September 9-11, 2017, 2017, pp. 2021–2031.

302. D. JIN, Z. JIN, J. TIANYI ZHOU, AND P. SZOLOVITS, *Is bert really robust? a strong baseline for natural language attack on text classification and entailment*, in The Thirty-Fourth AAAI Conference on Artificial Intelligence, 2020.

303. G. JIN, S. SHEN, D. ZHANG, F. DAI, AND Y. ZHANG, *Ape-gan: Adversarial perturbation elimination with gan*, in ICASSP 2019 - 2019 IEEE International Conference on Acoustics, Speech and Signal Processing (ICASSP), 2019, pp. 3842–3846.

304. N. D. JOHNSON AND A. A. MISLIN, *Trust games: A meta-analysis*, Journal of Economic Psychology, 32 (2011), pp. 865–889.

305. P. R. JORDAN, L. J. SCHVARTZMAN, AND M. P. WELLMAN, *Strategy exploration in empirical games*, in AAMAS, IFAAMAS, 2010, pp. 1131–1138.

306. K. JUN, L. LI, Y. MA, AND X. J. ZHU, *Adversarial attacks on stochastic bandits*, in Advances in Neural Information Processing Systems 31: Annual Conference on Neural Information Processing Systems 2018, NeurIPS 2018, 3-8 December 2018, Montréal, Canada., 2018, pp. 3644–3653.

307. S. KAMATH, A. ORLITSKY, D. PICHAPATI, AND A. T. SURESH, *On learning distributions from their samples*, in Proceedings of The 28th Conference on Learning Theory, P. Grunwald, E. Hazan, and S. Kale, eds., vol. 40 of Proceedings of Machine Learning Research, Paris, France, 03–06 Jul 2015, PMLR, pp. 1066–1100.

308. M. KANTARCIOGLU, B. XI, AND C. CLIFTON, *A game theoretic framework for adversarial learning*, in Proceedings of the 9th Annual Information Security Symposium, CERIAS '08, West Lafayette, IN, 2008, CERIAS - Purdue University.

309. M. KANTARCIOĞLU, B. XI, AND C. CLIFTON, *Classifier evaluation and attribute selection against active adversaries*, Data Mining and Knowledge Discovery, 22 (2011), pp. 291–335.

310. M. KANTARCIOGLU, B. XI, AND C. CLIFTON, *Classifier evaluation and attribute selection against active adversaries*, Data Min. Knowl. Discov., 22 (2011), pp. 291–335.

311. Z. KATZIR AND Y. ELOVICI, *Quantifying the resilience of machine learning classifiers used for cyber security*, Expert Systems with Applications, 92 (2018), pp. 419–429.

312. H. KAZEMIAN AND S. AHMED, *Comparisons of machine learning techniques for detecting malicious webpages*, Expert Syst. Appl., 42 (2015), pp. 1166–1177.

313. C. T. KELLEY, *Iterative methods for optimization*, Frontiers in applied mathematics, SIAM, 1999.

314. R. O. KEOHANE, *Counterfactuals and Causal Inference: Methods and Principles for Social Research By Stephen E. Morgan and Christopher Winship Cambridge University Press. 2007. 319 pages. 83.99 cloth, 28.99 paper*, Social Forces, 88 (2009), pp. 466–467.

315. T. KIM, M. CHA, H. KIM, J. K. LEE, AND J. KIM, *Learning to discover cross-domain relations with generative adversarial networks*, in Proceedings of the 34th International Conference on Machine Learning - Volume 70, ICML'17, JMLR.org, 2017.

316. D. P. KINGMA AND M. WELLING, *Auto-encoding variational bayes*, in 2nd International Conference on Learning Representations, ICLR 2014, Banff, AB, Canada, April 14-16, 2014, Conference Track Proceedings, Y. Bengio and Y. LeCun, eds., 2014.

317. J. KLEINBERG, C. PAPADIMITRIOU, AND P. RAGHAVAN, *A microeconomic view of data mining*, 1998.

318. M. KLOFT AND P. LASKOV, *Online anomaly detection under adversarial impact*, in Proceedings of the Thirteenth International Conference on Artificial Intelligence and Statistics, Y. W. Teh and M. Titterington, eds., vol. 9 of Proceedings of Machine Learning Research, Chia Laguna Resort, Sardinia, Italy, 13–15 May 2010, PMLR, pp. 405–412.

319. M. KOCAOGLU, C. SNYDER, A. G. DIMAKIS, AND S. VISHWANATH, *CausalGAN: Learning causal implicit generative models with adversarial training*, in International Conference on Learning Representations, 2018.

320. P. W. KOH AND P. LIANG, *Understanding black-box predictions via influence functions*, in Proceedings of the 34th International Conference on Machine Learning - Volume 70, ICML'17, JMLR.org, 2017.

321. A. KOŁCZ AND C. H. TEO, *Feature Weighting for Improved Classifier Robustness*, in Proc. 6th Conf. on Email and Anti-Spam, July 2009.

322. S. KOMKOV AND A. PETIUSHKO, *Advhat: Real-world adversarial attack on arcface face id system*, arXiv preprint arXiv:1908.08705, (2019).

323. V. KONDA AND J. TSITSIKLIS, *Actor-critic algorithms*, in Advances in Neural Information Processing Systems, S. Solla, T. Leen, and K. Müller, eds., vol. 12, MIT Press, 2000.

324. V. KÖNÖNEN, *Asymmetric multiagent reinforcement learning*, in 2003 IEEE/WIC International Conference on Intelligent Agent Technology (IAT 2003), 13-17 October 2003, Halifax, Canada, IEEE Computer Society, 2003, pp. 336–342.

325. J. KOS, I. FISCHER, AND D. SONG, *Adversarial examples for generative models*, in Proceedings of 2018 IEEE Security and Privacy Workshops (SPW), 2018.

326. J. KOS, I. FISCHER, AND D. SONG, *Adversarial examples for generative models*, 2018 IEEE Security and Privacy Workshops (SPW), (2018), pp. 36–42.

327. J. KOS AND D. SONG, *Delving into adversarial attacks on deep policies*, in 5th International Conference on Learning Representations, ICLR 2017, Toulon, France, April 24-26, 2017, Workshop Track Proceedings, 2017.

328. S. KOZIEL, *Computational Optimization, Methods and Algorithms*, Springer Publishing Company, Incorporated, 2016.

329. A. KRAUSE, P. PERONA, AND R. GOMES, *Discriminative clustering by regularized information maximization*, in Advances in Neural Information Processing Systems, J. Lafferty, C. Williams, J. Shawe-Taylor, R. Zemel, and A. Culotta, eds., vol. 23, Curran Associates, Inc., 2010.

330. K. Kreutz-Delgado, J. F. Murray, B. D. Rao, K. Engan, T.-W. Lee, and T. J. Sejnowski, *Dictionary learning algorithms for sparse representation*, Neural Computation, 15 (2003), pp. 349–396.

331. ——, *Dictionary learning algorithms for sparse representation*, Neural Comput., 15 (2003).

332. A. Krizhevsky, I. Sutskever, and G. E. Hinton, *Imagenet classification with deep convolutional neural networks*, Advances in neural information processing systems, 25 (2012), pp. 1097–1105.

333. V. Kuleshov, S. Thakoor, T. Lau, and S. Ermon, *Adversarial examples for natural language classification problems*, (2018).

334. B. Kulis, *Metric learning: A survey*, Foundations and Trends in Machine Learning, 5 (2013), pp. 287–364.

335. A. Kulkarni, S. Srivastava, and S. Kambhampati, *A unified framework for planning in adversarial and cooperative environments*, in AAAI, AAAI Press, 2019, pp. 2479–2487.

336. N. Kumari, M. Singh, A. Sinha, H. Machiraju, B. Krishnamurthy, and V. N. Balasubramanian, *Harnessing the vulnerability of latent layers in adversarially trained models*, in Proceedings of the Twenty-Eighth International Joint Conference on Artificial Intelligence, IJCAI 2019, Macao, China, August 10-16, 2019, 2019, pp. 2779–2785.

337. D. Kunin, J. Bloom, A. Goeva, and C. Seed, *Loss landscapes of regularized linear autoencoders*, in Proceedings of the 36th International Conference on Machine Learning, K. Chaudhuri and R. Salakhutdinov, eds., vol. 97 of Proceedings of Machine Learning Research, PMLR, 09–15 Jun 2019, pp. 3560–3569.

338. A. Kurakin, I. Goodfellow, and S. Bengio, *Adversarial examples in the physical world*, arXiv preprint arXiv:1607.02533, (2016).

339. A. Kurakin, I. J. Goodfellow, and S. Bengio, *Adversarial examples in the physical world*, in 5th International Conference on Learning Representations, ICLR 2017, Toulon, France, April 24-26, 2017, Workshop Track Proceedings, 2017.

340. ——, *Adversarial machine learning at scale*, in 5th International Conference on Learning Representations, ICLR 2017, Toulon, France, April 24-26, 2017, Conference Track Proceedings, 2017.

341. V. Kyatham, D. Mishra, and P. AP, *Variational inference with latent space quantization for adversarial resilience*, in 25th International Conference on Pattern Recognition, ICPR 2020, Virtual Event / Milan, Italy, January 10-15, 2021, IEEE, 2020, pp. 9593–9600.

342. A. Kyrola, D. Bickson, C. Guestrin, and J. K. Bradley, *Parallel coordinate descent for l1-regularized loss minimization*, in Proceedings of the 28th International Conference on Machine Learning (ICML-11), 2011, pp. 321–328.

343. H. Lakkaraju, S. H. Bach, and J. Leskovec, *Interpretable decision sets: A joint framework for description and prediction*, in Proceedings of the 22nd ACM SIGKDD International Conference on Knowledge Discovery and Data Mining, KDD '16, New York, NY, USA, 2016, Association for Computing Machinery.

344. G. R. Lanckriet, L. E. Ghaoui, C. Bhattacharyya, and M. I. Jordan, *A robust minimax approach to classification*, J. Mach. Learn. Res., 3 (2003).

345. M. Lanctot, V. Zambaldi, A. Gruslys, A. Lazaridou, K. Tuyls, J. Perolat, D. Silver, and T. Graepel, *A unified game-theoretic approach to multiagent reinforcement learning*, in Advances in Neural Information Processing Systems, I. Guyon, U. V. Luxburg, S. Bengio, H. Wallach, R. Fergus, S. Vishwanathan, and R. Garnett, eds., vol. 30, Curran Associates, Inc., 2017.

346. A. B. L. Larsen, S. K. Sønderby, H. Larochelle, and O. Winther, *Autoencoding beyond pixels using a learned similarity metric*, in Proceedings of the 33rd International Conference on International Conference on Machine Learning - Volume 48, ICML'16, JMLR.org, 2016, pp. 1558–1566.

347. A. B. L. Larsen, S. K. Sønderby, H. Larochelle, and O. Winther, *Autoencoding beyond pixels using a learned similarity metric*, in Proceedings of The 33rd International Conference on Machine Learning, M. F. Balcan and K. Q. Weinberger, eds., vol. 48 of Proceedings of Machine Learning Research, New York, New York, USA, 20–22 Jun 2016, PMLR, pp. 1558–1566.

348. T. LE, S. WANG, AND D. LEE, *MALCOM: generating malicious comments to attack neural fake news detection models*, CoRR, abs/2009.01048 (2020).

349. Y. LECUN, S. CHOPRA, R. HADSELL, F. J. HUANG, AND ET AL., *A tutorial on energy-based learning*, in PREDICTING STRUCTURED DATA, MIT Press, 2006.

350. Y. LECUN AND F. HUANG, *Loss functions for discriminative training of energy-based models*, in AISTATS 2005 - Proceedings of the 10th International Workshop on Artificial Intelligence and Statistics, 2005, pp. 206–213.

351. S. LEDESMA, G. AVINA, AND R. SANCHEZ, *Practical considerations for simulated annealing implementation*, in Simulated Annealing, C. M. Tan, ed., IntechOpen, Rijeka, 2008, ch. 20.

352. K. LEYTON-BROWN AND Y. SHOHAM, vol. 2, 2008.

353. G. L'HUILLIER, R. WEBER, AND N. FIGUEROA, *Online phishing classification using adversarial data mining and signaling games*, in Proceedings of the ACM SIGKDD Workshop on CyberSecurity and Intelligence Informatics, CSI-KDD '09, New York, NY, USA, 2009, Association for Computing Machinery.

354. B. LI AND Y. VOROBEYCHIK, *Feature cross-substitution in adversarial classification*, in Advances in Neural Information Processing Systems 27, Z. Ghahramani, M. Welling, C. Cortes, N. D. Lawrence, and K. Q. Weinberger, eds., Curran Associates, Inc., 2014, pp. 2087–2095.

355. ———, *Scalable Optimization of Randomized Operational Decisions in Adversarial Classification Settings*, in Proceedings of the Eighteenth International Conference on Artificial Intelligence and Statistics, G. Lebanon and S. V. N. Vishwanathan, eds., vol. 38 of Proceedings of Machine Learning Research, San Diego, California, USA, 09–12 May 2015, PMLR, pp. 599–607.

356. B. LI AND Y. VOROBEYCHIK, *Scalable Optimization of Randomized Operational Decisions in Adversarial Classification Settings*, in Proceedings of the Eighteenth International Conference on Artificial Intelligence and Statistics, G. Lebanon and S. V. N. Vishwanathan, eds., vol. 38 of Proceedings of Machine Learning Research, San Diego, California, USA, 09–12 May 2015, PMLR, pp. 599–607.

357. B. LI AND Y. VOROBEYCHIK, *Evasion-robust classification on binary domains*, 12 (2018).

358. C. LI, H. FARKHOOR, R. LIU, AND J. YOSINSKI, *Measuring the intrinsic dimension of objective landscapes*, in International Conference on Learning Representations, 2018.

359. D. LI, Y. ZHANG, H. PENG, L. CHEN, C. BROCKETT, M.-T. SUN, AND B. DOLAN, *Contextualized perturbation for textual adversarial attack*, arXiv preprint arXiv:2009.07502, (2020).

360. H. LI, X. XU, X. ZHANG, S. YANG, AND B. LI, *Qeba: Query-efficient boundary-based blackbox attack*, in Proceedings of the IEEE/CVF Conference on Computer Vision and Pattern Recognition (CVPR), June 2020.

361. H. LI, S. ZHOU, W. YUAN, X. LUO, C. GAO, AND S. CHEN, *Robust android malware detection against adversarial example attacks*, in Proceedings of the Web Conference 2021, WWW '21, New York, NY, USA, 2021, Association for Computing Machinery, p. 3603–3612.

362. J. LI, T. CAI, K. DENG, X. WANG, T. SELLIS, AND F. XIA, *Community-diversified influence maximization in social networks*, Information Systems, 92 (2020), p. 101522.

363. J. LI, S. JI, T. DU, B. LI, AND T. WANG, *Textbugger: Generating adversarial text against real-world applications*, arXiv preprint arXiv:1812.05271, (2018).

364. L. LI, W. CHU, J. LANGFORD, AND R. E. SCHAPIRE, *A contextual-bandit approach to personalized news article recommendation*, in Proceedings of the 19th International Conference on World Wide Web, WWW '10, New York, NY, USA, 2010, Association for Computing Machinery.

365. L. LI, R. MA, Q. GUO, X. XUE, AND X. QIU, *BERT-ATTACK: Adversarial attack against BERT using BERT*, in Proceedings of the 2020 Conference on Empirical Methods in Natural Language Processing (EMNLP), 2020, pp. 6193–6202.

366. T. LI AND L. LIN, *Anonymousnet: Natural face de-identification with measurable privacy*, in Proceedings of the IEEE Conference on Computer Vision and Pattern Recognition Workshops, 2019, pp. 0–0.

367. H. LIAGHATI, T. MAZZUCHI, AND S. SARKANI, *Utilizing a maximin optimization approach to maximize system resiliency*, Systems Engineering, 24 (2021).

368. B. LIANG, H. LI, M. SU, P. BIAN, X. LI, AND W. SHI, *Deep text classification can be fooled*, IJCAI, (2018).

369. X. LIANG AND Y. XIAO, *Game theory for network security*, IEEE Communications Surveys Tutorials, 15 (2013), pp. 472–486.

370. K. LIN, D. LI, X. HE, M. SUN, AND Z. ZHANG, *Adversarial ranking for language generation*, in NIPS, 2017, pp. 3155–3165.

371. S. LIN, *Rank aggregation methods*, WIREs Computational Statistics, 2 (2010), pp. 555–570.

372. Y.-C. LIN, Z.-W. HONG, Y.-H. LIAO, M.-L. SHIH, M.-Y. LIU, AND M. SUN, *Tactics of adversarial attack on deep reinforcement learning agents*, in Proceedings of the 26th International Joint Conference on Artificial Intelligence, IJCAI'17, AAAI Press, 2017, pp. 3756–3762.

373. M. LIPPI, *Statistical relational learning for game theory*, IEEE Transactions on Computational Intelligence and AI in Games, 8 (2015), pp. 1–1.

374. M. L. LITTMAN, *Markov games as a framework for multi-agent reinforcement learning*, in In Proceedings of the Eleventh International Conference on Machine Learning, Morgan Kaufmann, 1994, pp. 157–163.

375. B. LIU, M. DING, S. SHAHAM, W. RAHAYU, F. FAROKHI, AND Z. LIN, *When machine learning meets privacy*, ACM Computing Surveys, 54 (2021), pp. 1–36.

376. B. LIU, M. DING, T. ZHU, Y. XIANG, AND W. ZHOU, *Adversaries or allies? privacy and deep learning in big data era*, Concurrency and Computation: Practice and Experience, p. e5102.

377. B. LIU, J. XIONG, Y. WU, M. DING, AND C. M. WU, *Protecting multimedia privacy from both humansand ai*, in in Proc. IEEE International Symposium on Broadband Multimedia Systems and Broadcasting, 2019.

378. C. LIU, B. LI, Y. VOROBEYCHIK, AND A. OPREA, *Robust linear regression against training data poisoning*, in Proceedings of the 10th ACM Workshop on Artificial Intelligence and Security, AISec '17, New York, NY, USA, 2017, ACM, pp. 91–102.

379. D. C. LIU AND J. NOCEDAL, *On the limited memory bfgs method for large scale optimization*, Mathematical programming, 45 (1989), pp. 503–528.

380. L. LIU, Y. LUO, H. HU, Y. WEN, D. TAO, AND X. YAO, *xtml: A unified heterogeneous transfer metric learning framework for multimedia applications [application notes]*, IEEE Comput. Intell. Mag., 15 (2020), pp. 78–88.

381. N. LIU, H. YANG, AND X. HU, *Adversarial detection with model interpretation*, in Proceedings of the 24th ACM SIGKDD International Conference on Knowledge Discovery and Data Mining, KDD '18, New York, NY, USA, 2018, Association for Computing Machinery.

382. ——, *Adversarial detection with model interpretation*, in Proceedings of the 24th ACM SIGKDD International Conference on Knowledge Discovery & Data Mining, KDD '18, New York, NY, USA, 2018, Association for Computing Machinery.

383. Q. LIU, P. LI, W. ZHAO, W. CAI, S. YU, AND V. C. M. LEUNG, *A survey on security threats and defensive techniques of machine learning: A data driven view*, IEEE Access, 6 (2018), pp. 12103–12117.

384. W. LIU AND S. CHAWLA, *A game theoretical model for adversarial learning*, in 2009 IEEE International Conference on Data Mining Workshops, 2009, pp. 25–30.

385. ——, *Mining adversarial patterns via regularized loss minimization*, Machine Learning, 81 (2010), pp. 69–83.

386. ——, *Mining adversarial patterns via regularized loss minimization*, Mach. Learn., 81 (2010), pp. 69–83.

387. W. LIU, S. CHAWLA, J. BAILEY, C. LECKIE, AND K. RAMAMOHANARAO, *AI 2012: Advances in Artificial Intelligence: 25th Australasian Joint Conference, Sydney, Australia, December 4-7, 2012. Proceedings*, Springer Berlin Heidelberg, Berlin, Heidelberg, 2012,

ch. An Efficient Adversarial Learning Strategy for Constructing Robust Classification Boundaries, pp. 649–660.

388. Y. LIU, X. CHEN, C. LIU, AND D. SONG, *Delving into transferable adversarial examples and black-box attacks*, in Proceedings of 5th International Conference on Learning Representations, 2017.

389. ——, *Delving into transferable adversarial examples and black-box attacks*, in 5th International Conference on Learning Representations, ICLR 2017, Toulon, France, April 24-26, 2017, Conference Track Proceedings, 2017.

390. Y. LIU, M. OTT, N. GOYAL, J. DU, M. JOSHI, D. CHEN, O. LEVY, M. LEWIS, L. ZETTLEMOYER, AND V. STOYANOV, *Roberta: A robustly optimized bert pretraining approach*, arXiv preprint arXiv:1907.11692, (2019).

391. Y. LIU, W. ZHANG, AND N. YU, *Protecting privacy in shared photos via adversarial examples based stealth*, Security and Communication Networks, 2017 (2017).

392. S. LLOYD AND C. WEEDBROOK, *Quantum generative adversarial learning*, Phys. Rev. Lett., 121 (2018), p. 040502.

393. Y. LOU, R. CARUANA, AND J. GEHRKE, *Intelligible models for classification and regression*, in Proceedings of the 18th ACM SIGKDD International Conference on Knowledge Discovery and Data Mining, KDD '12, New York, NY, USA, 2012, Association for Computing Machinery.

394. D. LOWD AND C. MEEK, *Adversarial learning*, in Proceedings of the Eleventh ACM SIGKDD International Conference on Knowledge Discovery in Data Mining, KDD '05, New York, NY, USA, 2005, ACM, pp. 641–647.

395. R. LOWE, Y. WU, A. TAMAR, J. HARB, P. ABBEEL, AND I. MORDATCH, *Multi-agent actor-critic for mixed cooperative-competitive environments*, in Proceedings of the 31st International Conference on Neural Information Processing Systems, NIPS'17, Red Hook, NY, USA, 2017, Curran Associates Inc.

396. Y. LU AND K. YAN, *Algorithms in multi-agent systems: A holistic perspective from reinforcement learning and game theory*, CoRR, abs/2001.06487 (2020).

397. A. LUEDTKE, M. CARONE, N. SIMON, AND O. SOFRYGIN, *Learning to learn from data: Using deep adversarial learning to construct optimal statistical procedures*, Science Advances, 6 (2020), p. eaaw2140.

398. A. LUEDTKE, M. CARONE, N. SIMON, AND O. SOFRYGIN, *Learning to learn from data: Using deep adversarial learning to construct optimal statistical procedures*, Science Advances, 6 (2020).

399. S. M. LUNDBERG AND S. LEE, *A unified approach to interpreting model predictions*, in NIPS, 2017, pp. 4765–4774.

400. S. M. LUNDBERG AND S.-I. LEE, *A unified approach to interpreting model predictions*, in Advances in Neural Information Processing Systems 30, I. Guyon, U. V. Luxburg, S. Bengio, H. Wallach, R. Fergus, S. Vishwanathan, and R. Garnett, eds., Curran Associates, Inc., 2017, pp. 4765–4774.

401. ——, *A unified approach to interpreting model predictions*, in Advances in Neural Information Processing Systems, I. Guyon, U. V. Luxburg, S. Bengio, H. Wallach, R. Fergus, S. Vishwanathan, and R. Garnett, eds., vol. 30, Curran Associates, Inc., 2017.

402. Y. MA, K. JUN, L. LI, AND X. ZHU, *Data poisoning attacks in contextual bandits*, in Decision and Game Theory for Security - 9th International Conference, GameSec 2018, Seattle, WA, USA, October 29-31, 2018, Proceedings, 2018, pp. 186–204.

403. O. MAIMON AND L. ROKACH, *Decomposition Methodology for Knowledge Discovery and Data Mining - Theory and Applications*, vol. 61 of Series in Machine Perception and Artificial Intelligence, WorldScientific, 2005.

404. A. MAKHZANI, J. SHLENS, N. JAITLY, AND I. GOODFELLOW, *Adversarial autoencoders*, in International Conference on Learning Representations, 2016.

405. A. MAKHZANI, J. SHLENS, N. JAITLY, AND I. J. GOODFELLOW, *Adversarial autoencoders*, CoRR, abs/1511.05644 (2015).

406. M. T. MAMOUN ALAZAB, *Deep Learning Applications for Cyber Security (Advanced Sciences and Technologies for Security Applications)*, Springer Nature, Switzerland AG, 2019.

407. M. MANCINI, L. PORZI, S. BULO, B. CAPUTO, AND E. RICCI, *Boosting domain adaptation by discovering latent domains*, in 2018 IEEE/CVF Conference on Computer Vision and Pattern Recognition (CVPR), Los Alamitos, CA, USA, jun 2018, IEEE Computer Society, pp. 3771–3780.

408. A. MANDLEKAR, Y. ZHU, A. GARG, L. FEI-FEI, AND S. SAVARESE, *Adversarially robust policy learning: Active construction of physically-plausible perturbations*, in 2017 IEEE/RSJ International Conference on Intelligent Robots and Systems, IROS 2017, Vancouver, BC, Canada, September 24-28, 2017, 2017, pp. 3932–3939.

409. M. H. MANSHAEI, Q. ZHU, T. ALPCAN, T. BAÇSAR, AND J.-P. HUBAUX, *Game theory meets network security and privacy*, ACM Comput. Surv., 45 (2013).

410. X. MAO, Q. LI, H. XIE, R. Y. K. LAU, Z. WANG, AND S. P. SMOLLEY, *Least squares generative adversarial networks*, in ICCV, IEEE Computer Society, 2017, pp. 2813–2821.

411. D. L. MARINO, C. S. WICKRAMASINGHE, AND M. MANIC, *An adversarial approach for explainable AI in intrusion detection systems*, in IECON 2018 - 44th Annual Conference of the IEEE Industrial Electronics Society, Washington, DC, USA, October 21-23, 2018, 2018, pp. 3237–3243.

412. O. MARTIN AND S. OTTO, *Combining simulated annealing with local search heuristics*, Annals of Operations Research, 63 (1999).

413. O. C. MARTIN AND S. W. OTTO, *Combining simulated annealing with local search heuristics*, tech. rep., 1993.

414. N. MARTINS, J. M. CRUZ, T. CRUZ, AND P. HENRIQUES ABREU, *Adversarial machine learning applied to intrusion and malware scenarios: A systematic review*, IEEE Access, 8 (2020), pp. 35403–35419.

415. H. MASNADI-SHIRAZI AND N. VASCONCELOS, *On the design of loss functions for classification: theory, robustness to outliers, and savageboost*, in Advances in Neural Information Processing Systems 21, D. Koller, D. Schuurmans, Y. Bengio, and L. Bottou, eds., Curran Associates, Inc., 2009, pp. 1049–1056.

416. F. MATERN, C. RIESS, AND M. STAMMINGER, *Exploiting visual artifacts to expose deepfakes and face manipulations*, in 2019 IEEE Winter Applications of Computer Vision Workshops (WACVW), Jan 2019, pp. 83–92.

417. R. R. MCCUNE, T. WENINGER, AND G. MADEY, *Thinking like a vertex: A survey of vertex-centric frameworks for large-scale distributed graph processing*, ACM Comput. Surv., 48 (2015).

418. J. V. MEDANIC AND D. G. RADOJEVIC, *Multilevel stackelberg strategies in linear-quadratic systems*, Journal of Optimization Theory and Applications, 24 (1978), pp. 485–497.

419. S. MEI AND X. ZHU, *The Security of Latent Dirichlet Allocation*, in Proceedings of the Eighteenth International Conference on Artificial Intelligence and Statistics, G. Lebanon and S. V. N. Vishwanathan, eds., vol. 38 of Proceedings of Machine Learning Research, San Diego, California, USA, 09–12 May 2015, PMLR, pp. 681–689.

420. M. MELIS, A. DEMONTIS, B. BIGGIO, G. BROWN, G. FUMERA, AND F. ROLI, *Is deep learning safe for robot vision? adversarial examples against the icub humanoid*, in 2017 IEEE International Conference on Computer Vision Workshops, ICCV Workshops 2017, Venice, Italy, October 22-29, 2017, 2017, pp. 751–759.

421. M. MELIS, D. MAIORCA, B. BIGGIO, G. GIACINTO, AND F. ROLI, *Explaining black-box android malware detection*, in 26th European Signal Processing Conference, EUSIPCO 2018, Roma, Italy, September 3-7, 2018, 2018, pp. 524–528.

422. D. MENG AND H. CHEN, *Magnet: A two-pronged defense against adversarial examples*, in Proceedings of the 2017 ACM SIGSAC Conference on Computer and Communications Security, CCS '17, New York, NY, USA, 2017, Association for Computing Machinery, p. 135–147.

423. L. MESCHEDER, S. NOWOZIN, AND A. GEIGER, *Adversarial variational bayes: Unifying variational autoencoders and generative adversarial networks*, in Proceedings of the 34th International Conference on Machine Learning - Volume 70, ICML'17, JMLR.org, 2017, p. 2391–2400.

424. J. H. METZEN, T. GENEWEIN, V. FISCHER, AND B. BISCHOFF, *On detecting adversarial perturbations*, in Proceedings of 5th International Conference on Learning Representations (ICLR), 2017.

425. Z. MICHALEWICZ, *Genetic Algorithms + Data Structures = Evolution Programs (3rd Ed.)*, Springer-Verlag, Berlin, Heidelberg, 1996.

426. ——, *Genetic Algorithms + Data Structures = Evolution Programs (3rd Ed.)*, Springer-Verlag, Berlin, Heidelberg, 1996.

427. B. MILLER, A. KANTCHELIAN, S. AFROZ, R. BACHWANI, E. DAUBER, L. HUANG, M. C. TSCHANTZ, A. D. JOSEPH, AND J. TYGAR, *Adversarial active learning*, in Proceedings of the 2014 Workshop on Artificial Intelligent and Security Workshop, AISec '14, New York, NY, USA, 2014, Association for Computing Machinery.

428. D. J. MILLER, X. HU, Z. QIU, AND G. KESIDIS, *Adversarial learning: A critical review and active learning study*, in MLSP, IEEE, 2017, pp. 1–6.

429. G. A. MILLER, *WordNet: An electronic lexical database*, MIT press, 1998.

430. H. MILLER, P. HALLER, AND M. ODERSKY, *Tools and frameworks for big learning in scala: Leveraging the language for high productivity and performance*, in NIPS 2011, 2011.

431. P. MIROWSKI, M. RANZATO, AND Y. LECUN, *Dynamic auto-encoders for semantic indexing*, in Proceedings of the NIPS 2010 Workshop on Deep Learning, 2010, pp. 1–9.

432. T. MIYATO, A. M. DAI, AND I. J. GOODFELLOW, *Adversarial training methods for semi-supervised text classification*, in 5th International Conference on Learning Representations, ICLR 2017, Toulon, France, April 24-26, 2017, Conference Track Proceedings, 2017.

433. T. MIYATO, S. MAEDA, M. KOYAMA, AND S. ISHII, *Virtual adversarial training: A regularization method for supervised and semi-supervised learning*, IEEE Trans. Pattern Anal. Mach. Intell., 41 (2019), pp. 1979–1993.

434. A. MNIH AND K. GREGOR, *Neural variational inference and learning in belief networks*, in Proceedings of the 31st International Conference on International Conference on Machine Learning - Volume 32, ICML'14, JMLR.org, 2014.

435. D. MODESITT, T. HENRY, J. CODEN, AND R. LATHE, *Neural cryptography : From symmetric encryption to adversarial steganography*, 2018.

436. H. MOHAMADI, J. HABIBI, M. S. ABADEH, AND H. SAADI, *Data mining with a simulated annealing based fuzzy classification system*, Pattern Recogn., 41 (2008), p. 1824–1833.

437. C. MOLNAR, *Interpretable Machine Learning*, 2019.

438. A. K. MONDAL, S. P. CHOWDHURY, A. JAYENDRAN, H. ASNANI, P. SINGLA, AND P. A. P., *Maskaae: Latent space optimization for adversarial auto-encoders*, in Proceedings of the Thirty-Sixth Conference on Uncertainty in Artificial Intelligence, UAI 2020, virtual online, August 3-6, 2020, R. P. Adams and V. Gogate, eds., vol. 124 of Proceedings of Machine Learning Research, AUAI Press, 2020, pp. 689–698.

439. S. MOOSAVI-DEZFOOLI, A. FAWZI, AND P. FROSSARD, *Deepfool: A simple and accurate method to fool deep neural networks*, in Proceedings of Conference on Computer Vision and Pattern Recognition CVPR, 2016.

440. S.-M. MOOSAVI-DEZFOOLI, A. FAWZI, O. FAWZI, AND P. FROSSARD, *Universal adversarial perturbations*, in Proceedings of the IEEE conference on computer vision and pattern recognition, 2017, pp. 1765–1773.

441. S.-M. MOOSAVI-DEZFOOLI, A. FAWZI, AND P. FROSSARD, *Deepfool: a simple and accurate method to fool deep neural networks*, in Proceedings of the IEEE conference on Conference on Computer Vision and Pattern Recognition, 2016, pp. 2574–2582.

442. J. J. MORÉ AND S. M. WILD, *Benchmarking derivative-free optimization algorithms*, SIAM J. on Optimization, 20 (2009), p. 172–191.

443. R. MOTWANI AND P. RAGHAVAN, *Randomized Algorithms*, Cambridge University Press, Cambridge; NY, 1995.

444. N. MRKŠIĆ, D. O. SÉAGHDHA, B. THOMSON, M. GAŠIĆ, L. ROJAS-BARAHONA, P.-H. SU, D. VANDYKE, T.-H. WEN, AND S. YOUNG, *Counter-fitting word vectors to linguistic constraints*, in The 15th Annual Conference of the North American Chapter of the Association for Computational Linguistics, 2016, pp. 142–148.

445. Y. MROUEH AND T. SERCU, *Fisher gan*, in Advances in Neural Information Processing Systems 30, I. Guyon, U. V. Luxburg, S. Bengio, H. Wallach, R. Fergus, S. Vishwanathan, and R. Garnett, eds., Curran Associates, Inc., 2017, pp. 2513–2523.

446. Y. MROUEH, T. SERCU, AND V. GOEL, *McGan: Mean and covariance feature matching GAN*, in Proceedings of the 34th International Conference on Machine Learning, D. Precup and Y. W. Teh, eds., vol. 70 of Proceedings of Machine Learning Research, International Convention Centre, Sydney, Australia, 06–11 Aug 2017, PMLR, pp. 2527–2535.

447. A. NAGURNEY, P. DANIELE, AND S. SHUKLA, *A supply chain network game theory model of cybersecurity investments with nonlinear budget constraints*, Ann. Oper. Res., 248 (2017), pp. 405–427.

448. Y. NARAHARI, *Game Theory and Mechanism Design*, WORLD SCIENTIFIC / INDIAN INST OF SCIENCE, INDIA, 2014.

449. Y. NARAHARI, D. GARG, R. NARAYANAM, AND H. PRAKASH, *Game Theoretic Problems in Network Economics and Mechanism Design Solutions*, Springer Publishing Company, Incorporated, 1 ed., 2009.

450. R. NARAYANAM AND Y. NARAHARI, *A shapley value-based approach to discover influential nodes in social networks*, IEEE Transactions on Automation Science and Engineering, 8 (2011), pp. 130–147.

451. R. NARAYANAM AND Y. NARAHARI, *A game theory inspired, decentralized, local information based algorithm for community detection in social graphs*, in ICPR, IEEE Computer Society, 2012, pp. 1072–1075.

452. N. NARODYTSKA AND S. P. KASIVISWANATHAN, *Simple black-box adversarial perturbations for deep networks*, arXiv preprint arXiv:1612.06299, (2016).

453. N. NARODYTSKA, S. P. KASIVISWANATHAN, L. RYZHYK, M. SAGIV, AND T. WALSH, *Verifying properties of binarized deep neural networks*, in Proceedings of the Thirty-Second AAAI Conference on Artificial Intelligence, (AAAI-18), the 30th innovative Applications of Artificial Intelligence (IAAI-18), and the 8th AAAI Symposium on Educational Advances in Artificial Intelligence (EAAI-18), New Orleans, Louisiana, USA, February 2-7, 2018, 2018, pp. 6615–6624.

454. J. NASH, *Non-cooperative games*, Annals of Mathematics, 54 (1951), pp. 286–295.

455. J. F. NASH, *Equilibrium points in n-person games.*, Proceedings of the National Academy of Sciences of the United States of America, 36 1 (1950), pp. 48–9.

456. B. NELSON, B. RUBINSTEIN, L. HUANG, A. JOSEPH, S. LAU, S. LEE, S. RAO, A. TRAN, AND D. TYGAR, *Near-optimal evasion of convex-inducing classifiers*, in Proceedings of the Thirteenth International Conference on Artificial Intelligence and Statistics, Y. W. Teh and M. Titterington, eds., vol. 9 of Proceedings of Machine Learning Research, Chia Laguna Resort, Sardinia, Italy, 13–15 May 2010, PMLR, pp. 549–556.

457. A. NEMIROVSKI, A. JUDITSKY, G. LAN, AND A. SHAPIRO, *Robust stochastic approximation approach to stochastic programming*, SIAM J. on Optimization, 19 (2009), pp. 1574–1609.

458. A. NGUYEN, J. YOSINSKI, AND J. CLUNE, *Deep neural networks are easily fooled: High confidence predictions for unrecognizable images*, (2015).

459. T. NGUYEN, T. LE, H. VU, AND D. PHUNG, *Dual discriminator generative adversarial nets*, in Advances in Neural Information Processing Systems 30, I. Guyon, U. V. Luxburg, S. Bengio, H. Wallach, R. Fergus, S. Vishwanathan, and R. Garnett, eds., Curran Associates, Inc., 2017, pp. 2667–2677.

460. T. NGUYEN, C. NGUYEN, D. T. NGUYEN, D. NGUYEN, AND S. NAHAVANDI, *Deep learning for deepfakes creation and detection*, ArXiv, abs/1909.11573 (2019).

461. T. NGUYEN, M. P. WELLMAN, AND S. P. SINGH, *A stackelberg game model for botnet data exfiltration*, in GameSec, vol. 10575 of Lecture Notes in Computer Science, Springer, 2017, pp. 151–170.

462. T. H. NGUYEN, Y. WANG, A. SINHA, AND M. P. WELLMAN, *Deception in finitely repeated security games*, in AAAI, AAAI Press, 2019, pp. 2133–2140.

463. T. H. NGUYEN, M. WRIGHT, M. P. WELLMAN, AND S. P. SINGH, *Multistage attack graph security games: Heuristic strategies, with empirical game-theoretic analysis*, Secur. Commun. Networks, 2018 (2018), pp. 2864873:1–2864873:28.

464. N. NISAN, T. ROUGHGARDEN, E. TARDOS, AND V. V. VAZIRANI, *Algorithmic Game Theory*, Cambridge University Press, New York, NY, USA, 2007.

465. A. NISIOTI, G. LOUKAS, A. LASZKA, AND E. PANAOUSIS, *Data-driven decision support for optimizing cyber forensic investigations*, IEEE Trans. Inf. Forensics Secur., 16 (2021), pp. 2397–2412.

466. A. NOUY, *Low-Rank Tensor Methods for Model Order Reduction*, Springer International Publishing, Cham, 2017, pp. 857–882.

467. A. NOWÉ, P. VRANCX, AND Y.-M. DE HAUWERE, *Game Theory and Multi-agent Reinforcement Learning*, Springer Berlin Heidelberg, Berlin, Heidelberg, 2012, pp. 441–470.

468. S. NOWOZIN, B. CSEKE, AND R. TOMIOKA, *f-gan: Training generative neural samplers using variational divergence minimization*, in Advances in Neural Information Processing Systems, D. Lee, M. Sugiyama, U. Luxburg, I. Guyon, and R. Garnett, eds., vol. 29, Curran Associates, Inc., 2016.

469. G. M. D. NUNZIO, M. MAISTRO, AND D. C. ZILIO, *Gamification for machine learning: The classification game*, in GamifIR@SIGIR, 2016.

470. J. OCENASEK, E. CANTÚ-PAZ, M. PELIKAN, AND J. SCHWARZ, *Design of parallel estimation of distribution algorithms*, in Scalable Optimization via Probabilistic Modeling, 2006, pp. 187–203.

471. S. J. OH, M. FRITZ, AND B. SCHIELE, *Adversarial image perturbation for privacy protection a game theory perspective*, in 2017 IEEE International Conference on Computer Vision (ICCV), IEEE, 2017, pp. 1491–1500.

472. F. OLIEHOEK, R. SAVANI, J. GALLEGO, E. VAN DER POL, AND R. GROSS, *Beyond local nash equilibria for adversarial networks*, in Artificial Intelligence, M. Atzmueller and W. Duivesteijn, eds., Communications in Computer and Information Science, Springer, 2019, pp. 73–89.

473. F. A. OLIEHOEK, E. D. DE JONG, AND N. VLASSIS, *The parallel nash memory for asymmetric games*, in Proceedings of the 8th Annual Conference on Genetic and Evolutionary Computation, GECCO '06, New York, NY, USA, 2006, Association for Computing Machinery.

474. F. A. OLIEHOEK, R. SAVANI, J. GALLEGO-POSADA, E. VAN DER POL, E. D. DE JONG, AND R. GROSS, *Gangs: Generative adversarial network games*, CoRR, abs/1712.00679 (2017).

475. U. O'REILLY AND E. HEMBERG, *An artificial coevolutionary framework for adversarial ai*, in AAAI Fall Symposium: ALEC, vol. 2269 of CEUR Workshop Proceedings, CEUR-WS.org, 2018, pp. 50–55.

476. M. J. OSBORNE AND A. RUBINSTEIN, *A Course in Game Theory*, vol. 1 of MIT Press Books, The MIT Press, 1994.

477. H. OTROK, B. ZHU, H. YAHYAOUI, AND P. BHATTACHARYA, *An intrusion detection game theoretical model*, Information Security Journal: A Global Perspective, 18 (2009), pp. 199–212.

478. N. PAPERNOT AND P. MCDANIEL, *Extending defensive distillation*, ArXiv, abs/1705.05264 (2017).

479. N. PAPERNOT, P. MCDANIEL, AND I. GOODFELLOW, *Transferability in machine learning: from phenomena to black-box attacks using adversarial samples*, arXiv preprint arXiv:1605.07277, (2016).

480. N. PAPERNOT, P. MCDANIEL, I. GOODFELLOW, S. JHA, Z. BERKAY CELIK, AND A. SWAMI, *Practical Black-Box Attacks against Deep Learning Systems using Adversarial Examples*, ArXiv e-prints, (2016).

481. N. PAPERNOT, P. MCDANIEL, I. GOODFELLOW, S. JHA, Z. B. CELIK, AND A. SWAMI, *Practical black-box attacks against machine learning*, in Proceedings of the 2017 ACM on

Asia Conference on Computer and Communications Security, ASIA CCS '17, New York, NY, USA, 2017, ACM, pp. 506–519.

482. N. PAPERNOT, P. MCDANIEL, A. SINHA, AND M. P. WELLMAN, *Sok: Security and privacy in machine learning*, in 2018 IEEE European Symposium on Security and Privacy (EuroS P), April 2018, pp. 399–414.

483. N. PAPERNOT, P. MCDANIEL, A. SWAMI, AND R. HARANG, *Crafting adversarial input sequences for recurrent neural networks*, in IEEE Military Communications Conference, 2016, pp. 49–54.

484. N. PAPERNOT, P. MCDANIEL, X. WU, S. JHA, AND A. SWAMI, *Distillation as a defense to adversarial perturbations against deep neural networks*, 2016 IEEE Symposium on Security and Privacy (SP), (2016), pp. 582–597.

485. N. PAPERNOT, P. D. MCDANIEL, A. SINHA, AND M. P. WELLMAN, *Towards the science of security and privacy in machine learning*, CoRR, abs/1611.03814 (2016).

486. M. J. A. PATWARY AND X. WANG, *Sensitivity analysis on initial classifier accuracy in fuzziness based semi-supervised learning*, Inf. Sci., 490 (2019), pp. 93–112.

487. J. PAWLICK, E. COLBERT, AND Q. ZHU, *A game-theoretic taxonomy and survey of defensive deception for cybersecurity and privacy*, ACM Comput. Surv., 52 (2019).

488. G. PEAKE AND J. WANG, *Explanation mining: Post hoc interpretability of latent factor models for recommendation systems*, in Proceedings of the 24th ACM SIGKDD International Conference on Knowledge Discovery and Data Mining, KDD '18, New York, NY, USA, 2018, Association for Computing Machinery.

489. M. PELIKAN, D. E. GOLDBERG, AND E. CANTU-PAZ, *Linkage problem, distribution estimation, and bayesian networks*, Evolutionary Computation, 8 (2000), pp. 311–340.

490. M. PERC AND A. SZOLNOKI, *Coevolutionary games - A mini review*, Biosyst., 99 (2010), pp. 109–125.

491. C. PERLICH, F. PROVOST, AND J. S. SIMONOFF, *Tree induction vs. logistic regression: A learning-curve analysis*, 4 (2003).

492. D. PFAU AND O. VINYALS, *Connecting generative adversarial networks and actor-critic methods*, CoRR, abs/1610.01945 (2016).

493. S. PIDHORSKYI, D. A. ADJEROH, AND G. DORETTO, *Adversarial latent autoencoders*, in Proceedings of the IEEE/CVF Conference on Computer Vision and Pattern Recognition, 2020, pp. 14104–14113.

494. L. PINTO, J. DAVIDSON, R. SUKTHANKAR, AND A. GUPTA, *Robust adversarial reinforcement learning*, in Proceedings of the 34th International Conference on Machine Learning, ICML 2017, Sydney, NSW, Australia, 6-11 August 2017, 2017, pp. 2817–2826.

495. M. PIRLOT, *General local search methods*, European Journal of Operational Research, 92 (1996), pp. 493–511.

496. B. POOLE, A. ALEMI, J. SOHL-DICKSTEIN, AND A. ANGELOVA, *Improved generator objectives for gans*, 2016.

497. A. PRAKASH AND M. P. WELLMAN, *Empirical game-theoretic analysis for moving target defense*, in MTD@CCS, ACM, 2015, pp. 57–65.

498. D. PRUTHI, B. DHINGRA, AND Z. C. LIPTON, *Combating adversarial misspellings with robust word recognition*, in Proceedings of the 57th Annual Meeting of the Association for Computational Linguistics, Florence, Italy, July 2019, Association for Computational Linguistics, pp. 5582–5591.

499. Z. S. W. C. QIU S, LIU Q, *Review of artificial intelligence adversarial attack and defense technologies*, in MDPI Applied Sciences, 2019, p. 9(5):909.

500. A. RADFORD, L. METZ, AND S. CHINTALA, *Unsupervised representation learning with deep convolutional generative adversarial networks*.

501. A. RAGHUNATHAN, J. STEINHARDT, AND P. LIANG, *Certified defenses against adversarial examples*, in ICLR (Poster), OpenReview.net, 2018.

502. A. RAJABI, R. B. BOBBA, M. ROSULEK, C. V. WRIGHT, AND W.-C. FENG, *On the (im) practicality of adversarial perturbation for image privacy*, Proceedings on Privacy Enhancing Technologies, 2021 (2021), pp. 85–106.

503. S. RAJASEKARAN, *On simulated annealing and nested annealing*, Journal of Global Optimization, 16 (2000), pp. 43–56.

504. A. RAKHLIN AND K. SRIDHARAN, *Optimization, learning, and games with predictable sequences*, in NIPS, 2013, pp. 3066–3074.

505. D. RAM, T. SREENIVAS, AND K. SUBRAMANIAM, *Parallel simulated annealing algorithms*, J. Parallel Distrib. Comput., 37 (1996), p. 207–212.

506. S. RASS, S. KONIG, AND S. SCHAUER, *Defending against advanced persistent threats using game-theory*, PLOS ONE, 12 (2017), pp. 1–43.

507. L. RATLIFF, S. BURDEN, AND S. SASTRY, *Characterization and computation of local nash equilibria in continuous games*, 10 2013, pp. 917–924.

508. J. RAUBER, W. BRENDEL, AND M. BETHGE, *Foolbox: A python toolbox to benchmark the robustness of machine learning models*, in Reliable Machine Learning in the Wild Workshop, 34th International Conference on Machine Learning, 2017.

509. S. REN, Y. DENG, K. HE, AND W. CHE, *Generating natural language adversarial examples through probability weighted word saliency*, in Proceedings of the 57th Annual Meeting of the Association for Computational Linguistics, 2019, pp. 1085–1097.

510. S. REN, K. HE, R. B. GIRSHICK, AND J. SUN, *Faster R-CNN: towards real-time object detection with region proposal networks*, CoRR, abs/1506.01497 (2015).

511. S. RENDLE, *Factorization machines*, in 2010 IEEE International Conference on Data Mining, 2010, pp. 995–1000.

512. I. REZEK, D. S. LESLIE, S. REECE, S. J. ROBERTS, A. ROGERS, R. K. DASH, AND N. R. JENNINGS, *On similarities between inference in game theory and machine learning*, J. Artif. Int. Res., 33 (2008), p. 259–283.

513. I. REZEK, D. S. LESLIE, S. REECE, S. J. ROBERTS, A. ROGERS, R. K. DASH, AND N. R. JENNINGS, *On similarities between inference in game theory and machine learning*, J. Artif. Intell. Res., 33 (2008).

514. M. T. RIBEIRO, S. SINGH, AND C. GUESTRIN, *Why should i trust you?: Explaining the predictions of any classifier*, in Proceedings of the 22nd ACM SIGKDD International Conference on Knowledge Discovery and Data Mining, KDD '16, New York, NY, USA, 2016, Association for Computing Machinery, p. 1135–1144.

515. ——, *Why should i trust you?: Explaining the predictions of any classifier*, in Proceedings of the 22nd ACM SIGKDD International Conference on Knowledge Discovery and Data Mining, KDD '16, New York, NY, USA, 2016, Association for Computing Machinery, p. 1135–1144.

516. M. T. RIBEIRO, S. SINGH, AND C. GUESTRIN, *Anchors: High-precision model-agnostic explanations*, in Proceedings of the Thirty-Second AAAI Conference on Artificial Intelligence, (AAAI-18), the 30th innovative Applications of Artificial Intelligence (IAAI-18), and the 8th AAAI Symposium on Educational Advances in Artificial Intelligence (EAAI-18), New Orleans, Louisiana, USA, February 2-7, 2018, 2018, pp. 1527–1535.

517. P. RICHTARIK, M. JAHANI, S. D. AHIPASAOGLU, AND M. TAKAC, *Alternating maximization: unifying framework for 8 sparse pca formulations and efficient parallel codes*, 2020.

518. D. RIOS INSUA, R. NAVEIRO, AND V. GALLEGO, *Perspectives on adversarial classification*, Mathematics, 8 (2020).

519. ——, *Perspectives on adversarial classification*, Mathematics, 8 (2020).

520. T. ROEDER AND F. B. SCHNEIDER, *Proactive obfuscation*, ACM Trans. Comput. Syst., 28 (2010), pp. 4:1–4:54.

521. Y. ROMANO, A. ABERDAM, J. SULAM, AND M. ELAD, *Adversarial noise attacks of deep learning architectures: Stability analysis via sparse-modeled signals*, Journal of Mathematical Imaging and Vision, 62 (2020).

522. Y. ROMANO, A. ABERDAM, J. SULAM, AND M. ELAD, *Adversarial noise attacks of deep learning architectures: Stability analysis via sparse-modeled signals*, J. Math. Imaging Vis., 62 (2020), pp. 313–327.

523. J. ROMERO AND A. ASPURU-GUZIK, *Variational quantum generators: Generative adversarial quantum machine learning for continuous distributions*, Advanced Quantum Technologies, 4 (2020), p. 2000003.

524. L. ROSASCO, E. DE VITO, A. CAPONNETTO, M. PIANA, AND A. VERRI, *Are loss functions all the same?*, Neural Comput., 16 (2004).

525. K. ROSE, *Deterministic annealing for clustering, compression, classification, regression, and related optimization problems*, Proceedings of the IEEE, 86 (1998), pp. 2210–2239.

526. I. ROSENBERG, A. SHABTAI, L. ROKACH, AND Y. ELOVICI, *Generic black-box end-to-end attack against state of the art API call based malware classifiers*, in Research in Attacks, Intrusions, and Defenses - 21st International Symposium, RAID 2018, Heraklion, Crete, Greece, September 10-12, 2018, Proceedings, 2018, pp. 490–510.

527. A. ROSSLER, D. COZZOLINO, L. VERDOLIVA, C. RIESS, J. THIES, AND M. NIESSNER, *Faceforensics++: Learning to detect manipulated facial images*, CoRR, abs/1901.08971 (2019).

528. S. ROTA BULO, B. BIGGIO, I. PILLAI, M. PELILLO, AND F. ROLI, *Randomized prediction games for adversarial machine learning*, IEEE Transactions on Neural Networks and Learning Systems, 28 (2017), pp. 2466–2478.

529. B. D. ROUHANI, M. SAMRAGH, M. JAVAHERIPI, T. JAVIDI, AND F. KOUSHANFAR, *Deepfense: Online accelerated defense against adversarial deep learning*, in Proceedings of the International Conference on Computer-Aided Design, ICCAD '18, New York, NY, USA, 2018, Association for Computing Machinery.

530. S. ROY, C. ELLIS, S. SHIVA, D. DASGUPTA, V. SHANDILYA, AND Q. WU, *A survey of game theory as applied to network security*, in 2010 43rd Hawaii International Conference on System Sciences, 2010, pp. 1–10.

531. B. I. RUBINSTEIN, P. L. BARTLETT, L. HUANG, AND N. TAFT, *Learning in a large function space: Privacy-preserving mechanisms for svm learning*, Journal of Privacy and Confidentiality, Vol.4 : Iss.1, Article 4. (2009).

532. B. I. RUBINSTEIN, B. NELSON, L. HUANG, A. D. JOSEPH, S.-H. LAU, S. RAO, N. TAFT, AND J. D. TYGAR, *Antidote: Understanding and defending against poisoning of anomaly detectors*, in Proceedings of the 9th ACM SIGCOMM Conference on Internet Measurement, IMC '09, New York, NY, USA, 2009, ACM, pp. 1–14.

533. C. RUDIN, *Stop explaining black box machine learning models for high stakes decisions and use interpretable models instead*, Nature Machine Intelligence, 1 (2019), pp. 206–215.

534. K. SADEGHI, A. BANERJEE, AND S. K. S. GUPTA, *A system-driven taxonomy of attacks and defenses in adversarial machine learning*, IEEE Transactions on Emerging Topics in Computational Intelligence, 4 (2020), pp. 450–467.

535. P. SAMANGOUEI, M. KABKAB, AND R. CHELLAPPA, *Defense-gan: Protecting classifiers against adversarial attacks using generative models*.

536. S. SAMANTA AND S. MEHTA, *Generating adversarial text samples*, in Advances in Information Retrieval - 40th European Conference on IR Research, ECIR 2018, Grenoble, France, March 26-29, 2018, Proceedings, 2018, pp. 744–749.

537. W. SAMEK, G. MONTAVON, S. LAPUSCHKIN, C. J. ANDERS, AND K. MÜLLER, *Explaining deep neural networks and beyond: A review of methods and applications*, Proc. IEEE, 109 (2021), pp. 247–278.

538. W. SAMEK, G. MONTAVON, A. VEDALDI, L. K. HANSEN, AND K. MÜLLER, eds., *Explainable AI: Interpreting, Explaining and Visualizing Deep Learning*, vol. 11700 of Lecture Notes in Computer Science, Springer, 2019.

539. S. SANKARANARAYANAN, Y. BALAJI, C. D. CASTILLO, AND R. CHELLAPPA, *Generate to adapt: Aligning domains using generative adversarial networks*, in 2018 IEEE/CVF Conference on Computer Vision and Pattern Recognition, 2018, pp. 8503–8512.

540. T. SCHLEGL, P. SEEBÖCK, S. M. WALDSTEIN, U. SCHMIDT-ERFURTH, AND G. LANGS, *Unsupervised anomaly detection with generative adversarial networks to guide marker discovery*, (2017), pp. 146–157.

541. A. SCHLENKER, O. THAKOOR, H. XU, F. FANG, M. TAMBE, L. TRAN-THANH, P. VAYANOS, AND Y. VOROBEYCHIK, *Deceiving cyber adversaries: A game theoretic approach*, in Proceedings of the 17th International Conference on Autonomous Agents and MultiAgent Systems, AAMAS '18, Richland, SC, 2018, International Foundation for Autonomous Agents and Multiagent Systems, p. 892–900.

542. L. SCHMIDT, S. SANTURKAR, D. TSIPRAS, K. TALWAR, AND A. MADRY, *Adversarially robust generalization requires more data*, in Proceedings of the 32nd International Conference on Neural Information Processing Systems, NIPS'18, Red Hook, NY, USA, 2018, Curran Associates Inc., p. 5019–5031.

543. L. SCHOTT, J. RAUBER, M. BETHGE, AND W. BRENDEL, *Towards the first adversarially robust neural network model on MNIST*, in International Conference on Learning Representations, 2019.

544. D. SCHUURMANS AND M. A. ZINKEVICH, *Deep learning games*, in Advances in Neural Information Processing Systems, D. Lee, M. Sugiyama, U. Luxburg, I. Guyon, and R. Garnett, eds., vol. 29, Curran Associates, Inc., 2016.

545. G. SCUTARI, D. P. PALOMAR, F. FACCHINEI, AND J.-S. PANG, *Convex optimization, game theory, and variational inequality theory*, IEEE Signal Processing Magazine, 27 (2010), pp. 35–49.

546. Y. SELDIN AND A. SLIVKINS, *One practical algorithm for both stochastic and adversarial bandits*, in Proceedings of the 31st International Conference on International Conference on Machine Learning - Volume 32, ICML'14, JMLR.org, 2014.

547. C. SEN, T. HARTVIGSEN, B. YIN, X. KONG, AND E. RUNDENSTEINER, *Human attention maps for text classification: Do humans and neural networks focus on the same words?*, in Proceedings of the 58th Annual Meeting of the Association for Computational Linguistics, Online, July 2020, Association for Computational Linguistics, pp. 4596–4608.

548. S. A. SESHIA, S. JHA, AND T. DREOSSI, *Semantic adversarial deep learning*, IEEE Design Test, 37 (2020), pp. 8–18.

549. A. SHAFAHI, W. R. HUANG, M. NAJIBI, O. SUCIU, C. STUDER, T. DUMITRAS, AND T. GOLDSTEIN, *Poison frogs! targeted clean-label poisoning attacks on neural networks*, in Advances in Neural Information Processing Systems, 2018, pp. 6103–6113.

550. H. SHAH, V. KAKKAD, R. PATEL, AND N. DOSHI, *A survey on game theoretic approaches for privacy preservation in data mining and network security*, Procedia Computer Science, 155 (2019), pp. 686–691. The 16th International Conference on Mobile Systems and Pervasive Computing (MobiSPC 2019),The 14th International Conference on Future Networks and Communications (FNC-2019),The 9th International Conference on Sustainable Energy Information Technology.

551. S. SHAN, E. WENGER, J. ZHANG, H. LI, H. ZHENG, AND B. Y. ZHAO, *Fawkes: protecting privacy against unauthorized deep learning models*, in 29th USENIX Security Symposium (USENIX Security 20), 2020, pp. 1589–1604.

552. M. SHARIF, S. BHAGAVATULA, L. BAUER, AND M. K. REITER, *Accessorize to a crime: Real and stealthy attacks on state-of-the-art face recognition*, in Proceedings of the 2016 ACM SIGSAC Conference on Computer and Communications Security, CCS '16, New York, NY, USA, 2016, Association for Computing Machinery.

553. C. SHEN, J. KIM, L. WANG, AND A. VAN DEN HENGEL, *Positive semidefinite metric learning using boosting-like algorithms*, J. Mach. Learn. Res., 13 (2012).

554. J. SHEN, Y. QU, W. ZHANG, AND Y. YU, *Wasserstein distance guided representation learning for domain adaptation*, in Proceedings of the Thirty-Second AAAI Conference on Artificial Intelligence, (AAAI-18), the 30th innovative Applications of Artificial Intelligence (IAAI-18), and the 8th AAAI Symposium on Educational Advances in Artificial Intelligence (EAAI-18), New Orleans, Louisiana, USA, February 2-7, 2018, S. A. McIlraith and K. Q. Weinberger, eds., AAAI Press, 2018, pp. 4058–4065.

555. R. SHOKRI, M. STRONATI, C. SONG, AND V. SHMATIKOV, *Membership inference attacks against machine learning models*, in 2017 IEEE Symposium on Security and Privacy (SP), May 2017, pp. 3–18.

556. A. SHRIKUMAR, P. GREENSIDE, AND A. KUNDAJE, *Learning important features through propagating activation differences*, in Proceedings of the 34th International Conference on Machine Learning - Volume 70, ICML'17, JMLR.org, 2017, p. 3145–3153.

557. M. SIMAAN AND J. B. CRUZ, JR., *On the stackelberg strategy in nonzero-sum games*, J. Optim. Theory Appl., 11 (1973), pp. 533–555.

558. K. SIMONYAN AND A. ZISSERMAN, *Very deep convolutional networks for large-scale image recognition*, arXiv preprint arXiv:1409.1556, (2014).

559. A. SINHA, P. MALO, AND K. DEB, *A review on bilevel optimization: From classical to evolutionary approaches and applications*, IEEE Transactions on Evolutionary Computation, 22 (2018), pp. 276–295.

560. A. SINHA, H. NAMKOONG, AND J. C. DUCHI, *Certifying some distributional robustness with principled adversarial training*, in 6th International Conference on Learning Representations, ICLR 2018, Vancouver, BC, Canada, April 30 - May 3, 2018, Conference Track Proceedings, OpenReview.net, 2018.

561. C. K. SØNDERBY, T. RAIKO, L. MAALØE, S. R. K. SØNDERBY, AND O. WINTHER, *Ladder variational autoencoders*, in Advances in Neural Information Processing Systems, D. Lee, M. Sugiyama, U. Luxburg, I. Guyon, and R. Garnett, eds., vol. 29, Curran Associates, Inc., 2016.

562. C. K. SØNDERBY, T. RAIKO, L. MAALØE, S. K. SØNDERBY, AND O. WINTHER, *Ladder variational autoencoders*, in Proceedings of the 30th International Conference on Neural Information Processing Systems, NIPS'16, Red Hook, NY, USA, 2016, Curran Associates Inc.

563. J. SONG, H. REN, D. SADIGH, AND S. ERMON, *Multi-agent generative adversarial imitation learning*, in Proceedings of the 32nd International Conference on Neural Information Processing Systems, NIPS'18, Red Hook, NY, USA, 2018, Curran Associates Inc., p. 7472–7483.

564. L. SONG, X. YU, H.-T. PENG, AND K. NARASIMHAN, *Universal adversarial attacks with natural triggers for text classification*, arXiv preprint arXiv:2005.00174, (2020).

565. Y. SONG, T. KIM, S. NOWOZIN, S. ERMON, AND N. KUSHMAN, *Pixeldefend: Leveraging generative models to understand and defend against adversarial examples*, in International Conference on Learning Representations, 2018.

566. J. C. SPALL, *Introduction to Stochastic Search and Optimization*, John Wiley & Sons, Inc., New York, NY, USA, 1 ed., 2003.

567. P. SPIRTES, C. N. GLYMOUR, AND R. SCHEINES, *Causation, prediction, and search*, MIT press, 2000.

568. P. SPRECHMANN AND G. SAPIRO, *Dictionary learning and sparse coding for unsupervised clustering*, in 2010 IEEE International Conference on Acoustics, Speech and Signal Processing, 2010, pp. 2042–2045.

569. A. SPURR, E. AKSAN, AND O. HILLIGES, *Guiding infogan with semi-supervision*, in ECML/PKDD (1), vol. 10534 of Lecture Notes in Computer Science, Springer, 2017, pp. 119–134.

570. S. SRA, S. NOWOZIN, AND S. J. WRIGHT, *Optimization for Machine Learning*, The MIT Press, 2011.

571. N. SREBRO AND T. JAAKKOLA, *Weighted low-rank approximations*, in ICML, 2003.

572. B. K. SRIPERUMBUDUR, K. FUKUMIZU, A. GRETTON, B. SCHÖLKOPF, AND G. R. G. LANCKRIET, *On the empirical estimation of integral probability metrics*, Electronic Journal of Statistics, 6 (2012), pp. 1550–1599.

573. E. STRUMBELJ AND I. KONONENKO, *An efficient explanation of individual classifications using game theory*, J. Mach. Learn. Res., 11 (2010).

574. ——, *An efficient explanation of individual classifications using game theory*, J. Mach. Learn. Res., 11 (2010).

575. J. SU, Y. TSAI, K. SOHN, B. LIU, S. MAJI, AND M. CHANDRAKER, *Active adversarial domain adaptation*, in 2020 IEEE Winter Conference on Applications of Computer Vision (WACV), 2020, pp. 728–737.

576. M. SUGIYAMA, *Distance approximation between probability distributions : Recent advances in machine learning*, Transactions of the Japan Society for Industrial and Applied Mathematics, 23 (2013), pp. 439–452.

577. M. SUGIYAMA, S. LIU, M. PLESSIS, M. YAMANAKA, M. YAMADA, T. SUZUKI, AND T. KANAMORI, *Direct divergence approximation between probability distributions and its*

applications in machine learning, Journal of Computing Science and Engineering, 7 (2013), pp. 99–111.

578. ——, *Direct divergence approximation between probability distributions and its applications in machine learning*, Journal of Computing Science and Engineering, 7 (2013).

579. B. SUMAN AND P. KUMAR, *A survey of simulated annealing as a tool for single and multiobjective optimization*, Journal of the Operational Research Society, 57 (2006), pp. 1143–1160.

580. L. SUN, M. TAN, AND Z. ZHOU, *A survey of practical adversarial example attacks*, Cybersecurity, 1 (2018), p. 9.

581. Q. SUN, L. MA, S. JOON OH, L. VAN GOOL, B. SCHIELE, AND M. FRITZ, *Natural and effective obfuscation by head inpainting*, in Proceedings of the IEEE Conference on Computer Vision and Pattern Recognition, 2018, pp. 5050–5059.

582. X. SUN, Y. LIU, J. LI, J. ZHU, H. CHEN, AND X. LIU, *Feature evaluation and selection with cooperative game theory*, Pattern Recogn., 45 (2012), p. 2992–3002.

583. X. SUN, Y. LIU, J. LI, J. ZHU, H. CHEN, AND X. LIU, *Feature evaluation and selection with cooperative game theory*, Pattern Recognition, 45 (2012), pp. 2992–3002.

584. X. SUN, Y. LIU, J. LI, J. ZHU, X. LIU, AND H. CHEN, *Using cooperative game theory to optimize the feature selection problem*, Neurocomput., 97 (2012).

585. S. SURESH, N. SUNDARARAJAN, AND P. SARATCHANDRAN, *Risk-sensitive loss functions for sparse multi-category classification problems*, Inf. Sci., 178 (2008).

586. V. SURYAN, A. SINHA, P. MALO, AND K. DEB, *Handling inverse optimal control problems using evolutionary bilevel optimization*, in 2016 IEEE Congress on Evolutionary Computation (CEC), July 2016, pp. 1893–1900.

587. V. SYRGKANIS, A. AGARWAL, H. LUO, AND R. E. SCHAPIRE, *Fast convergence of regularized learning in games*, in Advances in Neural Information Processing Systems, C. Cortes, N. Lawrence, D. Lee, M. Sugiyama, and R. Garnett, eds., vol. 28, Curran Associates, Inc., 2015.

588. C. SZEGEDY, V. VANHOUCKE, S. IOFFE, J. SHLENS, AND Z. WOJNA, *Rethinking the inception architecture for computer vision*, in Proceedings of the IEEE conference on computer vision and pattern recognition, 2016, pp. 2818–2826.

589. C. SZEGEDY, W. ZAREMBA, I. SUTSKEVER, J. BRUNA, D. ERHAN, I. GOODFELLOW, AND R. FERGUS, *Intriguing properties of neural networks*, arXiv preprint arXiv:1312.6199, (2013).

590. C. SZEGEDY, W. ZAREMBA, I. SUTSKEVER, J. BRUNA, D. ERHAN, I. GOODFELLOW, AND R. FERGUS, *Intriguing properties of neural networks*, in International Conference on Learning Representations, 2014.

591. N. TAGASOVSKA, D. ACKERER, AND T. VATTER, *Copulas as high-dimensional generative models: Vine copula autoencoders*, in Advances in Neural Information Processing Systems 32: Annual Conference on Neural Information Processing Systems 2019, NeurIPS 2019, December 8-14, 2019, Vancouver, BC, Canada, H. M. Wallach, H. Larochelle, A. Beygelzimer, F. d'Alché-Buc, E. B. Fox, and R. Garnett, eds., 2019, pp. 6525–6537.

592. A. TAN, D. T. NGUYEN, M. DAX, M. NIESSNER, AND T. BROX, *Explicitly modeled attention maps for image classification*, in AAAI, AAAI Press, 2021, pp. 9799–9807.

593. G. TAO, S. MA, Y. LIU, AND X. ZHANG, *Attacks meet interpretability: Attribute-steered detection of adversarial samples*, in Advances in Neural Information Processing Systems 31: Annual Conference on Neural Information Processing Systems 2018, NeurIPS 2018, 3-8 December 2018, Montréal, Canada, 2018, pp. 7728–7739.

594. O. TARAN, S. REZAEIFAR, AND S. VOLOSHYNOVSKIY, *Bridging machine learning and cryptography in defence against adversarial attacks*, in Computer Vision - ECCV 2018 Workshops - Munich, Germany, September 8-14, 2018, Proceedings, Part II, L. Leal-Taixé and S. Roth, eds., vol. 11130 of Lecture Notes in Computer Science, Springer, 2018, pp. 267–279.

595. H. TEMBINE, *Deep learning meets game theory: Bregman-based algorithms for interactive deep generative adversarial networks*, IEEE Transactions on Cybernetics, 50 (2020), pp. 1132–1145.

596. H. THALLER, L. LINSBAUER, AND A. EGYED, *Feature maps: A comprehensible software representation for design pattern detection*, in 2019 IEEE 26th International Conference on Software Analysis, Evolution and Reengineering (SANER), 2019, pp. 207–217.

597. J. J. THIAGARAJAN, I. KIM, R. ANIRUDH, AND P. BREMER, *Understanding deep neural networks through input uncertainties*, in IEEE International Conference on Acoustics, Speech and Signal Processing, ICASSP 2019, Brighton, United Kingdom, May 12-17, 2019, IEEE, 2019, pp. 2812–2816.

598. S. THYS, W. V. RANST, AND T. GOEDEME, *Fooling automated surveillance cameras: Adversarial patches to attack person detection*, in 2019 IEEE/CVF Conference on Computer Vision and Pattern Recognition Workshops (CVPRW), 2019, pp. 49–55.

599. R. TOMSETT, A. WIDDICOMBE, T. XING, S. CHAKRABORTY, S. JULIER, P. GURRAM, R. RAO, AND M. SRIVASTAVA, *Why the failure? how adversarial examples can provide insights for interpretable machine learning*, in 2018 21st International Conference on Information Fusion (FUSION), July 2018, pp. 838–845.

600. L. TONG, B. LI, C. HAJAJ, C. XIAO, N. ZHANG, AND Y. VOROBEYCHIK, *Improving robustness of ML classifiers against realizable evasion attacks using conserved features*, in 28th USENIX Security Symposium, USENIX Security 2019, Santa Clara, CA, USA, August 14-16, 2019, 2019, pp. 285–302.

601. ——, *Improving robustness of ML classifiers against realizable evasion attacks using conserved features*, in 28th USENIX Security Symposium (USENIX Security 19), Santa Clara, CA, Aug. 2019, USENIX Association, pp. 285–302.

602. L. TONG, S. YU, S. ALFELD, AND YEVGENIY VOROBEYCHIK, *Adversarial regression with multiple learners*, in Proceedings of the 35th International Conference on Machine Learning, J. Dy and A. Krause, eds., vol. 80 of Proceedings of Machine Learning Research, PMLR, 10–15 Jul 2018, pp. 4946–4954.

603. F. TRAMÈR, A. KURAKIN, N. PAPERNOT, I. J. GOODFELLOW, D. BONEH, AND P. D. MCDANIEL, *Ensemble adversarial training: Attacks and defenses*, in ICLR (Poster), OpenReview.net, 2018.

604. F. TRAMER, N. PAPERNOT, I. GOODFELLOW, D. BONEH, AND P. MCDANIEL, *The space of transferable adversarial examples*, arXiv, (2017).

605. N. TRAN, T. BUI, AND N. CHEUNG, *Dist-gan: An improved GAN using distance constraints*, in Computer Vision - ECCV 2018 - 15th European Conference, Munich, Germany, September 8-14, 2018, Proceedings, Part XIV, 2018, pp. 387–401.

606. N.-T. TRAN, T.-A. BUI, AND N.-M. CHEUNG, *Dist-gan: An improved gan using distance constraints*, in Proceedings of European Conference on Computer Vision (ECCV), 2018.

607. E. TRIANTAPHYLLOU, *Data Mining and Knowledge Discovery via Logic-Based Methods*, no. 978-1-4419-1630-3 in Springer Optimization and Its Applications, Springer, September 2010.

608. C. TSALLIS AND D. A. STARIOLO, *Generalized simulated annealing*, Physica A: Statistical Mechanics and its Applications, 233 (1996), pp. 395–406.

609. D. TSIPRAS, S. SANTURKAR, L. ENGSTROM, A. TURNER, AND A. MADRY, *Robustness may be at odds with accuracy*, in ICLR (Poster), OpenReview.net, 2019.

610. C. E. TSOURAKAKIS, *MACH: fast randomized tensor decompositions*, in SDM, SIAM, 2010, pp. 689–700.

611. K. TUYLS AND A. NOWÉ, *Evolutionary game theory and multi-agent reinforcement learning*, 20 (2005).

612. K. TUYLS, J. PEROLAT, M. LANCTOT, J. Z. LEIBO, AND T. GRAEPEL, *A generalised method for empirical game theoretic analysis*, in Proceedings of the 17th International Conference on Autonomous Agents and MultiAgent Systems, AAMAS '18, Richland, SC, 2018, International Foundation for Autonomous Agents and Multiagent Systems.

613. E. TZENG, J. HOFFMAN, K. SAENKO, AND T. DARRELL, *Adversarial discriminative domain adaptation*, in 2017 IEEE Conference on Computer Vision and Pattern Recognition (CVPR), 2017, pp. 2962–2971.

614. J. UESATO, B. O'DONOGHUE, P. KOHLI, AND A. VAN DEN OORD, *Adversarial risk and the dangers of evaluating against weak attacks*, in Proceedings of the 35th International Conference on Machine Learning, J. Dy and A. Krause, eds., vol. 80 of Proceedings of Machine Learning Research, PMLR, 10–15 Jul 2018, pp. 5025–5034.

615. M. UMMELS, *Stochastic multiplayer games: theory and algorithms*, PhD thesis, RWTH Aachen University, 2011.

616. M. USMAN, M. A. JAN, X. HE, AND J. CHEN, *A survey on representation learning efforts in cybersecurity domain*, ACM Comput. Surv., 52 (2019).

617. L. VERDOLIVA, *Media forensics and deepfakes: An overview*, IEEE Journal of Selected Topics in Signal Processing, 14 (2020), pp. 910–932.

618. A. VERMA, X. LLORA, D. E. GOLDBERG, AND R. H. CAMPBELL, *Scaling genetic algorithms using mapreduce*, in 2009 Ninth International Conference on Intelligent Systems Design and Applications, Nov 2009, pp. 13–18.

619. M. VIDYADHARI, K. KIRANMAI, K. R. KRISHNIAH, AND D. S. BABU, *Security evaluation of pattern classifiers under attack*, International Journal of Research, 3 (2016), pp. 1043–1048.

620. P. VINCENT, H. LAROCHELLE, Y. BENGIO, AND P.-A. MANZAGOL, *Extracting and composing robust features with denoising autoencoders*, in Proceedings of the 25th International Conference on Machine Learning, ICML '08, New York, NY, USA, 2008, Association for Computing Machinery, p. 1096–1103.

621. P. VINCENT, H. LAROCHELLE, I. LAJOIE, Y. BENGIO, AND P.-A. MANZAGOL, *Stacked denoising autoencoders: Learning useful representations in a deep network with a local denoising criterion*, J. Mach. Learn. Res., 11 (2010).

622. Y. VOROBEYCHIK AND B. LI, *Optimal randomized classification in adversarial settings*, in Proceedings of the 2014 International Conference on Autonomous Agents and Multi-Agent Systems, AAMAS '14, Richland, SC, 2014, International Foundation for Autonomous Agents and Multiagent Systems, p. 485–492.

623. Y. VOROBEYCHIK, M. P. WELLMAN, AND S. P. SINGH, *Learning payoff functions in infinite games*, in IJCAI, Professional Book Center, 2005, pp. 977–982.

624. T.-H. VU, H. JAIN, M. BUCHER, M. CORD, AND P. PÉREZ, *Advent: Adversarial entropy minimization for domain adaptation in semantic segmentation*, in CVPR, 2019.

625. E. WALLACE, S. FENG, N. KANDPAL, M. GARDNER, AND S. SINGH, *Universal trigger sequences for attacking and analyzing nlp*, in Proceedings of the 2019 Conference on Empirical Methods in Natural Language Processing, 2019, pp. 2153–2162.

626. B. WANG, H. PEI, B. PAN, Q. CHEN, S. WANG, AND B. LI, *T3: Tree-autoencoder constrained adversarial text generation for targeted attack*, arXiv preprint arXiv:1912.10375, (2019).

627. B. WANG, Y. YAO, B. VISWANATH, H. ZHENG, AND B. Y. ZHAO, *With great training comes great vulnerability: Practical attacks against transfer learning*, in 27th USENIX Security Symposium (USENIX Security 18), Baltimore, MD, Aug. 2018, USENIX Association, pp. 1281–1297.

628. F. WANG, W. LIU, AND S. CHAWLA, *On sparse feature attacks in adversarial learning*, in 2014 IEEE International Conference on Data Mining, Dec 2014, pp. 1013–1018.

629. K. WANG, C. GOU, Y. DUAN, Y. LIN, X. ZHENG, AND F. WANG, *Generative adversarial networks: introduction and outlook*, IEEE/CAA Journal of Automatica Sinica, 4 (2017), pp. 588–598.

630. L. WANG, W. CHO, AND K.-J. YOON, *Deceiving image-to-image translation networks for autonomous driving with adversarial perturbations*, IEEE Robotics and Automation Letters, 5 (2020), pp. 1421–1428.

631. T. WANG AND Q. LIN, *Hybrid predictive model: When an interpretable model collaborates with a black-box model*, CoRR, abs/1905.04241 (2019).

632. T. WANG, X. WANG, Y. QIN, B. PACKER, K. LI, J. CHEN, A. BEUTEL, AND E. CHI, *Catgen: Improving robustness in NLP models via controlled adversarial text generation*, CoRR, abs/2010.02338 (2020).

633. W. WANG, L. WANG, R. WANG, Z. WANG, AND A. YE, *Towards a robust deep neural network in texts: A survey*, arXiv preprint arXiv:1902.07285, (2019).

634. X. WANG, C. HOANG, Y. VOROBEYCHIK, AND M. P. WELLMAN, *Spoofing the limit order book: A strategic agent-based analysis*, Games, 12 (2021), p. 46.

635. X. WANG, L. LI, W. YE, M. LONG, AND J. WANG, *Transferable attention for domain adaptation*, Proceedings of the AAAI Conference on Artificial Intelligence, 33 (2019), pp. 5345–5352.

636. Y. WANG, *Integration of data mining with game theory*, in Knowledge Enterprise: Intelligent Strategies in Product Design, Manufacturing, and Management, K. Wang, G. L. Kovacs, M. Wozny, and M. Fang, eds., Boston, MA, 2006, Springer US, pp. 275–280.

637. Y. WANG, X. MA, J. BAILEY, J. YI, B. ZHOU, AND Q. GU, *On the convergence and robustness of adversarial training*, in Proceedings of the 36th International Conference on Machine Learning, K. Chaudhuri and R. Salakhutdinov, eds., vol. 97 of Proceedings of Machine Learning Research, PMLR, 09–15 Jun 2019, pp. 6586–6595.

638. Z. WANG, A. BOVIK, H. SHEIKH, AND E. SIMONCELLI, *Image quality assessment: from error visibility to structural similarity*, IEEE Transactions on Image Processing, 13 (2004), pp. 600–612.

639. J. WEBB, *Game Theory: Decisions, Interaction and Evolution*, 01 2007.

640. X. WEI, S. LIANG, N. CHEN, AND X. CAO, *Transferable adversarial attacks for image and video object detection*, in Proceedings of the Twenty-Eighth International Joint Conference on Artificial Intelligence, IJCAI-19, International Joint Conferences on Artificial Intelligence Organization, 7 2019, pp. 954–960.

641. T. WEISE, *Global Optimization Algorithms - Theory and Application*, self-published, Germany, 2009.

642. M. P. WELLMAN, *Methods for empirical game-theoretic analysis*, in AAAI, AAAI Press, 2006, pp. 1552–1556.

643. M. P. WELLMAN, L. HONG, AND S. E. PAGE, *The structure of signals: Causal interdependence models for games of incomplete information*, in UAI, AUAI Press, 2011, pp. 727–735.

644. Y. WEN, B. LIU, R. XIE, J. CAO, AND L. SONG, *Deep motion flow aided face video de-identification*, in 2021 IEEE International Conference on Visual Communications and Image Processing, VCIP 2021, Dec 2021, pp. 269–272.

645. Y. WEN, B. LIU, R. XIE, Y. ZHU, J. CAO, AND L. SONG, *A hybrid model for natural face de-identiation with adjustable privacy*, in 2020 IEEE International Conference on Visual Communications and Image Processing, VCIP 2020, Dec 2020, pp. 269–272.

646. J. WEXLER, M. PUSHKARNA, T. BOLUKBASI, M. WATTENBERG, F. VIEGAS, AND J. WILSON, eds., *The What-If Tool: Interactive Probing of Machine Learning Models*, 2019.

647. L. D. WHITLEY, S. B. RANA, J. DZUBERA, AND K. E. MATHIAS, *Evaluating evolutionary algorithms*, Artif. Intell., 85 (1996), pp. 245–276.

648. A. WIECZOREK, M. WIESER, D. MUREZZAN, AND V. ROTH, *Learning sparse latent representations with the deep copula information bottleneck*, in 6th International Conference on Learning Representations, ICLR 2018, Vancouver, BC, Canada, April 30 - May 3, 2018, Conference Track Proceedings, OpenReview.net, 2018.

649. D. H. WOLPERT, *The supervised learning no-free-lunch theorems*, in In Proc. 6th Online World Conference on Soft Computing in Industrial Applications, 2001, pp. 25–42.

650. D. H. WOLPERT AND W. G. MACREADY, *No free lunch theorems for optimization*, IEEE Transactions on Evolutionary Computation, 1 (1997), pp. 67–82.

651. ——, *Coevolutionary free lunches*, IEEE Transactions on Evolutionary Computation, 9 (2005), pp. 721–735.

652. E. WONG AND J. Z. KOLTER, *Provable defenses against adversarial examples via the convex outer adversarial polytope*, in Proceedings of the 35th International Conference on Machine Learning, ICML 2018, Stockholmsmässan, Stockholm, Sweden, July 10-15, 2018, J. G. Dy and A. Krause, eds., vol. 80 of Proceedings of Machine Learning Research, PMLR, 2018, pp. 5283–5292.

653. ——, *Learning perturbation sets for robust machine learning*, in 9th International Conference on Learning Representations, ICLR 2021, Virtual Event, Austria, May 3-7, 2021, OpenReview.net, 2021.

654. D. WU, Y. WANG, S.-T. XIA, J. BAILEY, AND X. MA, *Skip connections matter: On the transferability of adversarial examples generated with resnets*, in ICLR, 2020.

655. X. WU, U. JANG, J. CHEN, L. CHEN, AND S. JHA, *Reinforcing adversarial robustness using model confidence induced by adversarial training*, in Proceedings of the 35th International Conference on Machine Learning, J. Dy and A. Krause, eds., vol. 80 of Proceedings of Machine Learning Research, PMLR, 10–15 Jul 2018, pp. 5334–5342.

656. B. XI, *Adversarial machine learning for cybersecurity and computer vision: Current developments and challenges*, WIREs Computational Statistics, 12 (2020), p. e1511.

657. Y. XIAN, T. LORENZ, B. SCHIELE, AND Z. AKATA, *Feature generating networks for zero-shot learning*, in 31st IEEE Conference on Computer Vision and Pattern Recognition (CVPR 2018), Salt Lake City, UT, USA, 2018.

658. Y. XIANG, Y. XU, Y. LI, W. MA, Q. XUAN, AND Y. LIU, *Side-channel gray-box attack for dnns*, IEEE Transactions on Circuits and Systems II: Express Briefs, (2020), pp. 1–1.

659. C. XIAO, B. LI, J.-Y. ZHU, W. HE, M. LIU, AND D. SONG, *Generating adversarial examples with adversarial networks*, (2018).

660. C. XIAO, B. LI, J.-Y. ZHU, W. HE, M. LIU, AND D. SONG, *Generating adversarial examples with adversarial networks*, in Proceedings of the 27th International Joint Conference on Artificial Intelligence, IJCAI'18, AAAI Press, 2018.

661. C. XIAO, J. ZHU, B. LI, W. HE, M. LIU, AND D. SONG, *Spatially transformed adversarial examples*, in 6th International Conference on Learning Representations, ICLR 2018, Vancouver, BC, Canada, April 30 - May 3, 2018, Conference Track Proceedings, 2018.

662. C. XIAO, J.-Y. ZHU, B. LI, W. HE, M. LIU, AND D. SONG, *Spatially transformed adversarial examples*, in International Conference on Learning Representations, 2018.

663. H. XIAO, B. BIGGIO, G. BROWN, G. FUMERA, C. ECKERT, AND F. ROLI, *Is feature selection secure against training data poisoning?*, in Proceedings of the 32nd International Conference on Machine Learning, F. Bach and D. Blei, eds., vol. 37 of Proceedings of Machine Learning Research, Lille, France, 07–09 Jul 2015, PMLR, pp. 1689–1698.

664. H. XIAO, B. BIGGIO, B. NELSON, H. XIAO, C. ECKERT, AND F. ROLI, *Support vector machines under adversarial label contamination*, Neurocomput., 160 (2015), pp. 53–62.

665. C. XIE, J. WANG, Z. ZHANG, Y. ZHOU, L. XIE, AND A. L. YUILLE, *Adversarial examples for semantic segmentation and object detection*, in IEEE International Conference on Computer Vision, ICCV 2017, Venice, Italy, October 22-29, 2017, 2017, pp. 1378–1387.

666. E. XING, M. JORDAN, S. J. RUSSELL, AND A. NG, *Distance metric learning with application to clustering with side-information*, in Advances in Neural Information Processing Systems, S. Becker, S. Thrun, and K. Obermayer, eds., vol. 15, MIT Press, 2003.

667. Y. W. S. M. E. S. W. G. S. D. S. M. E. H. XINGJUN MA, BO LI AND J. BAILEY, *Characterizing adversarial subspaces using local intrinsic dimensionality*, in ICLR, 2018.

668. H. XU, C. CARAMANIS, AND S. MANNOR, *Robustness and regularization of support vector machines*, Journal of Machine Learning Research, 10 (2009), pp. 1485–1510.

669. H. XU, C. CARAMANIS, AND S. MANNOR, *Robustness and regularization of support vector machines*, J. Mach. Learn. Res., 10 (2009), p. 1485–1510.

670. H. XU AND S. MANNOR, *Robustness and generalization*, Mach. Learn., 86 (2012), p. 391–423.

671. Q. XU, K. BELLO, AND J. HONORIO, *A le cam type bound for adversarial learning and applications*, in 2021 IEEE International Symposium on Information Theory (ISIT), 2021, pp. 1164–1169.

672. B. XUE, M. ZHANG, W. N. BROWNE, AND X. YAO, *A survey on evolutionary computation approaches to feature selection*, IEEE Trans. Evol. Comput., 20 (2016), pp. 606–626.

673. H. XUE, B. LIU, M. DIN, L. SONG, AND T. ZHU, *Hiding private information in images from ai*, in ICC 2020 - 2020 IEEE International Conference on Communications (ICC), Dublin, Ireland, IEEE, Jul 2020.

674. M. XUE, C. YUAN, H. WU, Y. ZHANG, AND W. LIU, *Machine learning security: Threats, countermeasures, and evaluations*, IEEE Access, 8 (2020), pp. 74720–74742.

675. O. YAIR AND T. MICHAELI, *Contrastive divergence learning is a time reversal adversarial game*, in ICLR, OpenReview.net, 2021.

676. Z. YAN, Y. GUO, AND C. ZHANG, *Adversarial margin maximization networks*, IEEE Trans. Pattern Anal. Mach. Intell., 43 (2021), pp. 1129–1139.

677. C. H. YANG, Y. LIU, P. CHEN, X. MA, AND Y. J. TSAI, *When causal intervention meets adversarial examples and image masking for deep neural networks*, in 2019 IEEE International Conference on Image Processing (ICIP), Sep. 2019, pp. 3811–3815.

678. J. YANG, R. XU, R. LI, X. QI, X. SHEN, G. LI, AND L. LIN, *An adversarial perturbation oriented domain adaptation approach for semantic segmentation*, in The Thirty-Fourth AAAI Conference on Artificial Intelligence, AAAI 2020, The Thirty-Second Innovative Applications of Artificial Intelligence Conference, IAAI 2020, The Tenth AAAI Symposium on Educational Advances in Artificial Intelligence, EAAI 2020, New York, NY, USA, February 7-12, 2020, AAAI Press, 2020, pp. 12613–12620.

679. L. YANG, P. LI, Y. ZHANG, X. YANG, Y. XIANG, AND W. ZHOU, *Effective repair strategy against advanced persistent threat: A differential game approach*, IEEE Transactions on Information Forensics and Security, 14 (2019), pp. 1713–1728.

680. P. YANG, J. T. ORMEROD, W. LIU, C. MA, A. Y. ZOMAYA, AND J. Y. H. YANG, *Adasampling for positive-unlabeled and label noise learning with bioinformatics applications*, IEEE Trans. Cybern., 49 (2019), pp. 1932–1943.

681. D. YE, T. ZHU, S. SHEN, AND W. ZHOU, *A differentially private game theoretic approach for deceiving cyber adversaries*, IEEE Trans. Inf. Forensics Secur., 16 (2021), pp. 569–584.

682. H.-J. YE, D.-C. ZHAN, AND Y. JIANG, *Instance specific metric subspace learning: A bayesian approach*, in Proceedings of the Thirtieth AAAI Conference on Artificial Intelligence, AAAI'16, AAAI Press, 2016, p. 2272–2278.

683. ——, *Instance specific metric subspace learning: A bayesian approach*, Proceedings of the AAAI Conference on Artificial Intelligence, 30 (2016).

684. S. YE, X. LIN, K. XU, S. LIU, H. CHENG, J.-H. LAMBRECHTS, H. ZHANG, A. ZHOU, K. MA, AND Y. WANG, *Adversarial robustness vs. model compression, or both?*, 2019 IEEE/CVF International Conference on Computer Vision (ICCV), (2019), pp. 111–120.

685. D. S. YEUNG, I. CLOETE, D. SHI, AND W. W. NG, *Sensitivity Analysis for Neural Networks*, Springer Publishing Company, Incorporated, 1st ed., 2009.

686. Z. YIN, F. WANG, W. LIU, AND S. CHAWLA, *Sparse feature attacks in adversarial learning*, IEEE Transactions on Knowledge and Data Engineering, PP (2018).

687. ——, *Sparse feature attacks in adversarial learning*, IEEE Transactions on Knowledge and Data Engineering, 30 (2018), pp. 1164–1177.

688. Z. YIN, F. WANG, W. LIU, AND S. CHAWLA, *Sparse feature attacks in adversarial learning*, IEEE Transactions on Knowledge and Data Engineering, 30 (2018), pp. 1164–1177.

689. Y. ZANG, F. QI, C. YANG, Z. LIU, M. ZHANG, Q. LIU, AND M. SUN, *Word-level textual adversarial attacking as combinatorial optimization*, in Proceedings of the 58th Annual Meeting of the Association for Computational Linguistics, 2020, pp. 6066–6080.

690. F. ZHANG, P. CHAN, B. BIGGIO, D. YEUNG, AND F. ROLI, *Adversarial feature selection against evasion attacks*, IEEE Transactions on Cybernetics, 46 (2016), pp. 766–777.

691. F. ZHANG, P. P. K. CHAN, B. BIGGIO, D. S. YEUNG, AND F. ROLI, *Adversarial feature selection against evasion attacks*, IEEE Trans. Cybernetics, 46 (2016), pp. 766–777.

692. H. ZHANG, Y. YU, J. JIAO, E. XING, L. E. GHAOUI, AND M. JORDAN, *Theoretically principled trade-off between robustness and accuracy*, in Proceedings of the 36th International Conference on Machine Learning, K. Chaudhuri and R. Salakhutdinov, eds., vol. 97 of Proceedings of Machine Learning Research, PMLR, 09–15 Jun 2019, pp. 7472–7482.

693. J. ZHANG, B. HAN, G. NIU, T. LIU, AND M. SUGIYAMA, *Where is the bottleneck of adversarial learning with unlabeled data?*, CoRR, abs/1911.08696 (2019).

694. J. ZHANG, Z. HUI ZHAN, Y. LIN, N. CHEN, Y. JIAO GONG, J.-H. ZHONG, H. S.-H. CHUNG, Y. LI, AND Y. HUI SHI, *Evolutionary computation meets machine learning: A survey.*, IEEE Comp. Int. Mag., 6 (2011), pp. 68–75.

695. J. ZHANG, X. XU, B. HAN, G. NIU, L. CUI, M. SUGIYAMA, AND M. KANKANHALLI, *Attacks which do not kill training make adversarial learning stronger*, in Proceedings of the 37th International Conference on Machine Learning, H. D. III and A. Singh, eds., vol. 119 of Proceedings of Machine Learning Research, PMLR, 13–18 Jul 2020, pp. 11278–11287.

696. J. ZHANG, Z. ZHAN, Y. LIN, N. CHEN, Y. GONG, J. ZHONG, H. S. H. CHUNG, Y. LI, AND Y. SHI, *Evolutionary computation meets machine learning: A survey*, IEEE Computational Intelligence Magazine, 6 (2011), pp. 68–75.

697. L. ZHANG, T. ZHU, P. XIONG, W. ZHOU, AND P. S. YU, *More than privacy: Adopting differential privacy in game-theoretic mechanism design*, ACM Comput. Surv., 54 (2021).

698. X. ZHANG, L. ZHAO, A. P. BOEDIHARDJO, AND C.-T. LU, *Online and distributed robust regressions under adversarial data corruption*, in 2017 IEEE International Conference on Data Mining (ICDM), 2017, pp. 625–634.

699. Y. ZHANG AND B. C. WALLACE, *A sensitivity analysis of (and practitioners' guide to) convolutional neural networks for sentence classification*, in Proceedings of the Eighth International Joint Conference on Natural Language Processing, IJCNLP 2017, Taipei, Taiwan, November 27 - December 1, 2017 - Volume 1: Long Papers, G. Kondrak and T. Watanabe, eds., Asian Federation of Natural Language Processing, 2017, pp. 253–263.

700. Y. ZHANG AND Z. WANG, *Joint adversarial learning for domain adaptation in semantic segmentation*, in AAAI, 2020.

701. J. ZHAO, Y. KIM, K. ZHANG, A. RUSH, AND Y. LECUN, *Adversarially regularized autoencoders*, in Proceedings of the 35th International Conference on Machine Learning, J. Dy and A. Krause, eds., vol. 80 of Proceedings of Machine Learning Research, PMLR, 10–15 Jul 2018, pp. 5902–5911.

702. J. J. ZHAO, M. MATHIEU, AND Y. LECUN, *Energy-based generative adversarial networks*.

703. M. ZHAO, B. AN, Y. YU, S. LIU, AND S. J. PAN, *Data poisoning attacks on multi-task relationship learning*, in Proceedings of the Thirty-Second AAAI Conference on Artificial Intelligence, (AAAI-18), the 30th innovative Applications of Artificial Intelligence (IAAI-18), and the 8th AAAI Symposium on Educational Advances in Artificial Intelligence (EAAI-18), New Orleans, Louisiana, USA, February 2-7, 2018, 2018, pp. 2628–2635.

704. P. ZHAO, P.-Y. CHEN, S. WANG, AND X. LIN, *Towards query-efficient black-box adversary with zeroth-order natural gradient descent.*, in AAAI, 2020, pp. 6909–6916.

705. S. ZHAO, J. SONG, AND S. ERMON, *Learning hierarchical features from deep generative models*, in Proceedings of the 34th International Conference on Machine Learning - Volume 70, ICML'17, JMLR.org, 2017, p. 4091–4099.

706. Y. ZHAO, B. LIU, T. ZHU, M. DING, AND W. ZHOU, *Private-encoder: Enforcing privacy in latent space for human face images*, Concurrency and Computation: Practice and Experience, (2021), p. e6548.

707. Y. ZHONG AND W. DENG, *Adversarial learning with margin-based triplet embedding regularization*, in Proceedings of the IEEE/CVF International Conference on Computer Vision (ICCV), October 2019.

708. C. ZHOU AND R. C. PAFFENROTH, *Anomaly detection with robust deep autoencoders*, in Proceedings of the 23rd ACM SIGKDD International Conference on Knowledge Discovery and Data Mining, KDD '17, New York, NY, USA, 2017, Association for Computing Machinery.

709. Y. ZHOU AND M. KANTARCIOGLU, *Modeling adversarial learning as nested stackelberg games*, in Advances in Knowledge Discovery and Data Mining, J. Bailey, L. Khan, T. Washio, G. Dobbie, J. Z. Huang, and R. Wang, eds., Cham, 2016, Springer International Publishing, pp. 350–362.

710. ——, *Modeling adversarial learning as nested stackelberg games*, in Proceedings, Part II, of the 20th Pacific-Asia Conference on Advances in Knowledge Discovery and Data Mining - Volume 9652, PAKDD 2016, Berlin, Heidelberg, 2016, Springer-Verlag, p. 350–362.

711. Y. ZHOU, M. KANTARCIOGLU, AND B. THURAISINGHAM, *Sparse bayesian adversarial learning using relevance vector machine ensembles*, in 2012 IEEE 12th International Conference on Data Mining, 2012, pp. 1206–1211.

712. Y. ZHOU, M. KANTARCIOGLU, AND B. XI, *A survey of game theoretic approach for adversarial machine learning*, WIREs Data Mining and Knowledge Discovery, 9 (2019), p. e1259.

713. ——, *A survey of game theoretic approach for adversarial machine learning*, Wiley Interdisciplinary Reviews: Data Mining and Knowledge Discovery, (2019).

714. Z. ZHOU, H. CAI, S. RONG, Y. SONG, K. REN, W. ZHANG, J. WANG, AND Y. YU, *Activation maximization generative adversarial nets*, in International Conference on Learning Representations, 2018.

715. C. ZHU, W. R. HUANG, A. SHAFAHI, H. LI, G. TAYLOR, C. STUDER, AND T. GOLDSTEIN, *Transferable clean-label poisoning attacks on deep neural nets*, arXiv preprint arXiv:1905.05897, (2019).

716. B. D. ZIEBART, A. MAAS, J. A. BAGNELL, AND A. K. DEY, *Maximum entropy inverse reinforcement learning*, in Proceedings of the 23rd National Conference on Artificial Intelligence - Volume 3, AAAI'08, AAAI Press, 2008, p. 1433–1438.

717. H. ZOU, T. HASTIE, AND R. TIBSHIRANI, *Sparse principal component analysis*, Journal of Computational and Graphical Statistics, 15 (2004), p. 2006.

718. ——, *Sparse principal component analysis*, Journal of Computational and Graphical Statistics, 15 (2006), pp. 265–286.

Printed in the United States
by Baker & Taylor Publisher Services